Court Culture in Dresden

By the same author

TRIUMPHALL SHEWS:
Tournaments at German Courts in their European Context, 1580–1730

THE CAMBRIDGE HISTORY OF GERMAN LITERATURE

FESTIVALS AND CEREMONIES:
A Bibliography of Works Relating to Court, Civic and Religious Festivals in Europe 1500–1800 (co-author with Anne Simon)

SPECTACULUM EUROPAEUM:
Theatre and Spectacle in Europe (co-author with Pierre Béhar)

Court Culture in Dresden

From Renaissance to Baroque

Helen Watanabe-O'Kelly

© Helen Watanabe-O'Kelly 2002

All rights reserved. No reproduction, copy or transmission of this publication may be made without written permission.

No paragraph of this publication may be reproduced, copied or transmitted save with written permission or in accordance with the provisions of the Copyright, Designs and Patents Act 1988, or under the terms of any licence permitting limited copying issued by the Copyright Licensing Agency, 90 Tottenham Court Road, London W1T 4LP.

Any person who does any unauthorised act in relation to this publication may be liable to criminal prosecution and civil claims for damages.

The author has asserted her right to be identified as the author of this work in accordance with the Copyright, Designs and Patents Act 1988.

First published 2002 by
PALGRAVE
Houndmills, Basingstoke, Hampshire RG21 6XS and
175 Fifth Avenue, New York, N. Y. 10010
Companies and representatives throughout the world

PALGRAVE is the new global academic imprint of
St. Martin's Press LLC Scholarly and Reference Division and Palgrave Publishers Ltd (formerly Macmillan Press Ltd).

ISBN 0-333-98448-X

This book is printed on paper suitable for recycling and made from fully managed and sustained forest sources.

A catalogue record for this book is available from the British Library.

Library of Congress Cataloging-in-Publication Data
Watanabe-O'Kelly, Helen.
  Court culture in Dresden / by Helen Watanabe-O'Kelly.
    p. cm.
  Includes bibliographical references and index.
  ISBN 0-333-98448-X
  1. Dresden (Germany)—Intellectual life. 2. Arts, German—Germany—Dresden. 3. Dresden (Germany)—Court and courtiers. 4. Dresden (Germany)—Civilization. I. Title.

DD901.D747 .W38 2002
943'.2142—dc21

2001056119

10 9 8 7 6 5 4 3 2 1
11 10 09 08 07 06 05 04 03 02

Printed and bound in Great Britain by
Antony Rowe Ltd, Chippenham, Wiltshire

Contents

List of Figures	vii
Acknowledgements	xii
Abbreviations	xiv
Genealogical table	xv

Introduction — 1

1 The Lutheran Legacy: The Albertine Electors and Protestant Court Culture — 5
- The Electoral burial chapel at Freiberg — 5
- Sectarian tournaments — 20
- Lutheran sacred music – the 'historia' — 22
- Biblical drama — 26
- Johann Georg II and the 'Joseph' plays — 30
- Dedekind and the biblical semi-opera — 34

2 The Italian Ideal: The Sixteenth-Century Reception of Italian Culture — 37
- Italian artists in Dresden — 37
- The new stables and portrait gallery (1586) — 43
- Arms, armour and Italian horsemanship — 45
- The tournament and Italian influence — 49
- Princely education and 'civil conversation' — 54
- Johann Georg I's Italian journey (1601) and its Dresden legacy — 59

3 The Management of Knowledge: The Dresden Collections – Their Origin and Development — 71
- Early modern collecting — 71
- The original Dresden *Kunstkammer* — 73
- Elector August's Library — 84
- The Electoral Library in the seventeenth century — 88
- The *Kunstkammer* under Christian I and Christian II — 90
- Johann Georg I's *Kunstkammer* — 91
- Storage and inventorisation of the collections — 96

4 The Secrets of the Heavens and the Earth:
   Alchemy, Mining and Astrology at the Dresden Court   100
   Early modern alchemy in the Empire   101
   Princely patrons of alchemy in the Empire   104
   Alchemy in Dresden – the theory   106
   Alchemical practice at the Dresden court   115
   Mining and astrology in court festivals   120

5 The Fabrication of an Image: Johann Georg II's
   Self-presentation   130
   Johann Georg II's emergence as Jason (1650)   130
   The Riesensaal and the ballet of 1653   132
   Johann Georg II as Knight of St George   140
   Johann Georg II as Nimrod   151
   Publishing the image   154

6 The 'Recreation of the Spirit': Theatre at the
   Dresden Court during the Seventeenth Century   166
   'Pleasant inventions and entertaining histories' –
      foreign drama at the Dresden court   166
   'Heroes changed to flowers' – ballet at the Dresden court   174
   'Gods among the Saxons' – opera in Dresden   189

7 The Saxon Hercules: August the Strong, Elector
   of Saxony, King of Poland   193
   From Lutheran Elector to Catholic King   195
   The cultural impact of France   204
   From *Kunstkammer* to museum   212
   From occult science to early manufacturing   220
   From Mercury to Apollo – August's festivals   229

Conclusion   238

Notes   242

Bibliography   273

Index   297

List of Figures

The following are thanked for permission to reproduce works in their collections:

Staatliche Kunstsammlungen, Dresden (Gemäldegalerie Alte Meister, Grünes Gewölbe, Kupferstichkabinett, Porzellansammlung, Rüstkammer and Skulpturensammlung);
Sächsisches Hauptstaatsarchiv, Dresden (HStA);
Sächsische Landesbibliothek, Staats- und Universitätsbibliothek, Dresden (SLUB)
Stadtmuseum Dresden

'Deutsche Fotothek' in the following list indicates that the photograph in question comes from the Sächsische Landesbibliothek, Staats- und Universitätsbibliothek, Dresden, Deutsche Fotothek, which has kindly given permission for the photograph to be reproduced. The name of the photographer is indicated in brackets.

1	Map of Electoral Saxony after 1547	1
2	Medal commemorating the discovery of silver deposits in the St Anna mine near Freiberg, Erzgebirge, in 1690. Tentzel, *Saxonia numismatica*. Tab. 68, No. 1	7
3	Monument to Moritz, Elector of Saxony, Freiberg Cathedral. Deutsche Fotothek (Nowak)	10
4	Electoral burial chapel in Freiberg Cathedral. The monument to Moritz is on the left. Deutsche Fotothek (Möbius)	11
5	Kneeling figure of Christian I in the Electoral burial chapel in Freiberg Cathedral by Carlo di Cesare. Bronze. Deutsche Fotothek (Möbius)	13
6	Christ coming in Judgement on the ceiling of the Electoral burial chapel in Freiberg Cathedral by Carlo di Cesare. Stucco. Deutsche Fotothek (Seifert)	14
7	Zacharias Wehme, Christian I and his family, 1591. Gemäldegalerie Alte Meister, Dresden. Inv. No. MO 1951. Deutsche Fotothek (Steuerlein)	16

viii *List of Figures*

8   Johann Heinrich Böhme the Elder, Johann Georg II.
    1674. Alabaster. Wooden frame. 131 cm in height.
    Skulpturensammlung, Dresden. Inv. No. ZV 3227   18
9   Medal commemorating the inauguration of the chapel in
    Moritzburg Castle. Johann Georg II kneels before the altar.
    1672. Tentzel, *Saxonia numismatica*. Tab. 58, No. 1   19
10 Daniel Bretschneider the Elder, Design for a sledge.
    1602. SLUB. Mscr.Dresd.B 104   22
11 Map of Electoral Saxony after 1648, augmented by Lusatia   34
12 Johann Azelt, A view of the Palace courtyard in Dresden
    showing the *sgraffito* decoration. From Gabriel Tzschimmer,
    Die Durchlauchtigste Zusammenkunft, Plate 23, S.207.
    Deutsche Fotothek (Richter)   38
13 Fresco by the Tola brothers in the Riesensaal or Room
    of the Giants in the Palace in Dresden. Drawing by
    Valentin Wagner. Pencil and red chalk. Sheet 22 from
    Wagner's sketchbook. Kupferstich-Kabinett, Dresden.
    Deutsche Fotothek (Rous)   39
14 The stables built by Christian I (1586). Engraving from
    Gabriel Tzschimmer, *Die Durchlauchtigste Zusammenkunft*,
    S.15. Deutsche Fotothek (Richter)   43
15 The Langer Gang or Long Arcade. Engraving from Anton
    Weck, *Der Churfürstl. Sächs. Weit beruffenen Residentz und
    Haupt-Vestung Dresden: Beschreib: und Vorstellung* (1680).
    Deutsche Fotothek (Rous)   44
16 Daniel Bretschneider the Elder, Float and Ethiopians
    in the running at the ring held in Dresden in 1609.
    SLUB Mscr.Dresd.J 18. Deutsche Fotothek (Rous)   53
17 Matthaus Merian the Younger, View of Dresden
    (after 1622). Engraving. Deutsche Fotothek (Rous)   66
18 Friedrich Hagedorn, The Belvedere in Dresden (1887). Oil
    on canvas. Stadtmuseum, Dresden. Inv. No. 1979/K 208.
    Deutsche Fotothek (Paetzold)   67
19 Rock crystal drinking vessel with a setting of gold, rubies,
    enamel and sapphires. The Sarachi workshop in Milan
    before 1580. Grünes Gewölbe, Dresden. Deutsche
    Fotothek (Heckmann)   74
20 The figure of a Moor by Balthasar Permoser holds the lump
    of Columbian emerald ore from the *Kunstkammer*. The
    setting is by the Dinglinger brothers. Lacquered birch, gilt
    silver, emeralds, rubies, sapphires, topazes, garnets,

	almandine and tortoiseshell. c.1724. Grünes Gewölbe, Dresden. H. 63.8 cm. Deutsche Fotothek (Heckmann)	77
21	Georg Wecker, Ivory stacking cup, 1588. Grünes Gewölbe, Dresden. Deutsche Fotothek (Heckmann)	81
22	The raven in the cucurbit from HStA Geheimes Archiv Loc. 4417/5	103
23	Angel raising a man from the dead. Pen-and-ink drawing from HStA Geheimes Archiv Loc. 4417/7	111
24	Two alchemists at work. Pen-and-ink drawing from HStA Geheimes Archiv Loc. 4417/7	111
25	Daniel Bretschneider the Elder, Mercury and his furnace in the mining invention for the running at the ring held in Dresden in 1591. SLUB Mscr.Dresd.J 9. Deutsche Fotothek (Franke)	122
26	Daniel Bretschneider the Elder, Astronomer. Design for a sledge. SLUB Mscr.Dresd.B 104. Deutsche Fotothek (Richter)	123
27	Johann Oswald Harms, Set design of a mountain scene with miners at work for the *entrée* of Saturn in the *Ballet von Zusammenkunft und Wirckung Derer Sieben Planeten*, 1678. Note the windlass in the centre at the back. Deutsche Fotothek (Richter)	126
28	Samuel Klemm, Freiberg, 1675–77. The 'Tscherpertasche', or bag for tallow, and other lighting materials in the miner's accoutrements called the 'Bergmannsgarnitur' commissioned by Johann Georg II and worn by him in 1678. Leather, silver, gilding, enamel, precious stones. The enamel plaque represents the Electoral mint in which several figures can be seen at work. W. 17 cm. Grünes Gewölbe, Dresden. Deutsche Fotothek (Heckmann)	127
29	Johann Mock, The Riesensaal in the Palace in Dresden on the occasion of the installation of Johann Georg IV as Garter Knight in 1693 (detail). Gouache. Kupferstich-Kabinett, Dresden. C1961-114. Deutsche Fotothek (Andrich)	136
30	Johann Mock, The British envoy ties the Garter on Johann Georg IV on the occasion of his installation as Garter Knight in 1693 (detail). Gouache. The empty throne represents the English King. Kupferstich-Kabinett, Dresden. C1961-113. Deutsche Fotothek (Andrich)	138
31	St George and the Dragon. Medal commemorating the installation of Johann Georg II as Garter Knight in 1671. Tentzel, *Saxonia numismatica*. Tab. 57, No. 4	142

List of Figures

32 Gottfried Leygebe, Charles II as St George. Iron. Grünes Gewölbe, Dresden. Deutsche Fotothek (Heckmann) — 145
33 H.W. Schober, Johann Georg II in his Garter robes. Gouache. Rüstkammer, Dresden. Inv. No. I 447. Deutsche Fotothek (Andrich) — 149
34 H.W. Schober, engraved portrait of Johann Georg II with the Garter motto from Gabriel Tzschimmer's *Durchlauchtigste Zusammenkunft* (1680) — 150
35 Johann Georg II as Nimrod in 1678. Engraving from Gabriel Tzschimmer's *Durchlauchtigste Zusammenkunft* (1680) — 153
36 The Indoor Riding School and the Shooting Gallery in Dresden. Engraving from Anton Weck's *Der Residentz- und Haupt-Vestung Dresden Beschreib: und Vorstellung* (1680) — 159
37 The procession of the seven planets moves through the streets of Dresden in 1678. Engraving from Gabriel Tzschimmer's *Durchlauchtigste Zusammenkunft* (1680) — 162
38 Johann Azelt, The Mohrenballett being performed in 1678 in the Riesensaal in the Palace in Dresden. Engraving from Tzschimmer, *Durchlauchtigste Zusammenkunft* (1680) — 185
39 Johann Oswald Harms, The final set for the *Ballet von der Zusammenkunft und Wirckung derer VII. Planeten* (1678). Engraving from the libretto. Deutsche Fotothek (Handrick) — 187
40 Johann Oswald Harms, The auditorium of the Playhouse in Dresden in 1678. Engraving from the libretto of the *Ballet von der Zusammenkunft und Wirckung derer VII. Planeten*. Deutsche Fotothek (Rous) — 188
41 Medal struck in Nuremberg to commemorate the accession of Friedrich August I in 1694. Tentzel, *Saxonia numismatica*. Tab. 73, No. 1 — 194
42 Firework display held in Danzig in 1698 for the entry of Friedrich August I, Elector of Saxony, as August II, King of Poland. Engraving from Georg Reinhold Curicke, *Freuden=Bezeugung der Stadt Danzig*, Danzig 1698 — 198
43 George Bähr, Frauenkirche, Dresden. Deutsche Fotothek — 202
44 Carl Heinrich Jacob Fehling, The carrousel of the Four Elements in the Zwinger, 1719. Pen, ink and wash. Kupferstichkabinett, Dresden. Ca 200-16. Deutsche Fotothek — 210
45 Christian Albrecht Wortmann, Frontispiece to Matthäus Daniel Pöppelmann's *L'Orangerie Royale de Dresden avec ses pavillons et embellissements Bâtie en 1711*, Dresden 1729. Deutsche Fotothek (Würker) — 211

46 Johann Georg Schmidt, The entrance to the Wallpavillon. From Matthäus Daniel Pöppelmann's *L'Orangerie Royale de Dresden avec ses pavillons et embellissements Bâtie en 1711*, Dresden 1729. Deutsche Fotothek (Würker) 213
47 Johann Georg Schmidt, The doorway on the far side of the Kronentor leading out of the Zwinger towards the moat. From Matthäus Daniel Pöppelmann's *L'Orangerie Royale de Dresden avec ses pavillons et embellissements Bâtie en 1711*, Dresden 1729. Deutsche Fotothek (Rous) 214
48 Johann Melchior, Georg Friedrich and Georg Christoph Dinglinger, A dromedary and his attendant from the Birthday of the Great Mogul Aureng-Zeb in Delhi. Gold, silver, gilding, enamel, jewels. 1701–8. Grünes Gewölbe, Dresden. Deutsche Fotothek (Heckmann) 218
49 White so-called 'Böttger porcelain'. C. 1716–17. H. 42 cm. Porzellansammlung, Dresden. Inv. No. P.E.2909a. Deutsche Fotothek (Karpinski) 224
50 Carl Heinrich Jacob Fehling, The Festival of Saturn, 26 September 1719. The smelters demonstrate their skill. Kupferstich-Kabinett, Dresden. Engraving. Deutsche Fotothek (Koch) 227
51 Carl Heinrich Jacob Fehling, The Festival of Saturn, 26 September 1719. A model of a working mine surmounted by Mercury. Kupferstich-Kabinett, Dresden. Engraving. Deutsche Fotothek (Koch) 228
52 Carl Heinrich Jacob Fehling, Four of the machines presented at the Festival of Saturn on 26 September 1719. Kupferstich-Kabinett, Dresden. Engraving. Deutsche Fotothek (Richter) 228
53 Carl Heinrich Jacob Fehling, The banqueting table decorated with sugar mountains and models of mining and metallurgical processes during the Festival of Saturn, 26 September 1719. Kupferstich-Kabinett, Dresden. Engraving. Deutsche Fotothek (Koch) 230
54 Carl Heinrich Jacob Fehling, The illumination during the Festival of Saturn, 26 September 1719. Kupferstich-Kabinett, Dresden. Engraving. Deutsche Fotothek (Richter) 231
55 Martin Klötzel, Apollo and his coachman Aurora von Königsmark. 1695. Engraving 233
56 Zacharias Longuelune, The Festival of Diana on the Elbe on 18 September 1719. Pen, ink and wash. Kupferstichkabinett, Dresden Sax. Top. Ca. 200. Deutsche Fotothek (Nagel) 236

Acknowledgements

It gives me great pleasure to record my gratitude to the many people who helped me during the writing of this book and during my visits to Saxony in 1988, 1991, 1997, 1998, 1999 and 2000. In 1988 I had frequent conversations with Monika Schlechte, then of the Technische Universität, Dresden. I am one of the many scholars working on Dresden who have been given generous help by Jutta Bäumel (Rüstkammer, Dresden), Claudia Schnitzer (Kupferstichkabinett, Dresden) and Thomas Rahn (Freie Universität, Berlin). Without their help I could not have written this book at all. Barbara Marx (Technische Universität) gave me generous access not only to her own knowledge and ideas but also, before publication, to the work of her research group on 'Schriftkanon und sozialer Kanon in Renaissance und Barock (1450–1680)', which forms part of the 'Sonderforschungsbereich Institutionalität und Geschichtlichkeit' at the Technische Universität, Dresden. Hans-Georg Hofmann (University of Berne) and A.J. Harper (University of Strathclyde) also allowed me to see their work before publication, for which I am deeply grateful. I am also indebted to the specialist knowledge of Anna Carrdus (University of Bristol), Gillian Lewis (University of Oxford), Katrin Keller (University of Leipzig), Ian Maclean (University of Oxford), Robert Oresko (London), Sara Smart (University of Exeter), Dirk Syndram (Grünes Gewölbe, Dresden), Sabetai Unguru (University of Tel Aviv), Mara Wade (University of Illinois at Urbana-Champaign) and Toshio Watanabe (Chelsea College of Art and Design, The London Institute). My understanding of the period covered by this book has been greatly enhanced by the work of Pierre Béhar (University of Saarbrücken) and Jörg Jochen Berns (University of Marburg). Thomas Bürger, Deputy Director of the Sächsische Landesbibliothek, Staats- und Universitätsbibliothek, Dresden, smoothed my path there on many occasions as did many members of his staff, foremost among them Karl W. Geck, head of the Music Department, and Kerstin Schellbach of the Manuscript Department, who helpfully answered queries. Like all scholars working on Dresden, I have much cause to be grateful to the endlessly cheerful and willing staff of the Sächsisches Hauptstaatsarchiv, Dresden, and of the Deutsche Fotothek, a branch of the SLUB. Alice Watanabe rendered invaluable assistance with the maps. Ekkehard Henschke helped me not only with access to the holdings of the Universitätsbibliothek, Leipzig, of which he is the Director, but also with his knowledge of early modern mining and of Saxon history. Jill Bepler (Herzog August Bibliothek, Wolfenbüttel) read the manuscript as a whole and gave me the benefit of her unrivalled knowledge of early modern German court culture.

I could not have written this book and carried out the archival research necessary without the award of a British Academy Readership in the Humanities from 1997 to 1999 and without the funding of the Alexander von Humboldt-Stiftung. I thank these two remarkable institutions for their support. I am also grateful to the Faculty of Medieval and Modern Languages, Oxford, for help with photographic and travel costs and with the cost of picture permissions. Exeter College, Oxford, also provided me with a travel grant.

My work on this book was made more than pleasurable by the people of Dresden, whose courage, pragmatism and humour have enabled them to survive the political systems and the onslaughts of every century, including the twentieth. It was their labour that built the city in the period covered by this book. It is they who are rebuilding it as I write. I dedicate this book to them.

Oxford, 2001

Abbreviations

BL	The British Library, London
Bodleian	The Bodleian Library, Oxford
HAB	Herzog August Bibliothek, Wolfenbüttel
HStA	Sächsisches Hauptstaatsarchiv, Dresden
OHMA	Oberhofmarschallamt
SLUB	Sächsische Landesbibliothek, Staats- und Universitätsbibliothek, Dresden
UBL	Universitätsbibliothek, Leipzig

A note on proper names

All proper names have been kept in the original language, e.g. Cosimo de' Medici, Johann Georg, August II, Johann Friedrich the Magnanimous, August the Strong.

Genealogical Table of the Albertine Electors of Saxony

Heinrich (1473–1541), r. as Duke 1539–41, m.1512 Katharina, Duchess of Mecklenburg

- **Moritz** (1521–53)
  r. as Duke 1541–53; Elector from 1547
  m. Agnes, Landgravine of Hesse (1527–55)

- **August** (1526–86) r. 1553–86; m.(1) 1548 Anna, Princess of Denmark (1532–85); (2) 1586 Agnes Hedwig, princess of Anhalt (1573–1616)

  Christian I (1560–91), r. 1586–91; m. 1582 Sophie, Margravine of Brandenburg (1568–1622)

  - **Christian II** (1583–1611), r. 1591–1611
    m. 1602 Hedwig, Princess of Denmark (1581–1641)

  - **Johann Georg I** (1585–1656), r. 1611–56
    m. (1) 1604 Sybille Elisabeth, Duchess of Württemberg (1584–1606)
    m. (2) 1607 Magdalene Sybille, Princess of Prussia (1587–1659)

    - **Johann Georg II** (1613–80), r. 1656–80
      m. 1638 Magdalena Sibylla, Margravine of Brandenburg-Bayreuth (1612–87)

    - August of Saxony-Weissenfels (1614–80)

    - Christian of Saxony-Merseburg (1615–91)

    - Moritz of Saxony-Zeitz (1619–81)

      - **Johann Georg III** (1647–91), r. 1680–91
        m. 1666 Anna Sophie, Princess of Denmark (1647–1717)

        - Erdmuthe Sophie (1647–70)
          m. 1662 Christian Ernst, Margrave of Brandenburg-Bayreuth

        - **Johann Georg IV** (1668–94), r. 1691–94
          m. 1692 Eleonore, Duchess of Saxony-Eisenach (1662–96)

        - **Friedrich August I** (August II, King of Poland) (1670–1733), r. 1694–1733
          m. 1693 Christine Eberhardine, Margravine of Brandenburg-Bayreuth (1671–1727)

          - **Friedrich August II** (August III, King of Poland) (1696–1763), r. 1733–63
            m. 1719 Maria Josepha, Princess of Austria (1699–1757)

Introduction

At the Battle of Mühlberg in 1547, Moritz, Duke of Saxony and a member of the Albertine branch of the house of Wettin, wrested the title of Elector of Saxony from his Ernestine cousin Johann Friedrich the Magnanimous (Figure 1). He then made Dresden his capital city. Moritz

Figure 1. Map of Electoral Saxony after 1547.

was killed at the Battle of Sievershausen in 1553, but his successors kept the Electorship and the role within the Holy Roman Empire that it gave them. As part of their panoply of power, the Albertines embellished Dresden architecturally, amassed world-class collections of jewellery and *objets de vertu*, patronised church music, opera, theatre and ballet, and financed the advancement of science and technology. It is because of their cultural legacy that we visit Dresden today. But how does their art patronage fit into the wider intellectual climate of the era in which they lived? What is the political and religious context of the various art forms the Electors encouraged? Why were certain genres encouraged at certain periods and not at others? How do subsequent rulers relate to traditions already established? These are some of the questions this book seeks to answer.

The approach taken is a thematic one. Lutheranism, Italianate court culture, collecting, alchemy, official image-making and court theatre are the subjects dealt with in turn in chapters 1–6. Although all six topics are of importance across the whole period, the chronological focus moves gradually forward, concentrating in the earlier chapters more on the second half of the sixteenth century and in the later ones more on the seventeenth. Seven Electors reigned during this period: August (r. 1553–86), Christian I (r. 1587–91), Christian II (r. 1591–1611), Johann Georg I (r. 1611–56), Johann Georg II (r. 1656–80), Johann Georg III (r. 1680–91) and Johann Georg IV (r. 1691–94). The seventh chapter is devoted to an eighth ruler, Friedrich August I (August II, King of Poland), who reigned from 1694 to 1733. Under the soubriquet of August the Strong, he is the best known of all the rulers of Saxony. This last chapter examines the ways in which he built on and transformed the six areas examined in the previous chapters, using the by now well-established traditions of his house but adding his own distinctive elements to them. Because August the Strong left such a mark on Dresden as we see it today, particularly on its art collections, Dresden court culture has become synonymous with him in many minds. He deserves a monograph all to himself, or at the very least a full biography. This book is not concerned to deal exhaustively with his reign, any more than it deals exhaustively with any one of the eight reigns it examines. It wishes rather to trace the main lines of cultural development in the most important Protestant German territory in the early modern period and to enter into its intellectual life by means of soundings taken at different periods over almost two centuries. This is not a political history of Electoral Saxony nor an administrative or economic history of the Dresden court. Its focus is on official artistic production, whether visual, aural or literary, and on the intellectual life which determined that production as manifested in the continuous engagement of the Electors with science and technology.

Those who know Dresden today may be expecting a discussion of official court painting. But the famous Old Master collection (the 'Gemäldegalerie Alte Meister'), which is the first port of call for most visitors to Dresden today, is to a large extent the creation of Friedrich August II (August III, King of Poland, the son of August the Strong, r. 1733–63) and his successors. His reign lies outside the scope of this book. Nor was court painting of a particularly high quality in Dresden during the period this book discusses. Lucas Cranach the Elder (1472–1553) was court painter to the Ernestine Dukes of Saxony and followed the last deposed Ernestine Elector Johann Friedrich the Magnanimous into captivity in Augsburg in 1548, dying at his court in Weimar. Though Lucas Cranach the Younger (1515–86) did paint Elector August, Moritz's brother and successor, he worked for most of his life in Wittenberg and not in Dresden. After his death, court painting was left to undistinguished artists throughout the seventeenth century, as is confirmed by the portraits of Johann Georg II discussed in chapter 6. This is in contrast to the high standard of goldsmith work and applied art generally throughout the entire period.

The important cultural contribution made by the women of the court as, among other things, writers, collectors and organisers of theatrical events is not considered here either, for the state of our current knowledge is simply not advanced enough. There is ample work here for the future.

In the ten years since the demise of the German Democratic Republic, the kind of research that has long been underway in such other court cities as Florence and Paris, Munich and Kassel has at last become possible in Dresden. Exhibitions have been mounted, works of art have been unearthed from stores, archives and libraries and have been catalogued and made accessible, architectural monuments have begun to re-emerge in their former glory, research groups have been set up and doctoral dissertations been completed. In 1988 it was forbidden to use a photocopier in Dresden. In 2001 all the types of information technology are readily available. The current political climate has not only opened up Dresden to scholars from all parts of the world in a way that was impossible previously, it has also made available the knowledge and encouraged the research of the many dedicated curators and librarians who in the GDR preserved their collections against the depredations and neglect of a philistine state. Publications on Dresden are therefore increasing in number every year. As the first monograph on court culture in Dresden in any language, this book cannot be the last word on the subject. It hopes rather to stimulate debate and encourage researchers to carry the investigation further. Perhaps even, when they next visit Dresden, they will look with increased enjoyment at what they see there.

1
The Lutheran Legacy: The Albertine Electors and Protestant Court Culture

Seven of the eight Electors of Saxony whose reigns are covered in this book were Lutherans. The exception is the last, Friedrich August I, who converted to Catholicism in 1697 in order to be elected King of Poland as August II. Court culture in Dresden until the end of the seventeenth century, therefore, was distinctively Lutheran and this manifested itself in architecture, art, music, theatre and court festivals. But, as we shall see, it did not do so uniformly throughout the period, for confessional and political factors demanded different emphases at different periods.

The Electoral burial chapel at Freiberg

When a Lutheran Elector of Saxony died, his body was taken in solemn procession from Dresden, his capital city, to the little town of Freiberg in the Erzgebirge some 52 km to the south-west.[1] There he was interred in St. Mary's Cathedral ('Dom St. Marien'), in the burial chapel of the Albertine Dukes of Saxony, an astonishing work of Italianate Mannerist interior design, which bears witness to central Lutheran beliefs and confirms the political claims of the Albertines.

Freiberg today is a picturesque town of some 50,000 inhabitants with many buildings from the fifteenth and sixteenth centuries. Its wealth and importance in earlier times were due to the discovery of silver ore in the vicinity in 1168. Tin began to be mined in the region in 1230. Indeed, 'Erzgebirge' means 'Ore Mountains'. This was the basis for the wealth of the Saxon dukes and the prosperity of their territory. Freiberg became the first so-called 'free mining town' ('freie Bergstadt') in the

Empire, free because anyone who found a seam of ore was allowed to mine it, provided they paid their dues to the duke. Silver production decreased at the end of the fourteenth and the beginning of the fifteenth centuries but, with new discoveries of silver ore elsewhere in the Erzgebirge, there was a second boom period after 1470. Indeed, between 1524 and 1550, new technology enabled the income of the Albertines from the Freiberg mines to increase fivefold, to reach a highpoint in 1572.[2] Freiberg was declared the administrative centre of the Saxon mining industry in 1542.

Cobalt began to be mined in the area in 1556 and iron was another important raw material. Significant new silver deposits were found in 1662 near Johanngeorgenstadt, a town founded in 1654, and the amounts of silver extracted at St Anna near Freiberg in 1690 were so large that a huge commemorative medal was struck, depicting in realistic detail the aqueduct and the inner workings of the mine[3] (Figure 2). As Ekkehard Henschke has shown, the Dukes functioned as entrepreneurs throughout the early modern period and kept control of the mines through their investment.[4] They were the ones whose capital employed the workers and built the machinery that was necessary to bring the ore to the surface and to process and transport it. They were therefore also the ones who reaped the rewards. The ordinary miners, liable to be laid off at any time, worked for a wage, which, as Henschke has demonstrated for the neighbouring region of the Harz Mountains, declined in real terms between 1546 and 1624.[5]

The presence of these minerals attracted related industries to the Erzgebirge. The Saxon mint was situated in Freiberg until 1556 when it was moved to Dresden, a dyeing works based on cobalt was founded in the same year in Oberschlema. Armourers had already established themselves in Freiberg in 1381 and silversmiths even earlier in the same century, though the first guild in Freiberg is not attested until 1466.[6] Glass-making was another important related industry. Vitriol and sulphur processing began near Geyer in 1581. A brass foundry opened in 1603 at Rodewisch. As late as 1700 kaolin, the basis for the important porcelain industry of the eighteenth century, was found at Aue near Schneeberg in the Erzgebirge. The documents in the 'Geheimes Archiv' in the Hauptstaatsarchiv in Dresden filed under the heading 'Bergwercks-Sachen' (Mining Matters) illustrate the full range of the mining and related interests of the Electors. Not only are there papers relating to 37 different silver, tin, lead and copper mines and one gold mine, but also to smelting works, to brass and iron foundries as well as to processing plants for saltpetre, sulphur, alum, salt, cobalt, arsenic and lime. We see

The Lutheran Legacy 7

Figure 2. Medal commemorating the discovery of silver deposits in the St Anna mine near Freiberg, Erzgebirge, in 1690. Tentzel, *Saxonia numismatica*. Tab. 68, No. 1.

here the extent to which the revitalisation of all these industries was encouraged by the Electors after the Thirty Years' War.[7]

The Electors of Saxony therefore had a strong interest in promoting both technological advance and exploration. We shall see in later chapters how this manifested itself in the books and tools collected by Elector

August and in his and his successors' preoccupation with alchemy. It is no accident that it was in Saxony in 1565 that the first geological museum in the world was founded by Johann Kentmann (1518–74). He was a doctor who had first been in practice in Meissen but who spent the last twenty years of his life in Torgau, where he began to collect and classify the minerals of the region.[8] In 1565 his treatise *Nomenclaturae Rerum fossilium quae in Misnia praecipue et in allis quoque regionibus inveniuntur* appeared with an illustration of his Cabinet of Minerals, showing the numbered drawers in which he stored them. In 1575 the architect and designer Giovanni Maria Nosseni (1544–1620), originally from Lugano, arrived in Dresden. Elector August commissioned him to look for marble in Saxony in that year. Nosseni also found alabaster, serpentine and jade. In a similar fashion, Johann Georg II commissioned his architect Wolf Caspar von Klengel to undertake geological exploration in 1656–59.[9] Klengel found amethysts, agates, garnets and topaz. Friedrich August I set the scientist Ehrenfried Walther von Tschirnhaus the same task in 1696.

The House of Wettin, whose ruling dukes became Electors in 1423, had divided its territory into two in 1485 in the so-called Leipzig Partition ('Leipziger Teilung'). According to this, the Ernestines, descendants of Elector Ernst (1441–86), retained control of Torgau, Wittenberg, Gotha, Coburg, Jena, the Vogtland and Weimar, which they made their capital city. The cadet branch, descendants of Ernst's brother Duke Albrecht (1443–1500) and therefore known as Albertines, kept the territories of Meissen and Thuringia, with such cities as Dresden, Chemnitz and Freiberg and, in the west, Leipzig. As the mention of Wittenberg shows, it was the Ernestines who were the protectors of Luther and it was their territory that could claim to be the cradle of the Reformation. The Albertine lands did not become Lutheran until 1539, when Duke Heinrich (1473–1541) introduced the Reformation on his accession. He is the first of the Albertines to be buried in the cathedral in Freiberg in 1541, after a reign of only two years.

Duke Heinrich's choice of Freiberg was a natural one: he had been born there, he had lived there for more than thirty years, his sons and successors were born there. It was only during his brief reign that he lived in his official residence in Dresden. Furthermore, the cathedral in Meissen, where his predecessors had been buried, was still Catholic, making it ineligible as the burial place of a Lutheran prince. The cathedral had been rebuilt after a fire and therefore largely dates to the years 1484–1509. Even without the burial chapel it is a remarkable building, decorated with large carved and painted wooden figures of the apostles and of the wise and foolish virgins attached to the pillars of the nave, and with two striking carved stone pulpits.

It was Duke Heinrich's son Moritz (1521–53) who won the Electorship of Saxony for the Albertines, a title they kept in perpetuity, acquiring at the same time a large tranche of Ernestine land including Wittenberg and Torgau. Having fought with his fellow Protestant princes in the Schmalkaldic League, Moritz changed sides and supported the Emperor Charles V against the league in 1545, defeating his cousin the Ernestine Elector Johann Friedrich at the battle of Mühlberg in 1547, with strong Imperial assistance.[10] Moritz changed sides again, fighting against the Emperor on behalf of the Protestants in 1552. He forced the Emperor to sign the Treaty of Passau, which ultimately brought about the Peace of Augsburg in 1555, thus assuring the legal rights of Protestants within the Empire. It was Moritz who made Dresden the capital city of the Albertines and the focus of its court. He was killed at the battle of Sievershausen in 1553, fighting this time against Albrecht Alcibiades of Brandenburg-Kulmbach, a former ally.

Moritz had no male heirs, a circumstance that led the Ernestines to hope for the restoration of the Electorship to them. However, he was succeeded by his brother August, and it is with him that our story properly begins. August's 33-year reign established Dresden as a cultural centre, enlarged the Duchy and laid the foundations for all subsequent developments until the eighteenth century. In the early years of his reign August had to secure his claim to the Electorship, which he did in the Treaty of Naumburg in 1554. He made his new security visible in the first great artistic commission of his reign, the monument to his brother in Freiberg Cathedral.[11]

Moritz, like August, had been born in Freiberg and was the first Elector to be buried in the cathedral there. Two years after Moritz's death August commissioned the brothers Benedetto and Gabriele Thola, artists from Brescia in the service of Moritz since 1550, to design an imposing free-standing tomb for his brother (Figure 3). Elector August commissioned the Lübeck goldsmith Hans Wessel to carry out the design and he in turn passed the commission to the Antwerp sculptor Antonius van Zerroen, who made the monument in Antwerp and shipped it from Hamburg down the Elbe to Dresden.[12] An enormous two-storey marble structure in black and white is set on a stepped plinth. It is decorated with twenty plaques bearing Latin inscriptions, with twelve allegorical female figures sitting on the steps of the monument and twenty-eight warriors in classical costume standing round the second storey, holding coats of arms of the Saxon territories. This

Figure 3. Monument to Moritz, Elector of Saxony, Freiberg Cathedral. Deutsche Fotothek (Nowak).

impressive structure carries a platform resting on the back of eight bronze griffons, taking the height of the monument up to some five metres. On this platform is a life-size alabaster sculpture of Elector Moritz in full armour, shouldering his sword, kneeling in front of the cross in an attitude of eternal adoration. He is represented here as the soldier for Christ, the man whose military service for the Emperor won the Electoral dignity for the Albertines. Ten of the twenty inscriptions on the plaques underline the faithful service of Moritz, his family and his brother August to the Emperor. That Moritz was killed fighting against the Emperor is glossed over.[13]

Figure 4. Electoral burial chapel in Freiberg Cathedral. The monument to Moritz is on the left. Deutsche Fotothek (Möbius).

In 1563 the monument to Moritz was placed behind the altar at the entrance to the choir, dominating the space. Some twenty years later, in 1585, on the death of Anna of Denmark, his wife of thirty-seven years, and after ten of August's children had been buried in the cathedral, August decided to turn the choir area into an official family burial chapel (Figure 4). The space was more or less fixed, for plans to pull down the choir and rebuild it completely were declared too expensive. Giovanni Maria Nosseni, the architect mentioned above in connection with the investigation of mineral deposits in Saxony, was given the task of creating something new within a long narrow area illuminated by six large windows. The result is one of the most surprising church interiors in the Empire, vibrant with life and colour, packed with religious and political significance. Nosseni began work on the burial chapel in October 1586, a month before August's death. It was therefore left to his son and successor, Christian I, and, after his short reign from 1586 to 1591, to the regent, Friedrich Wilhelm of Saxony-Weimar, to carry the project to completion in 1594.

Christian I sent Nosseni to Italy in 1588, notably to Florence, to hire Italian artists. Wolfgang May regards this visit as producing a strong Florentine influence on all of Nosseni's subsequent work in Saxony.[14] Indeed, he sees the Freiberg burial chapel as having been decisively influenced by Michelangelo's New Sacristy in San Lorenzo, Florence. The sculptor Giovanni da Bologna recommended Carlo di Cesare, his colleague at the Medici court, and Carlo arrived in Freiberg in 1590. He had worked on designs for the wedding festivities of Francesco de' Medici and Johanna of Austria in 1566 and probably on the Palazzo Vecchio in Florence under Vasari.[15] He therefore brought knowledge of Italian styles and techniques to Saxony. He produced a number of other sculptures for the Dresden court, but his work for the burial chapel was the most extensive. His contribution to it was essential. He created the figure of Christ Triumphant behind the altar, a bronze crucifix for the altar and the figures of John the Baptist and St Paul pointing towards it, four figures representing the cardinal virtues, eight larger than life-size Old Testament prophets, almost eighty putti in alabaster, bronze and plaster and, most dominant of all, life-size kneeling bronzes of the most important of the Albertines to be buried in the chapel to date: Duke Heinrich of Saxony and his wife Katharina of Mecklenburg, their son Elector August and his wife Anna of Denmark and August's son Elector Christian I (Figure 5). (In 1660 the reigning Elector, Johann Georg II, completed the group of six figures by commissioning a bronze of his father Johann Georg I by Pietro Boselli.) All the figures face the altar and the crucifix, the women kneeling, their hands joined in prayer, the men echoing the representation of Elector Moritz on his cenotaph described above – in full armour, shouldering a sword, in an attitude of eternal adoration.

These figures are set in niches of red and green marble, flanked by Corinthian columns and surmounted by coats of arms. Huge figures of prophets loom over them and the upper part of the walls and the ceiling are covered in a riot of painted stucco with putti in various attitudes

Figure 5. Kneeling figure of Christian I in the Electoral burial chapel in Freiberg Cathedral by Carlo di Cesare. Bronze. Deutsche Fotothek (Möbius).

holding musical instruments. The whole rises to the ceiling which, in a mix of painting and three-dimensional figures, depicts Christ coming in judgment and majesty accompanied by the Archangel Michael, the Weigher of Souls (Figure 6). These are both enormous figures, some 2.5 metres in length but foreshortened by the height at which they are placed. They are surrounded by cherubs' heads and putti blowing long, three-dimensional trumpets while other putti carry the nails, the crown of thorns, the cross, the ladder, the sponge soaked in vinegar and the pillar on which Christ was scourged. The crucified Christ depicted on

Figure 6. Christ coming in Judgement on the ceiling of the Electoral burial chapel in Freiberg Cathedral by Carlo di Cesare. Stucco. Deutsche Fotothek (Seifert).

the altar, the risen Christ above the altar outlined against the window behind, and Christ in judgement on the ceiling together sum up the Lutheran belief in the next life and the triumph over death that is vouchsafed to those who are justified by faith.

The chapel is simultaneously a statement of the Albertines' claim to the Electorship, exemplified by the date 1566 carved on the sword carried by the figure of Elector August. This was the year in which Johann Friedrich II, the rival Ernestine claimant for the Electorship and son of the Johann Friedrich defeated at the Battle of Mühlberg, was outlawed on the accession of Maximilian II as Holy Roman Emperor. At his first Imperial Diet in Augsburg Maximilian publicly invested August with the office of Imperial High Marshall ('Reichserzmarschall') and with the Electorship of Saxony.[16] August had a special sword made to commemorate this event and had himself depicted shouldering it in a portrait by Zacharias Wehme, his court painter, in 1586. The portrait, now in the Armoury in Dresden (Inv. Nr. H 208), shows him in full armour.[17] The figure of August's son Christian I, represented in one of the life-size figures kneeling in the burial chapel, underlines the succession of the electoral title into the next generation.

There was another reason for including Christian in the group: to allay suspicion that he had formally converted to Calvinism. His *rapprochement* with Calvinism goes back to his father Elector August. In the 1560s and early 1570s August had favoured those followers of Melanchthon known as Philippists rather than hard-line Lutherans. His most trusted adviser, Dr Georg Craco, and his personal physician, Caspar Peucer, were close adherents of Melanchthon. He used the Huguenot sympathiser Hubert Languet, who had moved from France to Wittenberg to sit at the feet of Melanchthon, as his informant and diplomatic representative abroad between 1559 and 1577, maintaining a constant correspondence with him during that time.[18] August's chaplain, Christian Schütz, leaned very strongly towards Calvinism.[19] In 1570 August gave his daughter Elisabeth in marriage to the Calvinist Johann Casimir, brother of Friedrich, Elector Palatine. But August clearly thought the drift had gone far enough. In 1574 he cracked down on the Philippists and threw Craco, Peucer and Schütz into prison. Craco died there the next year under torture. Peucer was nor released until 1586; while Christian did not pardon Schütz until 1587.

But August had made Schütz his son Christian's tutor and Schütz's influence was clearly a lasting one. After his twenty-first birthday in 1581 Christian had been gradually eased into government by his father. When he was given further responsibility in 1584, August assigned Dr Nikolaus Krell, a man with clear Calvinist leanings, to be his son's special adviser. When Christian came to power, Krell was made a Privy Councillor and in 1589 Chancellor, thus more or less fulfilling the function of a prime minister. Though Christian once said in a play on his own name that he was neither Calvinist nor Flacian (an adherent of Flacius Illyricus) but Christian, he was clearly moving towards Calvinism. During his short reign of six years, he made it possible for Calvinists to take up posts at Saxon universities, began to reorganise the Lutheran

Figure 7. Zacharias Wehme, Christian I and his family, 1591. Gemäldegalerie Alte Meister, Dresden. Inv. No. MO 1951. Deutsche Fotothek (Steuerlein).

Church in Saxony, allowed Calvinist books to be sold in Leipzig and decreed that exorcism should no longer form part of the baptism service – a move away from Lutheran doctrine.[20] In religious matters it seems he was gradually becoming estranged from his wife, Sophie, Margravine of Brandenburg, although an official portrait belies this. Zacharias Wehme painted Christian, Sophie and their seven children towards the end of the reign in 1591 in an ecclesiastical setting (Figure 7). They are all kneeling with hands joined in prayer in what appears to be a chapel lined with statues of the saints and under a crucifix, the three boys on their father's left, the four girls on their mother's right. Here the Elector, his consort and their children are presented as the epitome of the devout Lutheran family.

Had he lived, Christian might have made Saxony a Calvinist territory according to the principle of *cujus regio ejus religio* and the whole course of history might have been altered. But he died suddenly in 1591 and the Regent, Friedrich Wilhelm of Saxony-Weimar, removed Calvinists from positions of authority with great severity. Krell was held in the fortress of Königstein for ten years until his execution in 1601. Christian's death thus prevented the 'second Reformation' from taking place. So sudden was his death and so opportune for the hard-line Lutherans that there were even rumours that he had been poisoned.[21] His father-in-law, Johann Georg, Elector of Brandenburg, advanced these rumours in May 1592 as a good reason for completing the burial chapel in Freiberg. To inter Christian there in a magnificent space, in whose planning he had taken such an interest, would demonstrate that there was nothing suspicious about his death.[22] It is clearly part of the political programme of the chapel that the effigy of Duke Heinrich, the Albertine who introduced the Reformation to the Albertine territories, should be nearest to the altar, on which John the Baptist and the Apostle Paul point to the crucified Christ. It is only when one knows of Christian's wavering allegiance to Lutheranism that one understands that the central Lutheran message, conveyed by the depiction of Christ's triumph and judgement, that faith at the moment of death rather than correct conduct during life is what counts, is also political in this context.

Orthodox Lutheranism was restored and the Albertines held to it for the next century. They continued to make marriage alliances with other Protestant houses such as Denmark (Christian II and Johann Georg III), Württemberg (Johann Georg I's first wife), Brandenburg (Johann Georg I's second wife) and Brandenburg-Bayreuth (Johann Georg II and Friedrich August I). But they remained stubbornly loyal to the Catholic Habsburg Emperor, something that was a huge disappointment to their fellow Protestant princes throughout the Empire, particularly in the early decades of the seventeenth century.[23] Neither Christian II nor Johann Georg I saw their Protestantism as a reason to break faith with the Emperor. Their role as Electors, indeed as the premier secular Electors in the Empire, took precedence over their personal beliefs. Had they joined the Protestant Union, for instance, Johann Georg I, rather than Friedrich of the Palatinate, might have become King of Bohemia, and might indeed have been elected Emperor.

Later Albertines liked to have themselves depicted in a manner similar to that of the figures in the burial chapel and on the monument to Elector Moritz. In 1660, as we have seen, the arch image-maker Elector

18 *Court Culture in Dresden*

Figure 8. Johann Heinrich Böhme the Elder, Johann Georg II. 1674. Alabaster. Wooden frame. 131 cm in height. Skulpturensammlung, Dresden. Inv. No. ZV 3227.

Johann Georg II had an effigy of his father by Pietro Boselli placed in the burial chapel. In 1674 he had himself portrayed by his court sculptor Johann Heinrich Böhme the Elder (1636–79) in a striking alabaster relief (Figure 8).[24] Wearing full armour, with his Electoral hat and sword at his feet and clothed in an ermine mantle, we see the Elector on one knee with clasped hands raised to shoulder height in a church. He is gazing raptly over his right shoulder at rays of light on which Latin, Hebrew and Greek letters spell out Old Testament passages. The figure of Faith stands in a niche above and behind him. Allowing for the Baroque details – the drawn curtain, the tension of the Elector's dramatic pose with his right leg extended stiffly in front of him, the turn of the head, the heavy wig and the way he seems to be placed on a stage – Johann Georg is depicted in the same attitude of eternal adoration as the figures of his forebears in Freiberg.

The Lutheran Legacy 19

Figure 9. Medal commemorating the inauguration of the chapel in Moritzburg Castle. Johann Georg II kneels before the altar. 1672. Tentzel, *Saxonia numismatica*. Tab. 58, No. 1.

One of Johann Georg II's many architectural commissions was a new chapel in his hunting lodge of Moritzburg outside Dresden, designed by his chief architect, Wolf Caspar von Klengel (1630–91). The foundation stone was laid in 1661 but the chapel was not consecrated until 24 June 1672, the Feast of St John and therefore the name-day of the Elector. To commemorate the consecration Johann Georg II had a medal struck by Ernst Caspar Dürr depicting him on the obverse kneeling alone in front of the altar (Figure 9). He is dressed in his Electoral robes with the Electoral hat and sword on the ground beside him. The inscription reads: 'Herr ich habe lieb die Staedte Deines Hauses und den Ort da Deine Ehre wohnet. Ps.26.v.8' (Lord, I have loved the habitation of thy house, and the place where thine honour dwelleth). On the reverse we see Johann Georg II's motto 'sursum deorsum' and the word 'Jehovah' in Hebrew characters emitting rays of light. Beneath that is an obelisk crowned with a helmet and bearing Johann Georg's monogram. Behind it is a sword and a palm branch crossed. The inscription round the rim reads: 'Im Glauben Herr Zu Stehen Gieb Crafft und Bestaendge Christen-Lieb' (Lord, give me strength to stand firm in faith and steadfast Christian love). The initial letters of this inscription correspond to the initial letters of 'Johann Georg Herzog zu Sachsen, Gülich, Cleve und

Berg Churfürst' – Johann Georg, Duke of Saxony, Gülich, Cleves and Berg, Elector.[25] Johann Georg is stating that his Lutheran faith is an essential component of his identity as Elector.

On his accession in 1657 he had laid down the religious feasts that were to be kept throughout the year and the relevant document in the Dresden archive shows how numerous they were.[26] We expect the feasts of Christmas, Lent, Easter and Pentecost to be celebrated. In addition, however, there is the first Sunday of Advent, the Feasts of the Annunciation, the Ascension, St Michael, the Purification of Our Lady, the Visitation, Epiphany, John the Baptist and Mary Magdalen. There are also nine Apostles' Days, the Conversion of St Paul and the Feast of St Martin. This protocol remained in force until 1721.

Sectarian tournaments

A more ephemeral way of presenting a prevailing ideology is by means of the court festival. In the sixteenth century this meant first and foremost the tournament, which until around 1570 consisted predominantly of the joust or tilt, with the running at the ring or the quintain becoming more prominent thereafter.[27] It was usual for the contestants to parade through the streets of the city before the tournament, each accompanied by lance bearers, footmen, musicians and grooms leading the horses they would ride in the contest. Such groups were usually costumed and each was often accompanied by an elaborate float or festival car picking up the theme of costumes. Such a group was called an 'invention', though the Dresden sources often use the term 'part' (variously spelled 'Part', 'Partt' and 'Parth').

In the climate of sectarian division described above, it is not surprising to find the tournament articulating confessional tensions. In 1574, for instance, the year that marked a decisive change in Elector August's policies of tolerance towards other shades of religious opinion, the running at the ring held on 2 February as part of the carnival celebrations has a number of inventions with a pronounced religious content.[28] One such depicts David and Goliath. The giant Goliath is holding a club and a huge shield and is followed by a group of footmen, one bearing the giant's head on a pole and four others his enormous sword, his club, his shield and his helmet respectively. The hero of the encounter, the champion of True Religion against the Philistine, David, is played by none other than Elector August himself.[29] The theme of the cohorts of the Lord vanquishing the forces of Darkness is again presented in the same running at the ring by means of two other inventions: the winged

Archangel Michael bearing a sword, followed by four angels, leads a fire-spitting Devil captive; and Samson and the lion accompany the Whore of Babylon who is shown riding a seven-headed Hydra.[30] These scenes are reminiscent of some of the illustrations in Protestant Bibles. These biblical episodes of struggle between Good and Evil must be seen in the context of the mockery of monks and nuns, drawing perhaps on the depictions in polemical broadsheets, which we find in two other inventions in this running at the ring. There is a nun riding backwards on a horse disguised as a ram in one group, and in another we have a monk carrying twin babies, both implying unchastity, and two nuns wearing fool's bells on their heads. It is not difficult to relate these five inventions to the confessional difficulties in Dresden in the same year.[31]

Explicit anti-popish satire is to be found again in the running at the ring to celebrate the wedding of Christian I and Sophie, Margravine of Brandenburg in April 1582. The seventeenth invention presented a monk on horseback, while in the twentieth Rudolf von Bünau appeared as the Pope, with the Archangel Michael holding a huge flaming torch with the vanquished Hydra twining round his horse.[32] The Pope is thus presented as the adversary of the angelic warrior. On 2 March 1584 Christian I organised a running at the ring which also included a sectarian jibe: a group of Franciscan monks and the captive Pope with two cardinals holding prayer books.[33] In the running at the ring on 5, 6 and 7 June 1587 to celebrate the christening of Sophie, daughter of Christian I, the Archangel Michael again appears, standing on horseback holding a drawn sword and leading in chains a lion and a gryphon. In front of him is the Pope with two Cardinals.[34] In January 1591 for the christening of his daughter Dorothea, the running at the ring includes at least one invention of a group of monks.[35] Almost a generation later, the same point is made in a tournament for the carnival of 1609. A manuscript tournament book by Daniel Bretschneider relating to this event records a group with a monk and two bishops and another (the sixteenth) with a fox, a fool, a pope and a nun.[36] Bretschneider depicted a similar group in the design for one of his sledges in 1602 (Figure 10).

In these later events we also see gentler representations of biblical events without the sectarian animus. For the christening of Dorothea held in January 1591 and thus shortly after Christmas, the twelfth group presents the Three Magi following the star, coming to do homage, one might imagine, to the new-born Saxon duchess. The tournament of 1609 had a float which depicted Adam and Eve naked under a tree. In September 1614, for the christening of August of Saxony-Weissenfels,

Figure 10. Daniel Bretschneider the Elder, Design for a sledge. 1602. SLUB. Mscr.Dresd.B 104.

Adam and Eve are depicted in the Garden of Eden on a much larger scale.[37] On this occasion there were two floats both showing the Garden: on the first God could be seen creating Eve out of the naked sleeping Adam's side and on the second the apple tree with the snake wound round the trunk. Georg Petzold's rhymed account of the christening also describes a depiction of Elijah in the Fiery Chariot.[38] These inventions bring us much closer to the dramatic presentation of biblical stories which was so central to Lutheran culture and which are examined in the next two sections through the musical genre of the 'historia' and the dramatic genre of the biblical play.

Lutheran sacred music – the 'historia'

One of the most enduring legacies of Lutheranism in Dresden is its church music. Music was of great importance to Luther himself, not just as part of church services but as integral to daily Christian living.[39] He regarded music as a gift from God – 'donum et creatura Dei' – to be practised by man. Again and again, in the Prefaces to the *September-testament* (1522), the *Wittenberger Gesangbuch* (1524) and the *Bapstsches Gesangbuch* (1545) and in his *Table Talk*, Luther stresses how the Bible must be proclaimed through music as well as through the sermon, 'singen und sagen' (singing and proclaiming) being his characteristic phrase. Other early Reformers such as Bugenhagen and Melanchthon also lent their authority to this idea.

When Elector Moritz established his court at Dresden, one of his earliest actions in the cultural field was the foundation in 1548 of a court choir to perform sacred music, the so-called 'Churfürstliche Cantorey'. This was kept separate from the Italian musicians who played for secular occasions, the 'Welsche Music'. The 'Cantorey' consisted of boy trebles, male singers and one or two organists[40] in accordance with the new tenets governing church music laid down by Luther himself in collaboration with Johann Walther the Elder (1496–1570). Walther, who had previously served the Ernestine Electors at Torgau and who had known and worked with Luther since 1524, moved to Dresden in 1548 and became the new choir's first conductor. If his early importance resided in his collection of Lutheran choral works, the *Geystliches gesangk Buchleyn* published in 1525, his later significance is based on the manner in which he organised ecclesiastical music at the Dresden court and in the traditions which he laid down for his successors.[41]

Adequate coverage of Lutheran church music in Dresden is beyond the scope of this book.[42] Space permits me to discuss only one of the genres of church music invented and developed at court – the 'historia'. Lutheran music is remarkable for the range of forms it generated to promulgate the Scriptures – the hymn, the chorale, the cantata, the oratorio. The 'historia' is another such genre and can serve as a paradigm of the way in which Lutheran music was created and nurtured at the Dresden court over a period of at least 150 years.

The 'historia' was originally a dramatic reading of a Gospel passage as part of a church service. As a musical genre it is a setting of a biblical episode and a precursor of the oratorio. Johann Walther the Elder can be said to have created it.[43] There are three types of 'historia': settings of the events of Christ's Passion; settings of the Easter or Resurrection story; and settings of the Christmas story. The oldest type is the Passion 'historia' and we have settings by Walther himself of the Passions according to Matthew and John in the so-called Torgau Walther Manuscript. This is the inception of the genre.

The oldest surviving example of the Easter or Resurrection 'historia' can also be dated to a very early period (1560–65) in the life of the Dresden Cantorey, for it was composed by the tenor Jacob Haupt, a member of the Cantorey under Walther. The next important Easter 'historia' known to us, 'Die aufferstehung Jesu Christi, auss den vier Evangelien' (The Resurrection of Jesus Christ from the Four Gospels) was composed by Walther's second successor, the first Italian *kapellmeister* in Dresden,

Antonio Scandello (1517–80). The text for this 'historia', based on Bugenhagen's 'Evangelienharmonie', was used again in 1623 by Heinrich Schütz (1585–1672) when he composed his 'historia' with the title 'Der Frölichen und Siegreichen Aufferstehung unsers einigen Erlösers und Seligmachers Jesu Christi' (The Joyous and Victorious Resurrection of our Sole Saviour and Redeemer) in Dresden. This is the first 'historia' with orchestral accompaniment and is characteristic of the development of the genre towards ever greater musical elaboration. Schütz uses three choirs, for instance, and eight-part vocal harmony.

Rogier Michael (c.1552–after 1619), Netherlandish *kapellmeister* at the Dresden court from 1587 to 1619 and Schütz's immediate predecessor, created the Christmas 'historia'. The manuscript of two such works by him from the year 1602, 'Die Empfängnis unsers Herrn Jesu Christi' and 'Die Geburt unseres Herrn Jesu Christi' (The Conception of our Lord Jesus Christ), has survived and bears a dedication in the hand of the then court preacher, Polycarp Leyser.

Lutheran biblical drama came into being as a new genre in the same post-Reformation period, but it concentrated on episodes from the Old Testament and on parables from the New. It therefore turned its back on the old miracle and mystery plays of the Middle Ages which had dramatised the Christmas and Easter stories. The 'historia' fills precisely this gap. Although as a form it cannot be called a drama in the narrowest sense of the word, it inhabits an area between the church and the theatre, and its purpose is not narrowly ecclesiastical. The full title of Schütz's Easter 'historia' of 1623 makes this clear: 'Historia der frölichen und Siegreichen Aufferstehung unsers einigen Erlösers und Seligmachers Jesu Christi, In Fürstlichen Capellen oder Zimmern umb die Osterliche zeit zu geistlicher Christlicher Recreation füglichen zugebrauchen, In die Music ubersetzet Durch Henrich Schützen Churf. Sächs. Durchlauchtigkeit Capellmeistern' ('Historia' of the Joyful and Victorious Resurrection of our Sole Saviour Jesus Christ, to be Performed in Princely Chapels or Apartments at Eastertide for the Purposes of Christian Spiritual Recreation. Set to Music by Heinrich Schütz, *kapellmeister* to His Grace the Elector of Saxony). The work may, therefore, be performed for the prince in his chapel – that is, in an ecclesiastical space – but is equally suited to performance in a secular space – the prince's apartments. It is not part of a church service but serves the spiritual recreation of the faithful. Its purpose is therefore not very different from that of the biblical dramas considered in the next section.

During the more than fifty years of his association with the Dresden court, broken up by sojourns in Italy (1628–29), Copenhagen (1633–35 and 1642–44), Hanover and Hildesheim (1639–1641) and Braunschweig (1644–45), Schütz continued to write Lutheran church music in great quantity. Examples are the so-called 'Becker Psalter' first published in 1629 and revised and enlarged in 1661, the *Cantiones sacrae* (Sacred Songs, 1625), the *Symphoniae sacrae* (Sacred Symphonies, 1629, 1647 and 1650), the *Musicalische Exequien* (Funeral Music, 1636), the *Geistliche Concerte* (Sacred Concerti, 1636–39) and the *Zwölf Geistliche Gesänge* (Twelve Sacred Songs, 1657). But, in his old age, at a period when he was spending more and more time in Weissenfels rather than Dresden, he returned to the genre of the 'historia'. In 1660 his Christmas 'historia', 'Historia der freuden- und Gnadenreichen Geburt Gottes und Marien Sohns Jesu Christi' ('Historia' of the Joyful Birth, Full of Grace, of Jesus Christ, Son of God and of Mary) was performed in Dresden on Christmas Day. This composition was printed in 1664 and Schütz himself pointed out in the Preface that it was musically so elaborate that it could be performed only by well equipped princely chapels. The 'historia' is now all but an oratorio. On Good Friday, 24 March 1665, a Passion by Schütz based on the Gospel of St John, 'Historia dess Leidens und Sterbens...Jesu Christi aus dem Evangelisten S Johanno' ('Historia' of the Suffering and Death...of Jesus Christ taken from John's Gospel) was performed in Dresden. At Eastertide in April 1666 the court heard a series of three Passion 'historias' by Schütz. That taken from the Gospel of St Matthew was performed on 1 April, that from Luke on 8 April and that from John on 13 April.[44]

This flourishing of the genre in the hands of the ageing Schütz did not spell the end of the form by any means. 'Historias' continued to be composed and performed at the Dresden court, just as Lutheran music in general was encouraged at this period. (Johann Georg II, who came to the throne in 1657, composed sacred music himself and more works of Lutheran church music were written during his reign than at any other time.) In the second half of the seventeenth century, for instance, many of the Dresden court *kapellmeister* composed 'historias' – Christoph Bernhard (1628–92) in 1663, Marco Gioseppe Peranda (*c*.1625–75) in 1668, Johann Möller in 1676, Johann Wilhelm Furchheim in 1677 and Nikolaus Adam Strungk (1640–1700) in 1690, though in many cases the scores have been lost. The continuity and astonishing longevity of the form is documented by the fact that the text of Scandello's Resurrection 'historia' from before 1580 was reprinted in a collection of texts published in 1745 in a reworking by O.S. Harnisch from 1621.[45] Thus, in the century and a half from the establishment of the 'Cantorey' until the conversion of the Elector to Catholicism in 1697, we see how a local tradition, established in accordance with Lutheran principles, is carried on at court regardless of whether the *kapellmeister* is Netherlandish, as in the early days, Italian, as later became common, or German. The high quality of the compositions and the prestige of the Elector ensured that this tradition then spread to other Protestant territories in the Empire, where 'historias' continued to be performed well into the eighteenth century. This is particularly true of the courts of Weissenfels, Zeitz, Altenburg and Gotha, though 'historias' are also to be found in neighbouring Breslau.

Related to the 'historia' is another musical genre which dramatised Bible stories, the so-called 'actus musicus'. This came into being in the seventeenth century as part of the academic celebrations held on various formal occasions during the year in Lutheran grammar schools and presents such typical Lutheran New Testament stories as the parables of Dives and Lazarus and the Prodigal Son. The earliest work in this genre which has come down to us deals with the first of these topics. It is Fromm's *Actus musicus de Divite et Lazaro* (1649). Georg Calmbach's *Actus musicus de filio perdito* (before 1677) is another characteristic example. These works are known to us from the same geographical area as the 'historia' and are one step nearer to the most dramatic genre to present the Bible to the faithful, Lutheran biblical drama.

Biblical drama

Luther lent his authority to the notion that a specifically Protestant spoken drama in the vernacular was to be encouraged for the benefit of the faithful. He advocated taking its themes from the Scriptures, particularly the stories of Tobias, Esther, Susanna, Daniel and Judith. Two Saxon cities, Wittenberg and Zwickau, played a central role in the creation and dissemination of this type of drama. Wittenberg had an importance all its own, with its associations with Luther and other leading Reformers, its university and its publishing industry. Zwickau, in the south-west of Saxony, was the second Saxon city to have a printing press (from 1523) and the printer Wolfgang Meyerpeck was particularly important for the printing of biblical plays up to 1550 when he moved to Freiberg.[46] These plays then spread outwards from this heartland to other parts of Saxony and into neighbouring territories such as Magdeburg and the Lausitz. In addition to the Old Testament stories sanctioned by Luther, biblical drama also presented New Testament parables such as those of the Prodigal Son or of Dives and Lazarus and certain favourite episodes such as the story of Herod. A related type of drama aims to inculcate correct social behaviour according to Lutheran ideals, particularly within the family – obedience in children and observance of gender roles in marriage being two of the most important. Given the sudden upsurge of such drama from the 1530s on, we are not surprised to find it making an impact on the Dresden court during the sixteenth century. That it should still form part of court celebrations until the death of Johann Georg II in 1680 alongside Italian opera and French-influenced *ballet de cour* is far more surprising and constitutes one of the peculiarities of court culture in Dresden.

It seems highly likely that biblical drama was performed in Dresden at least from the beginning of August's reign in 1553, if not before. The first indication that it was popular at this time is the number of texts listed in the first inventory of the Electoral Library compiled in 1574.[47] At this date the library was kept in Annaburg, the summer residence of the dukes, near Torgau to the north-west of Dresden. It was very much the private library of Elector August, with German works predominating and always listed before the Latin ones (this is discussed more fully in chapter 3 below).[48] What is interesting in the present connection is that, under the heading of 'Theologia', after a whole collection of Bibles, catechisms, pamphlets, sermons and works by Luther, comes a list of fifteen religious dramatic works.

The list begins with plays dealing with episodes from the new Testament: 'Tragedia von Johannis Baptistæ entheuptung' (The Tragedy of the Beheading of John the Baptist), 'Comedia von der offenbarung des waren Messie unnd wie Herodes die unschuldigen kindlein hat toten lassen' (The Comedy of the Revelation of the True Messiah and Herod's Massacre of the Innocents) and 'Comedia oder Tragedia von Juda Ischariote dorinnen ein schrecklich Exempel meer wider gewissen sündigt' (Comedy or Tragedy of Judas Ischariot, in which there is another terrible example of sins against the conscience). The last-named is most probably Johann Chryseus's translation into German of Naogeorg's Latin play *Judas Ischariotes, Tragoedia nova et sacra* which first appeared in Basel in 1552. The list continues with 'Schöner Comedien und Tragedien zwölf aus heiliger göttlicher Schrifft unnd historien' (Twelve Pleasant Biblical Comedies and Tragedies), which is surely Sebastian Wild's collection of the same name published in Augsburg in 1566. The next play mentioned, 'Haustafell. Ein geistlich spiel von den fürnembsten stenden der menschen auff erden' (Model Household. A Religious Play about the Highest Estates on Earth) is likely to be the work by Johann Schuward published in Eisleben in 1565.[49] The next title in the inventory so far eludes identification: 'Comedia wie Got aus fürbit des herrn

Jesu Christi erste Eltern Adam und Evam zu gnaden aufgenommen hatt' (Comedy about how God pardoned Adam and Eve on the Intercession of Jesus Christ), followed by 'Haman die schöne unnd sehr trostliche histori Hester reim unnd spielweis' (Haman. The Beautiful and Most Consoling History of Esther in a Metrical Drama), which is most probably the translation by Johann Chryseus of Naogeorg's Latin play *Hamanus tragoedia nova*, which appeared in Wittenberg published by V. Creutzer in 1546.[50] Next comes 'Das gulden Kalb ein spiel aus der historia des 32. Capittels im andern Buch Moisi' (The Golden Calf from Moses Chapter 32), which can be identified as Heinrich Raetel's *Eine newe geistliche Action, die Histori vom Gülden Kalb Aaronis auss dem 32 Cap. Des andern Buchs Mose*, published by Ambrosius Fritsch in Görlitz in 1573.[51] 'Ein andächtig spiel wie Abraham seinen Sohn Isac aufopfern solte. Und von austreibung der magd Agar auch von Vertreibung Sodoms und Gomorre' (A Pious Play of how Abraham was to sacrifice his son Isaac. Also of how Hagar was driven out and of the expulsion of Sodom and Gomorrha) corresponds to the title of a play by Jakob Frey.[52] 'Comedia vom Reichen mann unnd Lasaro' (A Comedy of the Rich Man and Lazarus) could be either of the two plays on the Dives and Lazarus theme by Johann Krüginger, published in Zwickau in 1543 and in Dresden in 1555 respectively. 'Tragedia der Irdisch Pilgerer genandt' (The Tragedy of the Earthly Pilgrim)[53] is surely Johannes Heros's *Tragedia Der jrrdisch Pilgerer genandt*, published in Nürnberg in 1562. 'Tragedi oder Schauspiel der Kaufman genant darinnen die Apostolische und Babstische Lehre für augen gestellt wirt' (The Tragedy or Drama called The Merchant, in which the Apostolic and Papist Teaching is Presented) is likely to be Naogeorg's *Mercator* in German translation. 'Comedia vonn dem letzten tage des Jüngsten gerichts wie unns derselbe gar nahe fur der tühren dadurch zur buß zubereiten' (Comedy of the Last Day of Judgment and how close this is, so that we should repent) is possibly the work by Philipp Agricola published in Frankfurt an der Oder in 1573, while 'Comedia vom Kinderzucht mit figuren gezieret...' (Illustrated Comedy of Childrearing) may be the play on this theme by Johann Rasser (Strasburg, 1574). 'Comedia vom schalckhafftigen knecht aus dem 18. Capittel Mathei, Dadurch wie der fünfften bit im Heiligen Vater Unser erinnert worden' (The Comedy of the Wicked Servant from Mathew Chapter 18 and how in this we are reminded of the fifth clause in the Lord's Prayer) is probably by Johann Bischoff.[54] The last-named play in the list, 'Spiegel Gotseliger eltern unnd frommer Kinder ein lustige unnd nützliche Comedia durch Michel Druidam...1572' (An Amusing and Useful Comedy, The Mirror of Godfearing Parents and Pious

Children by Michael Druida), appeared in Frankfurt am Main in 1572. We can see from this that the Elector owned a good cross-section of the Lutheran biblical plays available in the middle decades of the sixteenth century. The same plays are listed in the second manuscript inventory of the library taken in 1580 and again in the third dated 1595.[55] By 1629 Georg Pfund's 'Susanna. Eine schöne und nützliche Action' (Susanna. A Pleasant and Useful Play) and Wenceslaus Huber's 'Comoedia Tobiae' (Comedy of Tobias) have been added.

However, we also have evidence of actual performances. Andreas Hartmann's *Christliche Comödia vom Zuestande im Himmel vnnd inn der Höllen* (Christian Comedy on the State of Heaven and Earth) was performed in Torgau in 1600 by 107 actors divided into eight groups. The copy of the text, published in Magdeburg in 1600, from the Electoral library is still in the SLUB.[56] In 1602, for the extensive wedding celebrations for the marriage of Elector Christian II and Hedwig of Denmark, Wolfgang Sommer's 'Comedia. Daß ist, Einn fein Christliches lustiges Spiel, vom Heiligenn Patriarchen Isaac' (Comedy, that is, A Fine Christian Amusing Play of the Holy Patriarch Isaac) was performed.[57] It is a typical biblical play with twenty-three characters, narrative rather than dramatic in its structure. In 1604 Heinrich Kunn had a copy made of his play 'Geistlige Gewissen ruerende Historische Comedia, von der Schweren Belagerung und Wunderbar Erlösung zu Samaria aus dem 2. Buch der Königen am 6. Und 7. Capittel genommen' (A Religious and Historical Comedy, calculated to touch the conscience, of the Fierce Siege and Wonderful Salvation of Samaria from 2 Kings, chapters 6 and 7) and sent it to Elector Christian II, although it is not clear if the piece was performed for the wedding.[58] Preserved in another beautiful manuscript in the SLUB is Cornelius Schonaeus's Latin play 'Triumphus Christi. Das ist Die historia von der Sieghafften Aufferstehung Jesu Christi von den todten' (The Triumph of Christ, Or, the History of the Victorious Resurrection of Christ from the Dead').[59] The manuscript contains the German translation by Elias Gerlach as a parallel text. It is dated 1606 and dedicated to the young prince August (1589–1615), the younger brother of Christian II and Johann Georg I. In September 1612 a whole series of biblical plays by Hans Zihler was performed for the christening of Christian Albrecht, Johann Georg I's firstborn son who died in infancy. On 2 September 'Ruth' was performed, on 8 September 'Isaac' and on 9 September 'Mose', 'Jael' und 'Jephte'. All these plays are preserved in manuscript in the SLUB.[60]

Our knowledge of dramatic performances at the Dresden court is largely based on the detailed diaries and assorted paperwork relating to festivities produced by the Oberhofmarschallamt, or Chamberlain's department, at the time and preserved today in the Hauptstaatsarchiv in Dresden. These records list in detail guests and their entourages, their accommodation, the programme organised for their visit, score sheets for the tournaments, sometimes drawings of inventions or costumes, all bound in great manuscript volumes. Sometimes printed programmes or libretti are also included. There are, however, several important gaps in these records that falsify our picture. The volumes relating to the wedding of Sophia, the sister of Johann Georg I, and Franz, Duke of Pomerania, in 1610, the engagement and wedding of Sophie Eleonore, eldest daughter of Johann Georg I, and Georg II, Landgrave of Hesse, in 1627 and the wedding of Maria Elisabeth, Johann Georg I's second daughter, and Friedrich, Duke of Schleswig-Holstein, in 1630 are all now missing, so we have to rely for our information on such older works as those by Fürstenau, Prölß and Sponsel.[61]

From them we learn that English strolling players, who are discussed in greater detail in chapter 6, also performed biblical plays at court on their visits. Their themes are all the familiar ones: 'Der verlorene Sohn' (The Prodigal Son) and 'Haman und Esther' (Haman and Esther) in 1626 and 1627, 'Die Geschicht von der Hebraeischen Heldin Judith und dem Holoferne' (The History of the Jewish Heroine Judith and Holofernes) in 1629, 'die Tragödie vom Reichen Mann und Lazaro' (The Tragedy of Dives and Lazarus), the Prodigal Son again in 1632 and 'die Komödie von der Erschaffung der Welt' (The Comedy of the Creation of the World) in 1646. The first two appear in the printed collection of plays of the strolling players published in Leipzig in 1620 and again in 1624.[62] The biblical play thus continued to flourish into the seventeenth century.

Johann Georg II and the 'Joseph' plays

We have seen above how various Lutheran art-forms had a resurgence during the long reign of Johann Georg II (1657–80). The building of the chapel at Moritzburg, Johann Georg II's commissioning of depictions of himself in attitudes of Lutheran piety and the recrudescence of Lutheran church music encouraged by a ruler who was a composer himself, are examples of this. Biblical drama also had a notable flowering during the reign. Johann Georg II, who was responsible for promoting Italian opera and French ballet in Dresden, included frequent performances of German biblical dramas on traditional themes in his festivities. For the christening of his grandson, Johann Georg IV, in 1669, for instance, a whole series of biblical plays was performed: 'Die Historia von Saul und David' (The Story of Saul and David), 'die Historia von Haman und Esther' (The Story of Esther and Haman), 'die Hebräische Heldin Judith und der Holoferne' (The Jewish Heroine Judith and Holofernes) and 'die Tragödie von Joseph und seinen Brüdern' (The Tragedy of Joseph and his Brothers).

The theme of Joseph was a particular favourite of Johann Georg II's which he used for his own purposes. During his reign, a play on this topic was performed for large social gatherings at court in 1665, 1669, 1671, 1672 and 1678, but with a particular slant. The story of Joseph had been a favourite subject for biblical drama since the Reformation, as is documented by Lebeau and Wimmer,[63] but the three aspects most frequently stressed in earlier versions were Joseph's chastity in the face of the seductive wiles of Potiphar's wife during his exile in Egypt, his ability to interpret dreams and his role as saviour and prefiguration of Christ. In 1602, for instance, the Dresden court preacher Matthias Hoë von Hohenegg translated Aegidius Hunnius's play on the Joseph theme from Latin into German for the wedding of Johann Georg Goedelmann, Imperial Count and Saxon Councillor. It stressed Joseph's virtues of chastity and filial obedience.[64]

The Joseph plays staged during the reign of Johann Georg II are quite different. Their theme is Joseph and his brothers, or, more exactly, the hatred of the envious brothers for the virtuous Joseph, their father's favourite son, and his triumph over their wicked wiles. The first recorded performance was at the carnival season in 1665. Johann Georg II's only daughter, Erdmuthe Sophie, and her husband, Christian Ernst, Margrave of Brandenburg-Bayreuth, were the guests of honour at the celebrations, which lasted from 19 January to 22 February. The Court Chamberlain's papers record that the story of Joseph 'and how he was sold by his brothers into Egypt until he revealed himself to them' was performed on 27 January.[65] We have far more information about the performances given in February 1669. These were in honour of Johann Georg IV, who had been christened the previous October. The celebrations lasted from 2 to 23 February and, as mentioned above, included five biblical dramas, of which the 'Comoedie von Joseph' was one. The biblical story has now been divided into two plays, the first of which is devoted exclusively to the theme of fraternal hatred. A printed plot summary, spoken by Joseph, is to be found in the relevant volume in the Chamberlain's papers.[66] Joseph addresses the assembled company and tells them that the subject of the first of the two plays will be 'the effect of fraternal hatred and how it has turned natural brotherly love into inhuman tyranny'. Other phrases used are 'the hatred my brothers had conceived for me', 'the white-hot heat (Gluth) of their hatred', the 'embittered hatred of the brothers' which leads them to criminal acts, and so on. The second play deals with Joseph in Egypt. On 1 and 2 May 1671, as part of the celebrations for the installation of Johann Georg II in the Order of the Garter (see chapter 5 below), the Comedy of Joseph was repeated. It was again divided into two five-act plays and would seem to have been a repeat of the work given in 1669. The innovation was that it was followed by a 'Ballet of the Twelve Tribes of Israel.[67] From 4 to 23 February 1672, Johann Georg II called a summit conference of his brothers and their families at carnival time. This meeting was given the official title the 'Vertrauliche und Fröliche Zusammenkunft' (the Confidential and Joyful Gathering). Again, the Joseph plays were performed, over three evenings, on 14, 15 and 16 February, and were again followed by a ballet of the Twelve Tribes of Israel. The printed summary, spoken as usual by Joseph, explains that his brothers begrudged Joseph his father's love.[68] Six years later, between 29 January and 1 March 1678, Johann Georg II called another summit conference, this time recorded in a huge printed festival book with commentary entitled 'die Durchlauchtigste Zusammenkunft' (The Illustrious Gathering).[69] Again, the Comedy of Joseph fills three evenings, 6, 7 and 8 February. Tzschimmer makes perfectly clear and at great length how the story is to be interpreted.

His plot summary of Part I of the *Comœdiæ von dem Ertzvater Joseph* (the Comedy of the Patriarch Joseph), which deals mostly with the selling of Joseph into Egypt and takes us up to Joseph's resistance to Potiphar's wife, begins by underlining the havoc which can be caused by hatred and enmity between close relatives and blood brothers unless God supports the weaker party.[70] It goes on to underline the piety, filial devotion and obedience of the beloved son Joseph and the jealousy and bitterness of his brothers. In a separate section entitled 'the Moral of the First Part of the Comedy of Joseph', Tzschimmer hammers home the message: He begins: 'Rara Concordia Fratrum' and continues:

> Niemand aber ist gehässiger als ein fleischlicher Bruder/ wenn es den Wechsel der Ehre/ und Hoheit/ oder das Theil einer Erbschafft betrifft: Selten lässet sich die Tugend blicken/ daß die Eintracht der Brüder zusammenhält.
>
> [No one is more filled with hatred than a blood brother when transfer of honour, rank or a portion of an inheritance is at issue. Seldom does one see the virtue of harmony between brothers.][71]

Tzschimmer then lists nineteen examples of brotherly enmity from Cain and Abel to Ferdinand of Castile, including many examples from ancient history. Part II of the Comedy focuses on Joseph's brothers' journey to Egypt to buy grain and the changed power relations between the sometime victim and his brothers. The moral commentary now is a disquisition on 'Des Josephs belohnte Frömmigkeit und erhöhete Tugend' (Joseph's piety rewarded and his virtue elevated).[72] This is a eulogy on the theme of Joseph's manifold virtues, as is the moral commentary on the third part, which deals with 'Das versöhnliche Bruder-Hertz Josephs / und die treue Versorgung seines Väterlichen Hauses' (Joseph's forgiving brotherly heart and his true care for his father's house).[73] The whole focus of these three plays and the commentary on them is on Joseph, the wise, forgiving, virtuous saviour of his people, rising above the envy and malice of his brothers.

If we examine the guest list for the festivities of which these performances formed a part, we see that in 1669, 1672 and 1678 Johann Georg II's three younger brothers, August of Saxony-Weissenfels (1614–80), Christian of Saxony-Merseburg (1615–91) and Moritz of Saxony-Zeitz (1619–81), and their wives and families were all present, summoned to Dresden by Johann Georg II. Of the younger generation present, Johann Georg III (1647–91) and Johann Adolf of Saxony-Weissenfels (1649–97) were the most important. We have to imagine the brothers and their families obliged to endure these performances at which, each time with increased vehemence, as well as at increasing length, the theme of brotherly hatred against the virtuous Joseph was emphasised. There is no doubt who the figure of Joseph represents and, as a reminder, the guests would have been given a printed plot summary to take away with them.

Only an intense rivalry between the brothers can explain these extraordinary circumstances.[74] Their father Johann Georg I divided his territory four years before his death, presenting his three younger sons with territories in the west of Saxony, territories which were thereby taken away from the patrimony of the eldest son (Figure 11). August was given Weissenfels, Christian Merseburg and Moritz Zeitz. Unclarity in Johann Georg I's will made a series of further agreements and compromises between the brothers necessary in the following decade. In 1657, for instance, they signed the so-called 'freundbrüderlicher Hauptvergleich' (the amicable and brotherly principal accord), but further agreements were necessary in the years 1660, 1661 and 1663. The gatherings in Dresden were in the nature of summit conferences between the four brothers. Johann Georg II seems to have felt especial rivalry towards his next youngest brother, the notable August of Saxony-Weissenfels, as a fat volume of documents in the SLUB entitled 'Acta Streitigkeiten zwischen Chursachsen und Fürst

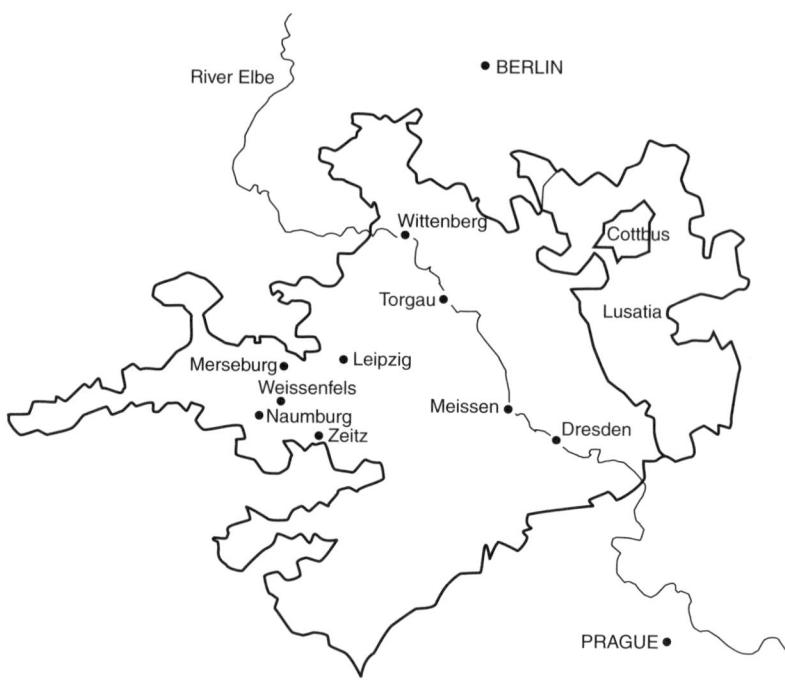

Figure 11. Map of Electoral Saxony after 1648, augmented by Lusatia.

August...betreffend' demonstrates.[75] One can speculate that the contrasting family circumstances of the two brothers fuelled Johann Georg's unease. The Elector had only one son and one daughter, while August had five sons and four daughters by his first wife and a further two sons by his second. A fall from a horse, an illness, could have wiped out the Elector and his heir and brought August or one of his sons to power. Only Johann Georg II's youngest brother Moritz seems to have been regarded with any favour, being paralleled in the plays by the beloved youngest son Benjamin. Biblical drama is thus being used here not for edificatory purposes but in the service of family politics. As we shall see in chapter V, Johann Georg used other dramatic forms for the same purpose.

Dedekind and the biblical semi-opera

At about the same time, the greatest original contribution to biblical drama at the Dresden court was being made by the composer, writer, bass, violinist and director of the court orchestra from 1666 to 1675,

Constantin Christian Dedekind (1628–1715). Dedekind published his first collection of biblical plays, *Neue geistliche Schau=Spiele, bekwehmet zur Music* (New Religious Plays Set to Music), in 1670 and dedicated them to Johann Georg II. As the title indicates, these works lie somewhere between plays and operas, and Dedekind presumably hoped that they would be put on in the new opera house in Dresden. As far as we know, this never happened. The collection consists of four plays: *Himmel auf Erden/ Das ist Gott als Mänsch im Freuden=Spiele der Gebuhrt Christi/ vohrgestaellet* (Heaven on Earth, that is, God Made Man in a Joyous Play on the Birth of Christ); *Stern aus Jakob und Kinder=Mörder Herodes/ verfasset in ein singendes Trauer=Spiel. Anderer Teil von Jesus Gebuhrt* (Star of Jacob and the Child-Murderer Herod in a Sung Tragedy. The Second Part of the Nativity); *Sterbender Jesus, auf Thraehnen=reicher Schau=Bühne eines bluhtigen Trauer=Spieles/ zu schuldigster Erinnerung / wehemütigst vohrgestaellet* (Dying Jesus on the Tear-soaked Stage of a Bloody Tragedy in Most Due Remembrance Most Movingly Presented); *Siegender Jesus/ in einem Freuden=Spiele Seiner triumphierlichen Höllen=Fahrt und Auferstehung vohrgestaellet* (Jesus Victorious in a Comedy on his Triumphant Descent into Hell and his Resurrection). As the titles make clear, these four plays cover the three themes that are typical of the 'historia' – the Passion, Resurrection and Christmas stories – and one can see them as a synthesis of the 'historia' and of the biblical play.

In 1676, Dedekind brought out a second collection, *Heilige Arbeit über Freud und Leid der alten und neuen Zeit / in Music-bekwehmen Schau= Spielen ahngewendet* (Sacred reworking of joyful and sorrowful events in ancient and modern times, in plays suitable for music), but this time dedicated to Johann Georg's younger brother and arch-rival, August of Saxony-Weissenfels. In this collection Dedekind concentrates on themes from the Old Testament. It begins with a group of short, sacred entertainments to be performed during banquets at court, 'Ahn=Hang zur geistlichen Taffel=Music'. It includes Jacob's Flight and Dream, the Lord Calling Moses, a Triumphal Song at Pharaoh's Destruction in the Red Sea, David's Fight with and Victory over Goliath, and Elija's Journey to Heaven. Then come five musical and dramatic renderings of the stories of Adam and Eve, 'der erster Märterer Abel', (Abel, the First Martyr), 'Der Wunder=gehorsahmen Isaak und großgläubiger Abraham' (The Wondrous Obedient Isaac and Most Faithful Abraham), 'Rebekka' and 'Samson' (the latter being a translation of Vondel's *Simson*). What is interesting to note is that the theme of brotherly discord is again treated in this collection dedicated to August of Saxony-Weissenfels. 'Jacob's Flight and Dream' begins with the statement that it is brotherly envy which is driving Jacob away ('Ach! Bruder=Zorn ist übel zuverschmerzen' [Oh, brotherly anger is hard to bear]) and the David play shows him rejected by his natural brothers, only to find a true brother in Jonathan at the end of the piece. The Abel play deals with the quintessential story of brotherly hatred, the murderous envy of Cain for Abel; and Abraham and Isaac depicts the obedient son, beloved of his father. One cannot but speculate that these plays represent the same conflict we saw in the Joseph plays, but from the point of view of the younger brother.

What genre do Dedekind's musical plays belong to? They are not operas on the Italian model nor are they oratorios. They are more dramatic than the 'historia' and are written expressly for theatrical performance. The tightness of their construction and the musical interludes distance them from biblical drama proper. Dedekind combines serious with comic scenes and is writing for a sophisticated stage with all its technical possibilities. We see this particularly in his scenes in hell in the fourth Act of the 'Birth of Christ' and in the Prologue to 'Jesus Victorious'. Yet a specifically Lutheran piety, a reverence for the Scriptures and for the message of Salvation, informs his works. The sacred drama of the Fall is combined in Dedekind's treatment with a search for a Saviour, for instance. Dedekind's works could only have been produced in Dresden, where Lutheran piety, a highly developed court stage and German church music of the highest quality could be found side by side.

If the Electoral burial chapel at Freiberg was planned as a statement of the political ambitions and religious beliefs of the Albertines, it was completed in a climate of unrest between Lutherans and Calvinists at the end of the sixteenth century, heightened by the suspicion that the recently deceased Christian I had actually been a Calvinist himself. If a musical genre like the 'historia' was created from within the core of the Lutheran faith, the sectarian inventions so common in the tournaments held at court in the 1570s and 1580s reflect Lutheran insecurities vis-à-vis Catholicism. If Johann Georg II reiterated his identity as a Lutheran prince after the Thirty Years' War by building the chapel at Moritzburg and by having himself depicted in various media as a pious Lutheran, his struggles with his younger brothers caused him to use the established genre of the biblical drama for propaganda purposes.

How this intensely Lutheran culture was intertwined with, indeed inseparable from, the Italianate ideal of the Renaissance prince is the subject of the next chapter.

2
The Italian Ideal: The Sixteenth-Century Reception of Italian Culture

Italian artists in Dresden

We saw in chapter 1 how the first Albertine Elector Moritz was glorified by his successor and brother August as the champion of Lutheranism in the great monument in the burial chapel at Freiberg. We also saw how Moritz and August assiduously patronised German Lutheran art-forms, in accordance with Luther's own linking of German values and the German language with the reform of religion. But the same two princes also wished to turn Dresden into a princely city and to establish themselves as rulers of European importance. This meant modernisation, particularly in the cultural field, and modernisation meant Italianisation. For this they needed to bring Italian architects, artists, craftsmen, engineers and musicians across the Alps and north to Dresden.

Almost immediately after wresting the Electorship from his Ernestine cousin, Moritz began this process. The first stage in his programme was the transformation of the medieval fortress in Dresden into a Renaissance palace, much larger than its predecessor and covered with striking and elaborate *sgraffito* depictions of scenes from the Old Testament, classical mythology and ancient history (Figure 12). This was a decorative technique hitherto unknown in Saxony.[1] Moritz travelled to Italy in 1549, and visited Venice, Mantua, Ferrara and Milan. Using a wealth of new archival material, Evelyn Korsch has demonstrated the extent of the diplomatic connections Moritz established with the court of Ercole II d'Este in Ferrara, which lasted from 1549 until Moritz's death in 1553.[2] These culminated in a plan being considered in 1552–53 for the Turks to take over the Kingdom of Hungary, but for Moritz to reign over it as their

38 *Court Culture in Dresden*

Figure 12. Johann Azelt, A view of the Palace courtyard in Dresden showing the *sgraffito* decoration. From Gabriel Tzschimmer, *Die Durchlauchtigste Zusammenkunft*, Plate 23, S.207. Deutsche Fotothek (Richter).

representative. He would thus provide a European barrier against Islam but also curb the power of the Emperor. But from the time of his Italian journey in 1549 these political manoeuvrings went hand in hand with cultural interests. In Mantua Moritz probably visited Giulio Romano's Sala dei Giganti in the Palazzo del Tè, completed in 1535. This may have influenced the design for the twelve larger than life-size frescoes of giants in the Riesensaal or Hall of the Giants completed in 1553 in the Palace in Dresden[3] (Figure 13). These frescoes were executed by the brothers Benedetto (1525–1572), Gabriele (1523–1569) and Guerino Tola from

Figure 13. Fresco by the Tola brothers in the Riesensaal or Room of the Giants in the Palace in Dresden. Drawing by Valentin Wagner. Pencil and red chalk. Sheet 22 from Wagner's sketchbook. Kupferstich-Kabinett, Dresden. Deutsche Fotothek (Rous).

Brescia, whom Moritz hired on this visit with the help of Cardinal Christoph Madruzzi, Archbishop of Trent. They and a fellow countryman, Francesco Ricchino, also provided the designs for the wall paintings in the three-storied gallery, or 'Altan', protruding into the Palace courtyard, and for the *sgraffito* decorations on the outside of the Palace.[4]

But the Tola brothers were also musicians and, with Antonio Scandello and Cerbonio and Mattia Besozzi, were members of a group of cornettists and sackbut players that Moritz brought back with him to Dresden. One of Moritz's early cultural initiatives had been the founding on 22 September 1548 of a 'Cantorey', or choir of boys and men, to sing at Lutheran church services. As discussed in chapter 1, this choir was directed by Johann Walther the Elder, who had worked with Luther himself and who remained in office until 1554. The Italian musicians hired early in 1549 were to form a separate group, the so-called 'Welsche Music' ('foreign musicians') whose task was to perform secular music. Of these musicians the one who is now remembered is Antonio Scandello (1517–80). On Moritz's death at the Battle of Sievershausen in 1553, Scandello wrote a memorial mass in the Elector's honour, the *Missa sex vocum super epitaphium illustrissimi principis Mauritii*. Though Walther was succeeded by the Netherlandish composer Matthaeus Le Maistre (c.1505–77) who held the post from 1554 until his retirement in 1568, Scandello was first made Le Maistre's assistant in 1566 and then his successor in 1568. Scandello was thus the first Italian *kapellmeister* not only in Dresden but at any German court. He was able to make his Italian tradition fruitful in his new home. The St John Passion of 1561 and his *Auferstehungshistorie* (Resurrection 'historia') are cases in point. Hoffmann-Erbrecht records how influential his collections of sacred and secular songs were on his contemporaries, for instance, the *Neapolitanische Kanzonen* (Neapolitan songs) of 1566 or the *Newe und lustige weltliche deudsche Leidlein* (The new and merry secular German songs) 'which synthesized the Italian madrigal and villanella styles with the older German cantus firmus technique'.[5] Among other duties, Scandello accompanied Elector August to the Reichstag in Nuremberg in 1575.

Scandello was succeeded by another Italian *kapellmeister*, the Genoese Giovanni Battista Pinello di Ghirardi (c.1544–87), who came to Dresden from Prague in 1580.[6] And it was to Prague that Pinello returned when fired from his post in Dresden in 1584, probably on the insistence of the German and Netherlandish members of the Court Chapel. Pinello's achievement was his contribution to the spread of the Italian secular vocal style at German courts.[7]

Thus, while August dropped the diplomatic links with Ferrara on his brother's death, out of loyalty to the Emperor, this did not mean a cessation of cultural connections with Italy. Indeed, it was typical of August that he both kept on the artists and musicians hired by Moritz and employed a whole series of fortification engineers, architects, designers, artists and art agents during his thirty-three-year reign. As an example of how contact with the latter could further the knowledge of Italian art in Dresden, we might cite the link between Jacopo Strada and Elector August.[8] Strada, a Mantuan by birth, was a painter and goldsmith by training and a great collector of antiquities, books and pictures. He worked as an art agent for both the Fuggers and Albrecht, Duke of Bavaria, and was employed by Emperor Maximilian II as Keeper of his collection of antiquities ('Antiquar'). In his heyday in the 1560s he had myriad connections with Italian and German princes. He appears to have made the acquaintance of Elector August, or at least his confidential secretary Hans Jeniss, in 1573 when August visited Vienna. At this time Strada was trying to raise money to publish a seven-volume work on ancient inscriptions as well as a dictionary of eleven ancient and modern languages. In the summer of 1575 August paid Strada the large sum of 500 talers. In return Strada made August a present of copies of Titian's twelve Roman Emperors painted for the Duke of Mantua between 1536 and 1539. Strada, still needing cash, hoped either to sell his own collections to August or to be taken into August's employment, but this did not materialise.

Far more intensive and extensive was the contribution of engineers, architects and designers to the Italianisation of Dresden. As we shall see in the next chapter when we examine the Electoral Library, August assiduously collected the most modern Italian works on perspective and architecture. He also employed Italian architects. One of the earliest was another Brescian, Giovan Battista Buonomia, employed from 1566 to 1571.[9] His contract states that he was engaged not only as a sculptor, fortification engineer and architect, but also as the designer of court festivities.[10] But two other architects left a greater mark on the city: Rocco Guerini, Conte di Linar (1525–96), and Giovanni Maria Nosseni (1544–1620).

In the most substantial investigation of early modern cultural relations between Dresden and Italy to date, Barbara Marx teases out in fine detail the migration of artists from Florence to Dresden and the context within which the cultural exchange takes place.[11] She shows how the rapprochement with Florence began in 1557 and how it was marked first by misunderstandings, then by mistrust. Cosimo I de' Medici was interested in having good relations with those German princes who could provide him with skilled mining and artillery specialists and August needed architects, artists and craftsmen for various projects in Dresden. Markus Castor points out that Rocco di Linar represented a completely new type of architect – an aristocrat, a man of education and polish, a diplomat and a courtier.[12] Born in Tuscany, he is said to have been educated with Cosimo de' Medici. He first worked as a fortification engineer at the court of Alfonso II in Ferrara in 1539 but fled to France where he had a spectacular career for almost twenty years in spite of his Huguenot sympathies. As the leader of a Huguenot rebellion in 1567 he had to flee and went first to Heidelberg to the court of Friedrich, Elector Palatine, and then in 1569 to Dresden as architect and artillery specialist, where he remained until 1578 when he entered the service of Elector Johann Georg of Brandenburg. During his time in Dresden, he took over the building of the fortifications of the city, already begun by Moritz in 1546, and hugely extended them according to the most advanced conceptions of the day.[13] He also worked on the palaces in Freiberg, Augustusburg, Sitzenroda and Lochar. In the spring of 1572 he was sent on a diplomatic mission to Florence, Ferrara and Mantua and on his return brought gifts to Elector August which, as Marx has shown, initiated an exchange of presents between the two courts. As a consequence of Linar's visit to Florence, the young Costantino de' Servi (1554–1622), afterwards to become an internationally sought-after painter, designer and architect moving round the courts of Europe, paid a first visit to Dresden in 1572.

But the architect who made the greatest contribution to the introduction of Italian ideas to the art and architecture of the Dresden court was Giovanni Maria Nosseni. Born in Lugano he was recommended to Elector August by Count Hans Albrecht von Sprintzenstein as sculptor, stone-carver, painter, designer of court festivities and someone who could carve vessels out of alabaster.[14] He was first employed in 1575 and in the course of his long career served four Electors – August, Christian I, Christian II and Johann Georg I – as well as the regent, Friedrich Wilhelm von Saxony-Weimar, during the minority of Christian II. We have seen in chapter 1 how he was first given the task of finding marble and semi-precious stones in Saxony and then how he was commissioned by Elector August just before his death in 1586 to design the Electoral burial chapel in Freiberg, a task he carried on under August's son, Christian I, and completed after Christian's death in 1591. In connection with this project he was sent to Florence in 1588 to hire artists for the burial chapel, the most notable of whom, was the sculptor Carlo di Cesare, who spent the years 1590–93 in Saxony. Meanwhile, August had taken Carlo Theti (1529–1589), a Neapolitan engineer, into his service in about 1581, though his first official contract was not made out until 1584. One of his tasks was to teach Christian I the art of fortification. Marx suggests that Theti probably taught Christian the Italian language and Italian etiquette. In addition, he served as a Saxon envoy to Florence in 1585.

The new stables and portrait gallery (1586)

The early inculcation of an Italian ideal certainly bore fruit when Christian I succeeded his father in 1586. His reign began in February and, as Walter May has pointed out, by April he had already given orders to recruit the necessary stonemasons and other craftsmen for the construction of a new stables in Dresden.[15] The foundation stone was laid on 6 June 1586.[16] The stables were housed in a Renaissance building with *sgraffito* decoration next to the Palace in the centre of Dresden and was completed in 1588. What is left of it today is known as the Johanneum and is much altered.[17] This U-shaped building could house 128 horses on the ground floor and was one of the most magnificent stable buildings in the Empire in its day.[18] It had two main storeys, two further storeys in the gables and three in the roof, as the illustration in Anton Weck's description of Dresden of 1680 makes clear (Figure 14). The first floor housed the ducal apartments and the collections of sledges and of tournament accoutrements (known as the 'Schlittenkammer' and the 'Pallienkammer' respectively). The upper floors were reserved for the armoury.[19] The actual architects of the stables were Paul Buchner and Hans Irmisch, though some of the inspiration at least came from Giovanni Maria Nosseni who was influenced by the buildings he saw in Florence. The stables are still linked to the Palace by the so-called 'Long

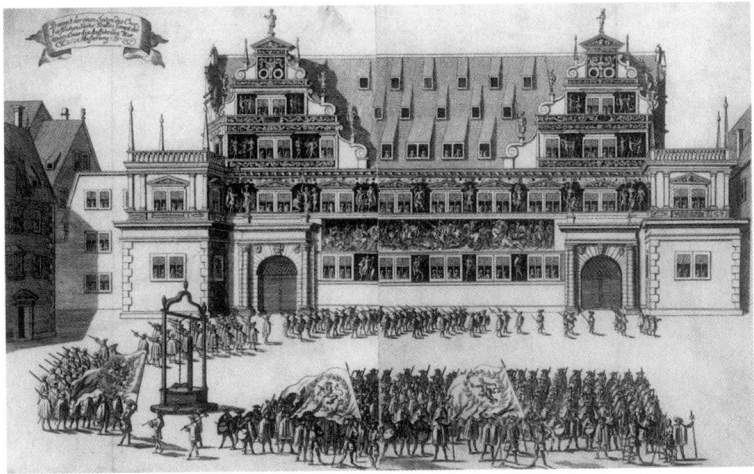

Figure 14. The stables built by Christian I (1586). Engraving from Gabriel Tzschimmer, *Die Durchlauchtigste Zusammenkunft*, S.15. Deutsche Fotothek (Richter).

Figure 15. The Langer Gang or Long Arcade. Engraving from Anton Weck, *Der Churfürstl. Sächs. Weit beruffenen Residentz und Haupt-Vestung Dresden: Beschreib: und Vorstellung.* Deutsche Fotothek (Rous).

Corridor' or 'Langer Gang' (also built between 1586 and 1588), an arcade of twenty-one arches 100 metres long with a covered upper storey and designed by Nosseni (Figure 15). The stables could be reached from the Palace under cover along this upper corridor, which Christian I made into a portrait gallery ('Ahnengalerie') with life-size paintings of Wettin ancestors and twenty-nine depictions of the tournaments of Elector August, all by Heinrich Göding.[20] Beginning at the Palace end, the portraits took the Wettin line back, quite fictitiously, to 90 BC. Accompanying each portrait was a motto – that of Elector August was 'Te Gubernatore' – and a depiction of that Wettin's famous deeds. Each subsequent Elector added his own portraits to the gallery. The diplomat and art dealer Philipp Hainhofer visited it in 1629 and described the portraits of the then ruler Johann Georg I and his four sons.[21] In his description of the stables published in 1680[22] Anton Weck lists the fifty portraits up to and including Johann Georg II. The 'Long Corridor' was thus a continuing monument to the Electoral family.

Visitors passing through this corridor came straight to the floor on which were exhibited and stored the collection of sledges and tournament armour. The 'Long Corridor' bounds on one side the outdoor riding arena or 'Stallhof', which was used for equestrian exercises and festivals at court. A ramp led down from the first floor of the stables into the Stallhof, so that it could easily be reached by tournament contestants who had put on their armour in the stables. As Jutta Bäumel points out, horses, arms and armour, princely magnificence and equestrian festivals are all visibly interconnected in the combination of Stallhof, stables and Long Corridor. The connection is further emphasised in the inscription Christian I had placed over one of the two imposing gates of the stables: 'equorum stationi areamque adjunctam militarium exercitationum causa'.[23]

Laurentius Peccensteinius, the court historiographer, writing some twenty years later, makes clear the close relationship that existed between the stables, the Stallhof and the portraits and other artworks which adorned them on the one hand, and the collections of arms, armour and accoutrements for festivites on the other. He places both in the context of the great deeds of the Wettins. He talks of the

> zierliche Gemelde und alten Römischen Triumphis... statuis des gantzen Wittichindischen Stambs / zu Roß sitzen/ sambt praefigurirunge jhrer insonderheit grossen Thaten/ Item den zierlichen Thurnier und Dummelplatz/ und dann den Königlichen Vorraht/ an Roßgeschmeiden/ allerhand Auffzügen/ zum Thurnieren und Ringelrennen/ auch anderer Fürstlichen lust/ so darinnen zubefinden...[24]

[the beautiful paintings and ancient Roman Triumphs... the statues of the whole line of the Widukinds on horseback with depictions of their particularly great deeds, then the beautiful arena for tournaments and *haute école* riding, and the royal store of tack and all sorts of costumes for tournaments and runnings at the ring and other princely diversions to be found there].

Arms, armour and Italian horsemanship

The combined functions of the stable building remind us how essential excellence in combat and horsemanship was to the public persona of the prince. The exhibiting of the prince's favourite horse and suit of armour in his funeral procession demonstrates the importance of his image as warrior-cavalier. Jutta Bäumel documents this with reference to Christian I.[25] She describes the armour for man and steed ordered by Christian some time in the late 1580s from the notable Augsburg armourer Anton Peffenhauser, the most extensive set ever made for an Albertine Elector. It was this suit of armour that was carried through the streets in Christian I's funeral procession in 1591.

The Armoury in Dresden (the 'Rüstkammer') is today the most important collection of arms and armour in Germany and one of the most important in Europe. It is in effect the personal collection of the Albertine Dukes and shows how assiduously they collected and commissioned arms and armour. The collection includes German,

Flemish, Spanish, French and Italian masterpieces. There is armour for the battlefield and for tournaments, armour for use and for display. There is every kind of weapon for war, tournaments and hunting. There are tournament accoutrements and textiles. This collection documents a whole area of activity essential to the self-definition of the early modern ruler. As soon as the princes of the House of Wettin were strong enough to wear it and old enough to appear in a tournament, a suit of armour was made for them. On exhibition in the Armoury are the exquisite suits of children's armour made for the sons of Christian I and Johann Georg I by such leading Augsburg armourers as Peter von Speyer the Younger and Anton Peffenhauser. In December 1592, a year after their father's death, Christian II, Johann Georg I and August, aged nine, seven and three respectively visited the court of their grandfather Johann Georg, Elector of Brandenburg, at Cölln an der Spree. A running at the ring was being held there for the christening of their uncle, Sigismund, Johann Georg's son by his third wife, an Anhalt princess. The two older boys may well have worn a suit of armour on this occasion.[26]

Another illustration of the importance of arms and armour is the way in which they were given as gifts from one ruler to another. The Armoury contains a Milanese *cordelas* and dagger possibly by Giovanni Battista Serabaglio, a gift to Elector August from Guglielmo Gonzaga, Duke of Mantua, datable to 1560–70. A shield depicting Judith and Holofernes was a gift from Francesco I de' Medici to Christian I on his accession in 1587 and formed part of a consignment of important objects, including three bronzes by Giambologna.[27] Another gift to Christian I in 1588 was a highly decorated suit of armour, covered in gods, putti, animals, vases, wreaths and love knots, from Carlo Emanuele I, Duke of Savoy. The Duke of Florence sent Christian II a Damascene sabre around 1609.[28] The princes themselves used their foreign journeys to acquire fine workmanship. Johann Georg I, for instance, brought back a rapier and dagger set decorated with cameos and pearls from his trip to Italy in 1601. These foreign influences naturally had an impact on the home-grown industry. The Dresden armourer Franz Kaphan, for instance, created a crossbow modelled on the Milanese pieces in the Armoury around 1570.[29]

An indispensable adjunct to the bearing of arms was horsemanship. Riding defined the gentleman but, beyond that, mastering a horse was an emblem of the ability to rule, and it is no accident that the prince is so frequently depicted on a rearing horse. The art of riding naturally formed an important part of the education of Christian I's three young sons, Christian II, Johann Georg I and August, still children on his death in 1591. In a document dated 16 June 1596, for instance, and discussed at greater length below, we see that the princes' programme of study, minutely set out for each day of the week, leaves room for both 'gallopieren' and 'tummeln'.[30] 'Gallopieren' means galloping, that is, riding fast straight ahead, but 'tummeln' is the word which in contemporary usage indicates the new riding which became codified in Italy in the middle of the sixteenth century in Federigo Grisone's famous riding manual *Gli ordini di cavalcare*.[31] 'Tummeln' indicates the so-called airs above and on the ground, riding what was called a 'collected' horse. This implies access to highly bred and highly trained horses with at least some Arab blood, and mastery of a sophisticated equestrian technique on the Italian model. The heavy medieval warhorse had made way for the lighter horse with Arab blood that came into the rest of Europe from Spain via Naples. One of the things Christian I had done was to send Heinrich von Hagen and Carlo Theti as envoys to Mantua, Florence and Ferrara in the early part of 1587 to bring back Italian horses.[32] Eleven years later, the new Elector of Brandenburg, Joachim Friedrich, sent Christian I's sons a horse each and had his own Italian groom, Hypolido de Marino, deliver them in person.[33]

That it was Christian I who introduced the new Italian riding to Dresden is borne out by the equestrian books in the Electoral Library. The inventory of Elector August's books dated 1574 contains only four books of equestrian interest, a small number considering the importance of the horse for transport, in war and for purposes of courtly display. Grisone is certainly there in German translation (1573),[34] but apart from that there is only one work to do with harnessing and bitting and two on farriery, and the inventory of 1580, also made during August's lifetime, does not alter this picture.[35]

The inventory of 1595, however, compiled four years after Christian I's death, shows us what books were bought during his reign, and we see a clear upsurge of interest in equestrian matters in general and in works on Italian riding in particular. It appears, for instance, that important equestrian works were finally acquired in this period, works that could have been purchased earlier. This time the section listing equestrian works is divided into books in German[36] and books in Italian and French.[37] Naturally both sections still include many books dealing with the important matters of farriery, harnessing and bitting. The German section, however, includes Johann Fayser von Arnstein's *Hippiatria. Grundlicher Bericht und aller ordennlichste Beschreibung der bewerten Rossärtzney* (Hippiatria. Thorough Report and Most Systematic Description of Effective Farriery, Augsburg 1576), notable because

Fayser von Arnstein is the translator of Grisone. That translation is listed again. A work entitled *Von der... Ritterlichen Kunst der Reutterey zu vier Bücher ordentlich getheilt* (The Knightly Art of Riding in Four Books, 1581) is likely to be by Hörwart von Hohenburg,[38] important because Hörwart was one of those who had assimilated and was disseminating the new principles taught by Grisone and his countrymen. It is in the Italian and French sections, however, that we see the chief innovations. Here are listed two editions of Cesare Corte's *Il Cavalarizzo*,[39] three editions of Grisone, two in Italian (Venice, 1552 and Pisa, 1550) and one in Latin (1557) respectively, Cesare Fiaschi's *Trattato del modo dell'imbrigliare, maneggiare, & ferrare cavalli...* (Venice 1561)[40] and Pasquale Caracciolo's *La Gloria del cavallo* (Venice, 1589). Any library that contains Grisone, Fiaschi, Carraciolo and Corte is the library of someone who is interested in the new riding of Italian provenance.

This section also shows a policy of purchasing the latest publications emanating from Italy and other Romance countries pertaining to farriery. The inventory lists what it calls 'Ars Equandi Gordani Ruffi', giving Venice, 1536 as its place and date of publication. This is one of the numerous sixteenth-century Italian editions of the thirteen-century writer Giordano Ruffo, possibly *Libro dell'arte de marascalchi per conoscere la natura de li Cavalli, medicarli nelle loro infirmità, et l'arte di domarli*. Francisco de la Reyna's *Libro de Albeyteria, en el qual se veran todas quantas enfermedades y desastres suelen acaescer a todo género de bestias, y la cura dellas* (Valladolid 1556) appears, though in Italian translation. Another item is referred to as Laurentius Rusius's *Ars Equitandi* (Venice, 1543 and 1548). This is most probably *Hippiatria sive marescalia ... in qua praeter variorum morborum... remedia, quadraginta tres ... frenorum formae excusae sunt*. Vegetius Renatus is represented,[41] and Xenophon by a work in French called *Oeconomia Xenophontis* published in Paris in 1548.

This is by no means a complete set of all important hippological works available at this date – Giovanni Battista Ferraro and Agostino Colombre are missing, to name but two important writers on equestrian matters, and one is surprised not to see the excellent work by Marx Fugger, *Von der Gestüterey* (1584). This latter, however, is present in the inventory of Johann Georg I's library made in 1612, just after he succeeded as Elector, when his books were integrated into the Electoral Library.[42] None the less, one could say that, by the end of the sixteenth century, the Electoral court was remarkably up to date, as far as works on the latest equestrian and veterinary developments are concerned.

The tournament and Italian influence

The development and assimilation of the new riding went hand in hand with two developments in the tournament itself as practised at European courts: on the one hand the actual martial exercises as trained and tested in the tournament evolved to take account of changing circumstances on the battlefield, and on the other Italian theatrical technology began to be increasingly used, as the element of spectacle assumed an ever greater importance.

The last manifestations of the medieval tournament in Dresden can be seen in the tournaments of Elector August around the middle of the sixteenth century. Between 1543 and 1566 he took part in fifty-five jousts, some of which are depicted in the twenty-nine oil paintings commissioned by Christian I from the painter Heinrich Göding around 1589/90, and therefore a generation later, of which nine survive today.[43] These paintings were designed to decorate the Long Corridor attached to the stables. They show us the traditional joust, the man-to-man collision of two riders in heavy armour, each riding a war-horse bred for strength rather than speed, each aiming to unseat his opponent by knocking him off his mount by sheer force. But warfare was changing and so was the function of the cavalryman on the battlefield.[44] His role as human projectile had been made obsolete by the rise of the handgun – the collections of the Albertine Electors show their intense interest in the development of this weapon – and of the pike. The cavalryman now needed to be both more mobile and more versatile in the use, not just of the heavy lance or the battleaxe, but of a range of weapons from lance to sword to handgun. Those tournament contests that demonstrated and trained speed and sureness of aim now superseded jousting and tilting. The equestrian exercise known as running at the ring enjoyed an increasing popularity at most European courts in the latter part of the sixteenth and the early part of the seventeenth centuries for this reason. It was at this time too that the running at the head was invented at German courts, the first tournament exercise to test ability with the handgun as one of a range of weapons used in quick succession. For all these exercises lighter and more agile horses were necessary, horses of a different breed from the heavy war-horse and which had been trained and were ridden differently.

The German courts, in a permanent state of confessional tension and war-readiness in the decades at the end of the sixteenth and beginning of the seventeenth centuries, thus continued to use the tournament as an opportunity to practise warlike skills and demonstrate their martial capability to one another long after the French court, for instance, had turned the tournament into the more theatrical and less dangerous carrousel, following the death of Henri II in a joust in 1559. Saxony was no exception to the general German pattern.

It reflects this development that in 1574 Elector August should stage a large-scale running at the ring for the carnival season, and that the Stallhof, which, as we have seen, came into being in the reign of Christian I, should be designed to accommodate the same contest. The running at the ring required a small metal ring divided into fields strung up above shoulder height between two pillars. The first running at the ring in the Stallhof took place in 1588 and the bronze pillars which we see there today date from the year 1601. The contestant rode at speed towards the ring in a 'lane' marked out by chains. These too are still in place. The contestant's aim was to pierce the ring with his light wooden lance – of which there are examples from as early as the 1570s in the Armoury in Dresden today – and carry it off on the tip. According to which part of the ring he pierced, he was awarded points. In moving from the joust or tilt towards this kind of contest against an inanimate object and in setting up an outdoor arena in which the exercise could be practised (it is not until the 1670s that an indoor riding school was built in Dresden) the Saxon Electors showed themselves to be in line with general German, and indeed European, developments. While many such events were small in scale – rather like golf or polo today – others were highly theatrical and political, designed to impress subjects and foreigners alike.

But what of the spectacular as opposed to the martial aspect of the tournament? The running at the ring held by Elector August for the carnival season on 23 February 1574 was fully costumed.[45] In general, the costumes for the running at the ring held in 1574, though mixed, were splendid and their imagery had a characteristically German, indeed Saxon, quality. That the theatrical aspect of the tournament had not yet reached Italian standards can be seen by comparing it with the tournament staged in Piacenza in the same year in honour of the same victory at Lepanto.[46] As in Dresden, the cumulative effect is one of surprise, as each new entry succeeds the previous one. What is very different from Dresden, however, is the extent to which the costumes draw on mythology and the fact that all the fifteen inventions except the last has its own 'machine'. Some of the machines were floats or carriages, such as that of the three Fates, the huge ship representing the Battle of Lepanto, the enchanted tower in which a lady is imprisoned or Sisyphus's mountain. These structures appeared to move of their own accord, thanks to men concealed within them who pushed them along, and usually carried costumed figures, often musicians, evidence of the much more sophisticated theatrical technology commonly employed in Italy at this date.[47] Dresden had to wait for an Italian designer to mount anything comparable in terms of imagery and technology and for us to be able to say that the Italian tournament spectacle had reached Dresden. That designer was Giovanni Maria Nosseni.

He designed the great tournament held in Dresden to celebrate the wedding of Christian I and Sophie of Brandenburg in 1582, and the Italian influence is perceptible.[48] As the Court Chamberlain's papers tell us, there were a number of contests: a costumed running at the ring on 26 April, a foot tournament on 29 April and a tilt.[49] Daniel Bretschneider's hand-tinted engravings bound together into a tournament book show us the twenty separate groups for the running at the ring, some of which resemble those seen in 1574. There is a group of Orientals, for instance, peasants, huntsmen and postal messengers and we have the sectarian depictions of monks and of the Pope and the Archangel Michael discussed in chapter 1. But by and large the costumes are far more Italianate. The bridegroom himself rides on to the lists, dressed in white and gold with golden wings and is accompanied by Neptune, who arrives on a float of the sea pulled by three hippocamps, preceded by a sea monster blowing a shawm. We have the Judgement of Paris and the naked Bacchus on a donkey with his companions Ebrietas and Crabula. The participants in the running at the ring are costumed as ancient heroes such as Pyrrhus, Hercules, Pompeius, Horatius, Aeneas, Achilles and Alexander the Great.

As we have seen, the young Elector Christian I was interested in the equestrian arts emanating from Italy and it is not surprising that his short reign should be characterised by the frequent staging of costumed tournaments in which a continued Italian influence is perceptible. It is clearly visible in the first important tournament of the reign, the running at the ring held on 5, 6 and 7 June 1587 for the christening of Christian's daughter Sophie, born in April of the same year.[50] This tournament was characterised by the increased use of Italianate machines. On a float depicting the sea, a ship, whose mast is crowned by a Cupid, carries two knights. Another horse-drawn machine depicting spring and dawn has a grove in which young ladies sit playing stringed instruments and tossing out wreaths. Summer is represented by a mountain, on which sit fauns making music, while Venus rides in front. Yet another machine represents a city surrounded by water at the foot of a mountain on which sit Jupiter and Mercury, a miner and a nun. The planetary gods follow the mountain. As well as these Italianate elements we have mixed groups of combatants in the usual manner: Moors, huntsmen, miners, Amazons, fools, shepherds and postal messengers.

Throughout his brief reign Christian I staged tournaments, either at the carnival season as in 1588, or to celebrate dynastic events such as the christening of his daughter Elisabeth in August 1588. The most magnificent tournament of all was held in January 1591, the year of his death, for the christening of his daughter Dorothea.[51] As the title of the tournament book tells us, it was a running at the ring held in the Palace courtyard over four days from 26 to 29 January. On the first day the defenders (the 'Maintenatoren'), Johann Georg zu Anhalt (Mandricardi) and Nicol von Miltitz, Master of the Duke's Horse (Rodomontes), entered the lists, followed by the challengers. On the second day a group of impressive machines appeared. The first was a group of four floats with a sea theme: a warship riding on the waves in which swim fish and sirens, a band of sirens making music with a Triton blowing a conch in front, the figure of Neptune guiding a shell-shaped boat pulled by two hippocamps in which are seated Christian I of Saxony and Christian, Duke of Anhalt, while a second warship brings up the rear. The machines are reminiscent of Buontalenti's designs for the Intermedii performed in Florence in 1589 for the wedding of Grand Duke Ferdinand I de' Medici and Christine, Princess of Lorraine. Knowledge of these designs could have been disseminated in Dresden by Carlo di Cesare, who had come to Saxony from Florence in 1590 and who worked for the court there until 1593.

There was a hiatus in tournament and indeed festival activity of any kind in Dresden during the ten-year regency of Friedrich Wilhelm of Saxony-Weimar and it was not until Christian II came of age in 1601 that it resumed. Nosseni's Italianate influence continued with the presentation on the Elbe in 1602 of a series of floating machines to welcome Christian II's bride, Hedwig, Princess of Denmark. These machines consisted of all kinds of sea monsters, the god Neptune and Glaucus blowing a trumpet surrounded by sirens. The numerous tournaments of this reign – in 1602, 1604, 1607 (two), 1609 (two again), 1610 and 1611 – also seem to carry on where the tournaments staged before the regency left off. The running at the ring held for the carnival in 1609 is much the most lavish of these. This event brought together in Dresden, in what looks very like a summit conference of Protestant allies, Margrave Christian Wilhelm of Brandenburg, Margrave Christian of Brandenburg, Margrave Joachim Ernst of Ansbach, Johann Casimir of Saxony-Coburg and Johann Ernst of Saxony-Eisenach.[52] For this reason

Figure 16. Daniel Bretschneider the Elder, Float and Ethiopians in the running at the ring held in Dresden in 1609. SLUB Mscr.Dresd.J 18. Deutsche Fotothek (Rous).

it is instructive to compare it with the tournament held in Stuttgart in the same year for the wedding of Johann Friedrich of Württemberg and Barbara Sophia of Brandenburg. It was this marriage which cemented the Protestant Union, an anti-Imperial power bloc to which Saxony emphatically did not belong. The Stuttgart tournament put forward an iconography which explicitly associated Protestantism with a Germanic identity, opposed it to Imperial policy and underlined the importance of Protestant unity. This iconography then spread from Stuttgart to the other courts of the Union.[53]

The Dresden tournament of 1609 is distinguished by a lavish exoticism that is very different. It was on a huge scale in terms of numbers of participants, in that it had forty-three inventions or costumed groups with some 500 costumed participants in all. Ethiopians constitute the commonest category (Figure 16). The procession opens with groups of naked Ethiopian drummers, nine trumpeters and attendants carrying lances. They are followed by an immense float pulled by two elephants with obelisks on their backs. Enthroned on top of the float is an Ethiopian chief. Below him are Ethiopian musicians and monkeys. This is followed by Ethiopian warriors, some carrying spears with helmeted European heads impaled on them, an Ethiopian king is carried on a litter under a palanquin and there are groups of Ethiopians leading horses. Magnificence, colour and exotic strangeness are the overwhelming impressions. Among the other costumes, occupational and national dress predominates. Examples of the latter include Moors, Romans, Turks, Hungarians, Gypsies and Persians, examples of the former are peasants, cavalrymen, miners, barbers, pilgrims, chimney-sweeps, huntsmen and postal messengers. The quantity and variety of costumes, the colourful heterogeneity are the chief features.

We might ask to what extent either the Electors themselves or their artists had access to accounts and engravings of festivals from other European courts when organising events in Dresden. The 1574 inventory of the Electoral library lists the official account of the Viennese tournament of 1560 and what is probably Hans Wagner's account of the Munich wedding of 1568, along with accounts of the coronation of Charles V in 1536, his entry into Munich in 1530 and into Rome in 1536, the festivals at Binche, Antwerp and Brussels held for him and his son Philip in 1549, the coronation of Henri de Valois in Cracow in 1574 and such compendia as Ruexner's *Turnierbuch*. The 1595 inventory lists the entries of Henri II, King of France, into Lyons in 1548 and into Paris in 1549. The inventory of the *Kunstkammer* dating to 1640 lists the Stuttgart festival books depicting the great festivals of 1609, 1616 and 1617. Claudia Schnitzer has investigated the library of Giovanni Maria Nosseni, the inventory of which is also preserved in Dresden.[54] She shows that two of these Stuttgart festival books came from his estate and that he owned such other works as Dilich's account of the christening in Kassel in 1596, Dürer's engraving of the *Great Triumphal Car* for Emperor Maximilian I, Mandeville's travel book, Ripa's *Iconologia* and Cartari's *Imagines Deorum*. This reference library would supplement what would have been at his disposal in the Electoral Library.

Thus, the Dresden court was aware of developments in international festive culture at the end of the sixteenth century and in the run-up to the Thirty Years' War and their festivals became visibly more Italianate under the guiding hand of Nosseni.

Princely education and 'civil conversation'

As we have seen, Christian I died unexpectedly in 1591 at the age of 31. His two eldest sons, Christian and Johann Georg, were eight and six respectively at the time of his death. Friedrich Wilhelm, the Ernestine Duke of Saxony-Weimar (1562–1602), had been named administrator of the Duchy until Christian II's majority and was joint guardian of the children with their maternal grandfather Johann Georg, Elector of Brandenburg (1525–98). In this latter capacity, Friedrich Wilhelm was responsible for the education of the young princes. The papers in the

Dresden archive document so thoroughly the care with which he discharged this duty that we can reconstruct the educational formation of the next two Electors of Saxony: Christian II, who reigned from his majority in 1601 until 1611, and his brother Johann Georg I, who reigned from 1611 until 1656.[55]

The first change made to the boys' education on their father's death was the appointment of a new tutor. Their first teacher, Sebastian Leonhart (1544–1610), was suspected of Calvinist leanings and so was immediately dismissed. Elias Reinhart took his place. He taught the boys until 1596. Given the strict Lutheranism of both the regent and the boys' mother, it is not surprising that a training in the doctrines of Lutheranism should be central to their education. What this meant in practice can be seen from the account of their schooling given to Friedrich Wilhelm by Elias Reinhart on 24 May 1592.[56] Their 'exercitia pietatis' include learning Luther's catechism, the psalms and other prayers from the Bible by heart. In another communication Reinhart attests that young Christian knows by heart the catechism in Latin and German, the commentaries on it in German, twenty-two Psalms, twenty important passages of the Bible, the most important passages of the Sunday gospel readings and a number of prayers. Little Johann Georg knows slightly less, as befits his age.[57] Reinhart fell out with the boys' mother and, as she had a great deal of influence over their education, a new tutor was appointed in 1596. Thus was Sigmund Röhling, the Electress's choice.

Shortly after his appointment, Röhling set out a new and detailed programme of study in a document dated 16 June 1596.[58] This document shows how their schooling was organised hour by hour throughout the week. It falls into four sections: I. 'Gebet Ordnung' (Rules for Religious Education and Prayer), II. 'Institution Ordnung' (Rules for Secular Education), III. 'Exercitia' (Physical and Artistic Education) and IV. 'Disciplin Ordnung' (Discipline). That the 'Gebet Ordnung' comes first does not surprise us. Indeed the stress on religious formation is only to be expected from the central importance of Lutheranism for the Albertines, as outlined in chapter 1, and the desire to extirpate any traces of the Calvinism which attracted their father.

In tandem with this, the boys were given an equally rigorous and much more varied secular education to prepare them for life as late sixteenth-century princes with European pretensions. The 'Institution Ordnung' lays down the study of Latin and, to a lesser extent Greek, but also shows that the boys were to be taught to speak well in German.[59] They are to read Cicero's letters on Monday afternoons, Aesop's Fables on Tuesday mornings and afternoons, and famous 'sententiae' on Thursday afternoons. Other documents make plain that they read Ovid, Terence, Virgil and Cicero and such ancient historians as Xenophon.

A further insight into their reading is given by two manuscript inventories in the SLUB in Dresden. The first lists the contents of three bookcases in 'the Young Gentlemen's Schoolroom' during this period.[60] Among the 565 books listed, a very large number by the standards of the time, we find as well as the Bible in German, Latin and Greek and Luther's works, classical authors such as Xenophon and Homer in both Latin and Greek, Ovid, Catullus, Propertius, Martial, Horace, Lucretius, Euripides, Appollonius, Seneca, Suetonius and Terence, all from the Aldine Press, Demosthenes, Cicero's letters, Aristotle, Plutarch's Lives, Aristophanes and Plautus. But Renaissance authors are also represented. Petrarch (his poetry as well as the Triumphs) and Boccaccio, Erasmus's *Colloquies*, *Adages*, *Apophthegmata* and *Enchiridion*, the poems of Petrus Loticius Secundus, Eobanus Hessus, Vitruvius, Lorenzo Valla's *De linguae latinae elegantia libri VI*, Johann Sturm, Paolo Giovio, Francesco Guicciardini, Comines's History, Roberto Valturio's *De re militari libri XII*, Sebastian Münster's *Cosmographia* and Scaliger's poetics.

The second inventory tells us which books 'the Young Gentlemen used in their studies and which were on Their Graces' desks'.[61] This is a more modest selection but includes on Christian's desk, as well as the catechism, Plautus and Terence, Cicero's *De officiis*, a Latin and German primer and the Psalter, Alciati's emblems and Aesop's fables. It is also clear from the tutorial programme laid down by Reinhart that the princes studied mathematics, astronomy and physics. In his account of the princes' education Richter gives more detail about which books were personal gifts to the princes on such occasions as Christmas, which their various tutors actually wrote themselves and which their guardian Friedrich Wilhelm of Saxony-Weimar had printed specially for them.[62] They were in general works of a morally uplifting and educational kind: dictionaries, grammar books, catechisms and prayer books, historical, geographical and mathematical works.

But if all of this comes under the heading of 'Institution Ordnung' in the 1596 programme of study, what was meant by the section headed 'Exercitia'? It is here that we see the princes acquiring the polish of a courtier. An earlier document dated 8 April 1594 had already expressed the twin aims of the princes' education as consisting of 'Gottesfurcht' and 'Fürstl. Höffliche Sitten' – fear of God and princely courtly (or courteous) manners.[63] This meant that they practised their music every day, the lute and the zither being favoured instruments, and that on

Mondays they were taught what is called 'welsch tanzen' or Italian dancing.[64] Riding was an important skill, as we have seen, and they also learned to play ballgames and to shoot with the crossbow or musket on Wednesdays and to play chess. In addition, mealtimes, particularly on Mondays, were to be given over to teaching the young princes conversation and etiquette. This is expressed as 'von löblichenn Schriften tiscurriren lernen, so wol zu reinlichem Essen und aller Fürstlicher zucht auch Höflichkeit erinnert, angeleitet und gehalten werden' (to learn to converse about praiseworthy books and to be taught how to eat cleanly and to show princely manners and courtesy).[65] This may seem a set of obvious skills and as such unworthy of remark. On the contrary, it is this passage, among others, which indicates the extent to which the Italian ideal of polished behaviour or 'civil conversazione' is being inculcated at the Dresden court.

One of the great Renaissance manuals of so-called 'civil conversazione' was Giovanni della Casa's *Galateo*, first published in 1558.[66] The German Humanist Nathan Chytraeus (1543–98) translated it into Latin in 1578 in Rostock,[67] a translation that was reprinted several times. He then produced an amended version published in 1597.[68] In the same year Chytraeus brought out a German translation of the work and this has hitherto been considered to be the sole German translation.[69] This is not, however, the case. Preserved in the SLUB in manuscript is a German translation of the *Galateo* by the Helmstedt scholar Friedrich von Gelhorn from Költschen in Silesia. It is entitled: 'Galatheus oder von Erbarkeit, vndt Höffligkeit der Sitten. Erstlichen in Welscher sprach geschrieben vndt itzundt erst, mit sonderem fleis aus dem Welschen in unsere hochdeutsche sprach vertiret vndt gebracht' (Galateo, or of the Honourable Nature and Courtesy of Manners. Written first in the Italian tongue and now for the first time with special diligence translated from Italian into our High German tongue).[70] It is dated 5 June 1595 and is dedicated to 'Cristianus, Joan-Georgius vndt Augustus, gebrüder, Hertzogen zu Sachsen' (Christian, Johann Georg and August, brothers, Dukes of Saxony). August is the youngest of Christian I's sons, at this date aged six. As the title makes clear, it has not been translated from Chytraeus's Latin version but from the original Italian and predates Chytraeus's German translation by two years.

The *Galateo* is concerned not with strict moral precepts but with manners. But to say that it is an etiquette manual is to simplify its aims and to fail to explain its vast and continued importance throughout Europe over a very long period.[71] The central concept is the vision of a civilised society. In order to achieve this, certain behavioural vices must be identified and then avoided. The areas covered include the unaesthetic (smacking your lips when eating), the irritating (whistling through your teeth), the embarrassing (failing to cover yourself up properly) and the boring (bragging). Pomposity and unnecessary ceremonial – bowing and scraping, the use of titles – are equally frowned upon, Della Casa going so far as to state that ceremonial acts are deceptive lies. Also to be avoided are showing off, flattery and unnecessary magnificence in dress.

There are positive traits to be inculcated too. By taking note of the feelings and reactions of others one will please them but one will also communicate better with them. Much of the treatise is devoted to how to speak to others in public and how to convey one's message clearly. Clothing and gestures also form part of social communication and attention must be paid to them. Sensitivity to and consideration of the feelings of others is of primary importance in social interaction, as illustrated in the story of how Galateo is asked by the Bishop of Verona to convey to a guest on his departure that he has unaesthetic eating habits. The lengths to which Galateo goes to communicate this without causing the guest to lose face are a classic demonstration of how to avoid social embarrassment. In short, the *Galateo* is concerned with how man, in a civil society, can rise above his purely animal needs to become a harmonious and pleasing entity, but without pride and ostentation. Proportion and harmony are the key terms here. If each man pleases others, then society will function better.

Giovanni Della Casa (1505–57), poet, later priest and Papal Nuncio to the Republic of Venice, aimed his treatise at the ordinary citizen and his Galateo is simply an older experienced man of no particularly high standing or family advising a younger one. Chytraeus turns him into a courtier and his pupil into a noble youth, though he addresses his German translation expressly to his bourgeois pupils in Bremen. Gelhorn in this respect is more faithful to Della Casa. In general, Chytraeus's and Gelhorn's translations are close to each other and to the original. Though Gelhorn's rendering of Italian personal and place names resembles the Italian more closely than Chytraeus's does, Gelhorn often leaves out Della Casa's examples and anecdotes, thus depriving the work of some of its Italianate character.

How closely the young princes studied Gelhorn's manuscript translation we do not know. It did not sit on the bookshelves of the schoolroom after they had moved on to adult life, however. Johann Georg I took it and kept it with his books – one of a relatively small collection – which he presented to the Electoral Library after his accession in 1612 on the death of his brother Christian II.[72] We may speculate that his reading of Della Casa, together with his lengthy sojourn in Italy in 1601, contributed to his interest in things Italian, as discussed below.

Johann Georg I's Italian journey (1601) and its Dresden legacy

In 1601, for the first time since Moritz's journey in 1549, a member of the princely family travelled to Italy. This was Johann Georg I, at that time a younger son with little hope of the succession. 1601 was the year in which his elder brother Christian II attained his majority and Johann Georg, then aged sixteen, set off on a thirteen-month journey which took him as far south as Naples. The significance which attached to this journey can be gauged from the fact that the historian Anton Weck includes an account of it in his book about the architecture of Dresden published in 1680.[73] Johann Georg I left Dresden on 16 January and travelled first via Nuremberg to Augsburg, where he arrived on 3 February. On 10 February he set off via Innsbruck, Bolzano, Trent, Brescia and Trieste for Mestre and then into Venice, where he must have arrived around 20 February. He journeyed incognito, that is, not as Duke of Saxony and brother of the Elector, which would have required a vastly greater entourage and a ceremonial welcome in each city he visited, but as Johann von Nissmitz, the cousin of his tutor, Georg von Nissmitz. Apart from these two, the group contained only four others. They stayed in Venice until 12 March in an apartment on the Grand Canal and must therefore have experienced the carnival. From Venice they proceeded to Padua, Ferrara and Bologna, where they matriculated at the University. On 23 March they arrived in Ancona and went to Rome on 31 March. After four days in Rome, they travelled on to the Kingdom of Sicily (not to the island but to the territory around Naples), passing through Sarmoneta, Terracina, Nola, Fondi and Capua, before reaching Naples itself on 7 April. Here they visited the sights, including Buzoli, Baia, Cuma, Mount Vesuvius, 'die Grotte Sibyllae / dann Centum Camerae (so ein wunderlich steinern Gebäude unter der erden) item die waarme Bäder / des Virgilii auch Ciceronis Palatium und Garten/ die rudera der alten Stadt Cuma und andere antiquität: und raritäten' (the grotto of the Sibyl, then the hundred caves, which are a wonderful stone building under the earth, then the warm baths, the palace and garden of Virgil and Cicero, the rubble of the old city of Cuma and other antiquities and rare things).[74] In every city they were concerned to live as simply as possible and to avoid recognition. They hurried away from Naples, for instance, on 12 April when an Antwerp merchant began to penetrate their disguise. They returned to Rome, where they spent twelve days, avoiding formal identification and thus an audience with the Pope. They then travelled back up to the Veneto again, arriving in Verona on 1 June. Here they set up house and lived for at least four or five months, not giving up their accommodation finally until 1 December. Johann Georg settled down to learn Latin and Italian with a tutor named Orlando Pescetti. In early October or thereabouts they set off towards Milan but were attacked and robbed. They did finally reach Milan where they spent five days. They then proceeded to Pavia where the prince became seriously ill. The Duke of Savoy sent his own doctor to Johann Georg and this subsequently meant a formal visit to Vercelli, where the Duke visited them and gave them presents, including a beautiful jewel and seven horses with embroidered saddles. This illness had also brought them into contact with a German merchant called Mattheus Fetzer, whom they afterwards visited on 3 November in Milan. On 8 November they returned to Verona and then to Mantua, where the Duke saw through their incognito and brought them to his Palace. It was now generally known who they were, so they were commanded sharply to return home. They managed to avoid the emissaries of the Dukes of Florence and of Parma and of the Pope. They hurried off to Venice again, leaving there on 9 December and travelling via Mestre, Treviso and Trent to Innsbruck again. On 24 December they reached Augsburg, on 27 December Ulm and visited Fetzer at his house in Nuremberg in February 1602. When they reached Nuremberg, Johann Georg lived *en prince* again. He visited his one-time guardian, Friedrich Wilhelm of Saxony-Weimar, and reached Dresden at the end of February 1602.

This journey of a young man who afterwards reigned as Elector of Saxony from 1611 to 1656 took him to many of the most famous centres of learning, art and architecture in Italy. Its outward form was dictated by the conflicting aims of acquainting him with the language and culture of Italy while keeping him uncontaminated by too much contact with Catholicism (what Weck calls the 'widrige Religion' or repugnant religion, of the country) at a period of great confessional unease in Saxony and in the Empire. This explains not just his jealously guarded incognito but also the places where he stayed. Had he spent lengthy periods of time in Rome or Florence, he would have had to associate with their respective rulers and would have been drawn politically into their ambit. Instead, he spent the bulk of his time in the

Republic of Venice. He visited Venice itself three times, spending in all about two months there, and he lived in Verona for four or five months. That he did study, as chronicled by Weck, is clear from the list of his books incorporated into the Electoral Library on his succession in 1612. From looking at the list, one can conjecture that many of them were bought on his Italian trip, for a high number of them appeared in the years 1599, 1600 and 1601 – that is, they were new or recent publications during the Italian visit.[75] However, Kristina Popova has unearthed twenty titles in the catalogues of the SLUB in Dresden and has found sixteen of the actual books, many inscribed with HvN (for Hans von Nismitz) or with V (for Verona).[76] Several are dictionaries or grammar books, as one might expect: Scipione Lentulo's *Italian Grammar* (1601), Filippo Venuti's *Dittionario volgare e Latino* in the 1600 edition and Tommaso Porcacchi's *Vocabulario Nuovo* (1596). The list also contains Henricus Hornkens's *Recueil de Dictionaires Francoys, Espaignolz & Latins* (Brussels, 1599), clearly a supplement to Johann Georg's linguistic studies, though where he acquired it we do not know. But we can also see the progress of the young Duke's political education. He owned Cesare Campana's *Delle Historie del mondo* (1599), the *Thesoro politico cioè Relationi, Instruttioni, ... Discorsi varii d'Ambri* edited by Ventura which was re-issued in 1598, Paolo Paruta's *Discorsi Politici* (1599) and Bartholomeo Zucchi's *L'Idea del Segretario ... rappresentata in un trattato de l'imitatione, e ne lettere di Principi e d'altre Signori* (1600). Also listed are Scipione Ammirato's *Discorsi* on Tacitus (1599) and Cicero's *Epistole Famigliari* translated by Aldus Manutius (1598). The only textual evidence of interest in Italian culture of a lighter sort is provided by the presence on the list of Lauro Settizonio's *Roselmina, favola tragisatiricomica*. This appeared in a second edition in both Novara and Venice in 1597, though the inventory gives the date as 1599. Perhaps he saw this play on one of his Venetian visits.

On the unexpected death of his brother, Christian II, Johann Georg I came to the throne in 1611 and immediately began to initiate his own programme of Italianisation, based not on that of his father twenty years before but on his own experiences in Italy. In 1612 he sent his court painter and 'Malerey-Inspector', Kilian Fabritius, to Rome.[77] But how do we know what aspects of Italian culture left a lasting impression on him? One of the ways to assess this is to ask what cultural achievements during his reign are both Italianate and without previous parallel in the local tradition in Dresden. Within the first four years of his reign he had made remarkable contributions to three areas of cultural life, all unthinkable without his Italian journey.

The first and best known is in the field of music. In 1614, Johann Georg invited the composer Heinrich Schütz to Dresden. At this time Schütz was fresh from having spent the years between 1609 and 1612 or 1613 studying with Giovanni Gabrieli in Venice, financed by a stipend from the Landgrave of Hesse-Kassel. Schütz never returned to the service of the Landgrave but remained in Dresden, becoming *kapellmeister* in 1617, on the retirement of Rogier Michael.[78] By bringing Schütz to Dresden Johann Georg ensured, over the next half-century, the cross-fertilisation between German and Netherlandish traditions in church music and the new Italian trends. Venetian music was the chief model, a style that Johann Georg would have become acquainted with in Venice. When the Augsburg art dealer and diplomat Philipp Hainhofer visited the 'Pfeiffenkammer' (Woodwind Room) in the Palace in Dresden in 1629, he noted the portraits of fourteen famous *kapellmeister* and composers ranged round the room on two cornices. Nine of the fourteen were Italians, and half had been employed in St Mark's in Venice.[79]

Schütz's contribution in the field of secular music was just as remarkable. One of his earliest works on becoming *kapellmeister* was performed on 15 July 1617 in honour of the visit to Dresden of Emperor Matthias, Empress Anna and their sons. This was the *Wunderliche translocation Des Weitberümbten und fürtrefflichen Berges Parnassi und seiner Neun Göttin/ mit ihren Großfürsten und Praesidenten Apolline/ Welche von den unsterblichen Göttern/ Ihr Kayser- und königliche Majestät auch Ertzherzogliche Durchleuchtigkeit zu empfangen und zu ehren in die Wolverwarte Hauptvestung Dreßden ablegiert worden sein* (The Amazing Translocation of the Famous and Wonderful Mount Parnassus and its Nine Goddesses, who have been delegated by the Immortal Gods to receive and honour His Imperial and Royal Majesty as well as Their Graces the Archdukes in the Well-Fortified Fortress of Dresden).[80] Schütz wrote the text as well as the music for this piece (the latter is mostly lost) and it is difficult to assign it to a genre: 'dramatic cantata' might be the most apposite. What is clear is that it was heavily Italianate in style and is another small step along the long road towards the introduction of Italian opera. In 1621 Schütz wrote another short semi-dramatic piece entitled *Glückwündschung des Apollinis und der neun Musen* (Tribute by Apollo and the Nine Muses),[81] this time for the birthday of Johann Georg I on 5 March of that year. Again Apollo and the Nine Muses appear, this time to congratulate the Elector. Each lauds him in turn, concluding with a chorus in which they praise 'Der mächtig Held von Sachsen' (the powerful Saxon hero).

But the work which has attracted most attention from modern scholars is that performed in 1627 at Torgau for the wedding of Sophie Eleonore, daughter of Johann Georg I, and Georg, Landgrave of Hesse-Darmstadt. This work, entitled *Dafne*, can claim to be the first opera in German. Its text was by Martin Opitz and the score, now lost, by Schütz. Opera as a genre had just come into being at the time of Johann Georg's Italian journey with the very work adapted by Opitz. This was *Dafne* with a libretto by Ottavio Rinuccini and music by Jacopo Peri and Jacopo Corsi and was put on in Florence in 1598, 1599 and 1600 for the carnival. In 1600 the *Rappresentazione di Anima e di Corpo*, with a libretto by Agostino Manni and a score by Emilio de' Cavalieri, was put on in the Church of the Oratory in Rome. These two works constitute the beginning of the genre. Opitz and Schütz's *Dafne* is a delightful little pastoral entertainment which dramatises one of the episodes from Ovid's *Metamorphoses*, interspersing the action with strophic *lieder*. However, since the score is lost, it is very difficult to draw conclusions about the nature of the music. Contemporary sources, also lost, refer to it as a 'Pastoral Tragicomedia', for instance,[82] and modern scholars have debated whether this really is an opera or a spoken play with vocal inserts. In the most recent contribution to the debate, Elisabeth Rothmund gives good reasons for claiming that it was an opera.[83] There has, in addition, been debate as to how much credit the Dresden court can claim for commissioning this work. Fechner has examined the circumstances in which the work was composed and performed and has demonstrated that it cannot be regarded as an official commission by the Elector.[84] None the less the performance took place and represents a signal step in the introduction in the Empire of one of the most important Italian musical genres.

The second area in which Johann Georg made an important innovation was in the presentation of the new developments in natural history and medicine, which came to fruition in Italy shortly before and during his stay there. In these developments, significantly, Verona had played a central part. Johann Georg's contribution was the creation in 1616 of a Chamber of Anatomy in the Palace in Dresden. This was situated near his grandfather's *Kunstkammer*, but resembled nothing to be found there. The *Kunstkammer*, discussed in the next chapter, was a scientific and technological museum in which, in direct contrast to the Chamber of Anatomy, *naturalia* were more or less absent. We have four accounts of what the Anatomy Chamber looked like, one by Hainhofer in 1617, a much briefer description by him in 1629, Tobias Beutel's account published in 1671, and another by Anton Weck published in 1680. From all the accounts it appears that the first impression of this room was of a garden or grove filled with artificial trees. But it was not just any garden. From Weck's description of the painted clouds on the ceiling and of the trees hung with artificial citrus fruit and pomegranates and of the palms and vines, it is clear that this was an Italian garden.[85] Indeed, we are reminded of the English traveller Sir Thomas Hoby's description of the countryside near Verona, which he visited in 1555: it was 'marvelouslie besett with citron trees, orenges, and lymones, verie plesant to behold'.[86]

Among these trees and bushes were placed a large number of all kinds of skeletons, both human and animal. Most of them had previously been domiciled at court. There were dwarves, male and female, and wild animals hunted by Johann Georg I, of all sizes from bear to mouse. Exotic animals such as dromedaries, lions, panthers and strange crossbreeds were also displayed and birds hung from the ceiling. Other skeletons stood on pedestals on which their fully-fleshed forms were depicted and labelled. But this display was not merely to be marvelled at or to be admired. It was intended for medical and scientific study. Hainhofer, writing in 1617 on his first visit when the Chamber had only recently been established, says that there was a separate little room within the Chamber, disguised as a mountain or rock on the outside and painted with mountain goats and reindeer on the inside. Here hung anatomical and surgical instruments and the name of the court surgeon who had done the dissection of the specimens was Melchior Mair.[87] The collection was therefore connected with medicine and with the technique of scientific dissection.

Paula Findlen has charted the evolution of the study of natural history and of medicine in Italy in the sixteenth and seventeenth centuries.[88] She shows how nature was brought into the museum and how the museum became a laboratory, yet was simultaneously to be understood as 'a repository of the collective imagination of ... society'.[89] One of the key figures in her account is the pharmacist and naturalist Francesco Calceolari (or Calzolari) (1521–1604), whose natural history museum in Verona drew visitors from far and wide, including that other notable naturalist Ulisse Aldovrandi.[90] Since Johann Georg spent four or five months in Verona and we know that Calceolari's collection was open to his pupils, it is highly probable that Johann Georg visited it. The collection was so famed that there were two printed catalogues of it. Giovanni Battista Olivi published one in 1584, Benedetto Ceruti and Andrea Chiocco the other in 1622.[91] The suggestion is not that Calceolari's museum provided a direct model for or actually resembled Johann Georg's Chamber of Anatomy, but that the scientific attitudes inherent in the former made the latter possible. In her sixth chapter, on 'Museums of Medicine', Findlen shows how collecting and dissecting became linked and how the medical curriculum changed during the sixteenth century in such a way that physicians and pharmacists needed to study the human body. Johann Georg's Chamber of Anatomy exemplifies this link and places it in the Italian setting in which it was born.

The third and most striking outcome of Johann Georg's Italian tour was the resumption and then completion of work on the 'Lusthaus', or Belvedere, an Italianate structure on the ramparts at Dresden overlooking the Elbe, which his father Christian I had begun in 1589. The engraving by Mathäus Merian the Younger shows both its position and its unmistakable silhouette well (see no. 6 at the left of the engraving) (Figure 17). This three-storey building was to have been used for festivities and commanded a delightful view over the river to the opposite bank. Giovanni Maria Nosseni was the architect and it has been suggested that he modelled his plans on the Forte di Belvedere in Florence which he had seen,[92] and on the Belvedere in Prague, whose roof is certainly reminiscent of that in Dresden.[93] While quarrying marble for the burial chapel of the Albertines in Freiberg, Nosseni had also cut marble slabs for the interior of the Belvedere but the project was suspended on the death of Christian I. His immediate successor, Christian II, merely had the lower storey roofed over. This consisted of a room fifteen by twenty metres and five metres in height. It was not until 1613, when Johann Georg I asked Nosseni for a list of the marble slabs put aside for the Belvedere, that thought was again given to this structure.[94] The slabs were brought to Dresden and work commenced. A second storey was added, various additions were made at the sides including a kitchen, and by 1622 at the latest the whole was roofed over (Figure 18). The upper chamber was roughly thirteen by nineteen metres and nine metres high. Round the outside of the upper chamber was a balcony with a railing.

Philipp Hainhofer describes in great detail the striking interior of this building as he saw it on 29 September 1629.[95] The first thing he mentions is that there was a workshop for polishing marble and for carving stone of various kinds just inside the entrance under the direction of Bartholomäus Börner the Younger (1590–1646), who, Hainhofer tells us, had studied with the famous carver Hans Kobenhaupt in Stuttgart. Hainhofer saw vessels of agate, jade and crystal in his workshop. Börner came from a family of carvers of serpentine (a semi-precious stone), in Zöblitz in Saxony, and was highly esteemed by his noble patron, who employed him from 1623 as a carver of drinking vessels from

Figure 17. Matthaus Merian the Younger, View of Dresden (after 1622). Engraving. Deutsche Fotothek (Rous).

The Italian Ideal 67

Figure 18. Friedrich Hagedorn, The Belvedere in Dresden (1887). Oil on canvas. Stadtmuseum, Dresden. Inv. No. 1979/K 208. Deutsche Fotothek (Paetzold).

semi-precious materials.[96] Then the visitor entered the lower chamber, whose walls were lined with all kinds of differently coloured marble. Around the walls were columns, and on each of them there was a plaster bust (later to be cast in bronze) of one of the sixty Dukes and Electors of Saxony up to the present day. Also in this chamber at the entrance on the left-hand side was a beautiful three-fold grotto with water pouring from a statue and a shell in it. All of this was made of marble but the cornice and the frieze were of jade, agate, lapis lazuli and calcedony, semi-precious stones which also decorated the doorframes. This grotto was to serve in future (implying that it was not yet finished) as a display area for drinking vessels and dishes made from every kind of semi-precious stone – crystal, jade, topaz, agate, set in gold, and for the ship of Bohemian crystal which was a present from the reigning Emperor to Johann Georg I. The fountain was by Carlo di Cesare.[97] The room also had an organ made of green serpentine. The walls were decorated with paintings of the most important deeds of the Saxon dukes. In this room one could dine but also walk out onto a terrace to admire the view across the river on one side and on the other through an arcade onto the ramparts where tournaments and firework displays were held. This whole lower chamber resembled an 'antiquarium'[98] and was decorated according to the rules of perspective.

A spiral staircase led up to the chamber on the floor above. This had four doors and twelve windows with a ceiling depicting the four elements, Day and Night, then lower down the seven planets and the twelve Signs of the Zodiac and the history of Troy, painted by Kilian Fabritius. There was a musicians' gallery high up on the inside, and a balcony on the outside, from which one could look out over the city. This room contained twenty stone statues of the last five Holy Roman Emperors, the last five Electors and the ten Virtues. Each figure had a shield with the arms of a different Saxon province on it and an emblem under it. The wall behind every statue was hollow, so that musicians could play in the room below and the music could be piped up to the upper chamber through tubes. Music could also be piped from the ceiling.

Correspondences with Italian models immediately come to mind. The similarity with the Belvedere in Florence has already been mentioned. The close proximity of the stone-working workshops to the display of sculptures and paintings is reminiscent of the Tribuna in Florence, set up only a few years before, which Nosseni would have seen on his visit in 1588. He may well also have seen the grotto in the Boboli Gardens (1583–85) or that in the Villa Medici (1565–1570/72).[99] A grotto linked with a dining room that Johann Georg himself is bound to have seen is that in the Giusti Gardens in Verona. The Elizabethan traveller Thomas Coryate, who visited Verona in 1608 shortly after Johann Georg and his party lived there, describes the grotto as follows:

> Also the Italian (Count Agostino Giusti) shewed me his garden, which is a second Paradise, and a passing delectable place of solace, beautified with many curious knots, fruites of divers sorts and two rowes of lofty Cypresse trees, three and thirty in a ranke. Besides his walkes at the toppe of the garden a little under St. Peters Castle, are as pleasant as the heart of man can wish; being decked with excellent fruits, as Figges, Oranges, Apricockes, and with Cypresse trees. In one of these walkes is a delicate litle refectory: at one side whereof there is a curious artificiall rocke, adorned with many fine devices, as scollop shels, and great variety of other prety shels of fishes brought from Cyprus: and mosse groweth upon the same as if it were a naturall rocke. This place certainly is contrived with as admirable curiosity as ever I saw, and moystened with delicate springs and fountaines conveighed into the same by leaden pipes.[100]

We find ourselves being led back to Verona yet again, though not only the grotto but the whole ambience of the Belvedere in Dresden, with its airy openness to the landscape around, its dedication to pleasure and its position above the Elbe, reminds us of Italy.

Two aspects of the interior decoration deserve further analysis. The first is the way in which the décor creates a monument to the Electors of Saxony, rising up through the floors of the building. In the lower chamber we have depictions of the *res gestae* of the Wettins and sixty busts representing their line back to its origins. This chamber therefore presents the place of the Albertines in history. As one ascends to the upper chamber, one emerges into the present. Here the five Albertine Electors from Moritz up to and including Johann Georg I himself are paralleled with the last five emperors, thus setting Electoral Saxony within the Empire. The arms on the shields of the statues present the provinces of Saxony, while the planets and the signs of the Zodiac on the ceiling give the cosmic context. This is a prefiguration of the programme of the Riesensaal in the Palace renovated by Johann Georg in 1627 with the help of the same artist, Kilian Fabritius, and discussed in chapter 5. When music emerges magically from behind each of the statues, it must have seemed as though they were producing the music of the spheres.

The other feature that deserves further comment is the lower dining chamber with its grotto, on which were displayed vessels made of semi-precious stones. In her discussion of artificial grottos in the early modern period, Claudia Maué quotes one of the most famous works of German literature of the early seventeenth century, *Die Schäfferey von der Nimfen Hercinie* (The Pastoral of the Nymph Hercinie) by Martin Opitz first published in 1630, though completed at the end of 1629.[101] This work, which introduced the pastoral genre into German, is dedicated to Hans Ulrich, Freiherr von Schaffgotsch, a Silesian nobleman, and many details of the landscape Opitz presents are taken from a work by Caspar Schwenckfeldt describing the area in the Riesengebirge where the Schaffgotsch family originated.[102] In the course of the work, the nymph Hercinie takes the four shepherds (Opitz and his fellow poets) into the underground cave of the rivers (among them the Oder and the Elbe) where nymphs sit weaving a beautiful cloth. This passage is closely based on Book XII of Sannazaro's *Arcadia*. But then the nymph leads them through a bronze door into the dwelling of Thetis. This is not a cave or grotto but a man-made dining-room lit by two windows, the floor and ceiling inlaid with semi-precious stones. It contains a long table carved from stone, many chairs made of amber, and a fountain.

On the walls are pictures and inscriptions. The nymph addresses the four shepherds:

> Wißet, sagte sie ferner/ daß alles was ihr biß anher gesehen undt noch sehen werdet/ in heimische außbeute/ in diesen gründen geseiffet/ in diesen wäßern gewaschen/ hier gefunden undt gearbeitet sey. Der weiße chalcedonier/ der schwartze cristall/ der violbraune amethist/ der blawe saffir/ der striemichte jaspis/ die tunckelrothen granaten/ der fleischfarbene carniol/ der rothgelbe gifftfeindt der hyacinth/ der gelbichte beryll/ der vielfärbichte achat/ der gelbe topazier...sindt alle hier zue hause. Diese perlen/ dieses silber/ diß goldt ist in flötzen und quärtzen/ flämmicht undt körnicht in hiesigen reichen gefilden undt gegenden an zue treffen; des zinnes/ kupffers/ eisens glases...zue geschweigen.[103]

[Know, she went on, that everything you have seen up to now and that you will see is local treasure, laid down as alluvial deposits in this soil, washed in these waters, found and worked here. White chalcedony, black crystal, violet-coloured amethysts, blue sapphires, streaky jade, dark-red garnets, pink carniol, the orange antidote to poison, the hyacinth, yellowish amber, iridescent agate, yellow topaz, they are all local to here. These pearls, this silver, this gold are to be found in mineral seams and ores, flame-coloured and grainy, in these rich fields and regions, not to mention tin, copper, iron and glass.]

This description does not resemble Sannazaro's and, while some of the minerals are described in a manner similar to that of Schwenckfeldt, the gorgeous, architectural, man-made setting is not. It does, however, closely resemble the lower chamber of the Belvedere in Dresden, which Opitz may have seen on his visit there in 1626, after which he began work on his translation of Rinuccini's *Dafne*. Opitz's pastoral pays homage in general to Hans Ulrich von Schaffgotsch but for the description of Thetis's dwelling Opitz drew on what he had seen in Dresden. Opitz, just like Johann Georg I, was concerned to modernise German culture, in his case German literature. One of the most important ways in which Opitz did this, as set out in his poetics *Das Buch von der deutschen Poeterey* (1624), was by mediating the literature of the Italian Renaissance – the poetry of Petrarch, the poetic theories of Scaliger, the opera libretto of Rinuccini, the pastoral of Sannazaro. It is therefore not surprising that Opitz should have responded to the Belvedere in Dresden and to the Italianising programme of its builder Johann Georg I.

3
The Management of Knowledge: The Dresden Collections – Their Origin and Development

Early modern collecting

The 1560s and 1570s saw the foundation of a number of important collections, so-called *Kunstkammern*, *Wunderkammern* or cabinets of curiosities, at major courts in the Empire.[1] The *Kunstkammer* of Emperor Ferdinand I is thought to have had its inception in 1553, the collection of Archduke Ferdinand of Tyrol in Schloss Ambras goes back to the 1560s and the *Kunstkammer* of Duke Albrecht V of Bavaria was installed in Munich in a purpose-built building between 1564 and 1567.[2] The Dresden court took part in this trend, the *Kunstkammer* there being founded, if we are to believe Tobias Beutel, its custodian of more than a century later, in 1560 by Elector August.[3]

As generally understood, a *Kunstkammer* is a forerunner of the modern museum in that it organises and presents various kinds of object which have been amassed to form a collection. They can be natural objects, *naturalia*, bearing witness to the multifariousness of nature, or man-made objects, *artificialia*, testimony to the skills of man. In both cases, the primary emotion the objects were expected to elicit was wonder. Natural objects were chosen for their extreme smallness or largeness, their aberrant shape or their exotic provenance. Man-made objects were collected for the intricate skill of their manufacture and the beauty and value of their raw materials. The natural objects usually included minerals of all kinds, exotic snails and shells, dried, stuffed or embalmed animals, birds and fish, bones, tusks and horns, as well as such things as Siamese twins or deformed animals. Some of the objects were thought to have special powers according to early modern ideas about medicine, alchemy and natural magic. Some of these natural objects could be enhanced by carving or by a precious or decorative setting. The man-made objects could have the most varied origins and purposes and be made from a range of materials. Some would come under the heading of what we would nowadays call antiquities (cameos, sculptures, vases) or art objects (paintings, sculptures, engravings), others we should designate as works of applied art (drinking vessels, inlaid cabinets, goldsmith work, jewellery) or even toys (automata, mobile drinking vessels). Other man-made objects would nowadays be classified as ethnographic objects (Brazilian featherwork, Turkish weapons, Japanese porcelain and armour), while other objects come under the heading of scientific instruments (astrolabes, armillary spheres, measuring devices, clocks) and books.

In a work called *Gesta Grayorum*, Francis Bacon, writing in 1594, has six counsellors advise the 'Prince of Purpoole' on the conduct befitting a prince. The Second Counsellor recommends what is called 'the Study of Philosophy'.[4] One of the things necessary for this study is a *Kunstkammer* and it is described as follows:

> a goodly, huge cabinet, wherein whatsoever the hand of man, by exquisite art or engine, hath made rare in stuff, form, or motion, whatsoever singularity, chance and the shuffle of things hath produced, whatsoever Nature hath wrought in things that want life, and may be kept, shall be sorted and included.

But to think of a *Kunstkammer* merely as a collection of objects is to miss the point. Samuel Quiccheberg, Flemish adviser to Duke Albrecht V of Bavaria and the author of a treatise on the *Kunstkammer*, called the Bavarian *Kunstkammer* a 'Theatrum sapientiae'.[5] The *Kunstkammer* was a system for organising knowledge about the universe and for demonstrating man's mastery of nature and often formed part of a larger group of collections. Each collector's organisation was different, each collector placed different emphases according to his or her tastes, means and opportunities, each collector used his or her collection differently and related to it in his or her own way.

Again Bacon's Counsellor illustrates this. The 'goodly cabinet' or *Kunstkammer* is only the third of 'four principal works and monuments' necessary to the Study of Philosopy. The first item in the overall scheme is 'a most perfect and general library, wherein whosoever the wit of man hath heretofore committed to books of worth, be they ancient or modern printed or manuscript, European or of the other parts, of one or other language, may be made contributory to your wisdom'. Then he envisages a garden stocked with all the plants in the universe, 'built about with rooms, to stable in all rare beasts, and to cage in all rare birds', and two lakes, one freshwater, one salt, stocked with all kinds of fish. These arrangements should provide 'in small compass, a model of universal nature made private'. The fourth essential element is 'a Stillhouse, so furnished with mills, instruments, furnaces, and vessels, as may be a Palace fit for a philosopher's stone' – in other words, an alchemical laboratory.[6]

The Electoral collections in Dresden formed part of such an overall scheme. This chapter examines their origins, organisation and purpose and charts their development from the mid-sixteenth century up to their radical re-organisation by Friedrich August I (August the Strong) in 1723, when he created the series of museums we see in Dresden today. Chapter 4 is devoted to the final element in the scheme, the alchemical laboratories.

The original Dresden *Kunstkammer*

The oldest of the Dresden collections is the Armoury or 'Rüstkammer'. This goes back to the Leipzig Partition of 1485, when the Albertine branch of the House of Wettin founded its own separate armoury in the Palace in Dresden. This formed the nucleus of the later Electoral collection of arms and armour. It was Elector August who had inventories made of the collection early in his reign and who renamed it the 'Rüst- und Harnischkammer' (the Armoury and Saddlery). The oldest inventory of part of the collection dates from 1561, there was a complete inventory dating from 1567 (lost in World War II) and another from 1568.[7] The 1567 inventory makes clear that some of the armour was already displayed at this date on carved wooden horses, so that it had some of the properties of a museum and was not merely a weapons store. Armour, weapons – for war, hunting and tournaments – harnesses, carriages and sledges for use by the ruler, his family and courtiers were some of the objects that came within the purview of the Armoury. As we saw in chapter 2, when August's successor, Christian I, built his new stables, considerable provision was made in it for the storage and display of this material.

Other important collections were of coins and medals (the 'Münzkabinett'), the collection of plate (the 'Silberkammer'), the treasury (the 'Schatzkammer') and the library. These groupings indicate the unusual character of the Dresden *Kunstkammer*, for several of the above categories would have formed part of the *Kunstkammer* at other courts, for instance, in Archduke Ferdinand's collection at Schloss Ambras. The treasury in particular contained such things as drinking vessels made from rock crystal which are often thought of as typical *Kunstkammer* pieces (Figure 19).

So what did the *Kunstkammer* contain and how was it organised? We owe our information about the early decades of the collection to the inventory compiled in 1587, a year after the death of its founder, Elector August, by the then custodian, David Ußlaub.[8] Unlike the inventories of the Armoury or those of the Library from the years 1574 and 1580, we have no inventory taken during the lifetime of the collector. Although it is clear that a number of pieces have been added by Christian I since his succession, the coherence and inner logic the inventory presents is such as to give us a good insight into the nature of Elector August's *Kunstkammer*.

The *Kunstkammer* was housed in seven rooms within the Palace in Dresden[9] and the collection was organised in 85 groups of objects. The first two rooms were the largest and contained the bulk of the collection and it is apparent that the rooms, as the visitor progressed through them, diminished in importance. The inventory takes us through the

Figure 19. Rock crystal drinking vessel with a setting of gold, rubies, enamel and sapphires. The Sarachi workshop in Milan before 1580. Grünes Gewölbe, Dresden. Deutsche Fotothek (Heckmann).

collection room by room. The first twenty-three groups of objects are described as being located 'In Meines gnedigsten Churfürsten und hern Reiß Cammer und kleinem Gemach' (In the small room in which my Most Gracious Elector and Lord did his drawing). Elector August therefore sat and worked here among his possessions, he was not merely a passive admirer of them. The next thirty-three groups of objects are said to be 'Im hindternn grossen Gemach kegen dem Vehsten Bau Gartenn' (In the large back room towards the garden at the fortifications). We are told that 'In der stubenn neben dem FrauenZimmer kegen dem Schloßhoffe' (In the room near the women's apartments towards the Palace Courtyard) there are eleven groups of objects. Three groups of objects are displayed 'In kleinem Gemach vor der grossen stubenn neben dem FrauenZimmer kegen dem Schloßhoffe' (In the small room in front of the large room near the women's apartments towards the Palace Courtyard), twelve groups 'In dem Gemach an der Librarey' (in the room next to the Library), two groups 'In dem außwendigen Vorsaall Zwischen der Kunst stuben und Librarey' (In the outer antechamber between the art room and the Library) and one 'In einer Cammernn unterm Dach nebenn deß Drechslers meister Egidius werckstadt' (In the chamber under the roof near Master Egidius [Löbenigk], the turner's, workshop).

The first three groups of objects and the very last group encountered in Room 1 (the so-called 'Draughtsman's Chamber') stand out for being heterogeneous in themselves and for not fitting in with the logical arrangement of the room or with the character of the collection as a whole. We therefore ask ourselves why it is that the collection begins with them. The first group, announced in the heading as 'Ahn schönen kunstreichen Schreibetischen, Schreib Zeugenn Probier Geheusen, und andern Kestleinn' (Beautiful artfully wrought desks, writing materials, a still and other little chests) begins with a desk given to August by the Emperor Maximilian II. The lengthy description tells us that it is in silver and gilt with coloured inlay depicting the Emperors from Albrecht II to Maximilian, and the seven Virtues. On it, and obviously part of it, is a chiming clock with the seven planets. There are twelve drawers filled among other things with various fine writing implements. Maximilian II was not only a personal friend of Elector August, but played a special role in the history of the Albertines. He it was who as recently as 1566 had conferred the Electorship and the office of Imperial High Marshall on August, thus finally securing the Electorship for the Albertines. This piece therefore reminds the visitor of the role Maximilian played in their history. In addition, the desk depicts the Imperial Succession through time (the clock), sanctioned by destiny (the planets) and allied to virtue (the depiction of the Cardinal Virtues), and its presence extends these desirable qualities to August. Another of the items in this group is a set of 'Indian' writing utensils given by the Duke of Florence to Christian I.[10] This must have been added by Christian after his succession. The second group consists of large crystals, crystal mirrors and silver candlesticks, presented to August in 1580 by Emanuele Filiberto, Duke of Savoy. One of the crystals, polished to a perfect sphere, weighs seven and a half kg and this was clearly used for scientific experiments, since one of the writings in the collection of books in the second room of the *Kunstkammer* describes the results of these experiments.[11] The last group in the room contains an 'Indian' dagger also donated by Emanuele Filiberto. The third group consists of 'precious stones, ivory and rhinoceros horn'. The first object here is a huge piece of Columbian emerald ore containing 16 uncut emeralds, a gift to August in 1581 from Rudolf II, an object so highly prized that the recipient made it the inalienable property of the Albertines[12] (Figure 20). This group also contains a very long rhinoceros horn and two others, one of which was presented by the Duke of Florence to Christian I, probably another new addition.

Such a grouping of objects is uncharacteristic of the collection as a whole and resembles rather the kinds of objects found in other *Kunstkammern* – the craftsmanship of the desk, the huge size of the crystal ball, the immense length of the rhinoceros horn, the magnificence and weight of the emerald ore, the exotic provenance of the 'Indian' writing utensils and dagger. But these things are all gifts, some of them to Christian I, and this explains both their divergence from August's own plan for his *Kunstkammer* and their prominence in the collection. Though these objects are not the kind of thing August himself placed in his *Kunstkammer*, they take on a particular lustre precisely because they are evidence of the friendly relations between the Elector of Saxony and such prominent figures as the Emperors Maximilian and Rudolf, the Duke of Savoy and the Duke of Florence. When another prince gave him an object that did fit in with his own collection, he placed it with similar objects of his own. Examples are the geometrical instruments and compasses given him by Wilhelm, Landgrave of Hesse, and Count Friedrich von Hohenlohe discussed below. Even gifts from the Emperor, if they fitted in with August's arrangement, could be placed within a group in the collection. An example is the pair of compasses listed on folio 56a of the inventory as being with the collection of other compasses in the first room.

After these groups of objects presented by prominent contemporaries, August's own collection begins. Seventeen groups of objects form a

Figure 20. The figure of a Moor by Balthasar Permoser holds the lump of Columbian emerald ore from the *Kunstkammer*. The setting is by the Dinglinger brothers. Lacquered birch, gilt silver, emeralds, rubies, sapphires, topazes, garnets, almandine and tortoiseshell. c. 1724. Grünes Gewölbe, Dresden. H. 63.8 cm. Deutsche Fotothek (Heckmann).

remarkably coherent series relating to measurement. The first group announces itself as consisting of clocks, clockwork and hourglasses but in its first item, a celestial globe, the main theme of the series is announced: the mapping of the heavens and the earth. This first item is the mechanical globe-cum-clock made in Augsburg in 1586 by Georg Roll and Johannes Reinhold. Georg Roll's description of this instrument is listed as No. 206 of the list of 288 books in the *Kunstkammer*, of which more below. This gleaming golden piece includes an eight-day chiming clock which rotates on its axis once in twenty-four hours, a calendar ring, a celestial globe, an armillary sphere, a compass, a terrestrial globe and four sundials, all worked by clockwork. The same group of clocks includes another celestial globe and a pedometer for measuring distance. The next group continues the theme of measurement and mapping and contains among other instruments astrolabes – one of the most important instruments in surveying and map-making – celestial and terrestrial globes, and compasses. One of the astrolabes is described as relating to the fifth book of Ptolemy's *Almagest*, the Arabic version of Ptolemy's famous work on astronomy and fundamental to the development of map-making, and another instrument is described as a 'Torquet' accompanied by a 'bericht' or instruction booklet.[13] This is a *torquetum*, the universal measuring instrument described by Petrus Appianus in 1532. Then the series goes on to other cartographic instruments – marine and underground compasses, surveying instruments, the brass plates for maps, and instruments for measuring distance by driving, riding or walking along the stretch of country to be measured. One group of such instruments is specifically credited to Thomas Rückert, originally an instrument-maker from Augsburg whom August brought to Dresden.[14] Then comes a quadrant and drawing implements presented by Wilhelm, Landgrave of Hesse-Kassel.[15] What are called in the heading to the next section 'astronomical and geometrical instruments' given by Count Friedrich von Hohenlohe to August and Christian I respectively turn out also to be surveying instruments: compasses and a 'Jakobsstäblein', the latter being a rod used predominantly for measuring buildings. Both Wilhelm of Hesse-Kassel and Friedrich von Hohenlohe were fellow Protestant princes with a strong interest in science.[16] Friedrich (1553–90) was the younger brother of Wolfgang II von Hohenlohe; we shall meet him again in chapter 4 as a noted alchemist and friend of Elector August.[17] Then comes a group of measuring and divining rods, another group of geometrical and mathematical instruments expressly labelled as measuring distance, height and depth, and then a set of models of geometric figures in wood and *papier maché* – pyramids, cubes, cones, octohedrons, etc. The next group is headed 'perspectival instruments', but the first item described is a surveying table ('Meßtisch') and what follows in this group are other measuring and drawing instruments. The next group begins with a pair of silver compasses presented by the Emperor to the Elector, then a group of other pairs of compasses and finally, rounding out the series, crystals, mirrors and spectacles. It is clear by now that what we have here bears little resemblance to other *Kunstkammern* where the objects (as at Schloss Ambras) are arranged according to the material they are made of or where the primary interest of the collector lies in the bizarre forms of nature or of man (as in the *Kunstkammer* of Ferdinand Albrecht, Duke of Braunschweig-Lüneburg, at Bevern). The Dresden collection is rather what Ludolf von Mackensen has called, with reference to the collection of the Landgraves of Hesse-Kassel, a 'Wissenschaftskammer', that is, a cabinet of science rather than of curiosities. As in Kassel, where the collection was founded by Landgrave Wilhelm and reflected his interest in astronomy, in Dresden the collection reflects August's interest in cartography and surveying. This is very different from those collections where it is thought that the collector understood little of the objects he was amassing.[18]

Still in the first room, the inventory goes on to a number of art objects and pictures which in total form a very small part of the *Kunstkammer*, though we should bear in mind that the very fine collection of goldsmith work and applied art collected in the same period was kept in other collections. The series here begins again with gifts and includes alabaster versions of Michelangelo's seasons, a number of small bronzes by Giambologna given to Christian I in 1587 by the Duke of Florence and another bronze also presented to Christian by the Duke of Mantua. Of the paintings and busts which follow, the majority consist of portraits of the Wettins and allied princes, or of religious works. The first group begins with the twelve Roman Emperors by Nosseni, portraits of August himself and of recent Holy Roman Emperors (Charles V, Maximilian II, Rudolf II) and goes on to Henri IV of France, and Christian III and Fredrik II of Denmark. There are a few depictions of classical themes such as the Judgement of Paris, Mercury's metamorphosis into an ox, and Meleager and Atalanta, but these are in the minority and we return to portraits of the Emperors, the Prince of Orange, the Duke of Braunschweig, the Kings of Poland and two more of August himself.

Then we get straight back to the topic of cartography because the next section is to do with maps and compass readings and begins with a complete illuminated map of his territories made by August himself and a red notebook or case containing various – we know them to have been sixteen – small-scale maps also made by him, as well as his own draughtsman's equipment and small desk.[19] Though it is thought that the fair copy of the map is by a draughtsman, the measuring and surveying, the actual cartography, are August's own work. He thus knew the practical application of the instruments he was collecting and used them himself. August's reign was characterised by territorial expansion, consolidation of power, development of trade, establishment of an administrative system and further exploitation of the natural resources of Saxony. For all of this, reliable maps and accurate calculations of distance were of prime importance. In 1586 August ordered an official cartographic survey of his territories, which was carried out by Matthias Öder and Balthasar Zimmermann and completed in 1591.

Unexpectedly, a small selection of snails completes the contents of this room before the last group – the Indian dagger presented by the Duke of Savoy.

Cartographic instruments and compasses spill over into Room 2, which begins with two groups of them. The inventory then lists Turkish bows and arrows, gifts from Archduke Matthias, before arriving at another of the major features of the *Kunstkammer* as a whole – groups of tools used in various crafts. Here we have builders' tools, followed by iron manacles and chains, more surveying and measuring equipment, then carpenter's, locksmith's, gunner's and draughtsman's tools. Then, set off by a special title-page in the inventory at folio 131a, we have seven groups of turned ivory and wooden objects (Figure 21). The title-page of the section points out that some of these ivories were made by August himself. Ivory-turning was one of his hobbies, as it was of many contemporary princes, and he had his son taught it.[20] Its significance was that the turner's lathe, or 'Drehbank', was a machine which could be used to manufacture art objects of the greatest intricacy out of the precious commodity ivory. Thus, like the complex mapping devices just mentioned, it enabled man – particularly the prince, who had access to such a valuable machine – to master nature by means of it. The group of ivories begins with August's pieces, then those made by the court ivory turners, Egidius Löbenigk and Georg Weckhardt, and then similar pieces presented to August, for instance by Archduke Karl and the Duke of Florence. Then come turned wooden objects from the King of Denmark followed by turned drinking vessels.

The next six sections deal with guns and shot of various kinds. This too is an area of the greatest practical relevance to the sixteenth-century ruler, just as it is to governments today. Then comes a group of parts for

Figure 21. Georg Wecker, Ivory stacking cup, 1588. Grünes Gewölbe, Dresden. Deutsche Fotothek (Heckmann).

compasses, before we come to stamps and moveable type, followed by fish-hooks. Then we have the book collection which consists of 288 numbered volumes quite separate from the books in the Electoral Library. Apart from about 37 volumes of engravings and a small number of illustrated festival books, costume books, books of heraldry and some miscellaneous items, it is a scientific collection which complements the scientific instruments, just as the engravings and illustrated works complement the groups of art objects.

We find here precisely the works which provide the theoretical underpinning for the instruments just described and in many cases explain their application. Naturally Euclid's *Geometry* is prominent in Greek, Latin and German and with various commentaries (at Nos. 38, 40, 56, 57, 64 and 236), as are his *Catoptrics* (Nos. 120, 124). So too is Archimedes (Nos. 40, 90, 223 and 238) and Apollonius of Perga (Nos. 71, 84). We find Ptolomy's *Almagest* with the commentary by Erasmus Oswald Schreckenfuchs (No. 66), as well as his *Geography* (No. 139) and his *Quadripartitum* (Nos. 148, 239). John of Canterbury (Nos. 84, 180) is here, as is Witelo's *Perspectiva* (No. 42). Petrus Aliacus (No. 176) is represented, as is Theodosius's work on spheres (No. 124). There is a good sprinkling of Arab mathematicians such as Albohazen Haly Filii Abenragel (Ali Ibn Abi Al-Rijal, al Shaibani) (Nos. 36, 37), Alfarganus (No. 137), Messahala (Nos. 146, 155), Albohali (Nos. 146, 155, 189), Alkabitius (No. 166) and Albumasar (No. 189).

Those works of Renaissance mathematics and astronomy which made the new techniques of navigation and cartography, not to mention gunnery, possible are also to be found in this collection. Regiomontanus is represented (Nos. 55, 59, 137, 144, 147), so is Heinrich Grammaticus (written as Schreiber, No. 210), Georg Peuerbach (Nos. 35, 39, 100), Johann Schöner (Nos. 41, 48), Johannes Stöffler (Nos. 145, 164), Orontius Finaeus's *Promathesis* (No. 28) and his *Geometria practica* (No. 210), Jakob Kölbel's work on surveying (No. 212), Balthasar Scultetus's *Gnomonice*, Johannes de Sacro Bosco (Nos. 227, 247, 259), Georg Joachim Rheticus (No. 128) and Copernicus (Nos. 86, 167). We have Walther Rivius (Nos. 46, 47, 48, 50, 62), Erasmus Reinhold's Prutenic Tables (Nos. 134, 135, 143), Gemma Frisius (Nos. 85, 168), Tilemann Stella (No. 106), Junctinus (Nos. 226, 227), Caspar Peucer (Nos. 244, 247, 250) and the Saxon arithmetician Adam Ries (Nos. 197, 286).

We have some practical works on the instruments themselves such as Christoph Schiessler's *Geometria* (No. 107) and Valentin Thaw's report on the use of the compasses and the curve (No. 19). We are not surprised, given the nature of the instruments we have been discussing, to find in the collection such landmarks of mapmaking as Abraham Ortelius's *Theatrum orbis terrarum* (No. 12), Petrus Appianus's *Cosmographia* (No. 168) and Sebastian Münster's *Cosmographia* (Nos. 65, 74).

The book collection also betrays an intense interest in architecture and work on perspective. We have Vitruvius in several editions (Nos. 119, 200) in addition to Giovanni Battista Bertani's version of the

Opera Ionica (No. 22), the commentary by Daniele Barbaro (Nos. 72, 83) and Walther Rivius's German translation (No. 67). We have Sebastiano Serlio (No. 20), Pietro Cataneo (No. 33), Girolamo Cataneo (Nos. 76, 162), Giovanni Battista Benedetti (No. 34), Cosimo Bartoli (No. 173), Giovanni Battista Carelli (Nos. 125–6) and the notable German writers on the subject such as Wentzel Jamnitzer (Nos. 17, 257, 263), Johannes Lencker (No. 78) and Albrecht Dürer (Nos. 44, 54, 59, 89).

The more speculative and mystical end of early modern science is represented by the astrologer Cyprian von Leowitz (Nos. 158, 209), the alchemist Leonhard Thurnneysser (No. 284), by Paracelsus (No. 201) and John Dee's *Monas Hieroglyphica* (No. 151). As we shall see, the Electoral Library also contained scientific books which relate closely to those just discussed in the *Kunstkammer*.

After the books, the next groups the inventory lists for this second room are eating and drinking vessels of marble, wooden 'Quadrant stoecklein' and measuring implements, a small group of portraits and pictures, elephant's teeth and corals, blowpipes, two small organs and gardening tools. Finally, a miscellaneous group including an 'Indian' table presented to Christian I by the Duke of Florence and a tin lantern, the gift of the Patriarch of Macedonia, round out the objects in this room.

Room 3 continues with collections of tools for various crafts. It contains the dies for minting coins, implements for wire-drawing, surgeons' instruments, carpenters' tools, tools for cutting agate, desks, another group of instruments for measuring distance made by Valentin Thaw, whose theoretical writing on the subject we encountered among the books, a group of clocks, a group of maps and engravings of landscapes and sieges, antlers and stags' heads, and another gift presented by the Duke of Mantua to Christian I, a costume.

Room 4 contains huntsmen's implements, more engraved maps and fortifications and a few paintings, for instance of animals hunted by Elector August, which complement the hunting implements.

Room 5 (next to the Library) holds a larger collection of objects, among which are geological samples of the semi-precious stones such as serpentine, jade, amethyst and marble found in Saxony by Nosseni and labelled as such in the inventory. Hunting implements, pictures of hunted animals, printing presses and an old scales, more geometric instruments, compasses, sundials, drawing and writing implements, transparencies (pictures on transparent parchment mounted on wooden frames), architectural models, samples of wood and brass, maps on wooden panels and more maps and pictures complete the contents of the room.

What little is contained in rooms 6 and 7 consists of cases for various scientific instruments and some miscellaneous objects such as a chair, a few pictures, a pulpit, and so on.

If we sum up the contents of this *Kunstkammer*, then, we can say that its emphasis is clearly on science and technology, since the bulk of the objects comprise scientific instruments and books, and tools of all kinds. Joachim Menzhausen estimates that, of the 10,000 objects listed, some 75 per cent are tools, 4.5 per cent are scientific instruments and clocks, 3 per cent are books, 2.5 per cent are turned ivory pieces, while art objects constitute only 1.5 per cent, and *naturalia* and furniture only 1 per cent each.[21] But this purely numerical analysis gives a false impression, implying that, because the inventory lists every screw and every spare part, the tools are far more prominent in the collection than the scientific instruments. A truer assessment can be made by looking at the 85 groups of objects. Here we find that roughly the same number of groups (about twenty-three) are devoted to scientific instruments and clocks as to tools (about twenty-four). In addition, since the inventory takes us through the seven rooms from the most important objects to the little lumber rooms at the back, the fact that the scientific instruments and books are presented before the tools underlines their greater importance.

It is also clear that the *Kunstkammer* closely reflected August's own interests. He was a mapmaker and, as we have seen, the collection focuses strongly on mapping the heavens and the earth. We have seen how the first and most important room was labelled as the room in which he drew and worked. But in fact every room in the *Kunstkammer* had desks and writing implements in it, so that one could work there. August was an ivory turner and the objects he produced are kept in the collection, as well as similar objects by the court ivory turners. He was interested in gardening and surgery and the Armoury in Dresden still preserves his gardening tools and surgical instruments from the *Kunstkammer*. The central importance of geology to the mining industry in Saxony is illustrated by the examples of Saxon minerals in the collection. The collection also contains books and implements that relate to such essential branches of knowledge for an expanding territory as architecture and gunnery.

Elector August's Library

Another great collection put together by August and equally related to his interests is the library. Unlike the inventory of the *Kunstkammer*, which was made only on his death, we have two inventories of the library taken during his lifetime, in 1574 and in 1580 respectively. As with the objects in the other collections, many of the books are still in Dresden today, preserved in the Sächsische Landesbibliothek, Staats- und Universitätsbibliothek (SLUB).

August began to collect books from about 1556 and we know from archival records that he took advice from the professors of the Universities of Wittenberg and Leipzig but also chose books himself from the catalogues of the German Book Fairs.[22] He also used Hubert Languet, his informant and diplomatic representative in the years from 1559 to 1577, as an agent abroad. Languet, a Frenchman and Huguenot sympathiser, sent a consignment of thirty books from Paris in 1566, for instance.[23] He sent another work from Vienna in 1574 which he thought would interest the Elector, paintings from Antwerp in 1577 and Bibles in English, Danish and Swedish from Antwerp in 1580, the year before his death.[24]

The first inventory of the library, that of 1574, is preserved in the SLUB in Dresden. It is entitled: 'Registratur der bücher in des Churfürsten zu Saxen Liberey zu Annaburg' (inventory of the library of the Electors of Saxony at Annaburg).[25] Annaburg was the ducal residence near Torgau to the north-west of Dresden, and a favourite of Duke August and his wife Anna, after whom it was named. That the books were kept there at this date rather than in the Palace in Dresden indicates that this is a collection for the personal use of the Elector and his family rather than for prestige or show. The organisation of the library underlines this.

The standard method of classifying books, as can be seen in the catalogues of the Frankfurt Book Fairs contemporaneous with this inventory[26] or in such later bibliographies as that of Georg Draudius,[27] lists works in Latin first, then in the vernacular languages, and groups them according to the University Faculties and subject areas: Theology, Law, Medicine, History, Philosophy and then Literature. In the Book Fair catalogues these categories are followed by those of Astrology and Mathematics, in Draudius by Music. Both the order in which the languages are listed and the order of the subject matter imply a ranking in order of importance. Draudius conveys this by means of a metaphor when, in his Preface to the Reader, he compares Theology to the head of the Colossus of Babylon, Law to its breast and arms, Medicine to its stomach and Philosophy to its legs.

August's collection, that of neither a bibliophile nor a scholar, is organised according to a system which reflects his interests. Of the

1,721 volumes the inventory lists, the majority are in the vernacular and all the vernacular (mostly German) works are listed together before the Latin works. How easily Elector August read languages other than German is open to question. We know, for instance, that he employed a translator, Georg Forberger, a Saxon who went to Basel to study and while there translated Paolo Giovio's *Historiarum sui temporis* and Francesco Guicciardini's *Historia di Italia* into German and was already working on Paracelsus.[28] After his appointment as 'Electoral Translator' in 1574 Forberger translated into German both Natale Conti's *Historiarum sui temporis* and Denys Zacaire's *Opuscule tres-excellent de la vraye philosophie naturelle des metaulx*. Forberger is notable for being the first editor of Paracelsus.

In the Elector's subject groupings 'Theologia' naturally comes first. Luther's Bible in various editions, other Lutheran writings, sermons and devotional works, catechisms and works relating to the Reformation, hymns, pamphlets, church ordinances, etc. In this section we also find the fifteen biblical plays discussed in chapter 1. The next category is 'Historica'. As well as German chronicles and genealogies of various kinds, we have translations of Justinian, Thucydides, Herodotus, Plutarch, Xenophon, Tacitus, Virgil, Polybius, Livy, Caesar, Sleidanus, Paulus Jovius, though the library contained many of these in the original languages also. We also have decrees of the Reichstag and many accounts of military matters, in addition to festival books relating to other courts, for example, the entries of Charles V or accounts of tournaments at Vienna and some travel literature. We also have a very complete set of the available printed early prose fiction in German from the late fifteenth and sixteenth centuries, some 99 titles in all. These include Maximilian I's verse epic of his own life, the *Theuerdank*, works by Elisabeth of Nassau-Saarbrücken (*Hug Schapler* and *Ritter Galmy*), Johannes Pauli (*Schimpf und Ernst*, Gaiety and gravity), Jörg Wickram (*Das Rollwagenbüchlein*) (The little carriage book) and what is called *Historia von vier Kaufleuten* (The history of four merchants), presumably his novel *von guten und bösen Nachbarn* (Of good and bad neighbours), Heinrich Bebel (the *Facetiae* in German translation), Sebastian Brant, the *Narrenschiff* (The Ship of fools) and Johann Fischart (*Gargantua* and *Floh Hatz Weiber Tratz*). This section also includes a long list of prose romances such as *Magelona, Lewfried, Melusina* and translations of the *Amadís* into German and French.

A group of works on military matters constitutes the next section and then comes the group of works on riding, horsemanship and farriery discussed in chapter 2. Medical books, herbals, works on midwifery and early pharmacology, a section labelled as being the medical works of Turneisser and Paracelsus ('Turneissers medicin' and 'Theophrasti Paracelsi medicin', both on fol. 73a), come next. After a small group of three titles relating to engraving and illumination we have a section listing books on mining and smelting. After two small groups of law books come two much larger groups which take up those interests of Elector August which we have already seen represented in the *Kunstkammer*. The first deals with mathematics (the section beginning at fol. 85a is called 'Geometria Astrologia Arithmetica unnd was deme anhengig' – Geometry, Astrology, Arithmetic and matters relating to them). Here we find twenty-eight titles mostly in German and in the corresponding Latin section a further thirty-three. The second group is entitled 'Architectur, Perspectiua, Kunststuck vom Kupferstichen Contrafacturn unnd sonst allerley figurn unnd gemähl' (Architecture, Perspective, Artworks such as engravings, depictions and all kinds of figures and paintings) and contains some sixty-three volumes with no corresponding Latin section. The question is how this collection of books relates to the scientific books in the *Kunstkammer*.

The composition of the list is remarkably similar and in some cases one wonders whether individual works which figure in the inventory of the library in 1574 have been moved to the *Kunstkammer* by 1587. For instance, the so-called 'Gros Planetenbuch' in the library may be identical with No. 208 of the *Kunstkammer* books, 'Practica Johann Carionis' in the library could be No. 264 of the *Kunstkammer* list, the work by Cyprian von Leowitz in the library could correspond to No. 158 in the *Kunstkammer* and the 'Geometrisch feldmessen' by Jacob Kölbel to No. 212. The account in the library inventory by Christoph Schießler of the quadrant he has made surely corresponds to No. 107 of the *Kunstkammer* books, especially as we know the instrument to which it refers was in the collecton, but Valentin Thaw's report on an instrument called a 'Triangulum' may relate to a different instrument than his report indicated at No. 19 of the *Kunstkammer* books which describes a compass with two semi-circular curves.

The section on architecture clearly contains many works which are either doubles of works in the *Kunstkammer* collection (works on perspective by Dürer and Jamnitzer, Tobias Fendt's *Monumenta Sepulchrorum* (No. 61), Erasmus Reinhold's work on surveying, Vergil Solis's Biblical figures (No. 194)) or actually are the same works which have been transferred. It is in this section too that we find works published in Paris, most likely those purchased and shipped by Languet. What is listed in the library inventory as 'Allerley Kunste von seltzamen fantaseÿen den Malern Goldschmiden Bildthauern dienlich Androuetÿ vonn Paris (fol. 88a)' (All kinds of pictures of strange fantastic creatures for the use of painters, goldsmiths and sculptors by Androuet of Paris) is surely *Les Grotesques* by Jacques d'Androuet du Cerceau,[29] but various other works listed as having been published in Paris (Androuet's *Livre d'architecture*, Vitruvius in French translation, portraits of the French kings) are probably from the same consignment.

A further detailed inventory of the electoral library was compiled in 1580, still during the lifetime of its founder.[30] It is very similarly organised to the 1574 inventory with most of the same categories, though the order of the categories is different and titles are given in a much more shorthand way. The most interesting thing it has to tell us is that the number of works has increased to 2,354, so that we can see that the Elector was purchasing books at the rate of about a hundred a year. This time too there is a supplement listing some 450 books owned by Anna, Princess of Denmark, August's consort – a marvellous source for our still very patchy knowledge of the role played by female consorts in the intellectual life of German courts. Her particular interests were pharmacy, medicine and horticulture, though a very high proportion of her books consisted of devotional works. Medicine was in general an interest of the Wettins, as we can see in another inventory in the SLUB which consists of a fifteen-page manuscript from the year 1590 entitled 'List of some manuscript medical books in a special cupboard in the Electoral Library'.[31]

In general, therefore, the library, like the *Kunstkammer*, is highly practical in its orientation and highly personal to its founder, containing those works that August (or his consort) needed for his (her) own use or for his various building, mining or surveying projects. That books were highly prized objects for August can be seen by the fact that he employed the bookbinder Jakob Krause (1531–85) to provide his books with beautiful parchment and calf leather bindings.

The Electoral Library in the seventeenth century

August's successors continued to add to the library he had founded and we have already seen how Christian I's interest in horses and riding can be seen in the books bought during his reign. He augmented his collection by buying the libraries of the Humanist Georg Fabricius (1516–71) and of the Saxon nobleman Dietrich von Werthern (1468–1536). We have a two-volume inventory from the year 1595 with additions up to 1629[32] and here we see some interesting innovations. The first thing to note is that volume I of the inventory now follows the standard pattern for organising books, that is, according to the University Faculties of Theology, Law, Medicine and History. Philipp Hainhofer, the Augsburg traveller and diplomat who visited the library in 1629 and whose account of Dresden is discussed below, actually calls the group of medical books 'the Medical Faculty' in his description of the library.[33] Another surprise is to find a collection of Calvinist works ('Calvinische Bücher') in the Theology section. Volume II of the 1595 inventory includes a separate section of music books for the first time and now labels its mathematical books 'Libri mathematici Welche ein stuck seind Philosophiae Contemplatiuae' (Mathematical books which are partly contemplative philosophy) (90A). It also contains a separate section of twenty-four works of prophecy (194 A and B) and a large group of 91 framed maps and engravings. Volume III up to 1629 follows the same scheme as 1595 and again has a section, though a very small one, of Calvinist books. In the later part of the inventory it is interesting to see how new scientific literature continued to be added to the collection: Tycho Brahe's *Astronomiae instauratae Mechanica* (1598), Mercator's Atlas (1609) and Kepler's *De stella nova in pede serpentarij* (1606) and *Astronomia noua seu Physica coelestis tradita* (1619), for instance.

A year after becoming Elector in 1611 Johann Georg I added his private library to the main collection and there is a list of those books included in volume II beginning at folio 231A. It includes many of the expected items – Bibles, sermons, legal works, festival books, etc. The most interesting item is the group of twenty-six works under the heading 'Bücher in Welscher sprach' (folio 250A – Books in Italian). As we surmised in chapter 2, it is likely that many of these books were purchased during his Italian tour of 1601.

After this period it is generally agreed that the library stagnated until the era of Friedrich August I at the end of the seventeenth century. We might note, however, that it had spread to three rooms by the time Anton Weck wrote his account of the city and Palace of Dresden, published in 1680.[34] Tobias Beutel, in his account of the Dresden collections from 1671 (reprinted and revised in 1683), relegates the Library to what he calls 'Neben=Wercke' ('Opera Affinia') or secondary features (of the Dresden court, he means), along with the Anatomy Collection, the Playhouse and the Lion House. This may indicate the relatively low importance now attached to the Library but it may also stem from Beutel's desire to reduce the status of a collection that did not come under his control. He was after all the custodian of the *Kunstkammer*.

The *Kunstkammer* under Christian I and Christian II

The changes to the *Kunstkammer* are rather more revealing of the development of taste during the century after its founder's death. As we have seen above, the original collection was very far from being an art collection, nor indeed did it resemble other *Kunstkammern* of the time. It is possible that Christian I wished to make it an art collection. In 1587 Gabriel Kaltemarckt, a knowledgeable artist who had travelled and who possibly taught Christian I drawing, wrote a report, proposing the establishment of an art collection in Dresden.[35] For him a *Kunstkammer* should include statues, paintings, *naturalia*, drinking vessels of semi-precious stones, skeletons and coins. He included long lists of the classical antiquities and the more recent artists from Italy, the Netherlands and Germany who should be included in this gallery. They would be represented not by paintings so much as by plaster casts and engravings. Naturally, this could be done only by removing from the present collection 'die Instrumenta zur Musica, Astronomia, Geometria, Item probir, Goldschmidt, Bildhauer, Tischer, Dressler, Balbier und andere werckgezeuge' 'dann weil solche nicht das Werck, sondern nur Instrumenta und gezeugk, damit mererley werck gemacht werden mögen' (the instruments for music, astronomy, geometry as well as tools for smelting, of goldsmiths, sculptors, carpenters, turners, surgeons and others' 'for these things are not the actual works but only the instruments and tools to make different works').[36] In other words, all that made August's *Kunstkammer* what it was should be removed to make way for a wholly different kind of collection.

Christian I's death intervened, so we shall never know if he would have acted on these recommendations. It is suggested below, however, that, just as Johann Georg brought to completion his father's project to build a Belvedere on the ramparts in Dresden, so he went some way towards realising Kaltemarckt's plan for the re-orientation of the *Kunstkammer*.

The next inventory was taken in 1595, during the minority of Christian II, and, as one would expect from the careful stewardship of the regent, Friedrich Wilhelm of Saxony-Weimar, it reveals that the collection was kept very much as it was in the inventory of 1587.[37] There are additions of similar or cognate items to the categories but the one tendency which we might say is a portent for the future is the perceptible one of including more paintings, engravings, sculptures and waxworks. We note the further inclusion of a gift of drinking vessels from the Duke of Florence in 1590[38] and that Bartholomäus Spranger is now represented by three canvases – *Sophonisba*, The *Triumph of Bacchus*, and *Judith and Holofernes*, demonstrating the cultural connections between Dresden and Prague, where Spranger was based at this date.[39]

Fifteen years later, in 1610, almost at the end of Christian II's reign, yet another inventory was taken.[40] This reveals a break with the original *Kunstkammer* whose inner logic and progression of ideas are no longer understood. We now begin with what was originally Room 6 in August's arrangement, proceed to Room 4 and then go backward through the collection from Room 3 to Room 2 and finally to Room 1. It is significant that the visitor now begins in the first two rooms with images – maps, landscapes, battle-scenes, portraits, hunting scenes, depictions of Troy, of Venus, of Diana and Actaeon, etc. Only then does he get to the tools and then only at the very end to the scientific instruments. The *Kunstkammer* has taken a further step away from being a technical museum towards becoming an art collection.

Johann Georg I's *Kunstkammer*

The next full inventory to be taken is that of 1619 which tells us little in that it is pretty close to that of 1610.[41] We gain a far better impression of the *Kunstkammer* some eighteen years into Johann Georg's I reign from the description of it by the art dealer and diplomat from Augsburg, Philipp Hainhofer (1578–1647). He visited Dresden in 1617 and again from 11 September to 17 September 1629. Hainhofer came as a member of a Protestant diplomatic mission that wanted the Elector to persuade the Emperor to relax his repressive measures against Protestants, particularly in Augsburg. Hainhofer was widely travelled and knew the *Kunstkammern* and other collections at Munich, Stuttgart and, Innsbruck, so his detailed account of all that he saw is of great interest. Hainhofer's description of his visit to the *Kunstkammer* on 16 September 1629 in the company of the custodian Theodosius Häsel (whom Hainhofer calls Theodorus) shows that certain rooms had hardly changed. We begin with the same room as in 1610, the ante-chamber. In it Hainhofer notes the paintings of animals and of August jousting. His description of the next room, Room 1, however, shows that the collection has for the first time acquired a considerable quantity of *naturalia*: what he calls the tongues of swordfish, snail shells with carvings on them, a bird of paradise, adders' tongues from Malta, crabs, rhinoceros horn (we know the collection already contained examples), various parts of whales, the shell and underbelly of a tortoise, tortoise-shell dishes, a turtle's egg, starfish, sea-horses' teeth, a buffalo horn out of which a tobacco pipe has been fashioned, and all kinds of misshapen antlers, etc. There is a giant's thigh-bone and a huge human tooth. Exotic objects from the animal kingdom such as elephants' teeth and Indian lizards are also listed, as is a group of what might be called ethnographic objects – all labelled as Indian. These are just a few of the curious and bizarre natural objects, sometimes enhanced by carving or setting, which Hainhofer lists. Here we have the kind of natural curiosities which are so common in other *Kunstkammern*. One of the objects in this room is a wooden effigy of Nebuchadnezar by Nosseni. This huge structure two metres high has little doors or drawers in every part of it – the head, the breast, the stomach, the arms and thighs – which contain emblems and depictions of the Kings and Emperors with details of their reigns.[42] This room also contains marble and bronze statues as well as Dutch and Italian paintings, many tools for drawing wire and Elector August's carpenter's bench, as well as nearly a hundred pieces of silver wire made by him and kept in his eternal memory. The original *Kunstkammer* is filling up with objects added during later decades.

This is equally true of Room 2, which corresponds to Room 4 in August's day. It originally contained mostly tools. Now it has acquired inlaid cupboards, a bird of paradise and more automata and clocks. Room 3 in the present arrangement actually was Room 3 in August's day and still contains mostly tools, desks and clocks, though there are many additions, particularly of the kind of goldsmith work and automata which are nowadays thought of as being typical *Kunstkammer* collectors' items. This room now contains a free-standing deer which, rather like the statue of Nebuchadnezar, is also a kind of cabinet, this time for medicines prepared from the deer by the court Apothecary, Johann Wechinger. Room 4 (previously Room 2) begins with a group of wax portraits and other depictions, beautiful drinking vessels, ivories, mirrors, a *pietra dura* table, the collection of scientific books from the original *Kunstkammer* and more automata – again typical *Kunstkammer* pieces. Hainhofer then went to Room 5, what was originally Room 1 in August's day. This contained Elector August's own mathematical instruments used by him and Hainhofer lists all the branches of science to which they related – astronomy, geometry, geography etc. He ended up in Room 6, what he calls the 'mineral Zimmer' or Geological Room, the old Room 5. All these rooms have acquired more pictures, particularly portraits.

We now have seven rooms, counting the ante-chamber, and it is clear that the collection by this time is rather different from that of its founder, Elector August. If we take Hainhofer's account and see it in the context of his description of the other Dresden collections, we see that Johann Georg has taken a huge step towards the sort of *Kunstkammer* envisaged by Kaltemarckt. According to Kaltemarckt, a *Kunstkammer* should contain first, statues, second, pictures, third, strange native and foreign plants, metals, stones, wood, herbs, fourth, drinking vessels made by nature and art, fifth, antlers, horns, claws, feathers and skeletons (to be got in Germany and Italy), coins and medals and finally 'bas reliefs, high reliefs and three-dimensional sculptures, embossed, carved and cast, of clay, wood, wax, plaster, stone and metal'.[43] While Johann Georg did not simply clear out his grandfather's objects, he set up his Chamber of Anatomy (discussed in chapter 2) where the skeletons are to be found, introduced a mass of *naturalia*, including antlers, claws, teeth and plant material into the *Kunstkammer* and above all, collected pictures and statues. One of the ways he did the latter was by buying up Nosseni's collection of pictures and casts on his death in 1621. In this way he acquired two fine Cranachs, for instance.[44]

The last of the *Kunstkammer* inventories to have survived dates from 1640. This was taken by Johann Christoph Werner and the same Häsel who showed Hainhofer round.[45] The inventory was necessary because the *Kunstkammer* had been reorganised. Now it could be viewed by selected visitors and the tendency towards turning it into an art collection had increased.[46] Many more artists' names are given and we note the appearance of Tintoretto, Titian and Parmigianino in the inventory, for instance. The third room now contains the kind of drinking vessels made out of semi-precious stone, Venetian glass and other precious objects that in Elector August's day would have been kept in the Treasury. There is even a new eighth room to accommodate all the new pictures which is designated as follows: 'Achte Zimmer oder große[n] Eckgemach auff einer seiten gegen dem gold: und dem Balhauß uf der andern Seite gegen der Churfürstin Gärtlein' (Eighth Room or large corner room on one side looking towards the Gold House and the Ballroom and on the other towards the Electress's garden). An extract from the inventory gives an impression of what the collection looked like and how it was displayed. On the two walls between the windows on the garden side of the new eighth room the inventory tells us on folios 507–509 that we would have seen the following:

> the figure of a Satyr and of Achilles standing, Venus with Cupid, an Ecce Homo, Andromeda chained to her rock (by Nicol Schwabe), two wax female figures on small panels, a ram with a dog, a wildman with a satyr, three plaster busts of Sigismund of Poland, Antonio of

Navarre and Duke Erich of Braunschweig and Lüneburg respectively, a carving of the Crucifixion in pearwood, a seated satyr in bronze with bagpipes, Adonis and Pallas in bronze, a bronze of Mercury by Hans Reisiger of Augsburg (1589), a standing figure of Hercules with a child, Leda with the swan, Thetis standing, two standing figures of children by Carlo de Cesare, a small Hercules in white wax, a black case with a gilt border with wax portraits of Christian I and his wife, a naked Roman bust of a woman, a wax crucified Christ on a black cross, a wax St. Sebastian tied to a tree, an alabaster relief of Danae with the shower of golden rain, three plaster portraits of the Emperor Ferdinand and of Emperor Maximilian and his consort, a flat carved pearwood sculpture 'de Iustificatione hominis coram Deo', a leaping unicorn in bronze, a figure of Adonis with a female in metal and a recumbent deer in bronze.

This reads very like Kaltemarckt's stipulations for what kinds of works, especially sculptures and reliefs, a *Kunstkammer* should contain.

By now, too, the inventory of 1640 shows that the whole *Kunstkammer* has turned into a monument to its founder, Elector August, no matter how many later additions there are to it. One is struck by the number of portraits of August it contains, at least one in every room more than fifty years after his death. This is corroborated by the account of the *Kunstkammer* given by Anton Weck in his lengthy illustrated description of the city and Electoral Palace in Dresden just mentioned. Weck begins his description of the *Kunstkammer* as follows:

Denn es bestehet dieselbe von Sieben Zimmern/ in welchen eine solche Disposition und gute Ordnung gemachet/ daß man darinnen Memoriam artificialem & localem haben kan/ darbey auch dieses wohl in acht zu nehmen/ daß/ weil der Höchstlöblichste Churfürst zu Sachsen/ U. Herr Augustus, Christmilden Andenckens/ als ein Kunstliebhabender: auch in Mechanicis und Mathematicis wohlerfahrener Potentat und Herr/ gleichsam dieses wichtigen Wercks Fundator und Urheber gewesen/ Sr. Churfürstl. G. Contrefait/ auf unterschiedene Arten/ zu mehrern Andencken/ in allen Gemächern der Kunst-Cammer zu befinden ist.

[For it consists of seven rooms which are so well ordered and displayed that they serve as an artificial and local memory system. It should be noted here that, because the most praiseworthy Elector of Saxony, our Lord Augustus of blessed memory, a lover of art and a master of technology and mathematics, was both the founder and onlie begetter of this important collection, His Grace's portrait in various modes is to be found in all the rooms of the *Kunstkammer* as a memorial to him. 34f.]

Weck begins his description of the first of the principal rooms with a list of the tools belonging to various crafts to be found there. Goldsmith work, clockmaking, gunnery, metalwork, carpentry, sculpture, mining, ivory turning, wire-drawing, surgery and gardening are mentioned. These are no ordinary tools but gilded and etched, inlaid with ivory or sandalwood, the point being that they belonged to Elector August. There is even a list of the people whose illnesses, wounds and broken limbs were cured by August using the surgeon's implements displayed here. This piece of myth-making implies that the Elector of Saxony had healing powers, rather in the manner of the Kings of England and France, and adds to the legend of the founder of the *Kunstkammer*. In the fourth room Weck notes a coat of arms of the Wettins which August drew with his own hand and in the seventh he mentions the turned ivory cups made by August and by Christian of Saxony-Merseburg. It is characteristic of Weck's presentation of the collections in relation to Elector August that, when he discusses the library, he should stress that it contained August's very own Bible.

The best-known published account of the *Kunstkammer* from this period is by its custodian, the mathematician Tobias Beutel. He wrote a bilingual guide to the collection in Latin and German *en face* called *Chur=Fürstlicher Sächsischer stets grünender hoher Cedern=Wald* (Lofty Evergreen Electoral Saxon Cedar Wood), telling us on the title-page that it is meant as a thanksgiving to God for His mercies to the House of Saxony, for the honour of his prince and as a service to travellers, that is, visitors to the *Kunstkammer*.[47] The first edition was published in 1671, the second in 1683 and there was a third in 1703, showing how popular it was. It is a description of what Beutel calls the Saxon 'Regal=Wercke' ('operum regalium') or collections, so it deals with all the collections of importance in his day. It is to this account that we owe the information that the *Kunstkammer* was founded by August in the year 1560, a piece of information generally not doubted but not corroborated by any other source. Since this piece of information is what Beutel begins with, he too is announcing the *Kunstkammer* as August's legacy.

Unlike the inventory of 1640 or Hainhofer's account of 1629, which both give the impression of clutter and disorganised profusion, Beutel makes the collection appear a place of order and logic. As its custodian, indeed, one might say that he was bound to do so. He focuses in his account of each of the rooms on one aspect of what is to be found there by listing it in the heading. Room 1, for instance, according to the heading, contains tools, and again we begin with those tools used by the founder August. Room 2 contains vessels of semi-precious stone, Room 3 jewel boxes and paintings, Room 4 mathematical objects, Room 5 mirrors, Room 6 *naturalia*, both those which are naturally strange ('rar') and those which are enhanced by art, and Room 7 sculpture, turned objects, automata and clocks. The short description of each room widens this perspective somewhat but not much, and Beutel refers the reader to the extensive inventories for more information. The *Kunstkammer* appears in this account to be a collection of objects acquired for their own sake rather than to exemplify and assist in the carrying out of a set of ideas, as was the case with the original *Kunstkammer*. Many of the standard curiosities of the collection are mentioned, as they are in every account – for instance, the cherry stone with 185 heads carved on it, the rhinoceros horn and the huge rock crystal sphere.

Storage and inventorisation of the collections

Though we have by no means discussed all the Dresden collections from the sixteenth to the end of the seventeenth centuries, their diversity as well as their sheer and growing size should by now be clear. This imposed a considerable problem of management.

The first aspect of this was storage. We have said enough about the seven, or at times eight, rooms in the Palace devoted to the *Kunstkammer* and have mentioned the three rooms to which the Library had expanded by the last quarter of the seventeenth century. According to Weck, the important Coin Collection was kept in the Ratsstube or Council Room, also in the Palace. We know in addition that the walls of many rooms were lined with paintings and that tables and cupboards everywhere were covered with precious objects. The more valuable items – objects of silver and gold, the most highly prized items of goldsmithwork and jewellery – were kept locked away in the four rooms of what was called the 'Gemeine Verwahrung' or Secret Repository in the West Wing of the Palace, the building of which began in 1548. It was this Repository which became known as the Green Vault or 'Grünes Gewölbe', a name in use in the sixteenth century and later applied by extension to the collection of jewels, *objets de vertu* and goldsmithwork now on view in Dresden displayed according to the arrangement made by August the Strong in the early eighteenth century. This repository had thick walls and iron grilles at the windows to protect the contents from fire and theft. That the latter did occur can be seen from the occasional cases of burglary from the *Kunstkammer*.

But all these objects – the tools and instruments, the paintings and sculptures, the desks and tables, the books, the drinking cups, the automata, the jewels – were relatively compact and easy to store and could be kept in the Palace. A storage problem of quite a different order can be seen if we look again at the Marstall or stables. In 1629 Hainhofer reports that he visited no fewer than 36 separate storage rooms, all full of different sorts of objects coming under the general purview of the Armoury. In the 1671 edition of his *Cedern=Wald* Beutel takes us through these 36 rooms one by one. He describes a room for sledges (the 'Schlittenkammer' – Room 1) which not only contained carved and decorated sledges but swords and armour, and a litter presented by the King of Spain. Room 7, the 'Ballienkammer', contained all the armour needed for jousting and tilting. A storey higher there was an area (Room 8) where all the lances and shields were stored. Then came the harnesses for processions (Room 9) and a room for embroidered saddles (Room 10). Another room again had embroidered tournament saddles and jackets for the pages (Room 11). The next room called the 'Rappier= Kammer' (Room 12) had hundreds of swords, rapiers and daggers, many of oriental, presumably Turkish, workmanship and covered in jewels. There was a separate room for Turkish arms and armour (Room 16), a store for sashes covered in pearls and gold embroidery (Room 17), a room for saddles for costumed tournaments (Room 18), another room full of feathers, again for use in tournaments and equestrian displays (Room 20), and several rooms devoted to handguns (Rooms 22–24). Another room contained hunting accoutrements (Room 25) and then we come to the so-called 'Indianische Kammer' or Indian Room (Room 28), reportedly full of exotic Indian *naturalia*, of which a large stuffed crocodile is one, and artefacts such as weapons, costumes and manuscripts. These sound like the kinds of things which might have been removed from the *Kunstkammer* to make space, but that is merely conjecture. Other rooms hold equipment for fencing (Room 29) and costumes for masquerades, ballets and plays (Rooms 30, 34). Of course what we are talking about here is just that part of the weapons collection for use by the princely family. Quite separate was the weapons store or Zeughaus where the weapons for the cavalry and the infantry and the cannon were kept. Among the buildings listed by Weck is a separate coach-house where presumably carriages for actual travel were kept. Claudia Schnitzer points out in her discussion of the organisation of storage in Dresden that even broken objects were kept.[48]

Each of the collections needed people to look after it. Hainhofer states that a staff of nine was needed to run the Armoury.[49] The *Kunstkammer* was in the care of a custodian or 'Kunstkämmerer' and we have already encountered the names of some of them – DavidUßlaub during the reign of August, Theodosius Häsel during the reign of Johann Georg I and Tobias Beutel during the reign of Johann Georg II. Lucas Brunn was the custodian during the early part of Johann Georg I's reign.

The Library was run by a librarian, an office which does not seem to have been conducive to a quiet life. Sebastian Leonhart, for instance, librarian from 1588 and also tutor to the sons of Christian I, was fired in 1591 as part of the purges of real and supposed crypto-Calvinists undertaken on Christian I's death. Johann Nienburg, appointed in 1611, was fired for negligence in 1638. Christian Brehme from Leipzig, a notable poet, was elected Lord Mayor of Dresden in 1656 and had to resign. David Schirmer, who acted as court poet, took over in 1650 but was relieved of his office in 1682. His successor Christian Philippi died in the same year.

The collection of turned ivory pieces was in the care of the Court Turner and the tapestries in the care of the Court Bedmaker ('Hofbettmacher'). Apart from keeping the collection in order and sometimes showing visitors round, one of the duties of the relevant custodian was to take an inventory whenever necessary and at the very least on the death of an Elector. In 1979 Elfriede Lieber made a catalogue[50] of such inventories of the Dresden collections as were held by the State Art Collections (Staatliche Kunstsammlungen) and she lists 122 inventories for the period 1550–1700 alone. We have already discussed the inventories of the *Kunstkammer* and the Library, but there are inventories of each of the storage rooms in the Armoury, of the tools and worked pieces in the ivory turner's workshop and of the coin collection. But these 122 inventories relate to only a part of the objects in the possession of the Elector. The State Archive in Dresden contains a further set of inventories of those objects that came under the purview of the 'Hausmarschallamt' or Steward's Department. Examples are the inventory taken in 1683 of the vault where the tapestries were kept,[51] the inventory of the Elector's bedroom taken between 1673 and 1682[52] and the inventory of the bedding and such bedroom accoutrements as candlesticks and commodes.[53]

The inventories are archival tools to register and keep check on Electoral possessions and also, by relating the objects to the space in which they were stored, to enable them to be found. We shall never know how precisely they corresponded to the reality and it is clear, when one reads a succession of them, that succeeding inventories were based on their predecessors. Indeed, the function of later inventories is to check that the objects previously registered have not been lost. In this way, one sometimes gets the impression that the inventories relate more closely to each other than to the collections they purport to catalogue.

Each successive Elector took on the burden of the possessions gathered by his predecessor and lived in the Palace in Dresden in the midst of an accretion of these objects. Many of the objects which surrounded him at all times took their value precisely from the fact that they had belonged to, been commissioned by or depicted one of the current ruler's predecessors. They often came equipped with the date when they were acquired and the name of their previous owner; in other words they functioned as visible reminders of the continuity of the House of Wettin. The inventories are naturally careful to give this important information. But as the inventory of the contents of Johann Georg II's bedroom makes clear, one gets the impression that in the end the possessions could come to possess their owner.

As we shall see in chapter 7, it took the radical reorganising zeal of August the Strong to institute a root-and-branch reform of the collections in 1723, breaking up the *Kunstkammer* of his namesake and reassigning the objects to new, clearer and more coherent groupings. It is he who created the Mathematisch-Physikalischer Salon for the scientific insturments, the Printroom (the present-day Kupferstichkabinett) for the prints and drawings, the Gemäldegalerie or Art Gallery for the paintings, the Porcelain Collection for the porcelain and the museum known today as the Green Vault or Grünes Gewölbe for a selection of the jewels, *objets de vertu* and pieces of goldsmith work. This meant a departure from the kind of personal collection favoured by his ancestors and the institution of a set of public museums. Knowledge was now to be managed in a wholly different way.

4
The Secrets of the Heavens and the Earth: Alchemy, Mining and Astrology at the Dresden Court

The previous chapter documented the intellectual interests of the Albertine Electors, which included a serious engagement with early modern scientific theory and its practical applications. In the period under discussion it was impossible to have such interests without also concerning oneself with the so-called occult arts. Indeed, the modern distinction between provable scientific fact arrived at by deductive reasoning and then tested through controlled experiment and intuitive and imaginative concepts which relate rather to the world of the spirit and the imagination simply did not exist for the early modern mind. For the latter the observable world gave but a glimmer of the reality which lay beneath, by definition a hidden reality which could be uncovered only by applying the techniques of natural or white magic. The physical world was thought to be peopled by spirit forces, which could, indeed had to be, harnessed to man's purposes. So the twin processes of understanding this occult world and manipulating it went hand in hand, and metaphysical speculation and practical experimentation were inseparable.

These endeavours were not incompatible with Christian beliefs. Since God had created everything, it followed that the occult dimension also emanated from Him and that it was only with His help that one could penetrate it. But because an interest in the occult implied on the one hand a willingness to explore and make fruitful the belief-systems of the Ancients, the Arabs and the Jews, and on the other an anti-rational approach to religion, it was often associated with mysticism and heterodoxy. Since it was hoped that natural magic would enable its practitioner to harness the vast spiritual forces inherent in nature, the power this would give was naturally thought too dangerous to fall into the hands of ordinary mortals and had, therefore, to be kept hidden. At the same time, if a prince financed extensive experimentation into natural magic, he wished, not unlike a modern multinational chemical company, to keep its fruits for himself. All of this contributed to the sense of the secret and the forbidden which clung to such experimentation, while the very belief in the forces which it was hoped to harness gave it an aura of danger.

Early modern alchemy in the Empire

The principal occult discipline that was used in these endeavours was alchemy. We saw in the last chapter how Francis Bacon included among the institutions necessary for the organisation of knowledge 'a still-house, so furnished with mills, instruments, furnaces, and vessels as may be a palace fit for a philosopher's stone' – in other words, an alchemical laboratory. The intense interest in alchemy of such fathers of modern science as Robert Boyle and Isaac Newton shows that there was still no separation between it and what we would now recognise as science, even in the second half of the seventeenth century.[1] That the pursuit of alchemy formed a necessary part of any quest for knowledge was a universal view and Evans, in his discussion of alchemy at the court of Rudolf II in Prague, says that alchemy was 'the greatest passion of the age in Central Europe'.[2] As we shall see, the Electors of Saxony shared in this passion.

We are sometimes tempted to damn alchemy with faint praise by according it the status of being a precursor of modern chemistry. The transmutation of substances, particularly base metals into gold, is after all one important aspect of it. But this is to praise only those aspects of alchemy that we find comprehensible and acceptable today and thereby to distort its nature and purpose. The making of gold was a mere offshoot of the far wider quest of the alchemist, who saw himself as seeking to penetrate 'the very secrets of Nature, Life and Death, of Unity, Eternity and Infinity'.[3] Alchemy was certainly a practical discipline, but it was also a spiritual one.

Fundamental to it was an attempt to understand matter itself. Alchemists saw themselves as the heirs of a great tradition which began with Adam. The great master was Aristotle with his theory of the four elements (earth, air, fire and water) and the four basic properties of all matter (cold, dry, hot and moist), as enunciated in *De caelo*, 302a f. and summed up again in Book IV of the *Meteorologica*. Then came the three great Arab authorities, Geber (Jabir ibn Hayyan, fl. c.760), Rasis (the physician, philosopher and poet Abu Bakr Muhammad ibn Zakariyya Al-Razi, c.825–c.924) and Avicenna (the physician and philosopher Abu Ali ibn Sina, 980–c.1036) and after them Albertus Magnus (c.1200–1280), Roger Bacon (c.1220–1292), Arnald of Villanova (c.1240–1311) and Ramon Lull (c.1235–1316).[4]

The alchemists of the early modern period inherited the ideas of these masters, but their actual method of working covered a broad spectrum according to the bent of the individual practitioner. At its most practical, early modern alchemy concerned itself with metallurgy and pharmacology.[5] It held to the Aristotelian idea that all metals, including gold, the most perfect metal, were composed of mercury and sulphur in varying proportions and that in the earth metals matured very, very slowly into gold. The alchemist could hasten this development by means of heat or by adding an elixir, an all-transforming agent known as the Philosopher's Stone. The first task of the alchemist, therefore, was to manufacture the Stone.

But alchemy was also concerned with increasing man's longevity and improving his health, which is where it impinged on pharmacology and medicine. As Leonhard Thurneysser says in the introduction to his illustrated verse account of the links between medicine and alchemy, the *Quinta Essentia*, published in Leipzig in 1574, 'So ist augenscheinlich daraus abzunemen/ das diese beyde künste/ Medicina und Alchemia unzerteilt/ und beyeinander sein müssen' (so it is obviously to be deduced that these two arts, medicine and alchemy, are indivisible and must be seen side by side).[6] Here the quest was for the Elixir of Life, which would do for man what the Philosopher's Stone would do for metals, that is, bring him to perfection.[7]

The combination of the interest in minerals and in pharmacology gave rise to the discipline of chemistry founded by the physician Theophrastus Bombast von Hohenheim, better known as Paracelsus (1493/4–1541). Chemistry had the twin goals of manufacturing medicines from minerals and also of comprehending the chemical processes of transmutation. Paracelsus displaced Aristotle's theory of the four elements in favour of the theory of the *tria prima* or three first principles by adding salt to the two elements of mercury and sulphur. These three fundamental principles were seen as being analogous to spirit, soul and body, the three fundamentals that constitute the nature of man.

According to Paracelsus, sulphur represents the combustible, mercury the liquid or soluble, and salt the fixed, permanent and incombustible. In order to produce actual substances from these three basic principles of matter, Paracelsus claimed that a spiritual principle was necessary. These spirits bound the three principles of matter together in the right proportion. He also held to the idea that there was a correspondence between the macrocosm and the microcosm. Medicine for Paracelsus had four pillars – alchemy, astrology, philosophy and virtue. Here we have again the combination of the physical or experimental with the spiritual so usual in the period.

Characteristic of alchemical writing is the hermetic visual language in which it is often couched. The process of transmutation is represented by means of colours – green being the colour of the beginning, the state that has to be overcome, and red the colour of the goal of the work, the state to be achieved. Sulphur is represented as red and mercury as white. During the process, when sulphur and mercury interact, they are thought of as being at war with each other, and the outcome of this struggle is a black substance called the *nigredo*. Out of this eventually emerges the white elixir or *albedo*. Various birds are used to represent stages in the process of distillation (Figure 22). The raven represents the

Figure 22. The raven in the cucurbit from HStA Geheimes Archiv Loc. 4417/5.

nigredo, the pelican cyclic distillation, the peacock with its iridescent tail the intermediate stage between the *nigredo* and the *albedo*, the dove or swan the *albedo*, the phoenix sulphur. The *albedo* or white elixir is also represented as the Queen or White Rose, the red elixir as the King or Red Rose. The King and Queen are then said to be united in a chymical wedding in which the red sulphur fixes the white mercury, and the Philosopher's Stone is born.

This kind of language illustrates the mysticism and hermeticism inherent in the pursuit of alchemy, features which made it both more fascinating to pursue but more difficult to comprehend. A characteristic Central European manifestation of it is the collection of alchemical emblems by Michael Maier called *Atalanta Fugiens* (Oppenheim: Theodor de Bry 1617). Each emblem has its accompanying musical fugue, which draws on classical myths and ideas of death, conception and rebirth, interpreting them allegorically in line with alchemical ideas.

There is a further strand of occult knowledge which is inseparable from alchemy and that is astrology. The connection between the world of the planets and that of metals and minerals is clear in the writings of Aristotle. In Book I of his *Meteorologica* Aristotle had maintained that all the elements were transformable into one another and that each was potentially latent in the others (339b). He maintained in the same discussion that there was a cold and moist vapour round the earth and that this contained exhalations from the earth which were hot and dry (340b–341b). At the end of Book III he took this further by saying that there were other 'exhalations' or 'secretions' below the earth and that these were the origins of minerals. Dry, earthy, hot, smoky exhalations produced stony, dusty minerals, while a moist vaporous exhalation produced metals that could be affected by fire, the only exception being gold. Thus, the same elements and their properties make up planetary bodies and metals and in alchemical writings the seven basic metals correspond to the seven planets of the Ptolemaic system. The Moon corresponds to silver, Venus to copper, Mercury to quicksilver, Saturn to lead, Mars to iron and Jupiter to tin. Astrology and alchemy are aspects of the same quest.

Princely patrons of alchemy in the Empire

Most of the important princes in the Empire in the sixteenth and seventeenth centuries were interested in alchemical inquiry and financed alchemical experiments. In the course of his study of the alchemical activities of Count Wolfgang II of Hohenlohe (1546–1610), Jost Weyer lists some of these princes: Joachim II, Elector of Brandenburg (1505–71), his son Johann Georg (1525–98), Wilhelm V, Duke of Bavaria (1548–1626), Georg Friedrich, Margrave of Brandenburg-Ansbach (1539–1603), Julius, Duke of Braunschweig-Lüneburg (1528–89), Friedrich I, Duke of Württemberg (1557–1608), Wilhelm IV, Landgrave of Hessen-Kassel (1532–92), and his son Moritz the Learned (1572–1632).[8] With all of the above, except Bavaria, the Albertines were closely connected either by marriage or by political alliance. Wolfgang von Hohenlohe himself, who not only collected alchemical manuscripts and books but engaged in intensive alchemical experimentation in the years 1587 to 1610 on his estate at Weikersheim in Württemberg, was bound by ties of friendship to Elector August. August visited him both at Weikersheim and at Hermersberg and Wolfgang von Hohenlohe in his turn visited August's successor Christian I in Dresden in 1590–91.[9]

But the most important patron of alchemy was the Emperor Rudolf II (1552–1612), who surrounded himself in Prague with a whole group of alchemists and practitioners of the occult.[10] We find frequent signs of connections between this circle and the Dresden court. One of those belonging to the Prague circle was the aforementioned Leonard Thurneysser (1530–96), physician, mining expert and metallurgist, alchemist, botanist and Paracelsian.[11] Thurneysser moved between Dresden and Prague and also worked at one time for Elector August's brother-in-law, Johann Georg, Elector of Brandenburg. Mardochaeus de Delle, who was said to have performed experiments with Rudolf, also went from Prague to Dresden and is thought to have worked with Elector August there.[12] The well-known Paracelsian Benedikt Figulus was associated with Rudolf and with Dresden. So was Sebald Schwertzer, as we shall see below. Lazarus Ercker (c.1530–94), before he became Rudolf II's superindent of mines in the 1580s, was for a time Elector August's so-called 'Generalprobationsmeister', or Master Assayer.[13]

Another patron of alchemical enquiry was the great lord Vilém Rozmberk (known in German as Wilhelm von Rosenberg, 1535–92), who conducted alchemical experiments in his residence in Prague, in his castle at Reichenstein in Silesia and in his vast palace at Krumlov in Southern Bohemia.[14] Rožmberk employed a number of important alchemists and collected alchemical manuscripts. Among the figures of international fame who worked at Krumlov were Nicolas Barnaud and Heinrich Khunrath (1560–1605) from Leipzig who became Vilém's physician in 1591 and who was also in contact with Rudolf II. The Hauptstaatsarchiv in Dresden contains correspondence from 1581 between Vilém and Elector August, mining being an important interest they had in common and one they shared with Rudolf II.¹⁵ There is a further collection of letters from Vilém to August and to Christian I between the years 1572 and 1588.¹⁶

That Kassel was an important centre of alchemical enquiry under Moritz, Landgrave of Hessen-Kassel, is well known.¹⁷ Moritz was in contact with several important alchemists who were part of the Prague circle, John Dee, for instance, and Michael Maier. They visited him in Kassel where he had laboratories for alchemical experiments and an important collection of alchemical manuscripts.¹⁸ For Moritz alchemy was connected to a utopian vision of a better and more peaceful world, beyond the sectarianism of the early seventeenth century. This vision was encapsulated in Rosicrucianism, a mystical brotherhood. The two Rosicrucian manifestos, the *Fama fraternitatis R.C.* and *Confesssio fraternitatis R.C.*, appeared in 1614 and 1615 respectively in Kassel, and Heiner Borggrefe is convinced that Moritz was the editor of the second of these works.¹⁹ The connections between Saxony and Kassel are well known – August was one of Moritz's godparents and visited Kassel for his christening in 1572 and again in 1584. Moritz in his turn paid a visit to Dresden in 1591, so while we have no evidence that the Saxon Electors shared Moritz's Rosicrucian ideas, they would have exchanged ideas about their mutual scientific interests in the same way that they exchanged gifts.

In their pursuit of alchemy the Electors of Saxony form part of this network of like-minded princes. What is exceptional about Dresden is the wealth of documentation still available to us today and the fact that it provides unbroken coverage over two centuries.

Alchemy in Dresden – the theory

The documentation gives us a picture of both the theory and the practice of alchemy in Dresden. We can tell a great deal, for instance, about which alchemical writings were available at court, either from the fact that they are still in existence in the SLUB and in the Hauptstaatsarchiv in Dresden and datable, or because various inventories from the period itself make them visible to us. In addition, a mass of paperwork gives us an insight into the practice of the Dresden laboratories, who was working there, how those laboratories were organised and what it all cost. This section and the next examine these twin aspects of theory and practice in Dresden up to the end of the seventeenth century. The eighteenth century development, which led among other things to the rediscovery of the process of porcelain manufacture, is discussed in chapter 7.

Many of the alchemical writings were kept behind closed doors in the laboratories in Dresden, as we shall see. But the public face of alchemy was its connection with mining. We saw in chapter 1 how essential the mining industry was to the Saxon economy and how the wealth of the Electors came from the extraction of metals and semi-precious stones and from associated chemical and metallurgical industries such as smelting, metal-working, dyeing and glass-making. These industries were closely connected with the more practical aspects of alchemy. One of the sections in the inventory of the Electoral library taken in 1595[20] shows this link very clearly. It is headed: 'Von Bergkwerk Muntzwerck Allchÿmeÿ Saltzkunst unnd Probieren', that is, 'Mining, Minting, Alchemy, Salt Extraction and Assaying', thus emphasising that for contemporaries these were cognate activities. The works listed under this heading fall into three main groups. The first consists of practical works, such as those by Georg Agricola, the great Saxon mining pioneer. Multiple copies of such key works of his as *De re metallica* (published in Basel in 1555 and 1556) as well as Philipp Beck's German translation of it (Basel, 1557), of *De mensuris et ponderibus* (Basel, 1550) and of *De ortu et causis subterraneorum* (Basel, 1558) are to be found here. Lazarus Ercker's Beschreibung *Allerfurnemisten Mineralischen Ertzt unnd Bergkwercks arten* (Prague, 1574) is also listed in this section. We also find here various sets of regulations promulgated by the King of France for the French salt mines and by the Elector of Saxony for the mines in his own territory, four different editions of Zacharias Löhner's work on assaying, the *Probierbüchlein*, a copy of Johann Neander's work on salt extraction and the manufacture of gold, *Virtutes extractionis solis siue Auri* (1577), Conrad Gessner's work on semi-precious stones and metals, *De omni rerum fossilium genere, Gemmis Lapidibus Metallis & huiusmodi libri aliquot...* (1565), Jacobus Theodorus Tabernamontanus's treatise on etching and gilding, *Rechte... Kunst zu Etzen und vergulden auf Stein Silber, Meßing, Kupffer...* (Frankfurt am M., 1585), and a number of other works on assaying, salt extraction and bronze working. Other practical works relate to the various mining towns in the Erzgebirge such as Freiberg.

The second group of works under the same heading consists of writings by Paracelsus or Pseudo-Paracelsus. Listed are *De spiritibus Planetarum sive Metallorum, lib. 3* (Basel, 1567), *Archidoxorum... Paracelsi de secretis naturae libri X* (Basel, 1581), *De secretis naturae* (Basel, 1570), *Etliche tractat Theophrasti Paracelsi...* (Strasburg, 1576) and *De Lapide Philosophorum; dreÿ tractetlein I. Manuele de Lapide Medicinali; II. de tinctura phisicorum; III. De tinctura Planetarum* (edited by Michael Toxites, Strasburg, 1572).

The third group consists of alchemical works in the narrower sense. Avicenna's *Artis chemicae Principes* (Basel, 1572), a work by Albertus Magnus entitled *De Mineralibus & rebus Metallicis lib. V* is listed, as is Wilhelm Gratarolus's *Verae Alchimiae artisque Metallicae, citra aenigmata, Doctrina, certusq modus comprehensus* (Basel, 1561). The *Alchimia* by Gilbert Cardinal and Richard of England's *Reformirte Alchimeÿ* (Strasburg, 1581) are followed by the *Ars Chemica Hermetis Trismegisti Aurej* (Argentorati, 1566), Gerhard Dorn's *Artificÿ Chymistici Phÿsici metaphysiqaue, opuscula*, his *Chÿmisticum artificium naturae* (Frankfurt, 1568) and his *Congeries Paracelsicae chemiae de Transmutationibus metallorum* (Frankfurt, 1581), as well as various other unidentified alchemical treatises simply labelled as such. There is thus a mixture of practical works with those of a more spiritual alchemical bent within the context of an intense interest in Paracelsus.

The focus on Paracelsus in particular is worthy of comment. From 1575 to 1576 Georg Forberger, a Saxon who had studied at Wittenberg before going to Basel, where he translated Paolo Giovio and Francesco Guicciardini into German and Paracelsus into Latin, was brought back to Dresden as official translator to Elector August.[21] In this capacity he translated Natale Conti's *Historiarum sui temporis libri X* and Denys Zacaire's *Opuscule tres-eccelent de la vraye philosophie naturelle des metaulx*, but we have to imagine that his close knowledge of Paracelsus's works was also fruitful in Dresden. Forberger went on to edit other Paracelsian works and continued to be associated with alchemical matters. Zaunick thinks that he is the probable translator of Bernardus Trevisanus's *De lapide philosophorum*, and he contributed a dedicatory poem to the first edition of Johann Thölde's *Triumph Wagen Antimonii*, which appeared in Leipzig in 1604.

We find works relating to the same complex of ideas among the scientific books listed in the *Kunstkammer* inventory for 1587.[22] There are works by Thurneysser (e.g., no. 284 on the planets), two copies of Paracelsus's *Astronomica et Astrologica*, (nos. 201 and 240) and John Dee's *Monas hieroglyphica* (no. 151). Astrology is represented here too. No. 70 is Martin Pegius's *Geburtsstunden Buch* or Book of Horoscopes. Cyprian von Leowitz's astrological prophecies can be found at Nos. 158 and 209, and No. 158 also contains a compendium of prognostications by nine other writers. The almanack listed at no. 285 belongs in the same category. We know that Elector August practised 'Punktieren', that is, the working out of horoscopes in answer both to personal and external political problems and questions, and some of the sixteenth-century astrological tables he may have used are preserved in the SLUB in Dresden (for instance, SLUB Mscr.Dresd.H 8).

But we have yet another sort of inventory from very much the same period as the two just mentioned. The immaculate record-keeping of the Albertines extended to the contents of the secret alchemical laboratories, the so-called 'Goldhaus' or Gold House, a separate building in the Palace complex in Dresden next to the theatre, as can be seen in engravings of Dresden. We have a series of inventories relating to the Gold House from the late sixteenth century roughly up to the end of the reign of Johann Georg II in 1680. The first of these inventories (Loc. 4419/3) was compiled in 1598 on the instructions of the regent, Friedrich Wilhelm of Saxony-Weimar, as part of his careful stewardship of the inheritance of his young orphaned nephews. Its detailed description of the physical layout and of the contents of the laboratories is discussed below. But books and papers were kept here too, for the use of those working in the laboratories. At folio 3a f. there is a list of these writings. We find here works on salt extraction listed as 'Salzwerg zu Franckenhaussen', 'Salzprobirbuch', 'Buch 4° über Salzsieden' (the salt mines at Frankenhausen, a book on salt extraction, a book in quarto on salt extraction by boiling), the statutes of the town of Magdeburg, and a description of the kingdom of Hungary, an unspecified work on assaying and another on horoscopes. Also listed is a bundle of unspecified papers said to relate to M. Figulus 'den Oeconomum zu Wittenbergk', that is, Benedikt Figulus, the well-known alchemist associated with Rudolf II. There is another bundle of writings said to be by the pioneering Saxon mathematician Abraham Riese. We also find here a report on Saxon mines dating to 16 July 1579 by the Councillors Hans von Bernstein, Hartman Pistoris, D. Pfeifer and Hans von Sebottendorf. Again mining, alchemy, medicine and mathematical and scientific enquiry emerge as indivisible.

If we examine the large collection of manuscripts relating to alchemy in the Hauptstaatsarchiv in Dresden, kept among the confidential papers in the Geheimes Archiv, we find many works dating to the same period.[23] These manuscripts comprise a wide range of documents in fifty bundles from the sixteenth to the mid-eighteenth centuries.[24] Here we find, for instance, a broad spectrum of typical alchemical treatises, mostly in manuscript but with some printed works scattered through the collection.

Loc. 4417/1 consists of a manuscript of the 'Hortus Divitiarum seu potius Arumnarum', 'the garden of all riches', by Georg Auracher of Strasburg. This is a set of instructions in twenty chapters for making the Philosopher's Stone, beginning and ending with a prayer. Loc. 4417/2 is headed 'Tractat von der Alchemie in XX Kapiteln', a practical treatise on alchemy. At Loc. 4417/3 is a document entitled 'Etzliche fürnehme Natürliche und Vornünfftige Regeln der Chymistarum oder

Philosophorum von Transmutation der Metallen, daraus viell guter nachrichtung zu nehmen, Irrthumb und betrug zuvormeiden' (Various important natural and rational rules of the alchemists and philosophers on the transmutation of metals, from which much good information may be taken and error and deception avoided). In a section called 'De lapide philosophorum' (On the Philosopher's Stone) it demonstrates the standard connection between the seven planets and the seven basic minerals and gives the commonly used symbols for them.

Loc. 4417/4 is labelled 'Alchymistische Fewerkunste belangende' (Papers relating to alchemical pyrotechnics. The term 'pyrotechnics' is used here not in the sense of fireworks but to mean transmutation by means of firing, as for instance in the famous work by Vanuccio Biringoccio, *De la pirotechnia*). A typical recipe is that on fol. 51a for turning copper into brass. This volume also contains a long treatise by Marcus Müller, an alchemist employed by Elector August in the 1580s, on the Philosopher's Stone and another entitled: 'Ex libro Hermetis sive Mercurij Trismegisti primi pos diluvium chÿmiae Imputoris'. The same file contains a third treatise on the Philosopher's Stone and finally a piece entitled the 'Bericht Jonas Georgen von Praga Probeschmeltzen belang' (Report by Jonas Georg of Prague relating to assaying). Here we see again the mixture of the occult and mystical with the practical.

Loc. 4417/5 is a folio manuscript entitled, on its vellum cover, 'Feuerkünste' (Pyrotechnics). This begins with a Paracelsian treatise that takes us through the various stages of transmutation and is illustrated with little coloured vignettes of typical alchemical motifs. Other pieces in this work deal with the 'mortification of metals' and are therefore rather practical guides to the manufacture of various substances. Loc. 4417/7 is a quarto notebook consisting of a 106-line poem in German rhyming couplets. It is headed: 'Ein kurzer und grüntlicher bericht der Alchimiae, und der Lapidus Philosophor' (A short and thorough report on Alchemy and the Philosopher's Stone). It is illustrated with six pen-and-ink drawings – of God wearing a halo and holding an orb, of naked angels astride or diving into cucurbits, of an angel raising a man from the dead (Figure 23), of two alchemists at work (Figure 24), and finally of the Christian alchemist on his knees before God the Almighty, who is blessing him from the Heavens. There is a similar notebook at Loc. 4416/4, again with a text in German verse and with very similar pen-and-ink drawings – the dragon biting a ring, two knights who have killed the dragon and are standing on him, etc.

Collections of spells make up a kind of sub-group of the alchemical recipes but tend to be more concerned with the conjuration of spirits by

The Secrets of the Heavens and the Earth 111

Figure 23. Angel raising a man from the dead. Pen-and-ink drawing from HStA Geheimes Archiv Loc. 4417/7.

Figure 24. Two alchemists at work. Pen-and-ink drawing from HStA Geheimes Archiv Loc. 4417/7.

means of diagrams and incantations rather than with chemical processes. The name of the early sixteenth-century necromancer Johann Faust often figures on these manuscripts. He was a historical figure first made famous in the anonymous early German novel *Historia von D. Johann Fausten* (1587) and later the basis for Marlowe's and Goethe's dramatic character. The novel, after all, moves him from southern Germany, where he is attested, to Saxony, making him a scholar at the University of Wittenberg who turns from the study of theology to become a devotee of the most advanced scientific learning of his day. Indeed, the terms in which he is described in the novel show that he is meant to be an alchemist. It is surely the fame of the literary character that attaches his name to material used by practising alchemists half a century later. Faust purports, for instance, to be the author of the little notebook at Loc. 4416/5 that contains magical signs and recipes and his name is also used on the tiny twenty-page notebook of spells measuring about 12 by 10 cm entitled: 'D. Johannis Fausti Zwang der Höllen und höllischen Geister. Erkundigung verborgener Schätze...' (Dr Johann Faust's Domination of Hell and its Spirits and the Location of Hidden Treasures (Loc. 4417/12)).

Another important group of materials in the Hauptstaatsarchiv consists of cabalistic writings.[25] Loc. 4417/4 is an example of such material. Folio 57 gives a table connecting the planets, zodiac signs, seasons, months, lunar quarters, days of the week and important political figures with numbers and symbols. The political figures range from Rudolf II himself, through the Electors, down to Julius, Duke of Braunschweig, and Wilhelm, Lord of Rosenberg (the Vilém Rožmberk mentioned above). Another bulging file labelled by a later more censorious age 'Einzelne Schriften allerhand Aberglauben 1579–1742' ('Various things relating to all kinds of superstitions 1579–1742') is to be found at Loc. 4417/8. It contains as document No. 3 a biblical justification for the Cabala. A battered edition of the 1663 edition of Steffen Michelspacher's well-known work, *Cabala, Spiegel der Kunst= und Natur: in Alchemia* (Cabala. The mirror of art and nature in alchemy, Augsburg 1616), is preserved here too. The same bundle contains a packet of cabalistic material labelled 'Magister Hutters sachen' (Master Hutter's materials). Elias Hutter (1553–after 1605), Professor of Hebrew at Leipzig University, was brought to Dresden in 1579 to teach Elector August Hebrew. Given Hutter's competence in the language, it is at least possible that he really knew the Cabala. There is also a 'Register Des geschriebenen Ebräischen alten Bücher in Teutsche [*sic*] Sprach' (a list of ancient Hebrew manuscripts in German), though the list does not state where these works are kept. There are other cabalistic works at Loc. 4417/13 and Loc. 4419/17.

Another file, Loc. 4419/18, contains as Document 4 a whole series of inventories from the 1660s of various sections of the working library kept in the laboratories. On 17 January, for instance, an inventory was taken of 'Etlicher Alchimistisch: und Chimischen Bücher und Schrifften, so uon Davidt Beuthern und Sschwertzern herrühren undt in einer schwarzen lade befunden undt auffgezeichnet worden' (Some alchemical and chemical books and papers which come from David Beuther and Schwertzer and were found in a black drawer and have been listed, fol.26 f). Nine bundles of papers are listed but the inventory is remarkably vague about what writings these were. 'Ein Convolut in Octavo' (A bundle of papers in octavo) is a typical description. But what is interesting is the fact that the papers are attached to the names of two notable alchemists who worked in Dresden at the end of the previous century. A local tradition is thus being kept alive several generations later.

On 18 December 1663 another inventory was taken. This is in the same document and begins at folio 41a. It is labelled 'Consignation. Etlicher Medicinischen Chÿmischen und zum Schmelz= auch Münzwesen gehörigen Bücher und Schrifften, welche uf Churf.Durchl. genädigsten Befehl aus dem geheimen Gewölbe uf das Laboratorium in das getaffelte Beÿstübgen am 18. Decembris Anno 1663. Gebracht worden und haben sich befunden' (A consignment of some medical and chemical books and papers and those relating to smelting and minting, which, on the orders of his Electoral Grace, were taken from his secret vault to the little panelled side-chamber in the laboratory). This tells us that these works had been kept in the Secret Repository in the Palace, along with other important papers, precious objects of all kinds and plate, and that it was on Johann Georg II's orders that they were transferred to the laboratories. This inventory is much more informative and systematic, and lists the works under the three subject headings mentioned above – medical works, chemical works and those to do with smelting and minting. Within these sections they are listed according to format and whether they are bound or unbound.

Under 'Medical Works', for instance, we find in folio a report by Marcus Müller on Paracelsus's 'Grund der Arzneÿ ' and Adam Lonicerus's printed and hand-coloured *Kräuterbuch* or herbal, in quarto an edition of the *Aphorisms* of Hippocrates, and Johannes Wolffius's treatise *De Acidis Wildungensibus* (Marburg, 1580) and in octavo an unbound manuscript treatise on the medical efficacy of minerals and a collection of pharmaceutical recipes by the Abbess of Weissenfels, Margarethe von Watzdorf.

The succeeding three pages of alchemical works again make reference to papers by alchemists in the time of Elector August, such as David Beuther and Marcus Müller, and in that of Johann Georg I such as Andreas Orthelius. One work is described as being by David Ußlaub, the Custodian of the *Kunstkammer* under Electors August, Christian I and II. Other descriptions give great detail about a particular book as an object and about its subject matter but still do not allow us to identify the author or authors, for example, 'Ein pergamen Buch in roht leder gebunden, vergüldet auf dem schnitt, darinnen allerhand Künste zum cementiren, gold und silber schmeidig zu machen, zum graviren, zum vergölden, zum goldscheiden, zu allerleÿ gießenn und steinen zu schmelzen, allerleÿ Metallen flüßig zu machen...glaß zu machen, zu färben und zu vergülden... (A work on parchment bound in red leather, the leaves gilt-edged, in which are all kinds of instructions on fusing metals, on making gold and silver malleable, on engraving, on gilding, on separating gold, on all types of pouring and smelting minerals and metals, on making glass, on dyeing and gilding...).

One might well have expected the above to have been listed in the next section, the ten and a half pages of works on smelting and assaying, but, as we have seen, the boundary between these subjects was a fluid one. The descriptions of the works in this latter section are much vaguer but there is a great deal of material on coinage and on minting. These books were checked on 4 October 1677 in the presence of Heinrich, Freiherr von Friesen, the head of the Privy Council, and various items were found to be missing.

The other detailed listing of alchemical works dates to the same period and is the inventory of the 'Chÿmischen Bücher und Schriften', found in the laboratory on the death of Dr Banzland. His collection consisted of thirty-three printed works and five manuscripts. Many of these are medical books: Daniel Sennert's *Practica Medicina* and his *Tractatus der Arthritide* (published in Wittenberg in 1653), Johannes Hornung's *Cista Medica* (Nuremberg, 1625), Martin Pansa's *Consilium Antinephriticum* (Leipzig, 1615) and his *Aureus libellus de proroganda vita* (Leipzig, 1615–20) and Henning Scheunemann's *Medicina reformata* (Frankfurt, 1617). The other works are a mixture of treatises on mining, metallurgy and alchemy. Banzland owned among other texts Geber's *Alchymia*, Thurneysser's *Archidoxa* and Johann Peucer's *Bergordnung*, Johannes Matthesius's *Berg-Postilla, oder Sarepta* (first published in 1571), Johannes Rhenanus's *Solis e puteo emergentis libri tres* (Frankfurt, 1613) and Rhenanus's edition of Hermann Condeesyanus's *Harmoniae Chymico-Philosophicae* (Frankfurt, 1625), Thomas Muffett's *De jure et praestantia chymicorum medicamentorum dialogus apologeticus* (Frankfurt, 1584), what is referred to as George Ripley's *Opuscula quaedam Chymica* (this is perhaps his *Opera omnia chemica* of 1649), Basilius Valentinus's (or rather Johann Thölde's) *Haligraphia*, his *Von natürlichen und übernatürlichen Dingen* and *Triumph Wagen Antimonii*, all published in Leipzig,[26] and of course Agricola's *De rebus metallicis*. Here too we find the Rosicrucian work, *Chymische Hochzeit Christiani Rosencreuz*. Among the few and not very precisely described manuscripts is a copy of the 'Donum Dei'.

These various listings of books, papers and manuscript treatises, which take us up to the year 1677, show that the Electors of Saxony and the alchemists working for them had access to the full range of theoretical and practical works available in their period and that, because much of the material was kept in a working library in the laboratories, the writings of their predecessors continued to be available to later generations. But what do we know of the actual workings of the laboratories themselves?

Alchemical practice at the Dresden court

The documents in the Hauptstaatsarchiv, again all in the Geheimes Archiv, provide a lot of information in answer to this question. They document, for instance, which alchemists were working for the Electors at what time. Activity under Elector August was particularly intense and Electress Anna was also a notable alchemist with her own laboratories at Annaburg.[27] Our first records date from the 1560s. Loc. 4418/1 consists of a huge bundle of letters relating to Daniel Pachmann or Bachmann, said to be a 'gold-maker and alchemist from London'. It was a risky profession to be an alchemist in the service of a noble patron. If one was suspected of not being able to manufacture gold, and so of being a charlatan, one could end up in prison or worse. If, on the other hand, it was thought that one had discovered the secret, one was just as likely to end up in prison to stop one taking the secret elsewhere. Bachmann was one of the many alchemists so incarcerated and there are letters of supplication from him and his wife. Loc. 4417/4 is a bundle of material relating to David Heideler, alchemist to Elector August in the 1580s. Esaias Stumpfeldt is another figure who appears here, and there are alchemical recipes both by him and by Heideler among this material. Loc. 4416/1 contains David Heideler's 'Probezettel über das ausbrachte Goldt' – the assayer's proof that he has made gold. There are many records relating to David Beuther, another of August's alchemists, particularly in the bundle at Loc. 4419/19, where we find a mass of papers from Annaburg where he too was incarcerated. This file contains a big bundle of recipes and lists of experiments, as well as letters to the Emperor from prison and various legal documents. Loc. 4419/1 tells us that Melchior Schirmer was Beuther's young assistant in 1582. A manuscript in the SLUB (Mscr.Dresd.N 36b) also relates to Beuther and his activities. We have already met Marcus Müller's name in our discussion of the alchemical writing. He was another of August's alchemists around 1583 with whom there is much correspondence (Loc. 4416/1). His treatise on the Philosopher's Stone is at Loc. 4417/4 and there is yet more relevant material at Loc. 4416/4. At Loc. 4417/17 there is a folio manuscript of alchemical recipes labelled 'Leonhardt Thurneysers Künste' ('The Arts of Leonhard Thurneysser'), which contains thirty pages of recipes for making the Philosopher's Stone (from folio 17a), for producing gold (from folio 25a) and for making pearls (from folio 33b).

One of the most controversial alchemists to be associated with the Dresden court in the late sixteenth century was Sebald Schwertzer (or Schwärtzer, d.1598). He clearly had entrepreneurial talents as well as alchemical ones and first became a commercial agent for Saxon wares for the Dresden court in 1584. He convinced Elector August of his abilities as an alchemist and enjoyed the patronage of Christian I who made him sole Director of the Slate Quarries at Eisleben, for instance. After Christian's death, his widow, Electress Sophie, became Schwertzer's patron.[28] However, rumours began to circulate that he was a charlatan and when a one-time business partner accused him of having poisoned the two previous Electors of Saxony, he fled to Prague.[29] He then became the Prefect of Mines at Joachimsthal (Jáchymov), the important mining centre in Bohemia, and enjoyed the protection of Rudolf II. Four full files relate to him and his affairs (Loc. 4417/18–21) and they include papers relating to Nuremberg, of which he was a citizen, correspondence between Elector August and Johann Georg of Brandenburg concerning him, accounts of gold given to Schwertzer by August and much else besides. As we saw above, papers purporting to come from Schwertzer were still in existence in the laboratories in the 1660s.

During the ten-year regency (1601–11), alchemical activity, like much else at the Dresden court, appears to have stagnated. Johann Georg I carried on the tradition of alchemical experimentation during his reign, as an undated manuscript on the transmutation of metals in the SLUB makes clear.[30] The many papers by Andreas Orthelius at Loc. 4416/1 show him to have been employed by the Elector as his 'Destillator' or chemist at least from January 1636 through to 1637. A printed work such as Johannes de Chastellet's *Philosophia metallica seu sempiterna veritatis demonstratio* from 1629 dedicated to Emperor Ferdinand III and still preserved among the alchemical papers in Dresden at Loc. 4416/5 must also have found its way into the laboratories at this period.

Petrus Colbovius also served under Johann Georg I and at Loc. 4419/4 there is a report by him dated 1654 on the manufacture of the Philosopher's Stone in which he calls himself 'Philosophiae et Medicinae Studiosus'. It is clear from the same file that he carried on working for Johann Georg II, who succeeded as Elector in 1656. That Colbovius had official status at court well into Johann Georg II's reign is shown by two poems published in the 1660s in Dresden by the court printer, Melchior

Bergen. The first is an epithalamium Colbovius wrote on the occasion of the wedding of Johann Georg II's only daughter, Erdmuthe Sophie, to Christian Ernst, Margrave of Brandenburg, in 1662.[31] The second is a verse treatise on alchemy in 192 seven-line stanzas in German published in Dresden in 1667.[32]

In general, the documentation shows that activity in the laboratories was particularly intense during the reign of Johann Georg II, rivalling that under Elector August a century before. This tallies with the revival of mining and mineral extraction in general during Johann Georg II's reign. From Loc. 4419/5, which contains bills and accounts, we learn that Amadeus Friedrich was director of what is called the 'Geheimes Laboratorium' or Secret Laboratory in 1663/4 and that his assistant was Augustus Hauptmann (4419/5). No less a sum than 1,500 thalers was spent, the same document tells us, on repairing the Secret Laboratory and the Assay House during this period. We also learn that other pieces of equipment were being repaired and that an (unnamed) 'Italian sculptor' was called in to repair an alabaster still (fol. 3a). Amadeus Friedrich appears elsewhere in the file under the title 'Churf. Saechs. Bergraht und Director des geheimen Laboratory' (Electoral Saxon Mining Councillor and Director of the Secret Laboratory), which shows yet again how closely the two specialisms of mining and alchemy were related. Friedrich was paid the impressive sum of 700 thalers for the six months from 12 January to 14 July 1663 and Hauptmann 150 thalers for almost the same period (26 January to 13 August 1663). We can see from Loc. 4419/6 that Hauptmann's contract of employment was renewed in 1670, 1672, 1675 and 1680. Another set of accounts at Loc. 4419/5 for 1664/5 talks about 'Der Goldschmied und Mechanicus Christoph Köhler', 'der geheime Probierer David Herman' and 'der laborant Georg Zuzschky' and 'der Junge' (the goldsmith and mechanic Christoph Köhler, the secret assayer David Herman, the laboratory assistant Georg Zuzschky and the boy).

Another notable figure to work under Johann Georg II was Johann Kunckel (see Loc. 4416/1), the alchemist and glass-maker (1630–1703). He was a figure of European fame who served successively Franz Karl and Julius Heinrich, Dukes of Lauenburg, the Elector of Saxony, the Elector of Brandenburg and the Swedish King Charles XI, who ennobled him. He is best known for his invention of ruby glass and for his annotated and expanded translation of Antonio Neri's *Ars vitraria experimentalis* (1679). But it was while in Saxon service before 1679 that he published his treatises on salts, *Nuetzliche Observationes Oder Anmerckungen/ Von den Fixen und fluechtigen Saltzen/ Auro und Argento potabili,*

Spiritu Mundi und dergleichen (Useful observations or notes on the fixed and volatile salts, Hamburg, 1676) and on phosphorus, *Oeffentliche Zuschrifft Von dem Phosophoro Mirabili und Dessen leuchtenden Wunder-Pilulen Samt angehaengten Discurs Von dem...Nitro, Jetzt aber unschuldig genandten Blut der Natur* (Public address on miraculous phosphorous and its gleaming wonder-pills, with an appendix on nitrate, now called harmlessly nature's blood, Wittenberg, 1678). He refers to himself on the title-page of the latter work as 'Electoral Saxon Chymicus'.

Information is sparser with regard to the reign of Johann Georg III, whose interests were military, and to the extremely brief reign of Johann Georg IV. However, in 1680 we have a letter from Christian Praetorius to Johann Georg III offering him a recipe for the manufacture of the Philosopher's Stone according to the 'Theophrastian' (that is, Paracelsian) method (Loc. 4417/15, fol. 42a/b) and at Loc. 4417/8 there is a letter relating to the Cabala addressed to Johann Georg IV by Simon Joachim Jüdiger dated 12 January 1694, so it was at least deemed possible by the writers of these letters that the Electors concerned might be interested.

We have three inventories of the laboratories themselves, taken in the years 1598 (Loc. 4419/3), 1603 and 1642 (both Loc. 4419/18). The laboratories are referred to on the title-page of the inventory of 1598 as the 'Probirhaus, allhier zu Dreßden hinder dem Schloß gelegen, so gemeiniglich das Goldthaus genannt wirdt' (the Assay House here in Dresden situated behind the Palace, usually called the Gold House). This inventory consists of eighty folio sides and takes us through the laboratories room by room, wall by wall, cupboard by cupboard, as was the common practice when compiling such inventories in Dresden. 'At the chest at the window near the stove on the lefthand side' is a typical heading for a section of the list of objects. The inventory begins with what is called the Big Room or Laboratory ('der Grosse Saal oder Laboratorium'), then goes on to the Little Round Corner Room ('das runde Eckstüblein'), then the Vault next to the Big Laboratory ('Das Gewelbe am grossen Laboratorium'), then another vault at the back and, within that, a separate vaulted room ('die gewelbte Stube, im hindersten Gewelbe, oder Laboratorio'). Of these the main laboratory is by far the biggest, taking up over half the space. Everything is listed, beginning with the pieces of broken glass to be found near the stove as the very first item and telling us on fol. 1b that the chest near the stove contains a bed in which David Heideler, the alchemist, used to sleep.

In general the material listed in the inventory falls into three groups: chemical substances, tools and equipment, and papers and books. The chemical substances are the usual selection to be expected in a centre of experimentation at that date and are corroborated by the inventories of Wolfgang von Hohenlohe's laboratories at Schloss Weikersheim.[33] They include metals such as iron, copper, silver, lead and mercury and the semi-metals arsenic and antimony. There are elements such as sulphur, and minerals and ores such as auripigment (yellow arsenic trisulphide), realgar (red arsenic tetrasulphide), 'Galmei' (carbonate of zinc) and verdigris (basal copper acetate). We also find salts such as cooking salt (natrium chloride), sal ammoniac (ammonium chloride), saltpetre (potassium nitrate), vitriol (sulphate of copper or iron) and alum (double sulphate of aluminium and potassium) and acids such as aqua regia or aqua fortis (nitric acid). Chalk, sand and alcohol are also listed, as well as a sediment of which the inventorist rather endearingly says 'man weis nicht was es ist' (no one knows what it is – fol. 2a.).

The equipment ranges from stills to retorts and cucurbits, crucibles, hammers, pestles and mortars, pots and pans. There is frequent mention of burnt skulls, which are used to hold various substances, and a large section of the equipment is related to assaying and consists of weighing scales and other implements for weighing and measuring.

The next inventory dated to 1603 is labelled on the title-page: 'Inventarium Uber das Probierstüeblein vndt den grossenn Saahll voran, vffn Schloss Dressdenn, Anno 1603. Im December vorzeichnet wordenn' (Inventory of the Small Assay Room and the Large Room in front of it in the Palace in Dresden Anno 1603. Compiled in December') and consists of thirty sides in folio. This was compiled in the reign of Christian II by Eusebius Hörsellen or Hörseln in the presence of Hans von Wolfframsdorff, Christoph von Schönberg, David Ußlaub and Christian Preusen. There is a separate inventory of the Little Room in the same file from folio 16a on. The former gives far more detail about the appearance of the furniture and equipment than before, which may be because of the presence of the Keeper of the Kunstkammer, David Ußlaub, who presumably had an eye for such things. We learn, for instance, whether a particular piece of furniture is inlaid and out of what rare wood it is made, that some of the utensils are of silver, that the vessels are gilt and decorated with coats of arms and that the scales for weighing precious metals have a nativity scene painted on them (4b). We are reminded here of Elector August's own furnace or 'Muffelofen' dating to 1575 and now in the Museum for Applied Art at Schloß Pillnitz outside Dresden, with its bas-relief panels and its finely engraved decoration of foliage and ribbons. The personifications and symbols of the seven planets with their corresponding symbols adorn the front of this princely piece of equipment (Inv. No. 40919). The Little Tower Room seems to be given over to assaying, as most of the equipment here is for weighing and measuring metals and coins. It is clearly in the Large Room ('Großer Saahl') that any major experiments take place, as this is where the various furnaces and other equipment are situated.

The inventory of the so-called Little Room ('das kleine Stübichen') tells us that the most secret matters were kept here. But it tantalisingly lists only thirty-two items, mostly chemicals, which are kept in a cupboard on the right-hand wall and a small number of other sundry items. An inventory dated 27 May 1643 (Loc. 4419/18, Document 3, fol.18a f.) is more wide-ranging, though much briefer than the earlier ones. It deals with the same two rooms as in 1603 – the Little Tower Room (now called 'Das kleine Erckerstüblein') and the Large Assaying Room ('die große Probirstube'), but groups the items under such headings as silver, copper and brass objects, instruments and tables, rather than taking us past them one by one.

We thus gain the impression of a functional set of laboratories, fully staffed, particularly during the long and peaceful reigns of Elector August and Johann Georg II, well equipped and well funded. Work was continuously being carried out in the Gold House behind closed doors in Dresden but any advances in science or technology which this work produced had great practical relevance for the local industries of mining and metallurgy.

This practical aspect as well as the more philosophical context of astrological and alchemical ideas were, however, also used artistically for the purposes of princely representation. These themes were made public down the centuries in the festivals of the Dresden court, in which mining and astrology are two of the enduring themes.

Mining and astrology in court festivals

We have seen how the planetary bodies and the metals were conceived of as having been produced by the same means and how the seven basic metals were thought to correspond to the seven planets of the Ptolemaic system, the Moon being linked to silver, Venus to copper, Mercury to quicksilver, Saturn to lead, Mars to iron and Jupiter to tin. In addition, man's destiny was envisaged as being dominated by planetary influence, and many trades, professions and human activities were thought of as being under the patronage of a particular planet or planetary deity. To harness the power of the planets by means of astrology and to penetrate the secrets of the earth and extract its riches by means of mining techniques were cognate powers, princely in nature and far beyond the capabilities of the ordinary mortal. It is thus natural that, in that supreme vehicle of princely self-representation, the court festival, the Electors of Saxony should again and again present astrology and mining as being part of their panoply of power. Mining, and all that is associated with it, and the seven planets are the two most prominent and often-repeated themes in court festivals at Dresden from the middle of the sixteenth century right up into the eighteenth. It is wholly characteristic of Friedrich August I (August II, King of Poland) that, as discussed in chapter 7, he should pick up precisely these two themes in 1719, in the greatest festival of his reign, and use them for his own purposes.

Once costumed tournaments become the norm in the Empire during the second half of the sixteenth century, it is common for the participants in these tournaments at other courts and in Dresden too to dress as hunters, boatmen or postilions. But that the theme of mining is presented again and again in court festivals is a phenomenon peculiar to Dresden. It is given great prominence, in that the Electors themselves commonly lead these mining 'inventions' and themselves dress as miners. Unlike the presentation of huntsmen or boatmen, mining is depicted as a highly complex process, associated with great technical know-how and productive of great and magnificent riches. Where a hunter will appear with his dogs or with a wild animal in a cage and a boatman will carry his oar, the miners are usually presented in these festivities in Dresden as actually engaged in extracting ore and precious minerals and frequently also in processing them. The level of technical detail, the working machinery which is presented on floats, the quantities of lumps of ore, the heaps of precious stones, demonstrate both the riches accruing to the Electors from these activities and also the mastery of nature which is fundamental to them.

A group of miners appears for the first time in Elector August's reign in the festivities he organised in 1561 for the wedding of his niece Anna, the daughter of his brother Moritz, to William, Prince of Orange. Wolf von Schönberg and Nicol von Miltitz appeared on that occasion with their attendants dressed as miners and were accompanied by a miners' choir with burning lamps.[34] Much more elaborate is the appearance of miners in the tournament Elector August put on at the carnival season in 1574. Here the miners appeared under the protection of the god Mercury, 'the God of all Metals', as he is called in a manuscript account of the tournament of 1574.[35] Mercury was Elector August himself and great care was taken in the realism of the miners' costumes and accoutrements. They appeared with their miners' lamps on their caps, they carried such tools of their trade as a divining rod, a hod of ore and a miner's axe, and were accompanied by a smelter and a coin-maker, each with his own tools or utensils.

The tournament in 1587 under Christian I presents a group of ten miners, four of whom are mounted, each carrying a big lump of ore in one hand, and four of whom are on foot, each holding a hod of ore. Christian I staged another costumed running at the ring in the Palace courtyard in Dresden in January 1591 to celebrate the christening of his daughter Dorothea. In the thirteenth invention, a fiery furnace was presented on a huge float. On the furnace Mercury stood blowing flames from a trumpet and simultaneously working a bellows (Figure 25). Two smelters walked in front of the float and five miners followed behind carrying hods of ore. Then came another pair of figures carrying lumps of ore and on a float a working mine, in whose shafts and passages the figures of six miners could be seen labouring away, with bonfires on the peaks of the mountain to symbolise good seams of ore. The Elector himself and the chief guest, Christian, Duke of Anhalt, as well as mining officials such as the 'Oberhauptmann' (or chief prefect) of the Erzgebirge, Heinrich von Schönberg, and the 'kursächsicher Berghauptmann' (or Electoral Saxon prefect), Christoph von Schönberg, formed part of this group and were costumed as miners. They were followed by two

Figure 25. Daniel Bretschneider the Elder, Mercury and his furnace in the mining invention for the running at the ring held in Dresden in 1591. SLUB Mscr. Dresd.J 9. Deutsche Fotothek (Franke).

pairs of miners, each pair carrying a stretcher full of uncut diamonds. Mining is presented here as an official state industry, presided over by the highest in the land.

But the mention of Mercury in 1574 shows that the planets and the planetary gods were presented in association with mining from the beginning. In 1587 the tournament which presented the miners also presented the seven planets in a separate invention. In 1591, the mining invention was under the patronage of Mercury, as we saw, but astrology appeared separately in the same tournament in the ninth invention in the shape of the Moon and a magician with an armillary sphere.

In 1602, Daniel Bretschneider the Elder, court artist to the Electors, executed a series of fifty-one designs for decorative sledges for festivities of various kinds.[36] One charming design places a device of a mountain on the front of the sledge, in which we see a functioning mine in which five miners are working (No. 4). The designs include a whole series relating to the planets – Saturn (No. 1), Mars (No. 15), the Sun (No. 21), Venus (Nos. 29 and 33), Jupiter (No. 8), Mercury (No. 36) and the Moon (No. 43). Astronomy is represented by an astronomer sited on the front of the sledge and pointing to the stars with one hand, while holding a dividers on a celestial globe with the other (No. 38) (Figure 26). Alchemy too appears in No. 14, in the form of two of the beasts most associated with alchemical processes, the pelican and the dragon.

During the next decade, astrological themes crop up again and again in tournament inventions. In 1604 the theme of the Seven Planets was presented in a running at the ring to celebrate Johann Georg I's marriage to Sibylle Elisabeth, Duchess of Württemberg. At his second wedding in 1607, to Magdalena Sibylle, Margravine of Brandenburg, in the seventh invention Saturn as Father Time leads the Sun and the

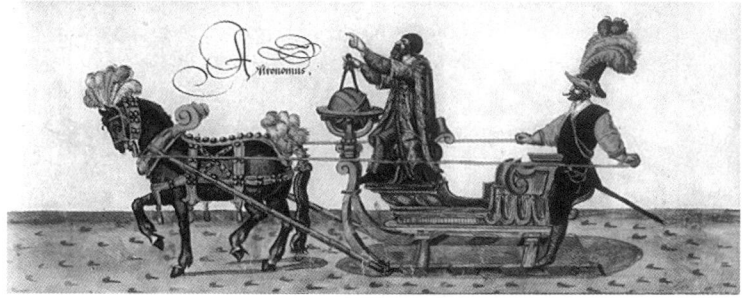

Figure 26. Daniel Bretschneider the Elder, Astronomer. Design for a sledge. SLUB Mscr.Dresd.B 104. Deutsche Fotothek (Richter).

Moon and they are followed by a figure on foot representing the stars. In 1609 in the third invention we have a very similar group of the Moon and the Sun with a figure on foot representing the stars and in the twenty-first invention the months and the signs of the zodiac followed by a small still on a float, thus linking astrology and alchemy.

But, in 1613, at the running at the ring held on 27, 28 and 29 June to celebrate the christening of Johann Georg I, one overarching theme unified the whole tournament for the first time in a festivity in Dresden and it was that of the Seven Planets. Father Time with his scythe came first and the Planets followed, each with its own float. Mercury appeared enthroned on a mountain which was, in the usual Dresden fashion, a working mine.

During the next decades, the theme of mining was not forgotten. Miners made their appearance in the tournament held in 1622 for the christening of Heinrich, Johann Georg II's younger brother. Here the second invention in the train of the reigning Elector, Johann Georg I, included eight miners bearing lumps of ore. In the sixth invention, Johann Georg I was followed by a large mountain in which miners could be seen making music and singing.[37]

Again, in the running at the ring held on 24 February 1630 for the wedding of Friedrich, Duke of Schleswig-Holstein, and Maria Elisabeth, the second daughter of Johann Georg I, the fourth invention consisted of the bride's four brothers, Dukes Johann Georg, August, Christian and Moritz (aged at this date seventeen, sixteen, fifteen and eleven respectively), dressed as miners. As usual, the Electoral family is associating itself publicly with the mining industry.[38]

In 1662 the youngest of these four brothers, Moritz of Saxony-Zeitz, as he now was, appeared as Mercury in the running at the ring to celebrate the wedding of his niece, Johann Georg II's only daughter, Erdmuthe Sophie, and Christian Ernst, Margrave of Brandenburg-Ansbach. The figure of Mercury was again accompanied by a float depicting a mine and by miners, smelters and minters.[39]

In February 1678 Johann Georg II held the 'Durchlauchtigste Zusammenkunft (Most Noble Gathering), discussed in chapter 1, in Dresden. In a reference to the tournament held in 1613 in celebration of his own christening, Johann Georg II chose the theme of the Seven Planets to unify the various events of the month-long festivities in 1678 and to remind his three younger brothers who were present, August of Saxony-Weissenfels, Christian of Saxony-Merseburg and Moritz of Saxony-Zeitz, of his pre-eminent position as head of the family and Elector. The reference would have been clear to all participants in 1678, for the running at the ring in 1613 was documented in a very large oil painting by Daniel Bretschneider the Elder,[40] which we know was still hanging in the stables in Dresden in 1671 (see chapter 5) and which is extant today. We should remember that the plays about Joseph and his brothers and the enmity between them discussed in chapter 1 formed part of the same festivities.

Johann Georg II presented the overarching theme of the planets in a ballet staged in the court theatre at the very beginning of the festivities on 3 February, the 'Ballet von Zusammenkunft und Wirckung derer VII. Planeten' (The Ballet of the Confluence and Influence of the Seven Planets).[41] It was a lavish stage work (see the discussion in chapter 6) with nine sets by Johann Oswald Harms, one for the prologue, one for each of the seven entrées dedicated to the seven planets and one for the grand ballet at the end. The planets are those of the Ptolemaic system, Saturn, Jupiter, Mars, the Sun, Venus, Mercury and the Moon. Of all genres of courtly entertainment, ballet is the most suitable for a representation of the planets, for it was created at the French court in 1581 to mimic the harmonious movement of the spheres and call down heavenly influences on man's affairs, linking the macrocosm and the microcosm.[42] But here in Dresden, the theme of the planets is linked with that of mining. This could hardly be more prominent, for it was presented in the very first *entrée*, that of Saturn (and for the first time in Dresden not in association with Mercury). Saturn is the planet furthest from the earth, it is cold and dark and therefore has a logical connection with mining. Harms's set depicts a wild scene of craggy rocks (Figure 27). Inside these rocks we can see miners at their work and it is miners who dance in the *entrée*.

Mercury has his own scene, the sixth *entrée*. From the text we see that he is particularly associated with alchemy, the hermetic (or mercurial) science. Harms's set for this *entrée* shows some of the arts and trades associated with Mercury in booths visible through a colonnade round the sides of the set – painting, sculpture, writing, astronomy, alchemy, etc. The figures who dance in the *entrée* are two alchemists and four fools, but also a scholar, a musician, an astronomer, an arithmetician, Geometry, a painter and a soldier.

At a later stage of the same festivities, on 21 February 1678, a running at the ring under the patronage of Mercury was held in the lists at the Riding School in Dresden and here the association of Mercury with mining has been restored. The participants processed through the city from the Zeughaus, or Weapons Store, across the Altmarkt and through the Schlossgasse and the Palace. Mercury was represented by Master of

Figure 27. Johann Oswald Harms, Set design of a mountain scene with miners at work for the *entrée* of Saturn in the *Ballet von Zusammenkunft und Wirckung Derer Sieben Planeten*, 1678. Note the windlass in the centre at the back. Deutsche Fotothek (Richter).

the Horse Goetze, who rode along enthroned, in a reference to the tournament of 1613, on a mountain in which miners could be seen at work. The procession included a flaming furnace and a hod of ore, smelters with their tools and minters tossing coins to the bystanders.

On this occasion Mercury was followed by Johann Georg II himself on horseback dressed as a miner. Part of his costume was a set of miner's tools and accoutrements, the so-called 'Bergmannsgarnitur', which he had had commissioned specially for this occasion and which bear his monogramm[43] (Figure 28). The set was made by Samuel Klemm, a Freiberg goldsmith, between 1675 and 1677 and consists of nineteen separate pieces. They include a sabre, a miner's axe ('Bergbarte'), a miner's lamp, a knife for cutting up tallow for the lamp ('Tscherpermesser'), the leather satchel ('Tscherpertasche') in which both lamp and tallow were carried, two decorative plaques for the black leather knee-protectors a miner wore, a hat badge, buckles, hatbands and spurs. These objects are richly embellished with semi-precious stones mined in Saxony – garnets, rock crystal, quartz, amethysts and opals. That these materials were available at this time is a direct result of the revival of mining in Saxony set in train by Johann Georg II.[44] The Thirty Years' War had caused both silver mining and the extraction of semi-precious stones to

Figure 28. Samuel Klemm, Freiberg. 1675–77. The 'Tscherpertasche', or bag for tallow, and other lighting materials in the miner's accoutrements called the 'Bergmannsgarnitur' commissioned by Johann Georg II and worn by him in 1678. Leather, silver, gilding, enamel, precious stones. The enamel plaque represents the Electoral mint in which several figures can be seen at work. W. 17 cm. Grünes Gewölbe, Dresden. Deutsche Fotothek (Heckmann).

fall into desuetude. Shortly after his accession in 1656 the new Elector commissioned his Chief Architect Wolf Caspar von Klengel (1630–91) to undertake a survey of all mineral and marble deposits in Saxony – just as Elector August had commissioned his architect, Giovanni Maria Nosseni, to do in 1575. Klengel presented his report in 1659. Among the deposits he found were garnets at Zöblitz which were used in the 'Bergmannsgarnitur'. The set is also decorated with silver, which came from the St Daniel mine near Schneeberg in the Erzgebirge. This mine had only become productive again in 1665, producing 175 kg of silver in that year. The 'Bergmannsgarnitur' is thus visible proof of the revival of an ancient source of wealth in Saxony and of an ancient industry.

But the set bears witness to the mining industry in another way also. The pieces are decorated with enamel plaques which depict in the most minute and realistic detail the various processes involved in silver-mining both below and above ground. The depiction begins on the hat badge with the figure of a diviner prospecting for silver and ends on the large plaque on the 'Tscherpertasche' showing a mint, in which seven figures are minting coins from the silver. The Elector as Overlord of the Saxon Mines both bears witness, and pays tribute, to his most important home-grown industry.

The festivities held in celebration of the 'Durchlauchtigste Zusammenkunft' were recorded in a lengthy official account by Gabriel Tzschimmer, a work which is discussed as a monument to the reign of Johann Georg II in chapter 5. This work has a second part, in which Tzschimmer discourses on matters related to the festivities he records in the first part. Here, on p. 496, he turns to a discussion of the planet Mercury. This is followed by a disquisition on alchemy (pp. 499–503) under the same general heading of 'Das edle Berg=Werk' (the noble art of mining) and relates mining and alchemy to Mercury. Tzschimmer shows a certain ambivalence with regard to alchemy. On the one hand he exhibits considerable knowledge of the topic – he relates that medicine and the manufacture of gold have to do with alchemy, he even gives a detailed and exact recipe for making gold on pp. 502–3, he mentions Thurneysser and Paracelsus and tells us that two Holy Roman Emperors, Maximilian I and Ferdinand III, were engaged in alchemical practices in 1510 and 1648 respectively. To bear this out, he narrates on p. 500 how Ferdinand III himself made three and a half pounds of pure gold out of three pounds of mercury with the help of a powder sent to him by an unknown philosopher from Prague. Tzschimmer also tells us on the same page of an iron nail preserved in the *Kunstkammer* in Florence which is gold at the tip. This has a kind of certificate vouching for it by Leonhard Turneysser!

So on the one hand, Tzschimmer appears to wish to enhance the reputation and credibility of alchemy by associating it with high-born people and famous collections, yet on the other hand he is clearly sceptical of its achievements himself. He then moves on to the safer ground of mining and metals. He takes us through all the metals in turn: silver, copper, pewter, iron, lead, mercury and then proceeds to a discussion of what he calls 'der unverdrossene Berg=Mann' (the cheery miner, p. 514) and so to the unexceptionable topic of minting (p. 524). One is not surprised to find such an extensive treatment of mining and related topics in an official publication such as Tzschimmer's festival book.

It is characteristic of the relationship of Friedrich August I (August II, King of Poland), to the Dresden tradition and to the cultural achievements of his grandfather Johann Georg II that he should take the Seven Planets as the overarching theme for the greatest festivity of his reign, the wedding in 1719 of his son to the daughter of the Emperor, Joseph I, and that the culminating event of the whole programme, a festival under the patronage of Saturn, should be devoted to a celebration of mining. As discussed in chapter 7, in this festivity mining is taken into the pre-industrial age but its prominence is still due to its importance as a symbol of the wealth and therefore the power of the Electors of Saxony.

5
The Fabrication of an Image: Johann Georg II's Self-presentation

The twenty-three-year reign of Johann Georg II from 1657 until 1680 was a pivotal one in terms of the development of Dresden as a court city and of the cultural achievements of the court. The reign was one of consolidation and reconstruction after the ravages of the Thirty Years' War and Johann Georg II's extensive programme of building bears witness to that. At the same time court entertainment, while retaining many traditional Saxon features, began to shake off any remaining provincial quaintness and to vie with the international festive culture of Vienna and Munich. That is the subject of the next chapter. This chapter is devoted to another of the cultural achievements of Johann Georg II – the elaboration of his own public image as warrior and hero over three decades, principally by means of court spectacles of homage focused on the person of the Elector.

Johann Georg II's emergence as Jason (1650)

Johann Georg II began to develop an image for himself already during his father's reign. Born in 1613 he began to function as the chief organiser of festivals at court at the latest from the 1630s. But before the 1650s these entertainments remained charming small-scale *divertissements* for the delectation of the Electoral family. Saxony's entry into the Thirty Years' War in 1632 made large-scale celebrations impossible, in any case. It was not, therefore, until the double wedding in 1650 of his two youngest brothers, Christian and Moritz, to two sisters, Christiane and Sophie Hedwig of Schleswig-Holstein, that Johann Georg had his first opportunity for public self-presentation.[1] This wedding was the first large-scale festivity he organised and it also functioned as a peace festival, marking the end of the Thirty Years' War. The two bridegrooms were officially the main participants, but Johann Georg gave himself a leading part in the festivities. The wedding festivities lasted from the arrival of the Schleswig-Holstein party on 17 November until 11 December 1650. The wedding itself took place on 19 November and the ballets and plays performed in the succeeding weeks are discussed in the next chapter. At the heart of the festivities were two other interconnected events: the running at the ring of Jason and the Golden Fleece on 25, 26 and 27 November and the firework display on the same theme on 1 December.[2]

Jason's challenge to those wishing to compete against him was promulgated in the usual way the evening before, on 24 November, and the running at the ring itself lasted for the three subsequent days. Much of this time was taken up with the processions of the costumed participants through the streets of Dresden. On the first day there was the procession of Jason himself, an imposing group of about a hundred people. He was supported by Telamon and Idas, by trumpeters, servants, grooms, musketeers leading horses and costumed figures on foot. Jason and his heroic journey to Colchis to capture the Golden Fleece was the subject of this so-called 'invention' and Jason was played by Johann Georg II. His brother Christian, one of the bridegrooms, appeared as Pax (Peace) in the next invention, riding on a triumphal car. His group included Revenge and Mercy, Discord and War, a terrestrial globe borne on a ship floating on the waves, and the four German rivers, the Rhine, the Elbe, the Danube and the Oder. His brother Moritz, the other bridegroom, appeared as Perseus in a much smaller invention with a float of Andromeda chained to a rock and a second triumphal car bearing the rescued Andromeda. On the second day Christian and Moritz appeared as Castor and Pollux, symbolising brotherly accord and harmony, and on the third day as Hercules and Admetus with Alcestis on a triumphal car. These other figures were the challengers ('Aventurier') who had to run against Jason (the 'Maintenator') and his supporters. Jason was thus the central figure, presiding over the whole tournament.

The firework display, in fact a firework drama in four acts with a text by David Schirmer,[3] elaborated on the Jason theme. In Act I the coats of arms and monograms of Johann Georg I and his wife and of the two bridal couples glowed against the night sky but the rest of the piece was devoted to Jason's exploits. In Act II he conquered the oxen and ploughed the field with them, in Act III he killed the dragon and sowed their teeth, and in Act IV he captured the Golden Fleece. His virtue is stressed in Act II, his courage in Act III and that most important of seventeenth-century virtues, constancy or 'Beständigkeit', in Act IV. By the very fact that it is the Electoral Prince, Johann Georg, who has earlier played the part of Jason in the running at the ring, these heroic deeds and noble qualities cannot fail but be associated with him. If the procession through the streets was a public presentation, visible to those who lined the route, a firework display was virtually unmissable, visible willy-nilly to the whole city. The organiser of the festivities made very sure that he played a central role at his brothers' wedding and that it was he who emerged identified with one of the indomitable heroes of the ancient world. From this point on, the myth of Jason was used and reinterpreted by Johann Georg as part of his personal iconography until his death in 1680. He combined it with the legend of St George, as we shall see below, and with the myth of Hercules. All three are heroes and warriors and this is one of the chief guises in which Johann Georg II presented himself.

The Riesensaal and the ballet of 1653

But Johann Georg was still only the Electoral Prince, not the Elector, and he needed to consolidate his position within his own family. We see a move towards such consolidation and at the same time towards a further elaboration of his persona as warrior in the untitled ballet he put on in honour of his father in 1653. It was danced in the Riesensaal in the Palace in Dresden on 3 July and the title-page makes very clear that this is a homage from Johann Georg, the Electoral Prince, to his father and that it was the former's dancing master, François Dolivet, who composed the choreography.[4]

The piece opens with a presentation of Saxony itself. The first scene depicts a landscape with a ploughman, a vintner and two female gardeners showing the fruits of their labours – corn, grapes, fruit and flowers. This is presided over by Ops and Cornucopia, the goddesses of Plenty. The second scene introduces two huntsmen, two miners and two fishermen, each again showing what they produce. Electoral Saxony is being put forward as a land of plenty, its prosperity reflecting well on its rulers.

The set changes to present the three chief cities of Saxony – Dresden, Wittenberg and Leipzig. Dresden is represented by two soldiers, who demonstrate how well the fortified city is equipped and how well tournaments and martial exercises are performed there. Wittenberg is represented by a group of those who inculcate important disciplines in the young: a philosopher, a rhetorician, a dancing master, a fencing master and a horseman. This shows that the famous Saxon Universities do not just teach academic subjects but make sure their alumni are also taught 'allerley Adeliche und nützliche übungen' (all kinds of noble and useful skills). Leipzig is represented by a merchant's wife. Thus Saxony is shown to be the home of martial skills, courtly pastimes, learning, social polish and commerce.

The third set presents the noble and ancient origins of the House of Saxony by means of the four ancient heroes, Harderich, Wittekind, Thimo and Friedrich the Quarrelsome, supposedly tracing their descent back to Harderich in 772.

Now the focus is widened to demonstrate, in allegorical dumb show, Saxony's position in the Empire and the key role played by its ruler, the premier secular Elector. On a swelling sea we see a ship bobbing up and down. This is Electoral Saxony. Then a second larger ship appears without a mast, though containing six passengers. This represents the Holy Roman Empire without an Emperor but with the other six Electors. The Ship of the Empire gets into difficulties and has to ask the Ship of Saxony for assistance. Saxony guides the Empire safely home and provides it with a mast. But the same thing happens again: a second time we see the Ship of the Empire without a mast and again it is Saxony which has to come to the rescue and help the six passengers to save their vessel. These incidents represent the occasions on which Johann Georg I functioned as Imperial Regent on the death of an Emperor, leading the Electoral College to a successful vote and the installation of a new Emperor.[5]

We are then shown the ruler – by implication Johann Georg I – engaged in the activities of government in three scenes. At the front of the stage in the first scene a military official, a lawyer and a diplomat show the emblems of their professions, while the back of the stage opens to reveal a table piled with letters and documents and a mighty statesman all alone at the head of it, with his councillors seated below him. The military man, the lawyer and the diplomat have their business settled. This represents, says the text, the great care, wise counsels and constant attention that the Elector devotes to all matters pertaining to his lands and subjects. In the second part of this section a rich usurer, a poor man and two women all come to ask for justice, which the Elector metes out fairly, irrespective of rank. In the third part two ambassadors representing Upper and Lower Lusatia present their coats of arms to the Elector. This is a tribute to his noble princely virtues and wise counsels.

The *grand ballet* which follows intensifies the claims made by the Electors of Saxony in terms of rank and status within the Empire, elevates the Electors by means of mythological parallels, yet personalises the homage proffered to them. It opens with what the text calls an impressive ('ansehnlich') figure wearing the Electoral robes and insignia. He is flanked by two kings who behave in a very friendly manner towards him, signifying that the Electoral dignity is without question equal in status to that of a king. Four knights in Roman dress, danced by Johann Georg's four sons, Johann Georg II, August, Christian and Moritz respectively, demonstrate their love and reverence for the figure of the Elector. Two courtiers representing the Elector's subjects also show their obedience. We might note that at this point, after their brief appearance, Johann Georg II's three younger brothers stand aside for the final homage.

Here again the quasi-royal dignity of the Electors is emphasised:

'Es ist billig daß der Kuhrhutt mit den Krohnen wird erhöht
Weil sein Purpur ihrem Golde gleich an Würd' und Ehre steht:
Denn in grader Waage bleibt Kuhr= und Königlicher Stand
Ihrer beyder rühmlich' Hoheit ist durch alle Welt bekant.'

(It is right that the Electoral Hat should be elevated to the same level as the crowns, for the Electoral purple is equal in dignity and honour to their gold. The estate of Elector and King are of equal weight, their praiseworthy status is known throughout the world.)

This astonishing claim is then taken onto the mythological plane but simultaneously brought home to the Albertines. We have another sea scene, this time a calm sea with the Ship of Saxony again sailing through it. It has Jupiter at the helm, Mars at the main mast and Cupid on the prow. Jupiter, the wise ruler, is Johann Georg I, Mars, representing martial strength and power, is Johann Georg II and Cupid is the six-year-old Johann Georg III. The Elector, we are told, is a Jupiter to his people, a Mars to his enemies and a Cupid to his friends. Two sirens approach the ship and three angels descend from Heaven, one of them going to each of the three Johann Georgs and placing a wreath on his brow. The verses they sing link the gods, the ancient Saxon heroes and the three Johann Georgs into the very embodiment of the perfect ruler, the wreaths being the symbol of their virtue, their achievements and their worthiness to rule.

This spectacle thus culminates in a glorification arranged by Johann Georg II for his father but also for himself in which he represents Mars, the god of war. The marked stress on the element of dynastic continuity provided by the existence of three generations of the same name alive together also underlines Johann Georg II's pre-eminent position as the eldest of four brothers, while the ballet symbolically represents the subordinate position of the three younger brothers.

But the room in which this ballet was danced, the Riesensaal, or Room of the Giants, is highly pertinent (Figure 29). The walls and ceiling of this room were entirely covered with frescoes whose programme presented the government and territory of Saxony, its position within the wider world, the Elector as overlord of his domains and Destiny dominating the whole.

The room took its name from the twelve larger than life-size frescoes of giants by the brothers Benedetto, Gabriele and Guerino Tola, which were commissioned by Moritz, the first Albertine Elector, and completed in 1553 when the Riesensaal came into being[6] (see Figure 13 above; p. 39). This was part of Moritz's efforts to turn the Palace in Dresden from a medieval fortress into a Renaissance palace. The Riesensaal was needed for gatherings of the Saxon Landtag or Council of Estates and for festive occasions and celebrations.

In 1627, however, repairs were necessary because of damp and it was decided to enlarge and redecorate the Riesensaal, a process that was not completed until 1650. The most important change was to remove the five-metre-high flat ceiling and replace it with a 9.6-metre-high vault. The architect employed was Wilhelm Dilich (1571–1650), who came to Dresden in 1625 after long service with the Landgrave of Hessen-Kassel as fortifications engineer, architect, mathematician, draughtsman, engraver and historian. The depictions of the giants were retained on the long sides of the room but otherwise the frescoes depicted a whole new iconographic programme. This was executed by Kilian Fabritius from 1628 until 1631, when the Thirty Years' War brought the work to a halt (he died in 1633) and from 1638 by his former apprentice, Christian Schiebling.

The huge vaulted wooden ceiling was painted blue and decorated with the stars of the northern and southern hemispheres and with the twelve signs of the zodiac. Below this were strikingly large depictions of the cities of Meissen and Electoral Saxony, of which Dilich had already executed topographical drawings by 4 July 1628. There were sixteen depictions of towns at the point where the vaulted ceiling met the walls, one larger depiction each on the east and west wall and further smaller depictions of towns in the window arches. As has been pointed out by Norbert Oelsner,[7] the order in which the towns were presented corresponded exactly to the order of precedence of the towns within the Landtag. Leipzig came first, as the leading city of the 'Engerer Ausschuß',

Figure 29. Johann Mock, The Riesensaal in the Palace in Dresden on the occasion of the installation of Johann Georg IV as Garter Knight in 1693 (detail). Gouache. Kupferstich-Kabinett, Dresden. C1961-114. Deutsche Fotothek (Andrich).

or central committee, followed by the other members of that committee, Wittenberg, Dresden and Zwickau. They were followed by towns of the second rank, Freiberg, Chemnitz, Langensalza and Torgau. The ten lesser members of the 'Weiterer Ausschuß', or Council, are depicted next and the less important towns again are depicted in the window arches. Each of the depictions was equipped with a Latin inscription which encapsulated its character. The coats of arms of noblemen, another of the important estates in the Landtag, also appeared between the depictions of the towns.

In the window embrasures were larger than life-size representations of twenty-nine nations in national dress, eleven from Europe, seven from Asia, six from Africa and five from America. The wider world, the new geographical discoveries, are represented here. A large battle scene was added at the northern end of the western long side.

But dominating the whole south wall was a *trompe l'oeil* depiction of a balcony the entire width of the room, the painted balustrade in front and three wide open archways behind (Figure 30). The balcony was at the same height as the projecting frieze that ran down the long walls of the room. On this balustrade, looking down into the Riesensaal, were Johann Georg I and his consort, Magdalena Sibylla, framed by a curtain. Their four living sons were lined up beside their father and their three daughters beside their mother. The other figures depicted at a distance from the rest of the group are surely their three dead sons and Johann Georg I's deceased first wife, Sibylle Elisabeth, Duchess of Württemberg. Karallus points out that such a presentation is usually reserved for kings and emperors.[8] An extremely large coat of arms of the Wettins was positioned above the heads of the Elector and his wife.[9] The Elector thus dominated the entire room, whose redecoration he commissioned. His position on the balcony, in the midst of his family, announced him as the unquestioned head of the government of Saxony, which was represented by the depictions of the cities and the coats of arms of the nobles. The large costumed figures of many nations positioned Saxony within the wider world. Yet Destiny, in the shape of the stars and the signs of the zodiac, was literally the overarching power, guiding the fortunes of the territory and its ruling house.

By no means all ballets held at the Dresden court in this decade were staged in this room. Many of them, particularly those for family rather than state occasions, were in another room on the same floor of the Palace, the Steinern Saal, or Stone Saloon, so called after the many different sorts of stone used in the floor. Only ballets danced on important occasions – for instance, for the double wedding of 1650 – were put on

Figure 30. Johann Mock, The British envoy ties the Garter on Johann Georg IV on the occasion of his installation as Garter Knight in 1693 (detail). Gouache. The empty throne represents the English King. Kupferstich-Kabinett, Dresden. C1961-113. Deutsche Fotothek (Andrich).

in the Riesensaal. That the 1653 ballet was held in the Riesensaal distinguishes it, therefore, from the purely family occasion it appears at first sight to be, and underlines its function as a major political statement.

It is in fact a danced version of the iconographic programme of the Riesensaal itself. It claims that the Elector of Saxony is the equal of kings, it presents him as ruler and emblem of good government, it depicts Saxony by means of its three principal cities and its people through its presentation of the estates and professions. The male members of the Elector's family are assigned those roles for which birth equips them, and Destiny crowns the present and future Electors. The audience was thus looking at the static presentation on the walls round them, the figures so large and so brightly coloured as to dominate the scene, and at the same time at the moving presentation in the dance. They cannot fail to have made the connection.

That this ballet should be performed in 1653 was no accident. This was a year of some importance in both the Empire and the internal politics of the Albertines. On 18 June 1653, two weeks before the ballet we are discussing, the reigning Emperor Ferdinand III ensured the Habsburg sucession, as he thought, by having his son Ferdinand IV crowned as Roman King, that is, as the putative next Emperor. (He could not have foreseen that Ferdinand IV was to die the following year.) At the time of the ballet, therefore, Johann Georg I was but newly returned from having played his part yet again as Imperial High Marshall in guiding the Ship of the Empire, as the ballet has it. In terms of internal Saxon politics, it was in this year that Johann Georg I made a will providing greater financial security for his three younger sons by giving them territories in the west of the Duchy. August, Administrator of the Archbishopric of Magdeburg whose seat was Halle, was given Weissenfels, Christian Merseburg, and Moritz, whose seat was Naumburg, Zeitz. At this juncture Johann Georg II, always jealous of his position as heir, was reminding his father, now 68 years of age, and his three younger brothers of what could be presumed to be his imminent succession to his father's title.

The ballet of 1653 was not only more ambitious in scale than previous entertainments in honour of Johann Georg I, its focus was far wider than just its principal addressee. It eulogised Saxony, set it within the Empire, highlighted the function of the Elector, showed the present incumbent engaged in the business of government as the perfect ruler and then claimed his rank to be kingly, his abilities to be godly and the succession assured. By presenting the Elector to himself and by having his four sons perform in the ballet, relegating the younger ones after their brief appearance to the status of onlookers, the ballet not only represented the ruler and the power-relations within his family, it was itself performative. By the very act of representing himself as eldest son and heir, Johann Georg II is making his power more secure.

Three weeks later, on 24 June 1653, Johann Georg II again underlined the theme of dynastic continuity with a celebration of the Feast of St John the Baptist. The importance of this feast was that it was the 'Dreyfacher Johannestag', or Threefold St. John's Day, the joint nameday of the three Johann Georgs, his father, himself and his son. Two pastoral entertainments were written for this occasion, David Schirmer's 'Dalliance of the Nymphs and Satyrs' and a translation of *Il Pastor Fido* by Ernst Geller.[10] Both stress the dynastic continuity made manifest in the three generations of Johann Georgs and Johann Georg II's unassailable position, not just as heir but as the father of the next heir again. In a sonnet written for the threefold nameday two years earlier, Schirmer had compared the three Johann Georgs to Anchises, Aeneas and Ascanius. In chapter 1 we discussed Johann Georg's rivalry towards his younger brothers which was expressed in his own reign in the performance of a series of plays on the theme of Joseph and his brothers. This harping on the succession ties in with his perceived need to bolster his position within the family. Johann Georg II as Jason and Mars was nothing if not combative.

Johann Georg II as Knight of St George

Almost twelve years into his own reign – he succeeded late in 1656 – Johann Georg received an honour that gave him hitherto unparalleled possibilities for focusing spectacles of homage on his own person. On 19 June 1668 he was elected to the British Order of St George, otherwise known as the Order of the Garter, as the 470th Garter Knight since its foundation in 1348. In fact, the election was a mere formality, for in the case of what was called a 'Stranger Prince' it was the sovereign – in this case Charles II – who chose to award the honour.[11] The rules stipulated that an embassy from the English sovereign should go to the foreign prince to offer him membership of the Order 'in respect of his renowned Prowess, Valour, Virtues, &c. and to establish and encrease the Amity that is between them'.[12] Sir Thomas Higgins and Thomas St. George duly set off for Dresden on 27 February 1669, arriving there on 5 April.[13] They brought with them, as was customary, the Garter itself, of blue velvet with buckles of gold and precious stones, the Collar of the Order made of 30 ounces of gold, the Mantle, the Gown and the Order of St George (both the so-called Great and Lesser George), the Garter Star for more everyday wear and a copy of the Statutes of the Order.[14]

The actual investiture, for which a very precise ceremonial was laid down in the Statutes in the case of a foreign national being invested on foreign soil, took place in the Riesensaal in the Palace in Dresden on 13 April 1669. (Since the Feast of St George fell on 23 April, investitures customarily took place as near to that date as possible.) The Court Chamberlain's papers in the Archive in Dresden present the ceremonial from the Dresden perspective on eighty-eight folio pages.[15] They show the Dresden court machine clicking into action: instructions as to where the Elector's throne and the other furniture should be placed, instructions to the Chief Marshals about the procession and the details of the ceremony, a memo to Marshal Kannen containing the same details in outline, instructions to Privy Councillor and Chief Chamberlain Hermann von Wolfframsdorff, to Master of the Horse von Götze, to Chief Trumpeter Johann Arnold and to the court victuallers. From folio 45a on there are instructions concerning the baldachin which is to be spread over the banqueting table, the red carpet for the floor, the cushions on which the insignia are to be carried and the colour of the herold's tunic. An inventory of the hangings and tapestries taken in 1683 shows how costly these fabrics were, gold, velvet and damask being the preferred fabrics.[16] From folio 41a on we have a list of the forty-nine courtiers who were in attendance on the Elector on this occasion. For the entertainment of the Ambassadors a bear hunt was organised and then they had an audience with the Elector, his son and daughter-in-law, and this too had to be organised.

To be made a Knight of the Garter constituted a very real distinction and these elaborate preparations show that Johann Georg II was well aware of it. This was partly due to the fact that this was the most ancient order of chivalry in Europe but also to the fact that there could not then (and still cannot now) be more than twenty-six Garter Knights at any one time, the number being limited by the number of stalls in the Chapel of St George at Windsor Castle. During the reign of Charles II, apart from the sons of Friedrich of the Palatinate, the only foreigners invested before Johann George II were Henri Charles de la Trémouille, Prince de Tarente, William, Prince of Orange, Friedrich Wilhelm, Elector of Brandenburg, the Comte de Granville and the future Christian V, King of Denmark. He was therefore not only the first Elector of Saxony to receive the Order, but was being accorded the same distinction as the Great Elector and the future King of Denmark.

Johann Georg made the most of the honour and used the anniversary as an occasion for further spectacles of homage, particularly apt in view of the personal symbolism attached to the name George. Indeed, by re-enacting his investiture in the Order of St George, Johann Georg was able to create what amounted to a second nameday festival for himself, the so-called 'Georgsfest'.

Having been actually invested in the order in 1669, Johann Georg was installed by proxy in Windsor in 1671 and to mark the installation Benjamin Leuber published a short history of the Order of the Garter up to the reign of Charles I.[17] Johann Georg had a medal struck for the occasion in honour of Charles II. On one side is a depiction of St George killing the dragon with round the edge the inscription 'En honneur du souverain du tres noble ordre de la iartiere' (Figure 31). On the back we read: 'Du tré haut tré puissant et tres excellent Prince Charles II par la grace de Dieu Roy de La Grande Bretag: Fran: et Irlande defenseur de la

Figure 31. St George and the Dragon. Medal commemorating the installation of Johann Georg II as Garter Knight in 1671. Tentzel, *Saxonia numismatica*. Tab. 57, No. 4.

foy. MDCLXXI.'[18] Parallel with the ceremony in Windsor, the installation was also enacted in Dresden on 26 April 1671 in the presence of Sir William Swan representing Charles II.[19]

The account in the Court Chamberlain's papers opens with an annotated diagram of the Riesensaal indicating the position of all those taking part. The three chief features were the altar (so-called) in the middle of the back wall on which the insignia were placed and the two baldachins at either side and in front of the altar, one for the British Ambassador, the other for the Elector. There is the same minute apparatus for organising the festival and its ceremonial and this time the court documentation in Dresden extends to 150 folio sides (fol.48a–123a).

Sir William Swan wrote an account of his trip to Dresden which is informative not only about the installation itself, which was held in what he calls the 'Riesen Sahl' in the Palace on 23 April (the Dresden account says 26 April), but about the festivities staged by the Elector in celebration of the event.[20] According to Swan, there was a running at the ring on 24 April, of which he gives no details, and that evening a 'Comedy of Jason and Medea in High Dutch' in the playhouse. On 25 April there was a firework display depicting Jason's conquering of the Golden Fleece. Sir William comments that it 'was an extraordinarie thing, & hardly better seene... This Fireworke has been kept for an extraordinary occasion these 24 yeares, & has cost above 20000 Crownes, the Elector (as he told me himselfe) having made most of it himselfe, when he was an Electorall Prince.' The next day there was 'an Opera... continyuing the matter of the Comedy. The words Hony soit qui Mal y pense [the motto of the Order of the Garter] were... burning all along about the Theater, and there were a Ship, fighting at Sea whereof one was called the Dragon, & the other St. George which later burnt and sunk the former...' (ibid.).

It is clear from this that Jason, the hero who conquers the monsters of the ancient world and with whom Johann Georg had long since identified himself, is to be seen as a prefiguration of St. George, the Christian dragon-slayer, since the symbolic presentation of the latter in the opera is said by Swan to be a continuation of the play depicting the former. The Dresden documents do not mention the opera.

Another prefiguration of St. George from the ancient world, namely Hercules, was also used in the installation celebrations in 1671, for there was a second firework display entitled *Hercules Britto-Saxonicus*.[21] This was staged on the ramparts overlooking the Elbe and consisted of a pillar of fire to represent the pillars of Hercules and was meant, so the account tells us, as a sign of the tie (or garter) uniting Johann Georg II and the British Hercules, Charles II. As part of the same celebrations, the Joseph plays discussed in Chapter I were performed – on 1 May the selling of Joseph into slavery and on 2 May Joseph's chastity in Egypt.[22] They were followed by the ballet of the Twelve Tribes of Israel. (Swan would not have seen these as he was visiting such sites in Saxony as Meissen, Stolpen and Pirna on the days they were performed.)

One of the court poets at this date, Constantin Christian Dedekind, who has already been discussed in chapter 1 as an exponent of biblical semi-operas, adds yet another dimension to the significance to be attached to the symbolism of St George. In a narrative poem in fifty-six rhymed Alexandrine couplets entitled 'C.Chr.D. Vom grausahmen Libyschen Drachen/ durch Georgium den Ritter/ erlösete Siläische Prinzessin/ poëtisch beschrieben/ und auf das Georgianische Ritter=Fest untertähnigst übergeben' (Of the Cruel Libyan Dragon and the Selenian Princess Saved by the Knight George, Described Poetically and Humbly Presented on the Chivalric Feast of St George by C.Chr. D) and written for the 1671 investiture, he tells the story of the city of Silena, which is terrorised by a dragon, which eats its flocks and then wants to devour its princess, until it is killed by St George, the knight in shining armour. Dedekind presents this as an allegory of Christ (St George) saving the world (Selena) from the devil (the dragon), who wants to devour the human soul (the princess). In both 1669 and 1671 the Feast of St George, and therefore the Garter Festivals, were very close to Easter, so this linking of St George and Christ is particularly apt, according to Dedekind. The last twelve lines of the poem bring the interpretation round to Johann Georg II. The Elector has knightly courage, he loves heroic deeds, he does homage to Jesus, he has a father's care for his domains. The Elector is not explicitly compared to Christ, he is merely linked to St George whose name he bears, but as St George has just been declared to be an allegory of Christ, the connection is clear. This poem is bound with the manuscript documents relating to the 1671 festival in the Chamberlain's papers.[23]

This concept of St George as the embodiment of the ideal of the Christian knight was also used by Charles II, the very king who brought Johann Georg II into the Order. The Order of the Garter was very important to Charles and he used it to bind allies to him both at home and abroad and to reward good service.[24] He liked to portray himself as St George, the patron saint of England. In 1667 the Elector of Brandenburg, already a Garter Knight, sent Johann Georg as a gift a small iron statue by Gottfried Leygebe of Charles II as St George triumphing over evil in the shape of the many-headed monster[25] (Figure 32).

Figure 32. Gottfried Leygebe, Charles II as St George. Iron. Grünes Gewölbe, Dresden. Deutsche Fotothek (Heckmann).

A further printed work bound in with the same papers shows how the anniversary of the investiture as Garter Knight continued to be used for propaganda purposes. This is a presentation copy, bound in blue satin with blue and silver ribbons, of the Latin oration held in Wittenberg to commemorate the investiture in 1673. The author is Johann Heinrich Sander and the thirty-four pages of the Latin text are followed by a German translation, each separately paginated.[26] Sander is very clear that the Garter cannot as a distinction be compared to the Electorship, but that it is a mark of the esteem in which Johann Georg is held by other rulers far and wide. Sander then discusses the origin of the Order and of the legend of St George, in the course of which he polemicises against the pre-Reformation papacy, which, he says, spread evil rumours about the life of this saint. Edward III made St George the patron of his

Order because St George is to be understood symbolically as the 'pater patriae' (the father of his country, Latin text p. 14) and 'ein ieder rechtschaffener Regent sey ein George' (each and every true ruler is a St George, German text p. 9). The dragon is the devil, but the princess represents the Christian Church, which a Christian ruler has to protect and save. But it is above all from the errors of Popery that she has to be saved and this is just what Johann Georg's forebears – Friedrich, Johann, Moritz and August – did (German text p. 10). A lengthy panegyric on Johann Georg I follows. He is the German Mars who saved the Lutheran Church in the Thirty Years' War. Johann Georg II's heroic stature resides, however, in the fact that he has brought peace to his people. This is not because he is an incompetent warrior (German text pp. 17–18), for he understands martial matters well, but because he places peace above war. He deserves to have the 'Bürgerliche Krone' (the bourgeois crown) placed on his head (German text p. 18). So here in this oration St George emerges not just as the embodiment of the Christian knight but as the champion of Protestantism, and Johann Georg II's heroic status is given a new twist.

Johann Georg himself celebrated the anniversary of his investiture, that is, the Feast of St George, in Dresden in 1675, 1676 and 1678, each time linking St George implicitly with Jason and Hercules. On the first two of these occasions the programme is very similar to what we have just been discussing.[27] At what is referred to as the 'Begehung des St. Georgen Fests 1675', or Celebration of the Feast of St George 1675, there was a banquet on 23 April and the announcement of next day's shooting contest, and after dinner the play *Jupiter und Amphytrion* was performed in the Electoral Playhouse. On 24 April the shooting contest took place in the Shooting Gallery. Its fictional framework was taken from the Hercules legend and the targets were the many-headed Hydra, Cerberus and the Dragon. On 25 April Jason issued his challenge for the running at the ring and at the head to be held under his patronage and a firework display depicted Hercules's victory over Cerberus. On 26 April Jason and the Argonauts processed through the streets, on 27 April the comedy of Jason and Medea was performed in the Playhouse and after that there was a firework display depicting Jason and the capture of the Golden Fleece. On 28 April Jason and the Argonauts again processed in triumph through the streets for the running at the ring. On 29 April there was the ballet of the Banquet of the Gods, the Judgement of Paris and the Rape of Helen. On 30 April the challenge for the running at the quintain was published and the opera *Achilles and Polixena* was performed. On 1 May the two opposing sides in the running at the quintain emerged from two different locations – Agamemnon and his thirty heroes from the Zeughaus, or Weapons Store, near the bastion overlooking the Elbe, and Priam and his heroes from the stables. That night the second part of the opera was performed.

At the Feast of St George the following year, 1676, the actual celebration of the investiture was held on 23 April, on 24 April there was another shooting contest depicting the deeds of Hercules and a fencing contest on 25 April. On 26 April the challenge for the tournaments was published and the comedy of the Thessalian King and Jason was performed, followed again by a firework display presenting the capture of the Golden Fleece. On 27 April the running at the ring presented Jason and the Argonauts competing against a group representing the Judgment of Paris, another depicting Hercules and a third the Trojans. There was again the ballet of the Banquet of the Gods, the Judgement of Paris and the Rape of Helen. The tournaments have now increased in number and magnificence. On 29 April there was a double running at the quintain (this meant that two knights ran simultaneously in two separate 'lanes' in the lists) between Priam and Agamemnon. On 30 April there was a foot tournament between the Greeks, Amazons and Trojans. On 1 May the same opera as before, *Achilles and Polixena*, was performed with the second part the next night.

In 1678 the Elector celebrated the anniversary of his investiture for what was to be the last time before his death in 1680. In 1678 a much more extensive account of the Order of the Garter was published in commemoration of the occasion by Johann Caspar Horn, bringing its history up to the reign of Charles II.[28] We have three sources for the festivities themselves. By far the most extensive is the huge volume of manuscript documents in the Court Chamberlain's papers. They have now swollen to roughly 200 folio sides.[29] Bound with the copy of Horn's history preserved in the SLUB in Dresden is the printed account of the firework display that took place on 25 April.[30] On the blank pages at the back of this work is a manuscript account of the festivities eight and a half pages long by an unknown writer.

The festivities started on 20 April with the reception of the English ambassador, who was again Sir William Swan ('Wilhelm Schwan', as the Court Chamberlain's papers call him on folio 64a). Johann Georg II had the same medal struck as in 1671 and merely changed the date.[31] On 23 April as usual there was a ceremonial re-enactment of the installation of Johann Georg II in the Order of the Garter in the Riesensaal in the Palace. (It is with this aspect that the manuscript account at Hist.Sax.C.146, misc.2 is mostly concerned.) Present were Johann Georg III, Moritz von Saxony-Zeitz and Christian von Saxony-Merseburg. In attendance was Samuel Benedict Carpzov. On 24 April there was a running at the ring with thirty-two contestants, among them the aforementioned noblemen. As the score sheet shows (folio 192a), Johann Georg was a rather unsuccessful participant in this event, with only one hit in contrast to his son's five. The firework display again took as its theme Jason and his capture of the Golden Fleece. In a speech printed in the account Jason tells the company that he will show them his victory over the fire-spitting oxen and the poisonous dragon and how he tamed the latter and sowed their teeth, before fighting the enemies which sprang up from them. A manuscript in the Court Chamberlain's papers (folio 321a) gives a list of the fireworks that were let off and in what order. After the very extensive celebrations of 1675 and 1676 this almost comes across as low-key.

But the consistency of the imagery is clear. Jason and Hercules, the ancient heroes, are precursors of St George, the Christian hero. St George is the defender of his people against all harm and evil. He also in some sense represents Christ and in the Saxon context he is clearly the champion of Lutheranism. Johann Georg, by virtue not just of his position within the state but by virtue of his name, is a latter-day St George, a heroic warrior. From the early presentation of himself as Jason in 1650 and as Mars in 1653 the image has merely become intensified and consolidated.

On the tenth anniversary of his election as Garter Knight, that is, in 1679, Johann Georg II had a commemorative medal struck showing himself on the obverse in armour wearing the garter and the George. The motto of the Order is engraved on the reverse.[32] Even on the medal struck on the occasion of his funeral and designed by Wolf Kaspar von Klengel which presents Johann Georg as Elector, the garter and the motto appear.[33]

Johann Georg also had himself portrayed in his Garter robes by H. W. Schober (Figure 33). The full-length portrait in gouache shows the Elector before a swagged, fringed and tasselled curtain that dominates the top half of the picture. On a table behind his left arm we see a mass of feathers and the actual Garter itself. In front, virtually engulfed in the billowing cloak and robes, stands Johann Georg, his pinched face framed by his full-bottomed wig, the Great George at his breast, the collar of the Order and the jewelled sword important accents in the picture. The robes seem to be wearing the Elector, rather than the other way about.

The Fabrication of an Image 149

Figure 33. H.W. Schober, Johann Georg II in his Garter robes. Gouache. Rüstkammer, Dresden. Inv. No. I 447. Deutsche Fotothek (Andrich).

In the preamble to Gabriel Tzschimmer's *Durchlauchtigste Zusammenkunft* of 1680, the massive festival book discussed below, there is an engraved waist-length portrait of the Elector by Philipp Kilian after Schober (Figure 34). The Elector is framed by a laurel wreath surmounted by the Electoral hat, and below the wreath we have the motto of the Order of the Garter – 'Hony soit qui mal y pense' – and the Garter arms. In the most extensive official publication of his reign, designed to

Figure 34. H.W. Schober, engraved portrait of Johann Georg II with the Garter motto from Gabriel Tzschimmer's *Durchlauchtigste Zusammenkunft* (1680).

disseminate and immortalise his cultural achievements, Johann Georg is presenting himself as a Garter Knight.

Other portraits of Johann Georg II either present him as Elector or as warrior. An example of the latter is the knee-length portrait in oils by Johann Fink, depicting the Elector as a man in his prime, perhaps soon after his succession to the Electorship. It shows him in full armour, holding a marshal's baton, with his helmet on a table behind his right arm. The helmet is lined with scarlet, the plumes on it are scarlet and so are the Elector's sash and sword belt. The Elector's clenched left fist, placed prominently at his waist, and his resolute countenance convey the impression of military strength and decisiveness. The curtain that provides a backdrop to the figure is pulled aside at the Elector's left shoulder to reveal a bust of the god Mars on a high plinth.

Later portraits show an increasingly pinched and emaciated figure exuding a kind of grim determination to cling to power. A striking example is the full-length gouache, again by Schober, of the Elector in full armour and wearing the Lesser George. His right hand grips the marshal's baton, which he is supporting on the table, his left hand rests on the head of a huge dog. The size and animal vitality of the dog stand in marked contrast to the wizened face of the Elector, whose thin lips are as always tightly pressed together. The appurtenances of war look quite out of place under such a face. We have only to contrast this depiction with portraits of his soldier son Johann Georg III, whose ruddy complexion and bursting good health appear wholly appropriate to his soldier's garb. Johann Georg II's presentation of himself in this guise is a willed image.

Johann Georg II as Nimrod

A further strand in this image is that of Nimrod, the great hunter, founder of Nineveh, builder of the tower of Babel. Johann Georg began to elaborate this persona for himself in the 1660s, the first occasion being the celebration of an important dynastic event, namely the wedding in October 1662 of his daughter, Erdmuthe Sophie, to Christian Ernst, Margrave of Brandenburg-Ansbach. The festivities lasted from 18 October until 13 November[34] and the theatrical presentations are discussed in the next chapter. At the heart of the celebrations was a huge tournament lasting a full five days from 27 to 31 October inclusive. This was the running at the ring of Nimrod and the Planets. The bridegroom appeared as Jupiter, the Sun and Venus, Moritz of Saxony-Zeitz as Mars and Mercury and Johann Georg III, brother of the bride, as Diana. Each so-called invention had its own festival car and a large group of suitable supporters. Diana was accompanied by hunters, foresters and satyrs, Mars by soldiers of many nations, the Sun by the months and Time, Mercury, as discussed in chapter 4, by miners, smelters and minters, and so on. But the whole was presided over by Nimrod assisted by Belus, Assur and Amraphel, that is, by Johann Georg II himself, riding into the lists on the first day in a triumphal car. The firework display for this wedding again depicted Jason and the capture of the Golden Fleece, a persona already associated with him, as we have seen.

Johann Georg II again appeared as Nimrod in 1672 at the family gathering or Albertine summit conference known as the 'Vertrauliche und Fröliche Zusammenkunfft' (the Confidential and Joyful Gathering) held in Dresden from 4 to 23 February. This time he presided over a running at the quintain in which the contestants were Babylonian and Assyrian heroes.[35] In 1678 for the next family gathering of the Albertines in Dresden, the so-called 'Durchlauchtigste Zusammenkunft' (Most Noble Gathering) Johann Georg II yet again played the role of Nimrod, assisted by thirty-six Babylonian princes, competing against the seven Planets (the Sun, the Moon, Mars, Mercury, Venus, Jupiter and Diana).[36] In the plates to the elaborate printed account of the festival discussed below, Gabriel Tzschimmer's *Durchlauchtigste Zusammenkunft*, we see Nimrod on a throne in Roman dress and wearing a plumed helmet, holding a baton and riding on a Roman chariot with a winged lion holding a globe in front (Figure 35). He is accompanied by four Roman spear-bearers. This tournament was held in the new Riding School, but on the first day, 4 February, the contestants processed through the streets of Dresden, with each of the seven planets on a festival car. The same festivities again presented a firework display depicting the deeds of Hercules.

The next year, 1679, Johann Georg II celebrated the Peace of Nijmegen in November by again appearing as Nimrod in a running at the ring and at the quintain on 4 November. In this tournament the six oldest monarchs in the world – Nimrod, Nebuchadnezar, Cyrus, Alexander the Great, Julius and Charlemagne – ran against the six planets.[37] On this occasion also, there was a firework display and a shooting contest under the aegis of Hercules.

Nimrod plays a prominent part in the mythology of the four ancient kingdoms. He is the first king of the first kingdom, that of the Assyrians or Babylonians. Gabriel Tzschimmer published a translation in 1676 of the best-known account of the four kingdoms, that by Sleidanus.[38] Sleidanus, in Tzschimmer's German, describes Nimrod as a mighty hunter and as the builder of Nineveh and writes: 'Die Schrifft nennet

The Fabrication of an Image 153

Figure 35. Johann Georg II as Nimrod in 1678. Engraving from Gabriel Tzschimmer's *Durchlauchtigste Zusammenkunft* (1680).

ihn einen gewaltigen Jäger/ und eignet ihm also eine Macht und Gewalt. Andere nennen ihn den Saturnum...'[39] (The Bible calls him a powerful hunstman and thus power and force are inherent in him. Others call him Saturn). In part II of Tzschimmer's *Durchlauchtigste Zusammenkunft* Nimrod is described as the founder of the first monarchy in the book of Daniel by the will of God and as the builder of the Tower of Babel. In the tournaments in which Johann Georg II appears as Nimrod he is above all a warrior king, doing battle against heroes and planets. In his challenge or 'Cartell' in 1678, for instance, Nimrod presents himself as being a great conqueror, the epitome of bravery.[40]

The theme of the four monarchies has a long association with the Albertines.[41] But there is a particular significance in its use by Johann Georg II in that it is a direct reference to his position within his family and his status as first-born, for Nimrod and the seven planets appeared for the first time in Dresden as the theme of the running at the ring to celebrate his own christening in 1613.

This tournament took place on 27, 28 and 29 June 1613. On the first day was the procession of Time and the Seven Planets in the courtyard of the Palace in Dresden. This is documented in a very large oil painting by Daniel Bretschneider the Elder[42] which we know was hanging in the stables in Dresden in 1671, clearly identified by its legend as depicting the tournament for the christening.[43] In the painting a huge figure of

Father Time with his scythe precedes the Planets, each with its own float – the Moon, Mercury, Venus, the Sun, Mars, Jupiter and Saturn. On the next two days we have the procession of Nimrod with Cyrus, Alexander the Great and Julius Caesar.[44] The presentation of the same subject matter in 1678 makes specific reference to the painting of 1613. The order in which the planets appear in the procession is different in 1678 but individual iconographic details are repeated, for instance, the depiction of Saturn riding on a cloud accompanied by skeletons or the huge figure of Father Time.

But Johann Georg II does not just re-use this motif in 1678. He makes it into the organising principle for one of the most splendid celebrations of his entire reign, the only festival to be dignified by being published in a festival book. For the first time all the parts of a month-long festival are subordinated to one overarching programme. The theme is first announced in the challenge thrown down to Nimrod and his supporters by the Seven Planets on 3 February. This is followed by the 'Musicalische Opera und Ballet von Wirckung der Sieben Planeten' performed in the Elector's Playhouse with nine different settings by Johann Oswald Harms and discussed in chapter 6. Nimrod and the other monarchs of the four kingdoms, Cyrus, Alexander the Great and Julius Caesar, appear in the scene devoted to Jupiter. The heart of the celebrations is the running at the ring and at the quintain mentioned above, which again is that of Nimrod and the Seven Planets. Two of the planets, namely Diana and Mercury, are later the patrons of other tournaments. The entire celebrations, then, are one huge homage to his own birth. Since his title and, allied to that, his constitutional role within the Empire as Imperial High Marshal and Elector are dependent on the accident of his birth, to remind his family and his court of his own christening is to draw attention to his own status and power.

Publishing the image

When examining such a carefully crafted image the extent to which it is promulgated is of paramount importance. The ballet – for instance, that staged in 1653 – is the ultimate internal presentation, both presented and seen by members of the court only. Its relevance is purely within that context. The Garter Festivals, in as much as they involve a foreign power and ambassadors from that power, have a wider resonance, but it is still limited to a relatively small elite group.

Within the city of Dresden festivals were made public to the citizens in two ways. The first was the procession through the streets which was an essential part of all tournaments. The actual contest may then have vanished into the courtyard of the Palace or into the Riding School. The costumed participants, the floats, the groups of musicians paraded through the centre of the city. In 1675, for instance, this was maximised by having the two opposing groups in the running at the quintain emerge from two different locations, before meeting for the actual contest. The firework display takes the public accessibility of festivals one stage further, though early modern displays often resembled dramas to be viewed close to rather than explosions of great height as in the modern firework show.

But to ensure a wider resonance and a greater permanence a ruler must construct permanent physical monuments in the form of architecture and permanent textual ones in the shape of publications. Johann Georg II took care of these two aspects also, in two publications which link festivals and architecture with the business of governance.

Weck's account of the city of Dresden (1680)

In 1680, the year of Johann Georg II's death, two large, illustrated folio volumes relating to the Dresden court appeared in Nuremberg. Both were published by Johann Hoffmann and printed by Sigismund Froberger and they complement and mirror each other. Notwithstanding the difference in their titles, they both address the twin topics of architecture and festivals. They are Anton Weck's *Der Chur=Fürstlichen Sächsischen weitberuffenen Residentz= und Haupt=Vestung Dresden Beschreib: und Vorstellung* (Description and Presentation of the Famous Capital City and Principal Fortress of the Elector of Saxony) and Gabriel Tzschimmer's *Die Durchlauchtigste Zusammenkunft/ Oder: Historische Erzehlung/ was der Durchlauchtigste Fürst und Herr/ Herr Johann George der Ander/...Bey Anwesenheit Seiner...Herren Gebrüdere/ dero Gemahlinnen/ Prinzen/ und Princessinnen/ zu sonderbahren Ehren/ und Belustigung/ in Dero Residenz und Haubt=Vestung Dresden im Monat Februario, des M.DC.LXXVIIIsten Jahres An allerhand Aufzügen/ Ritterlichen Exercitien, Schau=Spielen/ Schiessen/ Jagten/ Operen, Comoedien, Balleten, Masqueraden, Königreiche/ Feuerwercke/ und andern/ Denkwürdiges aufführen und vorstellen lassen...* (The Most Noble Gathering, Or, A history of what processions, knightly exercises, plays, shooting contests, hunts, operas, comedies, ballets, masquerades, *Königreiche*, firework displays and other notable things the Most Noble Prince and Lord Johann Georg II presented and had performed in Dresden in February 1678 in the presence of his brothers, their consorts, sons and daughters to honour and delight them).

That both of these works are official publications is clear. Weck, archivist and confidential secretary to the Elector, begins with a preface in which he states that Johann Georg II asked him in person to write the book and then gave him a written commission dated 16 January 1679. Weck further claims that he could not have completed the book without the Elector's assistance. Immediately after the preface he reproduces an instruction from Johann Georg to his Vice-Chancellor and Gentleman of the Chamber Johann David von Oppel to vet Weck's text before it is printed, to communicate any necessary changes to the author and to inform the Elector if it is suitable for publication. Von Oppel's official assessment of the book (the 'Gutachten') dated 28 November 1678 follows next and in it he claims that he did indeed read and comment on the content and that Weck adopted some of his suggestions. This in turn is followed by the actual licence to publish (the 'Privilegium') accorded by Johann Georg II to Johann Hoffmann in Nuremberg dated 25 August 1679.

And what does this highly official publication offer the reader? The title claims that it is a description of a princely city. Part I, the most heavily illustrated section of the work, indeed fulfils this brief. It describes the position of the city, its origins and its name, but then takes us on to the Electoral Palace, tracing its expansion through history. Successive engravings show us the original simple 'Burg', then the Renaissance Palace created by Moritz, the first Albertine Elector, with its elaborate *sgraffito* decoration on the façade, the relief of the Dance of Death which once adorned the Palace, the portal created by Christian I in 1589 and the Hausmannsturm erected by Johann Georg II in 1676. Inside the Palace itself, Weck singles out the Council Chamber, the Riesensaal, the coin collection, the *Kunstkammer*, the Anatomy Chamber and the Library. Chapter 7 describes the Chancellery or administrative building, constructed during the reign of Elector August between 1565 and 1567. Chapter 8, accompanied by two engravings, is concerned with the stables, the riding arena, the saddlery and the armoury (Figure 36). Here Weck takes us through the stables themselves, the ancestral portrait gallery and the various storage facilities for arms, armour, costumes and other objects relating to festivals and tournaments of all kinds. The weapons store and the Hunting Lodge are also described in detail. Weck then provides in chapter 11 a summary of all the other buildings associated with the court, from the playhouse to the food store, from the Powder Tower to the marble workshops. These buildings fall into three groups. The largest contains those buildings relating to princely magnificence such as the stables, the playhouse and the 'Invention-Haus'. The next contains those of a strictly utilitarian kind such as the cooper's workshop, the weapons store or the food store, and the third those buildings, few in number, associated with administration and government – the Council Chamber and the Chancellery, for instance. Six chapters are devoted to describing the principal buildings and monuments of the city, but the city appears as an appendage to the court, its skyline dominated by the Palace and the Belvedere.

But this is merely the first one hundred pages of a 548-page account. Part II, of roughly the same length, gives a history of the Margraves of Meissen, later Dukes and Electors of Saxony, describes the organisation of government in Saxony, then of the government of the outlying villages and finally extra responsibilities of the city, such as oversight over the hospital of St Materni. Part III covers all kinds of church matters. These first three parts are of roughly equal length – about a hundred folio pages each. Part IV, beginning on p. 305, is two and a half times as long as any one of the first three parts and gives an overview of historical events in Dresden from 1366 to the 1670s, but heavily slanted towards events of importance for the ruling family, as we might expect.

Chapter I deals with religious celebrations, such as jubilees, and Chapter II with births and baptisms, beginning with that of Duke Albrecht, the father of the Albertines, and continuing to close to the time of writing. Here Weck sometimes gives details of the tournaments and other festivities held to mark these events. Chapter III lists princely marriages and again the festivities are sometimes described. Weck even reprints part of August Buchner's text for the ballet *Orpheo* danced for the wedding of Johann Georg II in 1638. Chapter IV describes visits by foreign dignitaries, beginning in 1348, and chapter V funerals with details of many of the cortèges. Sessions of the Landtag are the subject of chapter VI, while chapter VII narrates changes in power relations between the Elector and the city. The occasions when the citizenry swear allegiance to the Elector are given in chapter VIII with a series of reprinted documents. Local laws, privileges, statutes and customs are the subject of chapter IX, again supported by a welter of documentation, and chapter X deals with those customs and laws which have partly fallen into desuetude. Chapter XI describes wars and sieges and chapter XII various disasters.

Weck could simply have chronicled the architecture of Dresden. He chooses instead to present that architecture as a kind of stage on which the drama of power is played out. His book is as much a history of the Albertines as it is an account of a city, as much a depiction of government in action as of a series of buildings. These latter are not seen as separate from the events that go on in them but are rather presented as emanating from the events and simultaneously reflecting them. The organic development of the city reflects the succession of dynastic events. Festivals bulk so large in his presentation because they are the first and most immediate way in which important dynastic, political and historical events are made manifest. But the festivals in their turn are made manifest in the buildings. The 'Most Noble Gathering' of 1678, the summit conference of the Albertines in Dresden, is celebrated among other things by a running at the ring and at the quintain (Nimrod and the Seven Planets). For this the new indoor riding school was inaugurated (Figure 36). The festival celebrates the event, but the building for evermore commemorates the festival held there.

Tzschimmer's festival book (1680)

Mention of the 'Most Noble Gathering' or *Durchlauchtigste Zusammen-kunft* brings us to the second great official publication mentioned above to come from the same printer and publisher in Nuremberg. The author is Gabriel Tzschimmer, Electoral Councillor. This enormous folio tells of the month-long carnival celebrations held in Dresden in February 1678 for the Albertine gathering just mentioned. It was organised by Johann Georg II and attended by August of Saxony-Weissenfels, Christian of Saxony-Merseburg and Moritz of Saxony-Zeitz, together with their wives and families. The poem to Tzschimmer by Johann Christian Schumann at the beginning of the work states that he is publishing his account on the orders of the Elector.

Such large-scale festivities in Dresden lasting a month were common during the reign of Johann Georg II. Indeed, there were at least seven major festivals between 1660 and 1672 similar to that of 1678 that were equally worthy of being the subject of a printed book: the carnival festivities held in 1660, 1661, 1663 and 1665, the wedding in 1662 of Erdmuthe Sophie, Johann Georg II's daughter, to Christian Ernst of Brandenburg-Ansbach, the blessing of the recently christened Johann Georg IV in 1669 and the gathering of the four ducal brothers at carnival time in Dresden in 1672. But, as pointed out above, it is this festival whose overarching programme of Nimrod and the Seven Planets is a re-creation of the tournament held in Dresden in 1613 for Johann Georg II's christening. The festival is Johann Georg's monument to his own pre-eminent position within his family as heir. The festival book is the monument to the festival.

Tzschimmer's account is a remarkable publication by any standard. It consists of two parts: Part I constitutes the festival account proper, fills

Figure 36. The Indoor Riding School and the Shooting Gallery in Dresden. Engraving from Anton Weck's *Der Residentz- und Haupt-Vestung Dresden Beschreib: und Vorstellung* (1680).

316 folio pages and contains thirty huge foldout plates plus the title engraving and four portraits; while Part II consists of what Tzschimmer calls his 'Kurtze Erläuterungen' or brief notes, which fill 562 folio pages, each containing almost twice as many words to the page as those of Part I. Part II is embellished with a further seventeen small illustrations. While the two parts are separately paginated, Tzschimmer instructs the binder that they are to be bound together and that the index he supplies to this mammoth volume refers to both parts equally.

Much of what is included in the first part of Tzschimmer's account closely resembles the immense volumes of documentation in the Court Chamberlain's files in the Archive in Dresden.[45] The lists of horses, of food to be provided, of numbers of guests to be accommodated, the processions set out on the page in the way they are going to appear on the street, the seating plans, and all the rest – these are part of the necessary paperwork prepared beforehand by the court bureaucracy when the festival is being organised. Into the same file after it is all over go the score sheets and lists of prizes given to the tournament contestants, copies of the printed challenges, the summaries of the plots of plays and operas. Just such a conglomeration of material is included in Part I of Tzschimmer's account. The journey and arrival of each individual guest, the ceremonial connected with the reception of each one and the details of where they are lodged is listed. Tzschimmer describes the church service for the feast of the Purification of the Blessed Virgin, noting the fact that Johann Georg II himself composed a setting for the Psalm 'Laudate Dominum omnes Gentes'. He gives us the seating plans and diagrams for each banquet, the cartels or challenges for the numerous tournaments, he details the processions into the field before each tournament, the numbers of horses ridden, the names of participants and the roles they played, he gives us the score sheets, he lists the prize money. The texts of the arias of the operas are included, ballets, shooting contests, hunting parties and plays are described, a 'Königreich' is presented, that is, a masquerade in which various courtiers represent all the functions, trades, etc. in the kingdom from the king down to the lowliest subject. The whole finishes with the description of the firework display.

What brings the documentation to life, though, is the number, quality and size of the engravings with which it is interspersed. The whole work begins with an engraving by J. A. Boener after Samuel Bottschild of 'Eintracht' (Concord) supported by Hercules (representing strength and courage), History, Truth, Wisdom and the goddess Pallas Athena.

Concord refers to the harmony between the ducal brothers, which is supposed to dominate their meeting. As we saw in chapter 1 when we discussed the series of dramas on the theme of Joseph and his brothers, this does not necessarily correspond to reality. Then, among the usual dedicatory material, there are engraved portraits of the four ducal brothers by Philipp Kilian, in the case of Johann Georg himself at least after H. W. Schober, accompanied by laudatory poems. Then come the engravings, many of them foldouts of considerable size, depicting the actual festivities. What is remarkable about them is that, apart from the schematic rendering of the entry of the guests into Dresden, the nine engravings of Johann Oswald Harms's sets for the ballet and opera entitled 'The Confluence and Influence of the Seven Planets' and the engraving of the firework display at the end, all the other plates depict the city and the Palace in considerable detail as the backdrop to the festivities, so much so that one could almost say these are architectural engravings as much as representations of festivities. An engraving of the muster of the Dresden militia, for instance (No. 1), is an opportunity for a large and detailed depiction of the stables and its *sgraffito* decoration. A second engraving of the muster shows us the troops marching six by six down the Wilsdrufferstrasse from the Altmarkt with every detail of the houses clearly presented. We even have a purely architectural engraving of the Electoral Playhouse (No. 5) with no figures in it at all. The most splendid of all the engravings – that of the procession of Nimrod and the Seven Planets before the running at the ring and the quintain – folds out to some 80 by 133 cm. In three rows one under the other the engraving depicts the floats and accompanying combatants and supporters winding their way through the Dresden streets towards the Riding School, so realistically depicted that one can recognise some of these locations today, in spite of the destruction wrought by subsequent wars (Figure 37). The procession of huntsmen with their cages of animals crossing the Elbe from the Hunting Lodge or Jägerhaus on the north bank to the south side of the river, where Diana's running at the ring is to take place, is a magnificent opportunity to depict not only the bridge but the bastions too (No. 20). Two further engravings show us the same procession further along on its journey. No fewer than five plates of hunts held in the Palace courtyard give us clear and detailed depictions of that space, as well as of the many animals alive and dead.

If Weck's architectural work turned out in practice to be just as much a history of the festive culture of Dresden and the government that the festivals represented and celebrated, Tzschimmer's work turns out to be

Figure 37. The procession of the seven planets moves through the streets of Dresden in 1678. Engraving from Gabriel Tzschimmer's *Durchlauchtigste Zusammenkunft* (1680).

just as much an overview of the architecture of Dresden as a description of a festival.

It is worth reminding ourselves that the *genre* Tzschimmer's work ostensibly belongs to is that of the printed festival book. This is an extremely numerous and by this date well-established category of texts, produced by most courts throughout Europe. Festival books often consist of a description with or without illustrations commissioned by the same patron who commissioned the festival itself. The books differ widely in format, length, degree of magnificence and artistic pretension.[46] But Dresden has no tradition of printed festival books at all, nothing to rival the great series of works to emerge from the court of the Dukes of Württemberg in Stuttgart before the Thirty Years' War, for instance. Apart from the so-called 'Pritschmeister' accounts in verse by such writers as Wolfgang Ferber[47] and Georg Pezold[48] earlier in the seventeenth century for the christenings of the sons of Johann Georg I, before the reign of Johann Georg II there is only the short and not very imposing printed account of the wedding of Maria Elisabeth, the daughter of Johann Georg I, and Friedrich, Duke of Holstein-Gottorp, in 1630.[49] For the same festival in 1678, the libretto of the ballet, *Ballet von Zusammenkunft und wirckung derer VII. Planeten Auf Ihr. Churfl. Durchl. Zu Sachsen großem Theatro gehalten Den 3. Februarii Anno 1678* was printed by Melchior Bergen, the court printer, in Dresden, embellished with Harms's nine engravings of the sets and a huge foldout engraving of the theatre itself. This resembles the illustrated libretti we know from Munich from the 1650s and 1660s, for instance.[50] But Tzschimmer's work is not only unusual within the Dresden context. It is safe to say that there is no festival book like it in any language between 1500 and 1800.[51] That it should emerge from a court which has no tradition of published festival books at all makes it all the more astonishing.

What makes the work so unusual? First, its length, which has been described above. Second, the size and quality of its illustrations, many of them large foldouts. But what makes the work unique is the quantity of discursive and explicatory material included by Tzschimmer alongside the actual description and documentation.

On seven occasions in the course of the first part of his book, ostensibly just an account of the festivals held in 1678, Tzschimmer adds to the pure description by giving us the benefit of his ideas on such themes as the usefulness of dance, drama and its history, the invention of guns, the moral lessons to be learned from the myth of Daphne, the fickleness of fortune, the impossibility of bringing back the past and the dissimulation of folly. In nearly every case these are brief articles of a couple of pages but it is this kind of moral explication which the second part of Tzschimmer's book provides. This immense treatise, roughly four times as long as the festival description to which it is attached, is divided up into six main sections. The full title of just one of these chapters, namely, chapter II, will suffice to give the flavour of Tzschimmer's method:

> II. Genauere Erklärung Uber [sic] Der Sieben Planeten und
> Des Nimrods Aufzug/ Auch was unter selbigem Welt-Monarchen/ und seinen im Reiche nachgefolgeten 36. Häuptern/ so wohl an geist- als weltlichen Dingen denckwürdiges fürgegangen: Ingleichen von allerhand Materien/ und zur Moralität dienenden Sachen.[52]

> [A more precise explanation of the procession of the seven planets and of Nimrod; also of what happened in both the spiritual and secular sphere in the reign of that monarch and his thirty-six successors, as well as all kinds of information and matter conducive to morality.]

Under these headings Tzschimmer groups a whole range of disparate material. The chapter on the planets gives rise, among many other things, to a discussion of the seven liberal arts, that on Mercury to a parade of the various metals, human qualities and trades he is associated with and so on. Some factual information of an encyclopaedic kind is delivered. For instance, the well-known list of tournaments beginning in 1487 taken from Georg Ruexner's *Turnierbuch* (Simmern 1530) and appearing in virtually every work of the age which deals with tournaments, makes its appearance here too. But the predominant tendency is to deliver a moral disquisition on each and every aspect of each and every theme, to draw out the moral meaning from the subjects the author is addressing. For instance, the chapter on Diana and hunting brings the author in due course to the subject of dogs. One of Tzschimmer's typical comments refers to the 'dog in the manger', who wishes to prevent others having what he cannot enjoy himself. A moral reflection on this kind of behaviour then follows. The chapter on Mercury has a sub-section on the many-eyed Argus, which gives Tzschimmer the chance to talk about adultery: 'Das gestohlne Wasser ist süsse/ und das verborgene Brod niedlich. Gleiche Bewandnis hat es mit der Hurerey' (Stolen water is sweet and hidden bread attractive. So too is it with adultery).[53]

A *sententia* such as this is characteristic of Tzschimmer and he begins virtually every paragraph with one. From these generalities he can develop his ideas in the same generalised and unoriginal way. As he says in his poem to the reader at the beginning of Part II of his book, the entertainments of Part I are evanescent but can be made to have a lasting value if they give rise to moral reflection:

> Kein Ding scheint hier so schlecht/
> Es hat gleich seinen Nutz und lauter gute Lehren/
> Und eben bloss darumb ist dieses Buch gemacht/
> Der Sitten=Lehre Grund und Tugend draus zu fassen.[54]
>
> [Nothing here appears so lowly but it has its use and provides many good lessons. And this is solely why this book was written, so that the fundamentals of the moral law and virtue could be drawn from it.]

Tzschimmer is using the depictions of Part I as the *pictura* of an emblem, of which Part II provides the *inscriptio* and the *subscriptio*. This general interpretative emblematic trend is followed through in the illustrations of Part II, most of which are vignettes accompanied by a moral *inscriptio* consisting of a rhyming couplet. By making the festivals the material for moral reflection Tzschimmer justifies their extravagance and gives them great importance and great permanence. The festival may have passed away but the moral improvement drawn from its contemplation will be lasting and will transcend the political moment. Among the subjects Tzschimmer discourses on are the nature of kingship, of right government and the role of the courtier.

These remarks are not interesting in themselves. Indeed, one is tempted to say that Tzschimmer is incapable of an original idea or of expressing any thought in an interesting manner. What is interesting though is that, just as Weck combined architectural description with an account of the government of Saxony and an overview of festivities in Dresden, so Tzschimmer, who is describing festivities and in doing so also conveying much information about the architecture, should also discourse on the nature of government. These three elements are presented as indissolubly connected.

As Ulrich Schütte has pointed out in a recent article, splendour or magnificence is one of the attributes of God Himself, one of the ways in which He manifests Himself to his people.[55] The ruler, as God's representative on earth, therefore has a duty to reflect this aspect of God's nature by being splendid himself. To exhibit splendour is one of the tasks of government, and the ruler complies with this requirement in peacetime principally in two ways: through the festivals and courtly pastimes he stages and through the architecture he commissions. These two aspects are both outward manifestations of his purpose and that of his court, which can be summed up as the representation of power. They thus both fulfil the same function, both are governance made manifest and Weck and Tzschimmer show themselves well aware of this.

But the festivals discussed in this chapter have to be seen against the background of theatre in general at the Dresden court – the round of ballets, operas and dramas that marked the cycle of the court's year, the ducal birthdays and namedays, the carnival season, the dynastic events such as weddings and christenings, the visits of other princes. They are all part of a coherent festive culture that only comes into being in Dresden after 1650 with the arrival of peace and which forms part of an immense effort of self-presentation by the man who commissioned the great works by Weck and Tzschimmer, Johann Georg II. This is the subject of the next chapter.

6
The 'Recreation of the Spirit': Theatre at the Dresden Court during the Seventeenth Century

In chapter 1 we discussed the tradition of native German drama in Dresden in the shape of the biblical plays which were performed continually during the seventeenth century, at least up to the death of Johann Georg II in 1680. In chapter 5 the firework drama emerged as one of the theatrical forms used by Johann Georg II in the elaboration of his personal iconography. This chapter considers three types of theatre which were foreign imports – the theatre of the strolling players, the *ballet de cour* and the opera.

'Pleasant inventions and entertaining histories' – foreign drama at the Dresden court

In 1620, with no indication of publisher or place of publication, there appeared a volume of ten plays and six interludes in German entitled: *Engelische Comedien und Tragedien. Das ist: Sehr Schöne/ herrliche und außerlesene/ geist= und weltliche Comedi und Tragedi Spiel/ Sampt dem Pickelhering/ Welche wegen jhrer artigen Inventionen, kurtzweilige auch theils warhafftigen Geschicht halber/ von den Engelländern in Deutschland an Königlichen/ Chur= vnd Fürstlichen Höfen auch in vornehmen Reichs= See= und HandelStädten seynd agiret und gehalten worden*... (English Comedies and Tragedies. That is: selected delightful and splendid sacred and secular tragedies and comedies which, because of their pleasant inventions, entertaining and also partly true histories, have been performed by the English players at royal, electoral and princely courts in Germany, as well as in important imperial, port and trading cities...).[1]

These English players were troupes of professional actors who, by that time, had been coming from England to tour the continent for forty years. The closing of the theatres in London because of plague and Puritan agitation, and the intense competition brought about by a surfeit of good actors and the popularity of the boys' companies, led such troupes to seek their fortune on the continent in considerable numbers. They were often led by highly proficient professional actors who had already made a name for themselves on the London stage and contained notable composers and musicians. They made the rounds of the important fairs from the Netherlands to the Baltic, covering the principal cities of Central Europe in between. Whenever possible, they spent the winters, when travelling was all but impossible, at the court of a great lord. Initially they acted in English but as time went on, they took more and more Germans into their companies and began to use German as their principal language.

'Englische Komödianten', or English players, went first to the Danish court and are recorded there as early as 1579/80 and again in 1585 and 1586. Because of the close connections between Dresden and Denmark, Dresden was one of the earliest courts they visited in the Empire.[2] Elector August had married Anna, Princess of Denmark (1532–85), in 1548 and, half a century later, in 1602, their grandson Christian II married Hedwig, Princess of Denmark (1581–1641). In 1586 five English musicians and actors came to Dresden from Copenhagen, namely, Thomas King, Thomas Stephens, George Bryan, Thomas Pope and Rupert 'Persten' and were employed by Christian I.[3] Once court life resumed in Dresden after the regency consequent upon Christian's unexpected death, English players began to appear at court very regularly. They performed in Dresden in 1600, 1601, 1605, 1609, 1610, 1617, 1626–27 and 1630–32. According to Fürstenau, they were particularly popular with the Dowager Electress Sophie, the widow of Christian I, and it was for her and her sons that they performed in 1600.[4] John Spencer's troupe came to Dresden for the first time in 1605 on the recommendation of the Electress of Brandenburg (Spencer was famous for his comic persona of 'Hans Stockfisch'). These actors appeared again at court in 1609, recommended to Christian II by the new Elector of Brandenburg, Johann Sigismund, in a letter written in Königsberg on 11 July 1609.[5] According to Limon, Spencer's company may have stayed in Dresden for almost two years before going back to the service of the Elector of Brandenburg in 1611. Cohn quotes another letter of recommendation for Spencer from the Elector of Brandenburg to Johann Georg I dated 16 April 1613.[6] We see the regard in which his players were held from the fact that they performed for the visit of Emperor Matthias and his family to Dresden in 1617. It appears to have been the Electress who paid them.[7] A notable troupe that performed in Dresden a generation later was that of John Green, which spent the season 1626–27 at court and was brought to Torgau for the wedding of Sophie Eleonore and Georg, Landgrave of Hessen-Darmstadt, in 1627.

The Thirty Years' War had an adverse effect on the ability of the players to travel safely. This drove many of the oldest established English companies, such as those of Robert Browne, John Green, John Spencer and Richard Jones, back to England, and cities with a long record of visits by the companies show a break of twenty years or more.[8] In Dresden, the gap occurred after 1632, the year Saxony entered the war. Strolling players had visited for the carnival season in 1630, during which the wedding of Maria Elisabeth, second daughter of Johann Georg I, and Friedrich III, Duke of Holstein-Gottorp, was celebrated. Players are attested in Dresden again on 26 September 1632 and on 3 February 1633.

The criticism voiced by Fynes Morrison, the Elizabethan traveller, in 1592 when he saw a troupe of English players perform at the Frankfurt fair is only valid for the very early period, when the troupes were still feeling their way on the continent. By the early seventeenth century we know from various reports that the players used splendid costumes, were accomplished actors and used music and dance effectively. Since they often stayed for long periods at a court, it is also thought that the stages they erected in the great hall of a palace were not inferior to what they would have used in England. Indeed, at Kassel from 1604–5 and in Warsaw from 1637 the players had access to permanent theatres, in the latter case with changeable sets and *periaktoi*.[9]

Whereas German actors were taken on by the English companies practically from the beginning, English troupes were still performing at German-speaking centres in the late 1650s. George Jolly is known to have played in Vienna in 1659 but is generally considered to be the last of the English actor-managers. In the decades before that, English troupes were still frequent visitors. Some of them, such as those led by Robert Reynolds, the famous Pickelhering, or by William Archer, had survived the war years by moving to areas where peace had been declared. Archer was permanently attached to the court of Vladyslav IV at Warsaw from 1636 to 1640.[10] When the Puritans closed the theatres in London during the 1640s, such continental stays became all the more necessary for the actors' survival.

Archer's troupe was taken over by William Roe, who joined forces with another of the leading actors in Archer's company, John Wayde.

This company is of particular interest to us because it played for the Dresden court in the autumn of 1646. Their return again illustrates how aware the players were of the progress of the war, for Saxony had made peace with Sweden at Kötschenbroda in the autumn of 1645 and was thus officially out of the war. On 8 July 1645 Roe had applied to play in Utrecht at the annual fair there. He then went to Cologne and from there to Dresden in September 1646,[11] before returning to Cologne in April 1647. This company is subsequently attested Königsberg, Gdańsk, at the Frankfurt fair, in 1649 and 1651, in Prague and even in Stockholm, where it performed for Queen Christina. According to documents in the Gdańsk archive dating to 1647, at that date the company was a thoroughly international one, containing English, Dutch and German players.[12]

What plays did these players perform? The answer is a wide range of the Elizabethan and Jacobean repertoire in German prose versions, many of which were performed again and again during the course of half a century or more. This is one of the most interesting examples of cultural transfer in the early modern theatre, all the more fascinating in that this English repertoire was not transmitted by scholars via the printed page but by the actors themselves. It is clear from the examination of their repertoire that many English plays reached a German-speaking audience before they had got into print in England and that the actors therefore brought the scripts with them in manuscript.

A list of the plays performed during the 1626–27 season in Dresden gives us an idea of the range of works presented.[13] *Romeo und Julia, Julius Cäsar, Hamlet, Prinz in Dänemark* and *Lear, König in England* are all versions of plays by Shakespeare. *Hamann und Esther* and *Der verlorene Sohn* (The Prodigal Son) are biblical plays on standard themes and could have been based on English or German originals. They and the plays *Fortunato*, a version of Thomas Dekker's *Old Fortunatus*, and *Jemandt und Niemandt* (Somebody and Nobody) had already appeared in the first published collection of the works of the 'Englische Komödianten' in 1620 mentioned above. The last-named is based on the anonymous English play *Nobody and Somebody with the true Chronical Historie of Elidure, who was fortunately three several times crowned kinge of England*. *Dr Faust* and *Barabas der Jude in Malta* are in all probability versions of Marlowe's *Dr Faustus* and *The Rich Jew of Malta* respectively. *Von der Märterin Dorothea* is thought to be based on Philip Massinger's *The Virgin Martyr* (written in 1620, printed in 1622).[14] *Die Komödie von Amphitrione* may be based on Damme's Dutch translation of Plautus and *Herzog von Florenz* on Philip Massinger's *The Great Duke of Florence*.

Though this was not actually published until 1636, it was given a licence to publish in 1627. This bears out the point that the players brought it with them in manuscript. Creizenach speculates that the play called *König in Spanien und Viceroy in Portugal* could be the first part of Kyd's *Spanish Tragedy*. He identifies *Von der Crysella* as *Patient Grissil* by Henry Chettle and thinks that *Herzog von Ferrara* is John Marston's *Parasitaster or the Fawn*. *König in Dänemark und König in Schweden* is possibly identical with George Peele's *Sir Clyomon and Sir Clamdydes* and *Orlando Furioso* with the play of that name by Robert Greene. *Tragoedia von Hyronimo Marschall in Spanien* is again the perennially popular *Spanish Tragedy* by Kyd. *Tragicomoedia von einem König in Aragonien* is probably Robert Greene's *Alphonsus, King of Aragon* and *Comoedia von Josepho dem Juden in Venedig* is a version of Shakespeare's *The Merchant of Venice*. *König in England und König in Schottland, Herzog von Mantua und Herzog von Verona, Cristabella, Vom behenden Diebe, Vom Herzog in Venedig und des Königs in Cypern Tochter, Vom alten Proculo, Vom Gevatter, Vom Graf von Angiers* and *Vom reichen Manne* (A play on the Dives and Lazarus theme) have so far not been identified. According to Fürstenau, these plays were mostly put on in the Kirchsaale (Room near the church) or in the Eckgemach (Corner Saloon) in the Palace in Dresden.[15] Clearly, Shakespeare's history plays dealing with the 'matter of Britain' were not thought to be of interest to foreign audiences, but dramas of power and kingship, political plays and plays with melodramatic and bloody plots were perennial favourites.

In 1630 the players performed *Ritter Arsidos, Agrippina, Isabella Konigin in Klein-Britannien* and *Prinz Celadon von Valentia*. Creizenach speculates that *Ritter Arsidos* could be *The Two Noble Kinsmen* attributed to Shakespeare and Fletcher or else that it is a version of an older piece, *Palamon and Arsett*, from the year 1594. In 1631 the players visited again, performing *Julius Caesar*, the *Tragödie vom Königreich Portugal, Vom Könige aus Gracia, Könige aus Frankreich, vom Königreiche Vanentia, Vom Könige in Engellandt, Von der Constantia Königs in Arragonien Tochter* (this could be the anonymous *Mucedorus*, first printed in 1598, according to Creizenach) and *Vom Prinzen Serale und der Hyppolita*.[16] On 26 September 1632 the court attended a performance of the *Tragicomedy of Marsiano und Cariel* and on 3 February 1633 one of *Orlando furioso*, a play performed in Dresden in the 1626–27 season.

After a break of some thirteen years, the players were back in Dresden in 1646. If we examine the list of performances and troupes, we find that Roe's troupe was not the only group performing at court that year. Fürstenau mentions a performance of the Prodigal Son on 1 July 1646 with a masquerade at the end and a dumb show before each act, for instance. Since this is a typical biblical topic, it is possible that it was put on by local German actors, as performances later in the autumn clearly were. On 9 October, for instance, the so-called 'Freybergische Springer', indicating a group of players from the Saxon mining town of Freiberg, put on a biblical play entitled 'eine comödie von Erschaffung der Welt' (A Comedy of the Creation of the World). On 17 October another relatively local German troupe, the so-called 'Erfurter Springer', performed a play on another favourite biblical topic, the parable of Dives and Lazarus ('Vom reichen Mann und dem armen Lazaro') in the Riesensaal in the Palace, followed again by a masquerade and a peasant dance.

Roe's troupe of highly experienced international actors had a somewhat different repertoire. On 12 September 1646 they performed the *Comödie vom stolzen Jünglinge Eucasto* (Cohn thinks this is a version of the English *Everyman*[17]) and on 13 September 'Eine Tragödie vom Lorenz' (A tragedy of Lorenz). Creizenach thinks that this is probably by Hans Sachs, though Limon speculates that it is Kyd's *Spanish Tragedy*.[18] The account quoted by Fürstenau adds that it was followed by 'ein Tanz von 8 personen wie bei den reichen Juden von Malta von den Engelländern getanzt' (the Englishmen did a dance for eight people like the one danced after *The Jew of Malta*). Whether it was the same troupe or not, on 15 October the court saw *Romeo und Julia*, followed by what is called a 'Mascarada' danced by eight people, rounded off by 'die singende Komodi mit der Kiste' (the sung comedy with the chest). This latter is probably Ayrer's *Pickelhering in der Kiste*, a version of the English comedy *Singing Simpkin*.[19] On 16 October the court saw the *Tragödie vom Herzog aus Burgund und den beyden Rittern Neudeckern und Lamprechten* and two 'Mascaradentänze' and on 19 October the comedy of two Pickelherings (or clowns) and their two naughty wives.

The trends established in the first half of the century were maintained. At the double wedding in 1650 English players performed *Diocletiano und Maximino* (possibly based on Beaumont and Fletcher's *The Prophetess*)[20] and the *Tragico-Comedia vom Könige in Cypern und Herzog von Venedig* (The Tragicomedy of the King of Cyprus and the Duke of Venice). Since the second of these plays was in the repertoire of the company of William Roe and John Wayde when they performed in Prague in December 1651, it is very likely their company which was in Dresden in 1650.[21] They had already played for the court in 1646 and were in Prague in 1649, so this makes it all the more probable. On the same occasion in 1650 the Electoral family put on *Tragico-Comoedia von ihren Vier Königlichen Brüdern in Engellandt* (The Tragicomedy of the Four Royal Brothers in England), which Creizenach says is a version of *Nobody and Somebody*.

During the reign of Johann Georg II, strolling players acted frequently at court, and plays from the English repertoire were just as prevalent as before. In 1660 the court saw 'Vom edlen Fremdling, so der Engländer übersetzt' (Of the Noble Stranger, translated by the Englishman, that is, Lewis Sharpe's *The Noble Stranger*[22]) and in 1661 'The Moor of Venice' (clearly *Othello*), and 'The Duke of Florence', presumably based on the play by Massinger mentioned above.

But we see the way that these foreign works are integrated seamlessly into the native tradition. In the celebrations held in 1669 at carnival time in honour of the christening of Johann Georg IV, for instance, the old favourite 'Trauer=Spiel von der heil. Märterin Dorothea (the Tragedy of the Holy Martyr Dorothea, based on Massinger's *The Virgin Martyr*) was performed alongside three biblical plays, the two-part 'Historia von Saul und David', 'die Geschichte von der Hebräischen Heldin Judith und dem Holoferne' and 'die Tragödie von Joseph und seinen Brüdern' (the History of Saul and David, the History of the Jewish heroine Judith and Holofernes, and the Tragedy of Joseph and his brothers. This latter work was discussed in chapter 1).[23] But the innovation is a play called 'Freuden=Spiel vom Jupitern und Amphitryonen' (Comedy of Jupiter and Amphitryon). From the printed programme it seems likely that this is a version of Molière's play first performed in Paris the previous year.

Molière in fact became one of the most popular dramatic authors to be performed at court during the next twenty years. The man largely responsible for this was Johannes Velten (1640–92), a new and much more highly educated kind of actor-manager. He was born in Halle and studied at Wittenberg, taking his Master's degree in 1661. He was thus justified in calling himself 'Magister Velten', as he frequently did. He joined the troupe of Carl Andreas Paulsen, the Hamburg actor-manager, and married Paulsen's daughter, eventually taking over management of the troupe himself. From 1678 on they were allowed to call themselves the 'Chursächsische Comödien-Bande' or 'the Elector of Saxony's Players'. Velten set about introducing the French repertoire into Germany, translating and performing many French plays for the first time there. Among these were no less than ten comedies by Molière, eight of which he presented for the first time in German. He published his translations in Nuremberg in 1694 under the title *Histrio Gallicus comicosatyricus sine exemplo*. Among the Molière plays he presented are *Tartuffe* (performed on 27 June 1677 in the Eckgemach in the palace in Dresden at 8 o'clock in the evening), *Amphytrion* (in 1678 for the 'Durchlauchtigste Zusammenkunft'), and *Sicilien ou l'amour peintre* ('Sicilianer'), *l'étourdi* ('Mascarilias') and *L'Avare* ('Der alte Geizhals'), all in 1684. In 1688 he presented *George Dandin ou le Mari confondu* in the Taubescher Garten (and Rechenbergischer Garten outside the Pirnaischer Tor), with *Tartuffe* again. In 1690 at the carnival season his troupe performed for the court at Torgau, presenting *Le Médecin malgré lui* ('Der gezwungene Arzt'), *Le Cocu imaginaire* ('Glückliche Eifersucht'), *L'école des hommes* ('Die Männerschule'), *Le Misanthrope* ('Die Verdrießlichen'), *Le bourgeois gentilhomme* ('Der bürgerliche Edelmann') and *Don Juan*. Velten also presented Corneille's *Le Cid* ('der gottlose Roderich').

Velten's was not the only troupe to act at the Dresden court, nor was he the only one to perform works from the French repertoire there. In 1674 what are called 'the Hamburg players' put on a wide range of material, including versions of *L'Avare* and *Le Cocu imaginaire*. In 1679 they performed a version of Scarron's *Jodelet ou le Valet maître* and Molière's *Les Fourberies de Scapin* as 'Scabins Betrügereien'. This troupe also performed works from the English repertoire and, like Velten, plays by Calderón.

For Velten did not restrict himself to Molière, whose plays formed merely a part of a large repertoire. He continued, for instance, to put on Shakespeare. In July 1676 he presented the 'Comedy of the Four Identical Brothers' (possibly *The Comedy of Errors*), while *König Lear aus Engellandt* was performed during dinner on 22 July 1676 for the Electress's birthday. *The Taming of the Shrew* (under the title 'Von der bösen Katharina' – Wicked Katharine) was put on in May 1678, as was a play called 'Die Jungfrau' (The Maiden), which could be a version of Beaumont and Fletcher's *The Maid's Tragedy*.[24]

Velten also had at least six plays by Calderón in his repertoire.[25] As early as 1669, his troupe performed Calderón's *Lances de amor y fortuna* in Danzig under the title of 'der künstliche Lügner'. Velten revived this play for the Dresden court in 1676 as 'Glück und Liebstück oder Aurora und Stella' and again in 1680 in Torgau as the 'Comoedie von Aurora und Stella', based, Sullivan says, on the Dutch version by Hendrik de Graef. In 1684 Velten presented Calderón's *El alcaide de sí mismo* in Dresden as 'Sein selbst gefangener' and in 1690 at Torgau *La vida es sueño* as 'Prinz Sigismund in Pohlen'. Velten also presented Calderón's *El mayor monstruo los celos* as 'Das größte Ungeheuer oder der eifersüchtige Herodes' (The greatest monster or jealous Herod) in Dresden in 1692. Sullivan is of the opinion that Velten knew and used Giacinto

Andrea Cicognini's Italian version of this play rather than the original Spanish.[26]

It should also be pointed out that in Torgau in 1690, Velten put on the now lost tragedy 'Wallenstein' by August Adolph von Haugwitz and *Papinianus*, the historical tragedy by the Silesian dramatist Andreas Gryphius.

In 1692 the troupe was dismissed by Johann Georg IV and in the same year Velten died. A distinguished episode in the development of drama at the Dresden court thus came to an end.

'Heroes changed to flowers'[27] – ballet at the Dresden court

Simultaneously with the developments charted above, another foreign theatrical genre was gradually being introduced at the Dresden court. This was the *ballet de cour*. In contrast to the professional theatre of the strolling players, whose performances the court attended, the ballet was a genre performed by the court for the court with the assistance of professional dancing masters.

Dance had always been one of the social forms practised at court. It readily lent itself to dressing up, to masquerading, to what was called in English 'disguising'. But in 1581 a new theatrical form came into existence in France, born, as Marie-Claude Canova-Green points out, from the fusion of four separate art-forms: music, dance, poetry and painting, and based on the theories of Antoine de Baïf's Académie de Musique et de Poésie in Paris.[28] This new form is the *ballet de cour*, the first known example of which is the *Balet comique de la Royne* by Balthasar de Beaujoyeulx, staged in the Louvre in September 1581. As mentioned in chapter 4, *ballet de cour* was supposed to mirror in dance the movements of the planets.

The genre took some time to manifest itself in the Empire and the first known ballet to be performed at a German court was *Die Befreiung des Friedens* (The Liberation of Peace), staged in 1600 in Darmstadt at the court of the Landgrave of Hessen-Darmstadt and in its theme of liberation clearly indebted to the *Balet comique*.[29] Smart speculates that it may be the proximity to France that made Darmstadt the innovator here. Interesting in our context is that the Dresden court was closely connected with this first known German ballet. The designer of both the scenery and costumes for it was none other than Giovanni Maria Nosseni, the architect whom we have encountered as a central figure at the Dresden court since 1575 and one who played a major part in the design of its festive culture. We can therefore assume that knowledge of this new form had reached Dresden by 1600. The other German court at which ballets are known to have been performed before the Thirty Years' War was Stuttgart, with ballets staged there in 1609, 1616, 1617 and 1618. Dresden had associations with this court too, for the first wife of Johann Georg I was a Württemberg princess, Sibylle Elisabeth, whom he married in 1604.

One can see a precursor of that combination of dance and drama which is essential to ballet in a danced insert in a play performed in Dresden in 1614. This is the 'Tragoedia der zweyer mächtiger Städt Rohm und Alba' (the Tragedy of the Two Powerful Cities Rome and Alba)[30] which was performed for the christening of August, later August of Saxony-Weissenfels, one of the sons of Johann Georg I. This is a five-act drama in couplets of iambic tetrameter, preserved in manuscript in the SLUB in Dresden (Mscr.Dresd.M 225). Towards the end of the third act there is a kind of interlude in which six young men and six young women wearing laurel wreaths and bearing olive branches come on. Each one in turn utters a six-line speech praising Rome and Roman youth and then the twelve take their places for a dance in three movements. These movements are referred to in the manuscript as 'clausulae' and the choreographic plans are given on folios 46A, 47A and 48A. The third 'clausula' is repeated (48 B). It is entirely possible that there were other dance inserts in performances at Dresden that we no longer know of.

Both Fürstenau and Prölß, the author of another standard work of nineteenth-century scholarship,[31] state that the first recorded performances of actual ballets took place in 1622, 1624, and 1625 and link them to the journey of the court dancing-master Gabriel Möhlich to Paris in 1620. The involvement of the Electress, Magdalena Sibylle of Brandenburg, the second wife of Johann Georg II, is also thought to be a factor. We do not know which of the several kinds of French ballet which had evolved by this date they were based on – that is, whether they were dramatic ballets, *ballets-mascarades*, melodramatic ballets or belonged to the recently created type, the *ballet à entrées*.[32] Smart points out that the celebrations in Torgau in 1627 for the wedding of Sophia Eleonore, daughter of Johann Georg II, and Georg, Landgrave of Hesse-Darmstadt, included a ballet entitled *Atalanta und Meleager*. Whether the Darmstadt connection is relevant here must remain an open question. Schütz and Opitz's *Dafne*, performed on the same occasion, also concluded with a balletic scene. *Ballet de cour* would thus appear to be established by the 1620s, but the genre was still not clearly defined.

Scholars are fairly unanimous, for instance, in stating that *Orpheus und Eurydice*, performed in the Riesensaal for the wedding of Johann

Georg II and Magdalena Sibylle of Brandenburg in 1638, and called a ballet by its author, is in fact an opera. The text was by August Buchner, the music by Heinrich Schütz and the choreography by Gabriel Möhlich. It was a five-act dramatic work with spoken, sung and danced portions, but in which dance played a secondary role.[33]

Johann Georg II must have been closely involved in devising the birthday entertainment for his father presented in 1648, since his four-year-old daughter Erdmuthe Sophie danced in it.[34] This is labelled a 'musical representation' and again combines song and dance. Mercury as herald ushers in Jupiter and Apollo. They praise the Elector and then the three Graces give him a wreath. The gods and the Graces sing an aria together and this is followed by a ballet of gods and goddesses. This clearly has similarities with the ballet, but we have to wait for the 1650s for the full-scale cultivation of ballet on the French model.

In this, the poet David Schirmer (1623–86) played a major role.[35] He arrived in Dresden in 1650 as the Elector's new librarian, a post he held until 1682. We know that he functioned as a court poet until 1663, writing occasional verse in honour of members of the Electoral family as well as libretti for a considerable number of dramatic works: ballets, musical entertainments, operas and firework dramas. It is possible, indeed likely, that some of the ballets performed in Dresden after 1663 are by him. He was also writing considerable quantities of accomplished lyric poetry of his own, which he published in two collections, both brought out by the court printer Melchior Bergen.[36] The most famous of these is the *Poetische Rosen-Gepüsche*, or 'Poetic Rose Bushes', poems from this collection appearing in most standard anthologies of German seventeenth-century verse.

In 1663 Schirmer had another collection published by Bergen, this time of his occasional poetry and dramatic works for the court, under the title *Poetische Rauten-Gepüsche* or 'Poetic Rue Bushes', the rue being the emblem of the Albertines.[37] It is dedicated to the Elector and his family and presents the texts in chronological order, so that we see the work of a busy court poet over a period of more than thirteen years. The first works in the collection show him already writing for the court before his official appointment in 1650, for it begins with a poem and the text of music performed at table on the occasion of Johann Georg I's visit to Wittenberg in 1646 and a 326-line poem on the birth of Johann Georg III written in 1647.

His first documented dramatic work for the court was the musical entertainment performed on 6 March 1650 for Johann Georg I's sixty-fifth birthday. It was put on in the Kirch-Saale in the Palace in Dresden and was brief enough to be performed before dinner.[38] In it, Time, Eternity and the Four Ages of Man honour the Elector in what was probably a kind of dramatic cantata. We do not know who wrote the music for this piece but during his time in Dresden Schirmer collaborated with Schütz, Philipp Stolle, Adam Krieger and Christoph Bernhard.

Later in the same year Schirmer had a chance to show what he could really do at the festivities in honour of the double wedding of Christian and Moritz, the two younger brothers of Johann Georg II, to two Schleswig-Holstein princesses. The celebrations lasted from 17 November until 11 December 1650 and Schirmer's contribution to them was considerable. First of all, he wrote the libretto for a firework display in celebration of Connubial Felicity.[39] The text describes two triumphal arches representing this quality of and the three Graces of 'Holdseligkeit' (Graciousness), while the firework display itself presented Hymen, Concordia, Fides, Comitas, Constantia, Prudentia, Foecunditas, Laetitia and Auctoritas, favourable, not to say necessary virtues for a successful marriage. Each of these virtues has two lines of verse to say and Schirmer points the contrast between Peace – one of the leitmotifs of the festivities – and Fire in a skilful poem consisting of four six-line stanzas.

On 1 December a much more impressive firework display was held, a firework drama on the theme of the Capture of the Golden Fleece ('Feuer=Werck/ von Eroberung des Güldenen Fellis') for which Schirmer wrote the libretto.[40] As pointed out in chapter 5 in our discussion of the Jason theme, this is a four-act drama in which Jason conquers the oxen, ploughs the field, kills the dragon and sows its teeth, and finally wins the Golden Fleece.

Firework dramas had not been that numerous in Dresden up to this point, largely because of the war.[41] An early example is the display let off in Dresden for the wedding of Maria Elisabeth, daughter of Johann Georg I, and Friedrich, Duke of Schleswig-Holstein, in 1630.[42] It depicted the Virtuous Knight being led by Virtue past a number of vices and temptations until he can pass through a triumphal arch into a mount which leads to the crown of glory. Another example of the genre is the firework drama organised by Johann Georg II for his mother's nameday on 22 July 1635. It was let off from the city ramparts overlooking the Elbe.[43] In the cartell Mercury announces the struggle of his father Jupiter against the forces of evil, as represented by Pluto, Proserpina and Circe who are vanquished by the fire of Jupiter. The initials of the Electress, Magdalena Sybille, glow against the sky. Anton Weck describes a firework drama for the wedding of Johann Georg II and

Magdalene Sibylle of Brandenburg in 1638.[44] Here the Mount of Virtue and Constancy is attacked by the Vices, by Heresy and by Mutability until they are repulsed.

Schirmer also wrote a text to be set to music as the bridal party went to table[45] and three songs to be sung by Poesis, Musica and Mimesis respectively.[46] But his most important contribution, and one which pointed most clearly to his future contribution to court culture at Dresden, was his text for what he calls the 'Singend Ballet' (sung ballet) *Von dem König Paris und der Helena* (King Paris and Helen) put on on 2 December in the Riesensaal.[47]

Like Buchner and Schütz's *Orpheus und Eurydice* of 1638, this work is also now generally regarded as an opera rather than a ballet, because only one scene in each of the first four acts was actually danced.[48] It is the synthesis of the two forms that is particularly interesting. In the Riesensaal a fully-fledged Baroque stage was constructed. It was technically advanced enough to be able to present four full scene changes. Act I takes place in the banqueting hall of the gods, Act II on Mount Ida, Act III in the Temple of Venus, Act IV before Troy in flames and Act V in the clouds. Cupids fly above the table of the gods in Act I, Mercury appears in a flash of lightning in Act II, there is a sea scene in Act III, Apollo appears in the clouds in Act V. The full height of the Riesensaal was therefore used to accommodate the flying machinery necessary for these special effects.

The work opens with the banquet of the gods celebrating the wedding of Thetis and Peleus. This banquet mirrors that of the Wettins in celebration of their double wedding. The gods have Chiron, their chamberlain, to organise things, who calls on the satyrs to bring on the produce of the earth (game), the sirens and Tritons to bring on fish and Ganymede and Hebe to pour the wine. This celebration of married love is interrupted by the ballet in which Eris comes to sow discord by setting the goddesses in competition with each other. Paris appears on Mount Ida in Act II, there is a ballet of shepherds and shepherdesses and Paris makes his choice of Venus. This introduces the element of illicit and destructive love, which is the theme of Act III. The capture of Helen is depicted in a ballet, there is a sea-battle, and Proteus prophesies the forthcoming war. The act ends with Troy in flames. Act IV presents martial combat – a mounted tournament by means of a ballet and a foot combat with drums and the letting off of muskets. Hecuba and Andromache lament their dead and a second ballet scene presents Ascanius, Aeneas and Anchises and the flight of Aeneas to Italy. Act V represents the coming of peace. Apollo prophesies the new Roman

Empire and links Aeneas and his line to the 'behertzte Sachsen' (the courageous Saxons), the successors to Rome. Apollo ends with a paean of praise to the Wettins, whose dynastic continuity is to be assured by the marriages being celebrated. The themes of married and illicit love, of war and peace are thus neatly linked in a work which ends with a glorification of the Albertines. The three generations of Johann Georgs are implicitly present in Ascanius, Aeneas and Anchises, and Schirmer links them explicitly six months later in a sonnet for the nameday of the Elector (the feast of St John the Baptist on 24 June). Johann Georg III, aged three and a half, was given his own show in 1650, for Schirmer's final work for the wedding was a short ballet in which Johann Georg III appeared as Cupid in the Riesensaal in what is called the 'Moren Gefängnüß' – the Moor's Dungeon.[49]

The next important dynastic event in Dresden was the wedding of Johann Georg I's third daughter Magdalena Sybille, in 1652. She had married Christian V, Prince Elect of Denmark, with great pomp in 1634.[50] Her husband had died in 1647 and there was no issue, so she returned to Dresden. She became engaged to her Ernestine relative, the widowed Friedrich Wilhelm of Saxony-Altenburg, in 1651 (marked by Schirmer with a madrigal and an ode to be sung before the engagement banquet), and married him in 1652. For this wedding Schirmer again wrote a lengthy opera libretto, *Der Triumphirende Amor* (Love Triumphant). He labels it a 'Singespiel', rather than a ballet. It had to be held in Altenburg, because the Dresden court was in mourning for one of the brides of the 1650 wedding. It tells the story of Jupiter and Io, is less ambitious scenically and lacks the historical and prophetic sweep of *Paris und Helena*. This is the story of Jupiter's love for Io, Juno's jealousy and Pan's parallel love for Syrinx. All of this demonstrates the power of the god Amor and takes place in a pastoral setting. There are four ballet scenes – of Io and her nymphs in Act I, of satyrs in Act II and of shepherds and shepherdesses in Act IV, while Act V finishes with a *grand-ballet* of the gods and goddesses. Apart from a chorus of praise to the bridal couple at the end and the tale of the beautiful Ruta (or rue, emblem of the Wettins) told by Argus in Act IV, there is none of the portentous political reference of the previous ballet. This is a court entertainment on the theme of love for a much more low-key occasion, the second marriages of two people no longer in the first blush of youth (the bride was 35, the groom 49), rather than the court officially presenting itself and its ambitions.

Schirmer is only one of a number of poets writing for the court at this time, as the performances during 1653 illustrate. Schirmer wrote a *divertissement* for the nameday of the three Johann Georgs on 24 June and a pastoral entertainment in five acts, *Liebes=Spiel der Nymphen/ und Satyren* (The Amorous Game of the Nymphs and Shepherds). Ernst Geller, who signs himself 'Kammerschreiber', or Confidential Clerk, to Johann Georg II, is the author of the *Arkadischer Hürten-Aufzug* (Arcadian Procession of the Shepherds),[51] a version of Guarini's *Il pastor fido*, also performed on 24 June, and the political ballet held on 3 July discussed in chapter 5 appeared under the name of the dancing master François Dolivet, though the text could have been by Schirmer. It would be interesting to know how fierce the competition was between the various court poets but at least in 1655 we see Geller and Schirmer collaborating on a joint publication. It is called *Entwurff Etlicher Chur- und Hoch=Fürstlicher Ergötzlichkeiten* (Sketch of some Electoral and Princely Entertainments)[52] and collects together the texts or plot summaries of the entertainments put on during the month of March 1655 in honour of the seventieth birthday of Johann Georg I and the visit of his son-in-law, Georg, Landgrave of Hessen-Darmstadt, who also had a birthday in the same month. The collection contains the summaries of three plays and a simple ballet by Geller, and a firework display, *Der Riese* (The Giant), and two ballets by Schirmer. Schirmer reprints his own texts in the *Rauten-Gepüsche*.

With these two ballets by Schirmer, the *Ballet der Glückseligkeit* (the Ballet of Happiness) and the *Ballet des Atlas* (The Ballet of Atlas), the French *grand ballet à entrées* became firmly established at the Dresden court. Unlike the dramatic ballet, the *ballet à entrées* does not have a plot or tell one unifying story. Instead, it consists of a sung introduction announcing the general theme and a series of *entrées*, usually four in number, loosely connected to this theme or illustrating aspects of it. Each *entrée* consists of a series of dances presented by costumed figures. There are sung arias between the *entrées* which give the dancers time to change costume. The pleasure of these ballets for the audience lies in the dance and in the costumes. The *ballet à entrées* did not demand elaborate scenery, but could be performed in a great hall. This kind of ballet was that being practised at the very same time at the court of Louis XIV. After a break in the 1640s, during which Mazarin concentrated on introducing Italian opera to the French court, this type of ballet began again in Paris in 1651 with the *Ballet de Cassandre*, which marked the debut of the young Louis XIV. He appeared in his most famous ballet role in 1653 as the Sun in the *Ballet de la Nuit*. It is central to the *ballet à entrées* that the ruler himself should appear in it. In concentrating on the *grand ballet à entrées*, therefore, the Dresden court was closely in step with contemporary developments at the French court. If the *Ballet der Glückseligkeit* and the *Ballet des Atlas* are modelled on the ballets of Louis XIV, the political ballet presented two years earlier in 1653 and discussed at length in chapter 5 follows the earlier tradition of the ballet under Richelieu, who promoted explicitly political ballets in the 1630s and 1640s, focusing in several of them on the political position of France at the time.[53]

The *Ballet der Glückseligkeit* and the *Ballet des Atlas* were put on in the Steinern Saal on 6 and 17 March respectively. The first, in honour of Johann Georg I, was danced by Johann Georg II's wife, Magdalena Sibylle, and had six *entrées*: Pantalons, the son of the gods ('der Junge Printz', probably Johann Georg II) with Victoria and the three Graces, the four seasons and a final *grand-ballet* of nymphs and shepherds. Landgrave Georg's wife, Sophie Eleonore of Saxony, and five of their seven daughters also took part. This heterogeneous mixing of comic, serious and pastoral characters is typical of the *ballet à entrées*. The *Ballet des Atlas* was danced by the Electoral Princess and Sophie Eleonore, again in honour of Landgrave Georg. Atlas, played by the dancing master François Dolivet, danced the first *entrée* and was followed by the four continents with associated groups in ethnic costumes. Some of the exigencies of the job of librettist on such an occasion become apparent in Schirmer's preface to the reader in which he apologises for the appearance of Egyptian women in the *entrée* of America. This is not his ignorance, he says, but those 'who most graciously wanted it thus had their reasons – for it is well known in which part of the world Egypt has always been situated'.[54] One can almost hear him gritting his teeth!

Judith Aikin points out that Schirmer's friend, the composer Phillip Stolle, who had collaborated with him on the song-book *Singende Rosen* (Singing Roses), left Dresden for the court of August of Saxony-Weissenfels at Halle in 1654. She thinks it possible that Schirmer wrote up to four texts for performance in Halle during Stolle's time there, *Die Hochzeit des Thetis* (The Marriage of Thetis, 1654) (now lost, so the nature of the text and even its existence is in doubt), *Charimunda*, a prose play with songs (1658), the operatic *Verwundeter und wiedergeheilteter Löwe* (The Wounded Lion, Later Cured, 1658) and the opera libretto, *Himlischer Gnaden-Segen* (The Blessing of Heavenly Grace, 1660). The only one of these to appear under Schirmer's name is the operatic *Verwundeter und wiedergeheilteter Löwe* and that has never been linked to Halle before.[55] Whatever the likelihood of these attributions, once the period of mourning for Johann Georg I was over and his son had been installed as Elector and Imperial High Marshal in 1657, Schirmer produced two new ballets for the Dresden court in 1659, the *Ballet der Tugend* and the *Ballet der Hygia*.[56] In the *grand-ballet* of the first of these works the Muses and gods spell out the name of the Princess. This is surely Erdmuthe Sophie, Johann Georg II's only daughter, so it is possible that it was performed on her birthday on 15 February 1659. It is relatively ambitious in its technical demands, since six sets are called for (a landscape, a vineyard, a garden, a copse, Mount Parnassus and the clouds), flying machinery is also necessary and there are thirty-seven characters. The *Ballet der Hygia*, perhaps in honour of the Electress's nameday on 22 September, is much smaller in scale, with about twenty characters in all in three *entrées* and no changes of set.

The next great dynastic event in Dresden was the wedding in October 1662 of Erdmuthe Sophie and Christian Ernst, Margrave of Brandenburg-Bayreuth. The opera staged on this occasion is discussed below. A few months later, in February 1663, the newly-weds came back to Dresden for the carnival season and Schirmer wrote two ballets for this visit: the *Ballet des Jahres* performed in the Riesensaal on 15 February, Erdmuthe Sophie's birthday, by her brother, and the *Ballet der Tugenden und Laster*, performed on 3 March in the Steinern Saal, in which Erdmuthe Sophie danced the part of Virtue. The *Ballet des Jahres* begins with the winds distributing the programmes from the clouds and the ballet then takes us through the four seasons and the twelve months of the year. We note again and again the four-part structure so characteristic of the *ballet à entrées*.

Schirmer's collection of his texts for the court, the *Rauten-Gepüsche*, does not take us beyond 1663. Aikin maintains that Schirmer's involvement with ballet in Dresden did not end there. Johann Georg II had a new playhouse, the 'neues Komödienhaus', built in 1664 and Aikin states that 'Dresden recycled a number of Schirmer's works on the new stage'.[57] This is a problematic statement on two counts. First, though two of the ballets performed in the 1660s, the *Ballet der Glückseligkeit* (1667) and the *Ballet des Atlas* (1669), have the same titles as earlier ballets by Schirmer, the texts, which exist in printed form, have nothing whatsoever in common with Schirmer's texts. They are new texts, not recycled versions of earlier texts by Schirmer. Second, while the second *Ballet der Glückseligkeit* (1667) was performed in the theatre, most of the other ballets were performed in the Riesensaal in the Palace.

The *Ballet der Glückseligkeit* was performed on 5 March 1667 for the arrival in Dresden of Johann Georg III's new bride, Anna Sophia, Princess of Denmark.[58] Though it is clearly attributed in the title of the printed libretto to the dancing master François de La Marche, there is a sonnet by Schirmer at the back addressed to the bride and it is at least probable that this second *Ballet der Glückseligkeit* is by Schirmer. As befits a stage work, rather than a piece to be performed by the court, professional dancers were drafted in for this performance, in the shape of the dancing masters from Dresden (La Marche himself, George Benteley, Anthonie du Pont and Charles Du Mesniel), from Bayreuth (François Maran) and from Halle (Louis de La Marche). The ballet is in four acts or *entrées*. It is introduced by Comus, the God of Good Cheer and Friendship ('Leutseligkeit und Freundschaft'). The first *entrée* represents the five senses by means of suitable gods and professions (Taste is represented by Ceres and a group of bakers, Smell by Flora and gardeners, for instance), the second the advantages of the body (e.g. Strength, Skill), the third of the spirit (e.g. Wisdom, Eloquence) and the fourth of happiness (e.g. Plenty, Honour, a Happy Marriage). Hymen and Cupid appear on a festival car at the end, Love and Happiness and six gods and goddesses dance in the final *grand-ballet*.

On 21 February 1669 for the festivities for the blessing ('Einsegnung') of Johann Georg IV (he had been christened the previous October), his mother, the Electoral Princess Anna Sophia, danced a *Ballet des Atlas*.[59] Again, this has nothing in common with the ballet of that name by Schirmer from 1655. Indeed, the wooden, jerky nature of the verse suggests that it is not by him. A random example can illustrate this. The 'Arie' of Atlas, sung before his dance at the beginning of the piece, begins as follows:

> Weicht/ ihr feurigen Planeten/
> Die ihr sonsten pflegt zu tödten!
> Es geht auff ein neuer Stern/
> Der mit seinen hellen Stralen
> Kan die Unter=Welt bemahlen.
> Weicht/weicht/weicht und bleibet fern!

[Give way, you fiery planets that usually kill! A new star is rising that can illuminate the underworld with his bright rays. Give way and keep your distance.]

The impossibly bumpy rhythm of the third and sixth lines is not the work of a skilled versifier such as Schirmer and the piece abounds with such clumsiness. Atlas's entrance is preceded by three Cupids who distribute the programmes at the beginning. Then the four continents appear in turn but with different texts and different ethnic groups in a different order from 1655, and the piece finishes with a *grand-ballet* of Apollo and the Nine Muses, instead of the Moors and Moorish women of the earlier work.

On 11 February 1672, for the Albertine gathering in Dresden known as the 'Fröliche Zusammenkunft', Johann Georg III and his wife, Anna Sophia, danced an untitled ballet in the Riesensaal. The printed programme listing the forthcoming entertainments at this gathering refers to it thus: 'ein kluger Tantz ist Ihr Beginnen// zu loben Dero Klugheit Schatz' (a clever dance is your purpose to praise the treasure of your cleverness), so let us call it the 'Ballet der Klugheit' or Ballet of Cleverness for convenience sake.[60] The printed text of the ballet[61] shows it to have four separate themes, one for each of the *entrées*. They are the four elements, the four seasons, the four continents and two virtues and two vices respectively and the work ends with a *grand-ballet* of the Indians. Both Johann Georg III and his wife danced in this ballet and the Dresden dancing master, Charles Du Mesniel, played several leading roles, as he did in the ballet of 1669. The verse here is, however, much more skilful than in that of 1669. There are flowing alexandrines for the two statues which open the piece, rattling dactyls for the windmills that represent the element air, comic dialect verse for the peasants who represent winter, and so on. Clearly this is the work of a highly competent poet and it would not be impossible to conceive of its being from Schirmer's pen.

During February 1678 Johann Georg staged one of the greatest festivities of his reign, the summit conference in Dresden with his three younger brothers, August of Saxony-Weissenfels, Christian of Saxony-Merseburg and Moritz of Saxony-Zeitz, together with their wives and families. Two ballets were performed during these festivities, the *Frauen-Zimmer- und Mohren-Ballet* (The Ballet of the Ladies and the Moors)[62] and the *Ballet von Zusammenkunft und Wirckung derer VII. Planeten* (The Ballet of the Confluence and Influence of the Seven Planets).[63] Aikin is convinced that both these ballets are by Schirmer on the basis of the verse-forms and because they re-cycle themes and ideas to be found in those earlier ballets which we know definitely to be by him. While this is possible, the kind of re-use she mentions is not necessarily conclusive – the association of the dark skin of the Moors with the darkness of night, for instance, is a seventeenth-century commonplace.

The two ballets are different from each other in almost every way one can think of. The *Ballet von Zusammenkunft und Wirckung derer VII. Planeten* is a lavish stage work put on in the theatre on 3 February with nine sets by Johann Oswald Harms, one for the prologue, one for each of the seven *entrées* and one for the *grand-ballet* at the end. One can imagine, in such a setting, the participation of a high proportion of professional dancers, that is to say the dancing masters at the Dresden and other courts. This ballet has the same problem with nomenclature that we have encountered previously in all such large-scale ballets, for, while the separately published libretto calls itself simply a ballet in the title, in his festival book Tzschimmer refers to it as the 'Musicalische Opera und Ballet von Wirckung der Sieben Planeten (Musical opera and ballet of the influence of the seven planets)'.[64] The *Frauen-Zimmer- und Mohren-Ballet*, on the other hand, was performed by the ladies of the court in the Riesensaal in the Palace and is therefore one of those more intimate pieces performed by the court for the court. From the engraving in Tzschimmer's *Durchlauchtigste Zusammenkunft* we can see that the dances were performed in front of a backdrop stretched across the width of the hall (Figure 38). Whether this was changed for every scene we do not know.

Figure 38. Johann Azelt, The Mohrenballett being performed in 1678 in the Riesensaal in the Palace in Dresden. Engraving from Tzschimmer, *Durchlauchtigste Zusammenkunft* (1680).

In content too, the two ballets could hardly be more different. The *Ballet der VII. Planeten*, while a *ballet à entrées* like the *Frauen-Zimmer- und Mohren-Ballet*, has one overarching theme, namely the seven planets and their influence on earth, an idea which links all the various parts of the month-long festivities into one programme. This central idea was announced in the first event of the celebrations, the promulgation of the 'cartel' or challenge for the running at the ring and at the quintain of Nimrod and the seven planets. The cartel was announced to the guests at a banquet on 3 February – the tournament actually took place the next day – and after the banquet they attended the ballet. This focuses on the seven planets: Saturn, Jupiter, Mars, Sol, Venus, Mercury and the Moon. Each appears in turn, with Jupiter presenting Nimrod and the other three monarchs in his *entrée*. During the course of the festivities, other events are under the patronage of planets such as Mercury, Diana and Saturn. Cupid, who claims to be more powerful than any of the other gods, flies down to sing the prologue in a set depicting ruins with the Temple of Venus visible at the back. Each of the other *entrées* presents one of the planets or planetary gods, each of which first appears in the clouds and then flies down at the beginning of the scene. They are in turn Saturn and the miners who appear in front of a rocky mountain containing a working mine (see Figure 27, p. 126), Jupiter and the four monarchs who dance in front of an elaborate arcade leading to a garden, Mars with his soldiers, Amazons and fencing masters in front of the gate and walls of a huge fortress, the Sun with the seasons, the continents and two Spaniards in an Italianate city, Venus with her Cupids, ladies and cavaliers in an Italianate garden, Mercury in front of an arcade with booths behind containing the arts and crafts associated with him – astronomy, alchemy, painting, writing, etc., the Moon in a wood with nymphs, shepherds, fishers, huntsmen and a bear. The piece culminates in the *grand-ballet* in which the set depicts the clouds, out of which emerge all the planets but Saturn, who appears out of the earth (Figure 39). Their chorus is a paeon of praise to the Albertines. The final huge foldout engraving depicts the Electoral Playhouse looking from the stage towards a full auditorium (Figure 40). We see the trumpeters to the right and left of the stage and the Electoral family seated in front. The score of this full-dress stage work, whose composer is uncertain, is preserved in the SLUB.[65] The *Frauen-Zimmer- und Mohren-Ballet*, on the other hand, consists of a series of unconnected *entrées* of a completely heterogeneous character. Fama, presumably the Electress, introduces the ballet. She is followed by eight *entrées* of Indians, shepherds and shepherdesses, old women and winter, Amazons, a

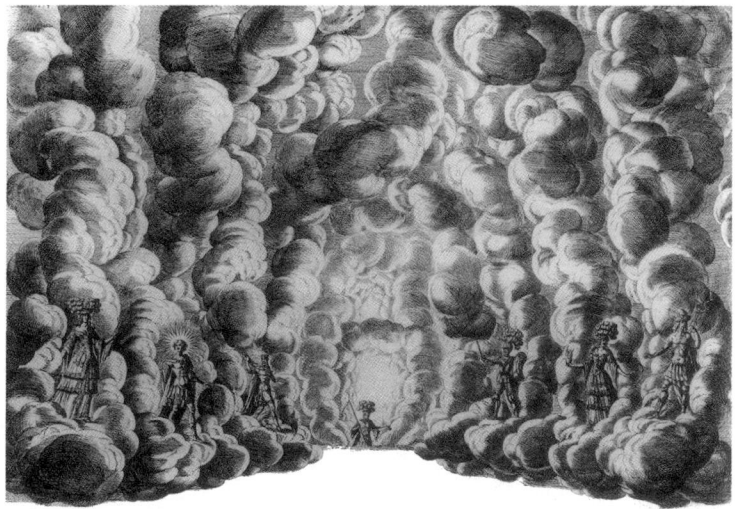

Figure 39. Johann Oswald Harms, The final set for the *Ballet von der Zusammenkunft und Wirckung derer VII. Planeten* (1678). Engraving from the libretto. Deutsche Fotothek (Handrick).

Turk, a Muscovite, a Hungarian and a Pole, Romans, Pantalons and Amouretten. The *grand-ballet* is danced by ten Moors. The text of the arias is in clumsy verse and what interest the piece has can only have resided in the contrast of the different costumes and the choreography by François Maran, the dancing-master at the court of Bayreuth. The quality of the verse could hardly be more different from that of the *Planeten-Ballet*.

The last ballet of the reign was held on 27 February 1679 in the Palace and was entitled *Ballet der vortrefflichen Schäffer und Schäfferinnen*.[66] This is a short pastoral entertainment in which the shepherds and shepherdesses mourn the winter which has robbed them of all greenery, until a young shepherd comes to tell them of the rue (the emblem of the Albertines), a plant that can never be touched by frost or snow.

It is worth noting that the last ballet held at the French court was performed in 1669, the *Ballet de Flore*. It is this work which was witnessed in Paris by the dramatist August Adolph von Haugwitz (1647–1706), the cousin of Friedrich August von Haugwitz, Court Chamberlain in Dresden from 1680. August Adolph von Haugwitz translated and adapted the *Ballet de Flore* as *Flora* (which he called a comedy) and published it in his *Prodromus poeticus* of 1684.[67] We do not know whether Haugwitz's version was ever performed in Dresden or anywhere else (the only

Figure 40. Johann Oswald Harms, The auditorium of the Playhouse in Dresden in 1678. Engraving from the libretto of the *Ballet von der Zusammenkunft und Wirckung derer VII. Planeten.* Deutsche Fotothek (Rous).

dramatic work by Haugwitz which the court is known to have seen is his lost tragedy *Wallenstein*) but at the date of the publication of *Flora* the French court had long since gone over to Molière's *comédie-ballet* and to Lully's *tragédie à musique*.

Johann Georg IV favoured Italian ballet rather than French and in 1691, for instance, a ballet entitled 'Il Tempio d'Amore' was performed at court. His wedding in Torgau in 1692 was celebrated by a ballet with the title 'Le Feste di Cupido'. But Johann Georg IV died in 1694 and his younger brother, best known to posterity as August the Strong, had other ideas, as we shall see in chapter 7.

'Gods among the Saxons'[68] – opera in Dresden

The combination of dance and sung text which we have observed in the works just mentioned shows the close relationship between ballet and that other new form, opera. This came into being in Florence at the very end of the sixteenth century. *Dafne*, with a text by Ottavio Rinuccini and a score by Jacopo Peri and Jacopo Corsi, was performed there at carnival time in 1598, 1599 and 1600 and the triumphal march of Italian opera had begun. As Werner Braun remarks, however, it is extremely difficult to generalise about German opera before 1660.[69] Mara Wade points out that it was not until Caspar Förster and Johann von Lauremberg's *Musicalisch Schawspiel* (Musical Drama, performed in Copenhagen in 1655) that German-language opera used madrigal verse and alternated recitative and arias.[70] Braun's definition of opera, following Anna A. Abert, is 'any kind of dramatic action, of which essential portions, if not the whole, are set to music'.[71] Plays with a few inserted songs therefore do not count as operas but, on the other hand, the absence of recitative is not of itself necessarily a barrier to calling a given work an opera. A greater difficulty is that so few scores survive. Only two operas were printed in the Empire in their entirety in the whole of the seventeenth century, one of which was the Dresden *Il Paride* (1662), discussed below.

An example illustrates the problems encountered when dealing with early opera. What, for instance, constitutes 'essential portions' set to music in Abert's definition of opera? In 1602 on the occasion of the marriage of Hedwig, Princess of Denmark, and Christian II, Martin Hass sent Christian a manuscript copy of his play *Philomena Tragoedia Germana*. This manuscript still exists in the SLUB in Dresden (Mscr.Dresd.M 14 B). It is a six-act verse dramatisation of the story of Gabriotto and Reinhard. We do not know if it was actually performed on this occasion but it has two noteworthy elements. The first is that there is a sung chorus at the end of each of the first five acts consisting of about twelve stanzas each and that at several key places in the course of the action there is a song (labelled each time a 'cantio'). When Philomena, the heroine, takes poison at the end of Act V, the following short song is sung:

> O Lieb, wie süß und bitter!
> Voll trauren furcht und zittern
> in anfang aller freud und leid
> Nichts allß ein süße Bitterkeit,
>
> Ein Brennend sehnlich Noth
> Bist herber denn der Thod.
> Wer dich nur recht wol kennet
> Wie Patrarcha dich nennet.

[O love, how sweet and bitter! Full of sadness, fear and trembling, in the beginning of all joy and sorrow nothing but a sweet bitterness. A burning longing need, you are more bitter than death. Only he who knows how Petrarch describes you knows you really well.]

This illustrates the other important aspect of this play – the fact that it is not in irregular 'Knittelvers', or doggerel, but in flowing iambs in the Petrarchan style, a decade earlier than one would expect to find such a style in German. The suggestion is not that this play can be termed an opera, but rather that we have here early evidence of the influence in Dresden of the new synthesis of music, text and theatre emanating from Italy.

In chapter 2, we saw how Johann Georg I, himself influenced by his stay in Italy in 1601, brought Heinrich Schütz, the most important musical talent to work in Dresden during our entire period, there in 1614. Schütz's early court entertainments and his 'opera' *Dafne* were also discussed there. This was one of a range of works performed in Dresden in which text and music played a central part but which were not labelled operas by contemporaries. These include what were called ballets (Buchner and Schütz's *Orpheus und Eurydice* of 1636 and Schirmer's *Paris und Helena* and *Der triumphirende Amor* of 1650 and 1652 respectively). There was also a number of small-scale musical entertainments at court, in which text, music and dance combined.

But for full-scale Italian opera, what had by then developed into *dramma per musica* in Venice under Francesco Cavalli, we have to wait until 1662 and *Il Paride* by Giovanni Angelini Bontempi (*c*.1624–1705). Bontempi wrote both the libretto and the music for this work. A castrato, he had entered the service of Johann Georg I in 1650, having sung under Monteverdi and Cavalli at St Mark's in Venice. He was the first castrato in Dresden and in 1656 was appointed joint *kapellmeister* with the now ageing Schütz and Vincenzo Albrici. Though he spent the years 1666 to 1670 in Italy, he was back in Dresden in 1671, returning to Italy finally on the death of Johann Georg II.

Il Paride bears the double distinction of being the first opera in Italian to be performed in northern Germany and one of only two operas to be printed in its entirety, both score and libretto, in the whole century. The work was performed for the wedding of Johann Georg II's daughter, Erdmuthe Sophie, and Christian Ernst, Margrave of Brandenburg-Ansbach. In the preface to the printed parallel text in German and Italian, Bontempi is very concerned to stress how different his work is from other operas from Italy. Though it has five acts, they do not follow Horace's scheme of the development of the action. His work is neither a comedy, a tragedy nor a tragicomedy. It should be a drama but the subject-matter does not fit this term. So he has decided to call it an 'Erotopaegnion Musicum (quod est, ludus de Amore, ad Musicam pertineus)'. In other words, it is an amorous or erotic musical. It treats the twin stories of the judgement of Paris and his capture of Helen, both illustrating the irresistible power of love. No fewer than nineteen sets were called for and there were four ballet scenes. We are not surprised to learn that Bontempi was appointed stage designer and master of machines at the court theatre in 1664.[72] While this work was an innovation for the Dresden court, it is none the less interesting to note that its subject matter picks up that used by Schirmer in his 1650 *Ballet von Paris und Helena*.

In 1671, on his return from Italy, Bontempi collaborated with Marco Gioseppe Peranda (*c*.1625–75) on the opera entitled *Drama oder Musicalisches Schauspiel von der Dafne*. The work was not actually performed until February 1672 when it was put on in the court playhouse in Dresden on the occasion of the Albertine gathering at carnival time, the so-called 'Fröliche Zusammenkunft', or Joyous Gathering.[73] The libretto was in German, and was based on Opitz's libretto for his *Dafne* of 1627. It is the first German opera to survive in full score. Peranda had been in Dresden since the early 1650s, having come there with Christoph Bernhard from Rome, where they had both been pupils of Carissimi. As well as the story taken from Ovid of Apollo's love for the nymph Daphne and the pastoral element provided by the chorus of shepherds,

Bontempi and Peranda introduce peasant characters who also exemplify the power of love. There is also the figure of the huntsman who represents the true lover. Wilsdorff points out that this was a part especially created for the bass Johann Jäger (Jäger means huntsman), one of the vocal stars at court at the time the opera was being written.[74] The next year (1672) Peranda and Bontempi collaborated on another opera, *Jupiter und Io*.[75] This is the story of Jupiter's love for Io and Juno's jealousy, with a whole series of other love intrigues organised around this central plot.

These works – German operas by Italians at a German court – did not lead to any further developments in Dresden. For the development of opera in German one has to look to the courts of Johann Georg II's brothers. It was his son Johann Georg III, who had spent time in Venice in 1685, who invited Carlo Pallavicino to Dresden in 1685. Pallavicino had been organist in Padua from 1665 to 1666 and during this time his first two operas were performed in Venice. He then came to Dresden as vice-*kapellmeister* in 1667 and spent the next six years there, returning to Italy in 1673. He went first to Padua and then in 1674 he was made musical director of the Ospedale degli Incurabili in Venice, where he stayed until 1685. It was from Venice that Johann Georg III brought him to Dresden and he put on his *Gerusalemme liberata* in 1687 in both Venice and Dresden. In Dresden Margherita Salicola, brought specially to Saxony in 1685 by Johann Georg III who had heard her sing in Venice, sang the role of Armida. Pallavicino's last opera, *Antiope*, was unfinished on his death in January 1688 but was completed by Nicolas A. Strungk and put on in Dresden in 1689. Pallavicino died in 1688, his patron Johann Georg III in 1691 and the reign of Johann Georg IV lasted not quite two and a half years. A further caesura in the development of theatrical and musical life in Dresden was brought about by the death in 1692 of *kapellmeister* Christoph Bernhard, who had served Johann Georg II so faithfully.

The next Elector, Johann Georg IV's younger brother, August the Strong, was to take opera in a new direction, as he did with most of the cultural forms of the Dresden court.

7
The Saxon Hercules: August the Strong, Elector of Saxony, King of Poland

In 1680 Johann Georg III (1647–91) succeeded his father. He had taken part in the war against France before his succession; as Elector he fought on the victorious side at the siege of Vienna in 1683; and campaigned against France in the Low Countries in 1688 and on the Rhine in 1689. He died on campaign in 1691 at the age of forty-four. It was he who created a standing army in Saxony and he who conceived the idea for a cadet school, which came into being after his death in 1692. His wife, Anna Sophia, Princess of Denmark, bore him two sons, who succeeded him in turn. The eldest, Johann Georg IV (1668–1694), died in July 1694 of smallpox contracted from his mistress Magdalena Sibylla von Neitschütz (1675–94). He had reigned for only two and a half years and had no heir by his wife Eleonore of Saxony-Eisenach (1662–96), the widowed Margravine of Brandenburg-Ansbach.

His younger brother Friedrich August I (1670–1733), often later referred to by the soubriquet August the Strong, thus became Duke and Elector of Saxony. In a medal struck in Nuremberg to commemorate his accession in 1694 he had himself depicted on one side in a shoulder-length portrait in profile. On the reverse we see the figure of Hercules with his club and lion-skin, standing in front of a panorama of the city of Dresden (Figure 41). The inscription reads: 'Hercules Saxonicus' – the Saxon Hercules.[1] Thus, from the very beginning of his reign, the young Elector was presenting himself in heroic terms and by means of one of the chief myths used by his grandfather, Johann Georg II. Friedrich August had spent his early years at his grandfather's court and was said to be his favourite. This may explain his frequent recourse, in the construction of his own image, to the symbolism used by Johann Georg II.

Figure 41. Medal struck in Nuremberg to commemorate the accession of Friedrich August I in 1694. Tentzel, *Saxonia numismatica*. Tab. 73, No. 1.

It is customary, looking back on Friedrich August's almost forty-year reign, to see him as the great innovator, the man who broke with the traditions of his house and who took Saxony in a new and dubious political direction. But this is not what we see when we look at the early years of his reign without the benefit of hindsight. Considered on their own terms, his actions seem logical and natural, the continuation of the line taken by his father and his brother in a number of areas. It is hard to imagine that they would have followed a different course, given similar circumstances. He had been destined for a military career and one of his formative experiences before his accession had been his participation in the war against France as an officer with the Imperial army on the Rhine at his father's side in 1689.[2] After his accession, he carried on his military activities just as his father and brother would have done. As Supreme Commander of the Imperial Army, Friedrich August fought in a number of campaigns, leading his troops against the Turks in Hungary in 1695 and 1696. He clearly enjoyed military involvement and took part in a third Turkish campaign in 1697. This time, however, he did not take the Supreme Command, for by now his attention was needed for another enterprise, one for which his own father had laid the ground.

From Lutheran Elector to Catholic King

Jan III Sobieski (1629–96), King of Poland, ruler of the vast territory to the East of Saxony which consisted of the combined Kingdom of Poland and Grand Duchy of Lithuania, had died on 7 (17) June 1696.[3] As with all kings of Poland since 1573, he had been elected by the Polish nobility, each member of which had an equal vote. Any new king had to agree to be bound by a contract with these nobles, the so-called 'Pacta Conventa'.[4] Jan III Sobieski had been in power since 1674, so it was natural that Johann Georg III, one of Poland's closest neighbours, should be anticipating the moment when the throne of Poland would again become vacant and he could put himself forward. It appears that he had secured the agreement of the Elector of Hanover to his candidature.[5] Johann Georg III must have been prepared to convert to Catholicism, for this was one of the conditions for election. But he did not live to be faced with this choice. His eldest son, Johann Georg IV, also died before the Polish throne became vacant. In the event, it was the younger son, Friedrich August, who was to realise his father's ambition. In seeking to become King of Poland, therefore, Friedrich August was not, as Karlheinz Blaschke seems to imply, merely gratifying an immature and incomprehensible whim for personal aggrandisement, but carrying out the foreign policy goals of his house.[6]

Other European powers with an interest in the region also began the necessary preparatory moves to get their candidate elected. The Poles themselves were divided and had ruled out the Queen Mother, Marie Casimire Louise de la Grange, and her son Jakub Ludvik Sobieski (1667–1737), whom the Emperor initially supported, preferring a foreign king who would stand above the internal faction-fighting. Louis XIV threw his influence behind the candidature of François Louis de Bourbon, prince de Conti, while the Elector of Brandenburg supported Ludwig Wilhelm, Margrave of Baden. The Pope had his own candidate in his nephew, Livio Odescalchi. Other great powers interested in events in Poland were Russia and Sweden. There were in total no fewer than twelve candidates. It appears that by the autumn of 1696 Friedrich August I had decided to put himself forward for election.[7] But a major obstacle in his way was his Lutheran religion, so in March 1697 he travelled to Austria where, at Baden near Vienna, he secretly became a Catholic on 23 May (2 June). He made his profession of faith in the presence of his cousin, Duke Christian August of Saxony-Zeitz, who had converted in 1691 and was now Bishop of Raab (Győr). The conversion had to be delicately handled. Friedrich August needed to be able to prove he was a Catholic in order to present himself as a plausible candidate to the Poles. However, there was no point in laying himself open to the difficulties his conversion would cause in Saxony if he had no chance of being elected as King of Poland, so his conversion could not yet become public. For, political expediency apart, it was nothing short of incredible that the ruler of Saxony, of all European princes, should convert to Catholicism. One would have to go back to the middle of the seventeenth century to the conversion to Catholicism of Christina, Queen of Sweden, the daughter of Gustavus Adolphus, the hero of Protestantism, to experience a conversion as shocking. It was the Electors of Saxony who had protected Luther when the Emperor put a price on his head, and Saxony was the cradle of the Reformation. August was therefore turning his back on one of the defining elements of the Albertine Electors. In addition, he was the head of the Lutheran Church in Saxony and the leader of the so-called 'Corpus Evangelicorum', the assembly of the Lutheran estates in the Reichstag.

His conversion was not received well in Saxony, where his subjects feared that their religious freedoms would be curtailed. One anonymous pamphleteer writes, probably in Dresden, in the persona of 'the Mother of the Christian Lutheran Church weeping at the loss of her most valued and dearly beloved son, who has now gone to the bosom of another ecclesiastical mother'.[8] Friedrich August's mother, the Danish princess Anna Sophia, and his wife Christine Eberhardine, Margravine of Brandenburg-Bayreuth, remained true to their Lutheran faith. Anna Sophia was devoutly pious and, until her death in 1717, remained close to Philipp Jakob Spener, the founder of Pietism and court preacher in Dresden in the 1680s. August was thus united in belief neither with his people nor with his family. In 1697[9] and again in 1709 August was forced to sign undertakings guaranteeing the freedom of worship of his Saxon subjects. When the Papal Nuncio celebrated Mass in public in Dresden at New Year in 1700 for the first time since the Reformation, there was an uproar.

There were critical Protestant voices raised abroad too. In 1700 in London Richard Burridge published a verse satire entitled *The Apostate Prince: Or, A Satyr Against the King of Poland*.[10] In 134 rhymed couplets of iambic pentameter he vents his spleen against the ruler he calls 'the least of Kings, and worst of Men' (p. 3):

> Fie, fie, a Christian Prince his God betray!
> Change his Religion, the Apostate play.
> ...

> Scandal to princes, scorn of Kings, and shame
> To Christendom, infernal is thy Fame!
> A Prince affront his God with Deeds so foul
> That they stain Heaven, and deform the Soul!
> O horror and amaze! What hast thou done?
> My Blood congeals, and scarce has pow'r to run.
>
> (p. 4)

Apart from his horror at what he calls Friedrich August's apostasy, Burridge also correctly assesses the problematic nature of the new king's actions – his power is trammelled by Poland's system of government which makes it a 'Republic of Nobles', he cannot automatically hand the Crown to his heirs and his wife does not support his conversion:

> Power you've none; for the Republick Rules
> As it thinks fit; Crowns are but lent by Poles:
> Your Queen durst not be there, unless, like you,
> She'll head-long damn her Soul, and Body too.
>
> (p. 12)

Friedrich August will be damned for his actions, in Burridge's eyes a latter-day embodiment of the greatest sinners in the Bible:

> Deserter of the Faith, what hast thou done?
> False Judas, cruel Herod, Cain, or none,
> Who are tormented in the Flames of Hell,
> Did, when they liv'd on Earth, so much Rebel
> Against their God as you ...
>
> (p. 15)

But, having professed his faith, Friedrich August set off for Poland on 12 (22) June, not to return to Saxony for two years. During the run-up to the election and at the election itself, the Prince de Conti emerged as August's chief rival. In the course of the open-air assembly of the Polish parliament held near Warsaw in May and June 1697, each was declared elected by different factions. Further diplomatic manoeuvrings, however, ensured that on 13 (23) July the Poles officially offered Friedrich August the crown of Poland, whereupon he signed the so-called 'Pacta Conventa' on 17 (27) July and his Catholicism professed publicly. On (5) 15 September 1697 as August II he was crowned King of Poland in Cracow.

Figure 42. Firework display held in Danzig in 1698 for the entry of Friedrich August I, Elector of Saxony, as August II, King of Poland. Engraving from Georg Reinhold Curicke, *Freuden=Bezeugung der Stadt Danzig*, Danzig 1698.

This however did not mean that all was plain sailing. Brandenburg was not at all happy with Friedrich August's election and Tsar Peter the Great supported Brandenburg until 1698 (Figure 42). Things began to look more settled after the so-called 'Pacification Parliament' in 1699, at which August was finally recognised by the entire Polish nobility. But in February 1700 the Northern War began when August marched into Livonia, which Poland was reclaiming from Sweden. (This war was not to end until the Peace of Nystad in 1721 between Sweden and Russia.) In 1701 Karl XII of Sweden defeated the combined Saxon/Polish forces at Riga, reaching Warsaw in March 1702. He defeated August at the battle of Kliszów in July and again at Pultusk in May 1703. In February 1704 Karl forced August to abdicate and had Stanislas Leszczyński elected King of Poland in his stead. The Saxon troops were again badly defeated at the battle of Fraustadt in February 1706. Later the same year Karl XII marched into Saxony and forced August to make peace at Altranstädt, according to the terms of which August was forced to give up his allegiance to Russia but was allowed to keep the title of king. In

August 1709 August renewed his claim to the Polish throne and marched into Poland. The Polish parliament swore allegiance to him and the Swedish army withdrew.

August remained King of Poland until his death in 1733 and so for the whole of this period ruled over two very different territories, divided by their system of government, their language, their traditions, their religion and even their calendar. Saxony was both more populous and more prosperous, but Poland-Lithuania was physically much more extensive. Geography did not make the task any easier. The two territories were separated by a strip of land about 50 km wide, which belonged in the north to Brandenburg and in the south to Austria. Including the period of August's forced abdication, an abdication which was not recognised by the Poles, August was King of Poland for thirty-five years and four months. During that time, he spent a total of some eighteen and a half years in Poland.[11] He was frequently absent from Saxony for more than a year at a time during the first twenty years of his reign, a period during which he spent two-thirds of his time in Poland. From 1717 on he spent more time in Saxony, spending some months in Poland each year and then returning to Dresden. It appears that the journey took about a week. It was naturally difficult to rule one territory when one was absent for long spells in the other. The Polish adventure and the military action that went with it cost Saxony a vast sum of money which it is difficult to quantify. One of the conditions for August's election, for instance, had been the payment of at least five million thalers to settle the back-pay of the Polish army, but this was only the beginning. The ten years of war which ensued cost far greater sums. In addition, the personal union of the two territories did not lead to the prosperity for either which August had hoped. August also had to fulfil his duties within the Empire as premier secular Elector, functioning as Imperial Regent on the death of the Emperors Leopold I in 1705 and Joseph I in 1711.

Catholicism continued to play a part in August's foreign policy ambitions when it came to the future of his son Friedrich August II. August II had him secretly convert to Catholicism in Bologna in 1712, in order that he should succeed him as King of Poland. The conversion was kept secret until 1717 and its revelation in the bicentenary year of the Reformation made it only the more unpopular in Saxony. Two years later, August II was able to win as his son's bride the deeply pious Catholic princess, Maria Josepha, the elder daughter of Emperor Joseph I. Viewed in terms of foreign policy, this was a brilliant diplomatic coup. Neither the Emperor Joseph nor his brother Karl VI, who had succeeded him in 1711, had male heirs. Though a pre-existing document called the *pactum mutuae successionis* gave precedence to Joseph's daughters, by the Pragmatic Sanction Karl minimised their claims and by 1719, when Friedrich August II married Maria Josepha, Karl had two small daughters of his own. He also made August II and the bridal couple sign a detailed renunciation of their claims on the occasion of the marriage.[12] But Karl's two daughters were then aged two and one respectively, so the chance of the Saxon prince succeeding to the Habsburg inheritance and the Imperial crown was not a negligible one. In the event, Karl VI did not die until 1740 and it was not Joseph's son-in-law but Karl's, François, Prince of Lorraine, who ruled as Emperor jointly with his wife Maria Theresa. The most dazzling of August II's goals was, therefore, never realised. A lesser ambition did come to fruition, however, when Friedrich August II was elected King of Poland in 1733 as August III, in spite of a contested election, in which Stanislas I Leszczyński was initially chosen.

In the 1730s and 1740s, too, an impartial observer would have said that, even though they had not achieved Imperial dignity, the Wettins' change of religion was a stroke of genius, for it enabled August III to make a series of brilliant marriages among the Catholic ruling houses of Europe for five of his eleven children. His heir, Friedrich Christian (1722–63), married Maria Anna, Princess of Bavaria, and his second daughter, Maria Anna, married Maximilian III Joseph, Elector of Bavaria. His eldest daughter, Maria Amalia, married the future Carlos III, King of Spain, his third daughter, Josepha, married the Dauphin, and his fourth son Albert, Duke of Teschen, married Christine, daughter of Empress Maria Theresa.

But this is to move ahead a generation. Given the opposition of August II's subjects and family to his new religion and his own very lengthy absences from Saxony until 1717, the extent to which a Catholic court culture could be instituted in Dresden was very limited. On his return to Dresden in 1699 he set up a Catholic chapel in the Audience Room reserved for foreign embassies in the Palace. This was open to members of the court only. In the same year, he designated the chapel at the hunting lodge at Moritzburg outside Dresden as the official Catholic court and parish church and opened it to other Catholics. This chapel had been specially built in the Baroque style under his grandfather Johann Georg II by the architect Wolf Caspar von Klengel (1630–91) and had been consecrated in 1672.[13] In 1708, August II gave way to the urging of the Pope and had Klengel's opera house at the Palace in Dresden remodelled by Johann Christoph Naumann (c.1664–1742) and designated a Catholic court and parish church. By re-using buildings under his own control, August did not need to seek outside permission for their reconsecration. It was August III and his consort Maria Josepha who built the Catholic court church, or 'Hofkirche', dedicated to the Blessed Trinity, what is now the Catholic Cathedral in Dresden, between 1738 and 1755. It was their architect Gaetano Chiaveri (1689–1770) who placed it in its present dominant position next to the Palace and the Augustusbrücke over the Elbe and who gave the building its clearly Roman character.

What the conversion of the Wettins did lead to, though indirectly, was the building of one of the principal landmarks of the city of Dresden until February 1945, the famous Lutheran church known as the 'Frauenkirche', or Church of Our Lady (Figure 43). The plan for a new church came about because the Dresden town council decided in 1722 to replace its structurally unsound medieval predecessor, the 'Kirche zu Unserer Lieben Frauen'.[14] The original church, founded in the tenth century, had been the only parish church in Dresden until 1539. It became Lutheran in 1559 and was the most important burial church in Dresden. At a time when not only the reigning Elector but his heir, his daughter-in-law and their son, born in that year, were Catholics, the building of the Frauenkirche reaffirmed the allegiance of the city of Dresden to Lutheranism. Its reconstruction from a heap of rubble in the last decade of the twentieth century, a reconstruction financed largely by public subscription, is a further testimony to the church's enduring symbolic importance to the city.

From the very beginning, however, the Royal Ministry of Works ('das königliche Oberbauamt') was involved in the planning of the church. Representatives of the Oberbauamt sat on the committee of experts which oversaw the building. Graf Wackerbarth, the head of the Ministry and Governor of Dresden, took a close interest in what was happening and involved the royal architect Johann Christoph Knöffel in the planning. The Oberbauamt had been working for some time on various plans for other new buildings in the area, for instance, Zacharias Longuelune's plans for a new Powder Tower, and on ambitious urban projects to transform the area. In addition, there was the inexperience of the City Council in dealing with architectural projects of this magnitude. Knöffel therefore produced plans of his own for the church which were not acceptable to the City Council. A new plan by George Bähr was given the go-ahead in 1726 and the foundation stone was laid. Various members of the court as well as of the City Council took part in the ceremony.

Figure 43.   George Bähr, Frauenkirche, Dresden. Deutsche Fotothek.

The church had a central construction with seating for 3,600 people arranged in the circular nave, in a raised tier which ran round the edge of this circular area and, rising above that, in three further galleries (see the engravings by Christian Philipp Lindemann after J.G. Schmidt).[15]

Its 95-metre-high cupola and immense capacity made it one of the largest Protestant churches in Christendom. The king himself took a direct interest in the building of the church and contributed two sums of 3,000 and 4,000 thalers respectively towards its construction. (This must be seen in the context of the total cost of the church, which was 230,000 thalers and of the fact that half of this sum was raised by the sale of pews and burial plots.[16]) George Bähr had an audience with the king on 18 August 1731 to present his plans and August made various suggestions.[17] Still incomplete, the Frauenkirche was consecrated on 28 February 1734. It was not finished finally until 27 March 1743.

Contemporaneous with the building of the Frauenkirche is a second Lutheran monument, but a text, not a building. In 1728, Christian August Hausen (1663–1733), Lutheran preacher ('Stadtprediger') in the city of Dresden since 1692, first at the Sophienkirche, then at the old Frauenkirche,[18] published a work entitled *Gloriosa Electorum Ducum Saxoniae Busta, Oder Ehre Derer Durchlauchtigsten und Hochgebohrnen Chur=Fürsten und Hertzoge zu Sachsen Leichen=Grüffte*.[19] As the full title makes clear, this work is concerned with the deaths and funerals of the Albertine Electors and Dukes of Saxony.

The 1,931 pages of the *Gloriosa Busta* consist of a compendium of funeral sermons, *curricula vitae*, eulogies, *epicedia*, portraits, epitaphs, descriptions of commemorative coins and of *castra doloris* or catafalques across two centuries. Saxony, the cradle of the Reformation, and the Saxon Electors as the champions of Lutheranism are the subjects of the work. It begins, therefore, not with the Albertines, for they did not become Lutheran until 1539, but with three Ernestine Electors, Friedrich the Wise (1463–1525), Johann the Constant (1468–1532) and Johann Friedrich I (1503–54), to whom Hausen devotes his first 220 pages. The very first two funeral sermons in the book are Luther's orations at the funeral of Friedrich the Wise in Wittenberg, preached on texts by St. Paul.

The next Elector, Friedrich's brother Johann the Constant, is given similar treatment – a sermon by Luther and by Melanchthon, for instance. In addition, Hausen strenuously refutes a rumour that Johann wanted to return to Catholicism at his death and to convert his son. Johann's son, Johann Friedrich I, is again presented as the guardian of Lutheranism – first in three funeral sermons, then in a testimonial to him written by Luther during his lifetime and lastly by Hausen himself, in an account of Johann Friedrich's life put together from the work of older historians. Hausen presents Johann Friedrich as a hero of the

Reformation in spite of the fact that it was his rebellion against the Emperor, his membership of the Schmalkadic League and his defeat at the battle of Mühlberg in 1547 that led to the Ernestines' loss of the Electoral title, the eventual outlawing of Johann Friedrich himself and the elevation of the Albertines to the Electorship.

Having dealt with those dukes who actually knew and supported Luther, Hausen can now turn to the Albertines, whose subject he is and in whose capital city of Dresden he is writing. He deals with the lives and deaths of eleven of them – Albrecht, the founder of the line (1443–1500), his sons Georg and Heinrich, Moritz, the first Elector, his brother August, then the two Christians and the four Johann Georgs, finishing in 1694 with the funeral of Johann Georg IV, the last Lutheran Elector.

As well as reprinting the funeral sermons for each Duke, Hausen gives us an account of their life and death, but from his particular point of view. The 33-year reign of Elector August, for instance, from 1553 to 1586, is reduced to his struggles to unite the Protestant German princes and fight Calvinism and Popery. Hausen's vision of August as defender of Lutheranism blots out any recognition of his achievements as a Renaissance prince. His focus on the six succeeding reigns is just as myopic, for Hausen's work is intended as a clarion call to the Lutheran faithful and a restatement of Saxon identity as Lutheran. In its way it is just as much a reaction against the conversion of Friedrich August I as is the building of the Frauenkirche.

The cultural impact of France

Whereas the cultural mecca for earlier generations of Albertines had been Italy, it was France for Friedrich August and his older brother, the future Elector Johann Georg IV. They were taught the French language at a young age and were thus exposed to French culture. When the two young princes set up their own household, Hans Ernst von Knoch (1641–1705) was put in charge of their education. He took up his post early in 1676, later accompanied Johann Georg IV on his Grand Tour and not released from his pedagogical responsibilities until 18 September 1687. Knoch had spent the years 1664–66 in France, particularly in Paris, and had devoted himself to the study of the French language.[20] In addition, the princes received instruction in French from Dieudonné Doncourt and after 19 September 1684 from Jean Rousseau.[21] It goes without saying that, as soon as each of the princes reached his seventeenth year, he was sent on a Grand Tour, which included a stay at the French court.

In the case of Friedrich August I, then merely a younger son, this lasted from 15 May 1687 until 28 April 1689.[22] Culturally speaking, this was the formative experience of his life. A third of his time away was spent in Paris, where he stayed for three months in 1687 from 14 June until 16 September and for five months in 1688, from 20 May until 7 November. He also visited Spain and Portugal, the Imperial court in Vienna and several of the major northern Italian cities including Turin, Milan, Pavia, Ferrara, Venice and Florence, but it was the court of Louis XIV that provided him with a model he tried to emulate for the rest of his life.

For one thing, the person of Louis XIV himself, aged around fifty at that date, made a deep impression on the young Saxon prince. Jutta Bäumel has unearthed a telling example of Friedrich August I's continued fascination with the French king some thirty years after he had met him, by which time Louis XIV was dead.[23] In 1719, at one of the most triumphant moments of his reign, namely, the wedding of his heir Friedrich August II to the daughter of the Emperor Joseph, August II wore on two successive days a magnificent dress of pale blue and salmon pink, covered in silver lace and decorated with ribbons. This costume, consisting of a short cloak, a doublet, wide, baggy, so-called 'Rhinegrave' trousers and gloves, is preserved in the Armoury in Dresden. According to a list of the costumes August was to wear during the wedding celebrations, a particular outfit is referred to as 'Montargon's costume'. Montargon was August's agent in Paris and had been in his service since at least 1705. On 25 December 1717 August wrote to Montargon, asking him to have a costume doll made in Paris and sent to Dresden wearing

> un habit tel que le Roy de France defunt a porté dans les grandes Ceremonies, telles que son mariage en manteau Pourpoint, etc Rhingra(ve) Il ne suffira pas qu'il envoyele dessein, de cet habillement; mais il foudra qu'il fasse habiller exactment une poupée dans cette sorte d'habit.[24]

> [A dress such as the late King of France wore on great occasions like his wedding – a cloak, doublet etc. and Rhinegrave trousers. A drawing of this costume will not suffice. Instead, a doll must be dressed precisely in this sort of costume.]

In addition, Montargon was to have a second doll made wearing the costume that a page would have worn on the same sort of occasion. August was therefore not asking for an example of Louis XIV's dress in the last years of his life (he had died in 1715) but of the costume he would have worn around 1660. Because the costume August wished to recreate was so out of fashion in 1717 a costume doll was truly necessary. Indeed, so outmoded was it that August would not have seen Louis XIV wearing it even in 1687 when he had spent time at Versailles, but only in portraits of the French king in the galleries there. One wonders if his tutor Knoch's accounts of life in Paris in the mid-1660s could have played a part here. Bäumel has also, with the help of Claudia Schnitzer, located a coloured sketch of Louis XIV wearing such a costume in the Prints and Drawings Collection in Dresden, possibly a sketch sent to Dresden by Montargon. On one of the most important occasions of his life, therefore, August II wished to look like Louis XIV on one of the most important days in his. This is just one example of the lasting impression the person of Louis XIV made on the young Friedrich August, then a younger son with no hope of succeeding. But French culture made an equally lasting impression. In the next section we shall see how this affected Friedrich August's art patronage and the arrangement of his collections. Court theatre and architecture were two other areas which were equally affected.

The travel journal of Friedrich August's tour devotes a considerable number of entries to his two sojourns in Paris, though it concentrates on only a limited range of the prince's activities. The most important topic is his reception by members of the French court, by ambassadors of other nations and by important German nobles, the next is his studies – visits to the riding academy, his dancing and language lessons – the third is his religious devotions (particularly important in a Catholic country) and the other activity which is listed is his visits to the theatre. He attended performances at the Comédie Italienne on 18 and 30 June 1687 and 13 September 1688 and the Comédie Française on 23 July, 4, 11 and 29 August and 3 September 1688. He saw plays at St Cloud on 4 and 8 July 1687, and went again to the theatre in Paris on 19 July 1687, though the journal does not specify which troupe he saw, and he attended the opera on 29 June, 20 July and 26 September 1688.

One of his first actions on his succession was to dismiss the Italian actors who had been in the service of his brother and to introduce the French theatre he had got to know during his stay in France. A troupe of French actors in the service of the Elector of Hanover played at the Dresden court from 1 January until 2 March 1696 during the carnival season.[25] In the autumn of 1696 Friedrich August decided that the existing opera house was inadequate for the performance of French plays and gave the order for a new playhouse, which was finished early in 1697. The same year he set about founding his own troupe of French actors and hired Angelo Constantini (1653–1729), an actor he must have seen in Paris at the Théâtre Italien. Though Constantini was Italian by birth, having been born in Verona, he made his acting debut in Paris in 1680 as a Harlequin, the year the Théâtre Italien, which performed *commedia dell'arte* pieces, moved to the Hôtel de Bourgogne. Constantini made a name for himself with his character 'Mézétin', a combination of servant and adventurer. He acted with one of the most celebrated of all seventeenth century *commedia dell'arte* performers, Tiberio Fiorilli (*c.*1605–94), best known for his character Scaramouche. Fiorilli may have been at the French court as early as 1639 and was patronised by Cardinal Mazarin. In the 1650s he acted with the Comédie Italienne at the Petit Bourbon, alternating with Molière's company and Molière was greatly influenced by him. Constantini wrote Fiorilli's life story under the title *La Vie de Scaramouche*.[26] This work went into at least four other editions and an English translation before 1700.

Constantini left Paris in 1697 to enter the service of Georg Wilhelm, Duke of Braunschweig and Lüneburg, whose residence was in Celle. However, he arrived in Dresden in the spring of the same year. No sooner had he been brought to Dresden than his employer set off for a stay in Poland that was to last two years. While a troupe called the 'Zellische Comoedianten' were putting on French comedies in Warsaw for the carnival in February 1699,[27] Constantini was sent from Warsaw to Paris as an impresario to assemble a troupe of French actors, singers and dancers and other theatrical personnel such as costumiers and set designers.[28] In May 1700, when he arrived in Warsaw from France with these artists and their families, the group numbered ninety-three – a director, thirty-one actors and singers of both sexes, fifteen dancers, three musicians, eleven other personnel and thirty-two family members. Constantini had also purchased costumes and sets. This troupe performed the plays of Corneille, Racine and Molière and, for the first time in Warsaw, Lully's operas, which August II had got to know in Paris. It appears that August II also hired a troupe of French players in Holland between March and May 1699. This troupe performed at the Michaelmas Fair in Leipzig in October of that year and in November and December in Dresden, putting on no less than fourteen comedies and a ballet there.[29] The famous French dancer Louis de Poitiers was also hired for the Warsaw court on 17 April 1700. But the Northern War, begun in the same year, put a stop to theatrical and musical performances in Warsaw for a long time to come.

Constantini fell into disfavour at the end of 1701 and spent the years from 1702 to 1708 in the fortress of Königstein. He was released because the king had engaged a new troupe of French actors in Lille, where he was on campaign in 1708, and needed Constantini to direct them. This was because the visit of the Danish King Fredrik IV, August II's first cousin, in June 1709, which marked Saxony's departure from the war, was in preparation. This was celebrated with the first large-scale festivities since those of 1695 for Friedrich August's accession. Constantini produced a theatrical piece for the festivities called *Le Théâtre des plaisirs*.[30] That he was back in favour is indicated by the titles he lists after his name on the title-page of this work: 'Camerier intime, Tresorier des menus plaisirs & Garde de bijoux de la Chambre du Roy' (Privy Councillor, Organiser of Festivals and Keeper of the Jewels of the King's Bedchamber). The tone of Constantini's prologue implies the same kind of familiar relations with the king as he had chronicled between Fiorilli and Louis XIV. Constantini writes, for instance: 'Il faut que je finisse, puisque Votre Majesté toute pleine d'esprit (soit dit sant luy deplaire) n'aime pas que l'on caquete toujours pour ne rien dire' (I must finish, for Your Majesty, full of *esprit* as you are (if I may say so without displeasing you), does not like one to chatter on without saying anything).

The printed text provides further information about the kind of theatrical display performed under Constantini's aegis. The participants were divided into three groups. First, there were the seventeen actors who made up 'la Troupe des Comediens François entre tenüe par sa Majesté'. Then come the thirteen 'personnages qui chantent dans la Piece' and we are told that all the music was composed by Sr. Schmidt (that is, Johann Christian Schmidt, 1664–1728), the King's *kapellmeister*. There were forty male and female dancers who made up 'les Ballets de la Cour de sa Majesté'. The choreography was by Louis de Poitiers and there were *entrées* of warriors, Sailors, Chinese, Heroes, Peasants, a 'Tableau Italien' and a final 'Carnaval Mascarade'. As well as this, the piece contained *commedia dell'arte* figures in various disguises and singers representing Momus, Mars, sailors, Chinese, a Roman Lady, a farmer, a philosopher, a shepherd and a nymph. The piece thus consists of an unconnected series of heterogeneous scenes, any one of which could be detached without harming the spectacle as a whole. Constantini does not attempt to disguise this fact, making a virtue of it in the preface: 'Ce sont toutes Scenes detachées, a fin d'y pouvoir introduire aisément les Musiques, les Chansons, et quantité de dances differentes l'une de l'autre' (These are all detached scenes, so that music, songs and a number of different dances, each different from the next, can easily be introduced). This is pure entertainment, a visual show without any intellectual or political content.

One of the *divertissements* that formed part of the great wedding celebrations of 1719 was called *Les Quatre Saisons*. The prologue states that both the plot and the characters were entirely conceived by August II.[31] *Les Quatres Saisons* is a typical, though rather simple, *ballet à entrées* with a libretto wholly in French. It has the characteristic four-part structure of such ballets, one *entrée* for each season rounded off by a *grand-ballet* (referred to here as the fifth *entrée*). About sixty members of the court sang and danced in it, quite apart from the one hundred or so professional members of the chorus and the orchestra. The preface congratulates the sixty courtiers on their mastery of 'la delicatesse de la langue françoise', pointing out that it would be difficult to find so many persons at another court whose French was so good! It should be noted that several of these excellent French speakers were Polish grandees such as Prince Lubomirsky and Count Oginski. If the aim of every German nobleman was to exhibit the polish and speak the language of the French court, clearly Dresden had succeeded in its aims better than most.

Another example where French influence is dominant is in Matthäus Daniel Pöppelmann's vision for that notable piece of court architecture that we know today as the Zwinger (Figure 44). He immortalised his vision in 1729 in a volume of twenty-four engravings in large folio format with an explanatory text, once he had given up hope for its realisation in built form.[32] The Zwinger began as an Orangery, the first idea for which can be traced to 1699. During his time in Paris, August II frequently visited the gardens at Versailles, St Cloud and Chantilly, he had seen the terraced gardens of Spain and Portugal, the citrus groves near Lisbon, the parks of the Medici. All of this must have played a part in his desire to create such a garden himself. Like so much else, however, it had to wait for the end of the Northern War to be put into execution. We have a sketch in August's own hand from 1709, setting out a semi-circle of terraces and arcades to house his orange trees in winter.[33] At the same time, plans were afoot to build a new Palace in Dresden, necessitated by a serious fire in the old Palace in 1701. August wanted a structure befitting his twin dignities as Elector and King. Pöppelmann was sent via Prague to Vienna to discuss the plans for the new Palace with such leading architects of the day as Johann Bernhard Fischer von Erlach and Lucas von Hildebrand. He then continued on to Rome. As plans for the Orangery evolved, the idea was to join it on to

Figure 44. Carl Heinrich Jacob Fehling, The carrousel of the Four Elements in the Zwinger, 1719. Pen, ink and wash. Kupferstichkabinett, Dresden. Ca 200-16. Deutsche Fotothek.

the new Palace. The latter was never built, but Pöppelmann was sent to Versailles and Paris in 1715 to get ideas for the interior decoration of the pavilions which formed part of the complex. For the great wedding festivities in 1719, the Zwinger took on the form that we know today. It is reminiscent in many aspects of the temporary wooden ampitheatre for the festivities in honour of the visit of the Danish King in 1709, torn down in 1714 and probably also designed by Pöppelmann. The famous grand entrance to the Zwinger, the Kronentor, was completed in 1718, but the fourth side of the Zwinger complex, where Semper's art gallery now stands, was still open towards the Elbe. Pöppelmann always intended to close it off and, when it became certain that this would never be realised, he published his plans in 1729 in the above-mentioned volume of engravings.

The bilingual nature of the volume picks up the French cultural ambience of the Dresden court. The dedication is entirely in French, the explanatory text in French and German. Pöppelmann explains the political symbolism readily apparent in the decoration of the building, particularly in the figure of Hercules bearing the globe which appears in various prominent positions. When the building was begun in 1711, August the Strong was fulfilling several political functions at once. As well as King of Poland and Elector of Saxony he was also Imperial High

Marshall and, since the death of Emperor Joseph I, Imperial Regent. The engraved frontispiece by C.A. Wortmann is concerned to stress these political functions in the various allegorical figures that frame the depiction of the westernmost tract of the Zwinger that fills the centre ground of the picture (Figure 45). The Zwinger is depicted as a site of elegant urbanity. The niches in the curving side wings are filled with

Figure 45. Christian Albrecht Wortmann, Frontispiece to Matthäus Daniel Pöppelmann's *L'Orangerie Royale de Dresden avec ses pavillons et embellissements Bâtie en 1711*, Dresden 1729. Deutsche Fotothek (Würker).

orange trees and among the elegant courtiers strolling in front of the building, we see gardeners carrying more trees. What was left of the old Palace, a couple of hundred metres away, seems in its Renaissance and Baroque monumentality in another world. In the 'Avertissement' on page 2 Pöppelmann lists the elements of his recreational complex. There are various large saloons for dining, gaming and dancing but smaller rooms too. There are baths, grottos, arcades, walks, rows of trees and pillars, grass and flower beds, jets of water and other fountains, places for recreation, benches, balustrades. Then there is the magnificent adjoining opera and play house and the central space in which the almost innumerable orange trees kept in the galleries in winter can be placed but which can be used for all kinds of tournaments, shows and other *divertissements* of the court.

The other engravings, all by Johann Georg Schmidt, show the Zwinger as a civilising and civil space, a place of public recreation and social interaction, where the members of society can disport themselves in urbane communication, not behind the closed doors of the Palace, but in a semi-public manner (Figure 46). Figures, both men and women, can be glimpsed through the windows, ascending the stairs or strolling in the gardens, talking, interacting, gesticulating or accompanied on occasion by little dogs (Figure 47). Pöppelmann stresses in the 'Avertissement' that both the principal ladies and gentlemen of the court and many inhabitants of the city stroll here of an evening, enjoying the delightful views in all directions. We are reminded of the way the parks and gardens at Versailles were used. The 'civil conversation' of the sixteenth century has given way to the Frenchified urbanity of the eighteenth.

From *Kunstkammer* to museum

One of the areas on which August the Strong left the most visible mark was the Dresden collections. He was not only a notable artistic patron and collector himself, he thoroughly reorganised the existing collections. This was yet another area in which his sojourns in France exerted a profound influence. In his most recent book, Dirk Syndram documents this.[34]

According to Syndram, collections at three of the courts the young Friedrich August visited – Versailles, Florence and Vienna – made a particularly deep impression on him. First among these were those of the French court. In Versailles, he had the opportunity to see the collections of Louis XIV and of his son, the Grand Dauphin, both of whom

Figure 46. Johann Georg Schmidt, The entrance to the Wallpavillon. From Matthäus Daniel Pöppelmann's *L'Orangerie Royale de Dresden avec ses pavillons et embellissements Bâtie en 1711*, Dresden 1729. Deutsche Fotothek (Würker).

214 *Court Culture in Dresden*

Figure 47. Johann Georg Schmidt, The doorway on the far side of the Kronentor leading out of the Zwinger towards the moat. From Matthäus Daniel Pöppelmann's *L'Orangerie Royale de Dresden avec ses pavillons et embellissements Bâtie en 1711*, Dresden 1729. Deutsche Fotothek (Rous).

collected vessels of semi-precious stone and jewels. Both the collections and the manner in which they were displayed left an abiding impression on the young August. Between his two French visits, he also travelled to Spain and Portugal, visiting many important collections and palaces as well as the two capital cities. In late 1688 he set off for Italy, visiting Turin, Genoa, Milan, Venice and Ferrara. The Italian trip culminated in a visit to Florence, where he saw the treasures of the Medici displayed in the Uffizi.

August was called home by his father in the spring of 1689 and on the way back he visited Vienna. Here he was able to study the Imperial collections, which contained many objects commissioned in Prague around 1600 by that remarkable collector and art patron, Emperor Rudolf II. The arrangement of this collection with its express purpose of bearing witness to the glory of the House of Habsburg again influenced August's own later ideas about the display and arrangement of his treasures. All the collections he saw contained precious stones, beautifully wrought jewellery, silver, silver gilt and gold vessels, uncut stones, drinking cups, automata, ivory objects, small bronzes and goldsmith work.

In Dresden were the remarkable collections of such objects amassed by August's forebears. In chapter 3 we discussed the *Kunstkammer*, founded by Elector August in 1560, and the Library, together with the additions and innovations carried out by subsequent Electors to both. But a number of other collections were kept elsewhere in the Palace whose contents corresponded more closely to August's tastes. These were locked away for safekeeping in a fire- and burglar-proof suite of rooms on the ground floor of the west wing of the Palace in Dresden. These rooms were known collectively as the 'Geheime Verwahrung', or Secret Repository. Since part of the largest vaulted room was painted lime green, by 1572 these rooms had acquired the name 'Grünes Gewölbe', or Green Vault. An inventory of 1588 shows that pieces of rare ore were kept there, as well as gold and silver boxes, amber objects, silver-gilt tableware and sixty vessels made of rock crystal. Valuable papers were another important item, as well as snuff for the ruler's personal use.[35] It is also possible that the Electors' reserves of gold and silver to be used for coinage were kept there, but the Repository certainly contained large silver objects such as basins and dishes to be used on important ceremonial occasions. The function of the Green Vault as a secret store for objects of great value remained unchanged throughout the seventeenth century. It was administered by a Privy Chamberlain who was also responsible for the *Kunstkammer*, but control over what it contained and when it was to be opened remained strictly in the hands of the Electors themselves.

Jutta Bäumel has shown how, when August the Strong was campaigning for his election as King of Poland in 1697, he sent for 120 silver objects from the Green Vault to be sent to Poland to convince the Polish parliament of his financial standing.[36] As the detailed inventory of these pieces compiled at the time makes clear, these included some of the best pieces collected by August's ancestors in the late sixteenth and early seventeenth centuries. Among them were silver-gilt drinking vessels in various forms, many of them the playful clockwork objects in the form of animals and mythological figures so beloved of that period, basins, ewers, dishes, other drinking vessels made of rock crystal and of semi-precious stone. The inventory also shows that a number of other similar valuables were kept in what was called the 'Elector's Oratory' ('Bethstübgen'), clearly a room on the first floor of that tract of the Palace known as the 'Georgenbau', near the living quarters of the Elector.

August's own patronage of goldsmiths and jewellers led to an extraordinary flowering of such work in Saxony during his reign. He had a passion for jewels and for small intricate *objets de vertu* combining gold, silver, precious stones and enamelwork. Some of these were the kind of small luxury items known to his age as 'Galanterien' – snuff-boxes, seals, perfume bottles, small containers of various kinds and objects of daily use – but executed in precious metals, bejewelled and enamelled. Figurines combining goldsmith work, enamel and precious stones, particularly baroque pearls, and depicting dwarves, tradesmen of various kinds and *commedia dell'arte* figures were especially treasured. August's older brother, Johann Georg IV, had already begun to collect such objects, which he bought through agents abroad and at the Leizpig Trade Fair. In addition, he was already employing two notable craftsmen who were to become even more prominent during the long reign of his brother August, the Dresden goldsmith Gottfried Döring (?1666–1718) and the Swabian jeweller Johann Melchior Dinglinger (1664–1731). The latter probably arrived in Dresden from Vienna in 1691 or 1692 and it is from his workshop, where he collaborated with his brothers, the enameller Georg Friedrich Dinglinger (1666–1720) and the goldsmith Georg Christoph Dinglinger (1668–1746), that some of the most remarkable works to be seen in the Green Vault today emanated.

The first work we know to have been made by Johann Melchior Dinglinger for Johann Georg IV is the figure of St George killing the dragon, made of gold, enamel and jewels. This was in honour of the

Elector's installation in the Order of the Garter in 1693. Other early works by Dinglinger include a number of collaborations with the sculptor Balthasar Permoser (1651–1732), whose little figures of Africans carved of ebony and ivory Dinglinger set in gold. Dinglinger advanced to the position of Court Jeweller to August the Strong in 1698 and the happy conjunction of these two contemporaries – the passionate collector and patron and the artist of extraordinary flair and inventiveness – led to the production of a series of masterpieces. Dinglinger's first great work for August was the golden coffee service (1697–1701), consisting of 45 little vessels – cups, saucers, dishes, little flagons – of gold, enamelled gold and crystal. The whole is presented on a gold pyramidal structure which in its present form dates from between 1714 and 1729 and embodies four ivory figurines of the elements by Paul Heermann as well as various other smaller ivory figures. It is decorated with more than 5,600 diamonds and semi-precious stones, and Dinglinger had to travel to Warsaw in person to present the coffee service to August on 23 December 1701.

At his own risk and as a speculative venture Dinglinger and his brothers began work in 1701 on another masterpiece, the unique collection of 132 figures known as 'the Throne of the Great Mogul Aureng-Zeb', completed in 1708. Aureng-Zeb was a contemporary of August the Strong who ruled over almost the whole of the Indian subcontinent from 1658 and died aged 88 in 1707.[37] The work in question depicts the five-day birthday celebrations held at the Mogul's court in Delhi. The Great Mogul is depicted seated on a throne in the courtyard of his palace, a structure more than a square metre in extent. Subjects, ambassadors and courtiers come to do him obeisance and present him with gifts (thirty-two of which can still be seen), servants hold parasols and wave fans, and each of the figures is in itself a marvel of detail and imagination (Figure 48).

All the while this work was in execution, the Dinglingers were making the usual figurines and other precious objects for the Elector, and such craftsmen as Guillaume Ferbecq, a Huguenot jeweller living in Frankfurt am Main, were acting as his agents abroad. While August was in Warsaw, he empowered his Privy Councillor Georg, Freiherr von Rechenberg, to deal with Ferbecq and Dinglinger and to buy such works as would find a worthy place in August's collection.

In the autumn of 1704 part of the collection was taken out of the Green Vault and moved up to what was called the King's 'Praetiosen Cabinet' near his private quarters.[38] The 'Cabinet' was a specially constructed display case in which August himself placed some of the

Figure 48. Johann Melchior, Georg Friedrich and Georg Christoph Dinglinger, A dromedary and his attendant from the Birthday of the Great Mogul Aureng-Zeb in Delhi. Gold, silver, gilding, enamel, jewels. 1701–8. Grünes Gewölbe, Dresden. Deutsche Fotothek (Heckmann).

precious objects from his treasury and the keys to which he had in his own keeping. This arrangement enabled him to have some of his treasures close at hand so that he could enjoy them and it remained in place until 1709, when the 'Cabinet' and its contents were taken back down to the Green Vault. Shortly afterwards he acquired a considerable number of new works from Dinglinger for the 'Cabinet', among them a beautiful drinking cup made of chalcedony depicting the Bath of Diana. The cup represents the pool, at one side of which the ivory figure of Diana is seated, attended by Cupid. Her toilet articles, hunting dog, the reeds by the pool, the baldachin over her head surmounted by a sphynx are made from gold, silver, steel, ivory, diamonds, pearls and enamelwork. The cup is balanced on the antlers of the head of the stag into which Diana has transformed Actaeon. Rechenberg continued to buy for the collection during 1705, but at this point August lost the war and the crown of Poland. In 1706 he had to pawn 102 of his most precious works, in some cases before he himself had paid for them. They included the golden coffee service, which was sent to Hamburg with the rest.[39] August was unable to redeem them until 1715, though as soon as his financial position began to ease in 1709, he began to collect again.

The financing of the collection was at all times precarious because of the huge sums of money involved, money which the Elector did not have because of the cost of the Northern War. The risk was borne mostly by the goldsmiths and artists themselves, who had first to purchase the precious materials with which they worked before selling their work to August. His middlemen also frequently had to pay for works they were acquiring on his behalf and then hope that they would get their outlay back. Syndram charts at length the financial side of both creation and purchase and the difficulties that even Dinglinger had in getting the remuneration that was due to him, right up to his death in 1731.

In 1715 August again set about displaying his collection and selected some objects from the Secret Repository to be placed in what were called the 'Queen Mother's Rooms'. They consisted of four rooms on the first floor of the west wing of the Palace. In the same year August, clearly influenced by what he had seen in Versailles in his youth, decided to set up a Mirror Room in which to display his jewels. He ordered the mirrors for the walls from Paris via his agent Baron Raymond Leplat, as well as a number of marble and bronze statues and paintings by such French artists as Nicolas Poussin and Louis de Silvestre. August was now clearly moving away from the earlier practice of locking precious objects safely away in the Secret Repository and only taking them out on state occasions, and moving towards the idea of a museum in which they would be permanently visible.

In the years 1717 and 1718 August was giving much thought to the reorganisation of all of his collections, including the *Kunstkammer*. In 1707 he had removed 614 paintings from it to decorate the so-called Redoutensaal, or ballroom. Twenty-eight small bronzes were removed in 1712 and added to the paintings.[40] In 1717 what was left of the *Kunstkammer* was taken across the river to a building August had acquired, the Holländisches Palais, soon to be renamed the 'Japanisch-Ost-Indisches Palais' after of the royal porcelain collection which was housed in it. There are several plans in the king's own hand from these years, documenting various concepts for the display and organisation of the collections.

The solution was to place the *objets de vertu*, the jewellery and the silver back in the Green Vault, but to reconstitute this as a permanent exhibition and not just as a store. Some time between 1720 and 1723 August decided to allow visitors to see this display, which necessitated some rebuilding in the four rooms of the Green Vault. The rebuilding was carried out under the direction of the Elector's Chief Architect, Matthäus Daniel Pöppelmann. The vaulted ceiling was painted and the walls were lined with mirrors in front of which the various objects could be displayed. August himself took a very close interest in any developments to do with his collection, and this first stage of the remodelling was largely completed by 1723. Between 1727 and 1730 four further rooms were created, as well as an entrance lobby for visitors.[41] The objects were organised according to the material they were made of. The visitor began with the Bronze Room, progressed to the Ivory Room, the Silver Room, the Silver-gilt room, the Corner Tower Room for the figurines, the so-called 'Pretiosen' Room, and the Jewel Room and ended finally back where he had started in the Bronze Room.

Many of the objects in these rooms came from the original *Kunstkammer* which was now dissolved. In 1728, the scientific instruments from the *Kunstkammer* were placed in a separate collection, the so-called 'Königliches Cabinett der mathematischen und physikalischen Instrumente', the books from the *Kunstkammer*, which related closely to the scientific instruments, were placed in the Library and the paintings were gathered into a Picture Gallery (what is nowadays called the 'Gemäldegalerie Alte Meister', though we have to remember that the collection now on display in Dresden owes a great deal to the collecting activities of the next Elector Friedrich August II, August III, King of Poland. August the Strong also created the porcelain collection discussed below, and the engravings and drawings were put into the Prints and Drawings Collection ('Kupferstichkabinett'). The museums we see when we visit Dresden today were thus brought into being and the *Kunstkammer* created by Elector August in 1560 ceased to exist.

From occult science to early manufacturing

Chapter 4 documented the interest throughout the centuries of the Electors of Saxony in alchemy in all its manifestations – shading off at one extreme into hermeticism and magic, while at the other connecting with the research insights and practical techniques necessary for the expansion of such important Saxon industries as mining and metallurgy. More generally known are the alchemical experiments in the reign of August the Strong, since it was because of his interest in the making of gold and the production of the Philosopher's Stone that the process of making porcelain was rediscovered.

Papers in the Dresden archive at Loc. 4418/4 (Geheimes Archiv) imply that August the Strong was interested in the mystical aspects of alchemy as well as in its practical and chemical ones. A folder within this large file is labelled 'From the Papers of King August II of Poland' and contains a collection of cabalistic wheels and crosses, some on vellum, and an anonymous thirty-six-page treatise in folio on the manufacture of the two elixirs – the universal tincture which would transform all base metals, and the Elixir of Life. We do not know whether these papers were read by Friedrich August or not, of course. This file also contains letters dated 1737 offering his son, August III, King of Poland, various recipes for making the Philosopher's Stone. Whether he made any use of these offers is not known, but they show that at this date it was still considered a possibility that he might be prepared to buy such material.

What we can state with certainty is that alchemical experiment in the reign of August the Strong bore fruit in a major new wealth-creating industry in Saxony, one that is still important today. This new industry was the manufacture of porcelain. Friedrich August was a passionate collector of Chinese and Japanese porcelain, an enthusiasm he shared with such contemporaries as Philip II, Duke of Orléans, Louis-Henri, prince de Condé, and Sophie Charlotte, Queen of Prussia. But he was also interested in discovering the secret of its manufacture. The discovery of the process is due to two men: the Saxon scientist and polymath Ehrenfried Walter von Tschirnhaus (1651–1708) and the alchemist Johann Friedrich Böttger (1685–1719).

Tschirnhaus was a remarkable man. He came from an ancient aristocratic family whose seat was Kieslingswalde in Lusatia, east of Görlitz.[42] In 1668 at the age of seventeen he went to Leiden, where he studied medicine and natural science. In about 1671/2 he became acquainted with the philosophy of Descartes. On Louis XIV's invasion of the Netherlands, Tschirnhaus fought on the Dutch side for eighteen months, before resuming his studies. In 1674 he came into contact with Spinoza, with whom he carried on a lively correspondence. In 1675 he travelled to London to conduct experiments with members of the Royal Society, founded in 1660. Here he worked with such men as Oldenburg, Papin and Boyle. From there he went to Paris to work with Christiaan Huygens who introduced him to the Académie Royale des Sciences, founded in 1666. During his time in Paris he became acquainted with Leibniz and with Colbert, whose son he tutored in mathematics. It appears that it was through Colbert's influence that Tschirnhaus began to apply his scientific knowledge to the practical problems of technology with the aim of wealth-creation. By 1675 Tschirnhaus was undertaking experiments with potter's clay using the heat produced by burning-mirrors, to fire the clay. In 1676 he left Paris for Lyons where he carried out further experiments with F. Villette using larger burning-mirrors and then continued over the Alps to Turin and Milan. In Milan he met the famous scholar Manfredo di Settala, then continued down to Rome, where he met Athanasius Kircher, Giovanni Alfonso Borelli and Cardinal Ricci. All this time he was corresponding with Leibniz, visiting him in Hanover in 1679 on the way back to Kieslingswalde. Here he carried on with his experiments with burning-mirrors, arriving at the notion of making them from copper rather than iron, and at the same time working on the physics of the reflection of rays. In 1682 he travelled again to Paris where he became the first German member of the Académie Royale des Sciences. Hoping for a pension from the French king, Tschirnhaus dedicated one of his philosophical works, *Medicina mentis sive artis inveniendi praecepta generalia*, completed in 1682 but published in Amsterdam in 1687, to Louis XIV, but without success. His philosophical ideas brought him into contact with the Pietist Philipp Jacob Spener, who was Court Chaplain in Dresden from 1686 before his departure for Berlin. Tschirnhaus's ideas on the teaching of mathematics and physics greatly influenced another Pietist, August Hermann Francke, the founder in Halle of the famous orphanage and school known as the Franckesche Anstalt, and also Christian Weise, the headmaster of the grammar school ('Gymnasium') in Zittau. One of Tschirnhaus's most cherished projects was the founding of an Academy of Sciences in Saxony on the lines of the Académie in Paris or the Royal Society in London. On his estates in Kieslingswalde he brought a kind of unofficial research group into being which was the closest he got to his ambition.[43]

But Tschirnhaus was still working intensively on technological problems. By 1686 he had made a burning-mirror which could melt all known metals, even iron, and with which he could produce glass. Tschirnhaus's next problem was how to make a large burning-glass. This meant first working out how to pour (rather than blow) glass, then how to produce it in blocks and finally how to grind it. He evolved a grinding mill driven by water power and furnaces that used less wood.[44] By 1691 he had made a burning-mirror sixty-five cm across.[45] These mirrors made him famous throughout Europe and Johann Georg IV gave him the title of Electoral Councillor. On the basis of Tschirnhaus's development of these glass-making techniques, glassworks were founded in Dresden in 1700, in Glücksburg and, after Tschirnhaus's death, in 1709 in Friedrichsthal near Senftenberg.[46] The Dresden glassworks, for instance, produced candelabra, pillars, tables and mirrors, as well as fireproof crucibles and receptacles for chemical experiments. Mirrors and other objects could be ground and polished in the mill also founded in Dresden by Tschirnhaus. In the winter of 1693–94 Tschirnhaus began to work systematically on the problem of the chemical composition and firing of porcelain. Many attempts to produce it had been made previously but they had produced either fine stoneware, milky glass or at best softpaste porcelain.

In 1696 Friedrich August I commissioned Tschirnhaus to look for semi-precious stones and valuable minerals in the Saxon countryside, just as Elector August had commissioned Giovanni Maria Nosseni in 1575 and Johann Georg II Wolf Caspar von Klengel in 1656–59. He was then sent by Anton Egon, Prince of Fürstenberg, Regent of Saxony during the absences of Friedrich August in Poland, on a study trip to Holland and France in the winter of 1701–2. On this journey Tschirnhaus visited those places where attempts to make porcelain were also in progress – Delft and St Cloud were two. By the time he returned to Dresden in March 1702, the young Johann Friedrich Böttger was already incarcerated there.

Böttger had claimed falsely to have manufactured gold in Berlin and had fled to Wittenberg in 1701. August the Strong was naturally interested in anyone who could apparently produce gold and had him brought to Dresden in November of the same year and imprisoned so that he could make good his claims. He was not to be released until 19 April 1714. Böttger was forced to continue his experiments under the eye of the Freiberg Mining Councillor ('Bergrat') Gottfried Papst von Ohain (1656–1729) and of Michael von Nehmitz (1670–1739). In 1703, realising that his attempts to make gold were not bearing fruit, Böttger attempted to flee to Austria but was brought back. In 1704 Tschirnhaus was asked to direct his work. In the autumn of 1705 Böttger was taken to the Albrechtsburg in Meissen, the ancient fortress of the Wettins, and given five Freiberg miners as assistants. Here he managed with Tschirnhaus's help to make the red stoneware which is known today as 'Böttger stoneware'.[47] It was not until 1707, when Böttger was installed in a research laboratory in the Jungfernbastei in Dresden, that he actually produced white porcelain made from a combination of kaolin, alabaster and quartz (Figure 49). Kaolin had been found at Aue near Schneeberg in the Erzgebirge in 1708.[48] In April 1708 the decree to found a porcelain manufactory in Dresden was signed, but in October of that year Tschirnhaus died.

Figure 49. White so-called 'Böttger porcelain'. C. 1716–17. H. 42 cm. Porzellansammlung, Dresden. Inv. No. P.E.2909 a. Deutsche Fotothek (Karpinski).

Böttger continued his work, solving the problem of the glaze by March 1709. He made another decisive contribution to the development of the new material by concerning himself with its aesthetic qualities. A sculptor, a glass-engraver and a potter were working with him as early as 1708.[49] Developments now followed swiftly, with porcelain objects being exhibited for the first time in 1710 at the Easter Fair in Leipzig. Work also continued to produce underglaze decoration. On 6 June 1710, a workshop for the production of porcelain was installed in the Albrechtsburg in Meissen and white porcelain was sold for the first time in May 1713 in Leipzig. Meanwhile Böttger did not cease his alchemical experiments, producing for the king by whatever means a lump of gold and one of silver on 20 March 1713. Shortly after, he became seriously ill, poisoned by the chemicals with which he came into daily contact, and died in 1716.

The two men who together created one of Saxony's most lasting products could not have been more different in their mental worlds, each representing a different trend in the development of science and manufacture. Tschirnhaus was a mathematician, philosopher and scientist, a friend of the foremost thinkers of his day, widely travelled and a representative of the dawning era of Enlightenment rationalism. His great ambition, as we have seen, was to found an Academy of Sciences in Saxony. Böttger began as an apprentice to the pharmacist Friedrich Zorn in Berlin and achieved early notoriety by claiming to have produced gold. This remained his great ambition. Alchemy and chemistry joined together in the service of technology as so often in Saxony's past.

The move of the related industry of mining into the pre-industrial age can also be seen in the event in which the great wedding festivities of 1719 culminated. This was the festival of Saturn held on 26 September.[50] These are Saturnalia with a difference. Saturn rules over the earth and the treasures within it and, as Saxony is rich not only in metals but in minerals and fossils, they are celebrated here. In the Plauenschen Grund outside the city Saturn has therefore built a temple in the rocks and has illuminated it by means of hundreds of miners' lamps. The miners appear in massed groups, bringing their ores, the various types of rock and precious stones they quarry, as well as the smelted metals, treated minerals and those things manufactured from the products of mining. They also bring all their mining and smelting tools, their machines and instruments. One has to imagine the elegantly dressed courtiers, the foreign dignitaries, the ladies in their perfumes and silks watching for hours hundreds and hundreds of men from the mountains, led by their bosses, march past, demonstrating all aspects of their profession, in what amounts to an early version of an industrial or trade fair (Figure 50). Of course, the miners did not wear their dirty and ragged working clothes but were suitably costumed for the occasion in versions of miners' dress, as we can see from the pen and wash drawing of the costumes by Carl Heinrich Fehling.[51] Twenty-four different costumes were made for the different groups in the procession and it was led by the Court Chamberlain Woldemar, Freiherr von Löwendal, representing the Director of the Saxon Mines, who was of course the Elector himself. In an emphatic reference to the Dresden tradition, Johann Georg II's bejewelled and enamelled miner's accoutrements, the 'Bergmannsgarnitur', made especially for him for the 1678 festivals and discussed in chapter 4, were taken out of store in 1719 and worn by Baron von Loewendel.

But the miners do not just show a few attractive and symbolic lumps of ore or precious metals or wheel on a couple of small furnaces amusingly spouting flames. As the programme of the procession makes clear ('Specification des Bergmännischen Auffzuges'), this was a display of what the mines and quarries in the Saxon domains could produce in the way of raw materials, of the specialised techniques needed to extract the materials and then of what the various related metallurgical and chemical industries produced from them. Natural resources and technical know-how are equally on display, and a specialist in mining and metal-working techniques would not have been disappointed by this display.

The demonstration falls into two parts, each consisting of thirty-five sections. The first demonstrates actual mining and the mineral wealth of Saxony, the second the processing techniques. In part I, for instance, section 11 demonstrates surveying underground and shows the necessary instruments, section 15 consists of a huge lump of all kinds of ore in which the whole workings of a mine are demonstrated by clockwork (Figure 51) and section 16 shows an example of the windlasses and other machines that move the mined ore along underground and up to the surface (Figure 52). This was a structure at least three metres high, for instance, as we can see from the depiction of it by Fehling.[52] Section 32 consists of a furnace which a whole troupe of workmen demonstrates to the assembled company, casting the smelted ore before their eyes. This same first part of the show also demonstrated not only gold and silver ore, precious stones and pearls but a whole range of different kinds of ore, gravel, bismuth, cobalt, vitriol, sulphur, alum, marble, serpentine and fossils. These are all specified in the programme of the

Figure 50. Carl Heinrich Jacob Fehling, The Festival of Saturn, 26 September 1719. The smelters demonstrate their skill. Kupferstich-Kabinett, Dresden. Engraving. Deutsche Fotothek (Koch).

Figure 51. Carl Heinrich Jacob Fehling, The Festival of Saturn, 26 September 1719. A model of a working mine surmounted by Mercury. Kupferstich-Kabinett, Dresden. Engraving. Deutsche Fotothek (Koch).

Figure 52. Carl Heinrich Jacob Fehling, Four of the machines presented at the Festival of Saturn on 26 Septembert 1719. Kupferstich-Kabinett, Dresden. Engraving. Deutsche Fotothek (Richter).

procession with indications of where they were extracted in many cases. The spectators must have had this programme, since even a specialist could not be expected to recognise 'gravel from Johanngeorgenstadt and Reichenbach' by lamplight and at a distance (section 20). The programme also emphasises that all these ores and minerals were deposited, extracted and prepared in Electoral Saxon domains. Part II of the procession demonstrates smelting of various metals by means of furnaces, assaying with all the necessary tools, minting both from casts and dies (and coins were made then and there before the spectators' eyes), the production of cast-iron, glass-making with differently coloured glass, polished marble, alabaster and serpentine, objects of brass and various kinds of wire. For each industry, wherever a machine or piece of apparatus can be demonstrated, it is. Part II also stresses that all these processes are carried out in Saxony. The camaraderie of the miners is demonstrated by the mining songs they sing and their characteristic cry 'Glück auf'.

This extraordinarily technical presentation is followed by a banquet in the Temple of Saturn. This is in the form of a hollowed-out mountain decorated with all kinds of miners' implements, and the patron of the festivity appears in effigy with a miner's axe in his left hand and a lump of ore in his right. The table is set all down its length with sugar mountains interspersed with little models of machines and figures of miners and other workers (Figure 53). On the mountainside opposite the temple the king's name glows in lights surrounded by the seven planets each with its own metal. The words 'constellatio felix' are to be seen lit up on the mountain (Figure 54).

Princely glorification is not absent, indeed the King-Elector is portrayed as overlord of all these treasures and master by proxy of all these techniques, which, in their ability to transmute metals and create such marvellous new materials from them as glass, have quasi-magical qualities. But the Elector has also demonstrated a whole series of saleable commodities and processes to a group of foreign ambassadors and princely guests.

From Mercury to Apollo – August's festivals

Since August the Strong spent so much time in Poland, particularly in the first half of his reign, Dresden did not see the constant succession of festivities through the year and every year that was characteristic of Johann Georg II's reign. Saxony's involvement in the Northern War and the expense associated with that were other inhibiting factors. Friedrich August's reign is characterised rather by infrequent but large-scale festivals to mark significant political events, of which four in particular are noteworthy. The first is the event he staged in 1695 to mark his unexpected accession. He staged another group of festivities in

Figure 53. Carl Heinrich Jacob Fehling, The banqueting table decorated with sugar mountains and models of mining and metallurgical processes during the Festival of Saturn, 26 September 1719. Kupferstich-Kabinett, Dresden. Engraving. Deutsche Fotothek (Koch).

The Saxon Hercules 231

Figure 54. Carl Heinrich Jacob Fehling, The illumination during the Festival of Saturn, 26 September 1719. Kupferstich-Kabinett, Dresden. Engraving. Deutsche Fotothek (Richter).

the summer of 1709 in honour of the visit of his cousin Fredrik IV, King of Denmark, and to mark the end of Saxony's involvement in the Northern War. There were festivities again at the carnival in 1728 for the visit of the King and Crown Prince of Prussia. But by far the most lavish were the celebrations in September 1719 for the wedding of his son and heir to the Emperor's daughter.[53] As was usual in Dresden these celebrations all lasted about a month.

It is clear from the themes he chose that the Dresden festival tradition, as August had experienced it in his grandfather's and father's day and as it was physically represented by the huge store of costumes and accoutrements in the Armoury, was Friedrich August's constant frame of reference. The carnival celebrations after his accession in 1695 included, for instance, a humorous tournament in which the participants were dressed as *commedia dell'arte* characters, a running at the ring in national costume on 29 January, and a so-called 'Grand Carousel' on 5 February, in which the four quadrilles (or teams) were led respectively by Nimrod, Cyrus, Alexander the Great and Julius Caesar.[54] But the humorous *commedia dell'arte* characters had been seen shortly before, during the reign of his brother, in a running at the quintain between the 'Truffaldini' and the 'Scaramuzzi' staged for Friedrich August's own wedding in February 1693,[55] a running at the ring in national dress had been held for this wedding as well as for the carnival in 1687 in his father's reign[56] and a running at the ring and at the quintain, in which the six planets competed against the six oldest monarchs of world history – Nimrod, Nebuchadnezar, Cyrus, Alexander the Great, Julius Caesar and Charlemagne – had been held in November 1679 in the time of his grandfather, Johann Georg II.[57] The only innovatory event in the month-long festival in 1695 was the 'Magnificent Procession of the Pagan Gods and Goddesses' ('Heidnischer Götter und Göttinnen prächtiger Auffzug'), which moved through the streets of Dresden on 7 February before the male participants took part in a double running at the ring that night in the indoor riding school. (Such contests in which two participants ran at the ring simultaneously in parallel 'lanes' were already well established in Dresden. There had been one already, for instance, in 1692.[58]) The participants in the procession consisted of equal numbers of men and women, in direct contrast to the traditional tournament procession in which the female roles were all played by men. Twenty double-page oblong engravings of the procession were published in book form with an accompanying explanatory text.[59] There were fifty-three different groups in the procession and Klötzel's text gives us not only the names of the various deities in each group but of the 136 members of the court who represented them. The procession also contained thirty-three floats and festival carts, many of them moving invisibly. Examples are the low hill on which Iris sits under her rainbow or the spectacular cloudscape out of which Saturn emerges clutching his scythe and holding a naked child up by the heel. Other floats consist of magnificent architectural constructions such as the Temple of Vesta with its flaming torches on the roof or of huge landscapes such as Mount Parnassus or the rocky cave in which Vulcan's smithy can be seen in action. The most striking float is the second last, representing the jaws of hell. Pluto and Proserpina are enthroned between the yawning jaws of a monstrous head, out of whose throat and nostrils belch smoke and flames. Cerberus sits on the tip of the monster's tongue, Alecto, Tisiphone and Megaera holding flaming torches are seated further back and the float is surrounded by dancing monsters. It is preceded by Charon's boat bearing corpses, with grave-diggers and skeletons in attendance. The final float shows the tortures of the ancient world.[60]

In this festival the young Elector rides at the head of the procession as Mercury. While the members of the court apparently drew lots for their roles, chance was not allowed a free hand in the assignment of parts. Aurora von Königsmark, for instance, the Elector's mistress at that date, appeared as Aurora, the Dawn, driving the coach of the Sun God Apollo (Figure 55). It is therefore entirely possible that August elected to represent Mercury and that he did so as a reference to the appearance of his ancestor and namesake Elector August in a festival in 1574 in that very costume.[61]

In 1709 for the visit of the Danish King, his cousin and ally Fredrik IV, Friedrich August, by now August II, King of Poland, staged a series of

Figure 55. Martin Klötzel, Apollo and his coachman Aurora von Königsmark. 1695. Engraving.

festivities lasting from 26 May until 29 June. This time the ladies actually took part in the contests in the ladies' running at the ring ('Damenringrennen') held on 6 June. This was a charming, decorative event in which twenty-four ladies of the court, each dressed in a different colour, were driven down the lists seated in an open chariot. As well as her coachman, each lady was accompanied by two gentlemen riding alongside, each holding a lance like the lady herself. The lady and her two cavaliers ran at the ring simultaneously, one in each of three lanes. Such a ladies' contest was not an innovation introduced by August II but again belongs to the Dresden tradition. Possibly influenced by the Danish court with which the Electors of Saxony had so many links through marriage, August's great-aunt Magdalena Sibylle, the widowed Princess of Denmark, had staged such a contest in 1654 for her second wedding to Friedrich, Duke of Saxony-Altenburg.[62] More importantly, she had had it published in an illustrated festival book, so that it would have been available for consultation fifty years later in the Electoral Library.[63] On 10 June 1709 there was a tournament on foot in which the cadets of the military academy staged a historicising contest using pike and sword, the weapons of yesteryear. On 19 June there was a running at the head in which each of the quadrilles represented one of the four continents. The costumes for this were modelled on Louis XIV's 'Grand Carousel' held in Paris in 1662, particularly those of the Africans who were led by Friedrich August.[64] On 22 June a re-run of the 'Magnificent Procession of the Pagan Gods and Goddesses' was held, using the same costumes as in 1695, but with August this time representing Apollo, wearing the golden sun mask made by Johann Melchior Dinglinger still to be seen in the Armoury in Dresden today.

We should not be surprised that August used the costumes and floats from 1695 fourteen years later. Claudia Schnitzer has documented in great detail the manner in which costumes and props were stored for generations in Dresden. They were then used, re-used, cut down and remodelled extensively.[65] This was true even for such a large-scale festival as the wedding celebrations of 1719. Indeed, as Schnitzer shows, the larger the scale of the festivity, the more likely the court was to re-use existing material in order to save both time and money. The effect, of course, was one of visual continuity not just from one festival to the next but from one reign to the next.

The celebrations for the wedding of Friedrich August II (later August III, King of Poland) in 1719 to the Imperial Princess, the most magnificent festivity of August II's reign, also built on the pre-existing Dresden tradition. It was the scale of the festivities that distinguished them from any festivity held in Dresden before. Elisabeth Mikosch has calculated, for instance, that the guest list included 'a total of 1257 foreign and non-local guests, including 11 princes, 87 counts, 55 barons and 356 other aristocrats'.[66] The actual wedding took place in August 1719 in Vienna, and in September the bride made her solemn entry into her new capital city of Dresden,[67] where the union between the Wettins and the Habsburgs was marked by a month of celebration.

For this, the triumphant assertion of his foreign policy ambitions, August II chose as a unifying theme for the whole celebration lasting from 2 to 30 September that of the seven planets. It is no accident that this is exactly the same theme his grandfather had used in 1678 in the greatest festival of his reign, the 'Durchlauchtigste Zusammenkunft', discussed in chapter 5 above.

In 1719, as in 1678, each of the seven planets was the patron of a different festivity. The programme was announced in the first event, an open-air opera, *La Gara degli Dei*, with music by Johann David Heinichen. This took place in the gardens of the Holländisches Palais (later the Japanisches Palais) on the northern bank of the Elbe.[68] The planets entered on a chariot and each told of the virtue or quality he or she had given the Electoral Prince. They then vied with one another to provide the finest event in honour of the bridal couple. Apollo would be the patron of the firework display, Diana of the hunt, Mars of the tournament, Mercury of the Fair, Venus of the ladies' running at the ring, Jupiter of the Grand Carousel of the Four Elements and Saturn of the concluding Miners' Festivity. This contest of the gods was concluded by a three-act firework drama on the Elbe depicting the heroic deeds of Jason and the Argonauts.[69]

The text of *La Gara degli Dei* is in Italian, as is that of the operatic prologue to the hunt and of the opera *Teofane* by Antonio Lotti, which was also part of the festivities. French prose versions were supplied as a parallel text in the printed versions. The tournament entitled *Li quattro Elementi: Carrosello*,[70] is a running at the head held in the Zwinger and is reminiscent of the Carousel of the Four Continents in 1709. The quadrille of the Air is led by Friedrich Ludwig, Duke of Württemberg, that of Fire by August II, that of Earth by Johann Adolf, Duke of Saxony-Weissenfels, and that of Water by the bridegroom himself. It is in fact a tournament opera on a small scale, with Jupiter (the castrato J. Boschi) entering on a float at the beginning and singing an aria composed by Antonio Lotti.

Again we note the many similarities with earlier festivities in Dresden. The hunt under the patronage of Diana (here in an aquatic version with the goddess's chariot floating down the Elbe accompanied by water nymphs and followed by the animals to be slaughtered) is a familiar Dresden theme (Figure 56) and the tournaments in the marketplace under the patronage of Mars and the ladies' running at the ring under Venus are simply expanded versions of similar events held in 1709. The ladies' running at the ring, for instance, has now increased to four groups running simultaneously to illustrate the contest between the four seasons. The grand finale to the celebrations, the concluding Festival of Saturn or Miners' Festivity discussed in the previous section, picks up another characteristic Dresden theme going back, as we saw in chapter 4, to the mid-sixteenth century.

There were some innovations, however. After the running at the head and at the ring, there came what is called in contemporary sources the 'jet de boules'. This is the team game, originally of Moorish origin, in which two teams bombard each other with hollow earthenware balls. It was known in Italy as the 'giuoco de' caroselli', in Spain as the 'juego de alcancías' and in the Empire in the early seventeenth century as the 'Carisell'. August has perhaps seen this game in older accounts of German tournaments, in particular in that of the Stuttgart 'Carisell' of 1617 which also had the Four Elements as its theme.[71] Elisabeth Mikosch

Figure 56. Zacharias Longuelune, The Festival of Diana on the Elbe on 18 September 1719. Pen, ink and wash. Kupferstichkabinett, Dresden Sax. Top. Ca. 200. Deutsche Fotothek (Nagel).

also draws attention to the Turkish Fête which was held on 17 September as part of these celebrations. This consisted of a banquet in Turkish dress held at night in the illuminated Turkish Palace in the Turkish Garden which culminated in a firework display.[72]

But the traditional elements far outweigh these innovations. The festivities of 1719 represent a refashioning and a grand synthesis of the Dresden tradition, not a departure from it. It is thus misleading to claim that 'Augustus followed the fashion for public expressions of grandeur that had been set for other monarchs such as Leopold I and Louis'.[73] Of course, August was influenced by Louis XIV, but he did not need the example of the Emperor and the French king, who in any case staged very few festivals in the course of their long reigns and those few mostly before he was born, to hold festivals himself, for he had the practice of his own brother, father and particularly grandfather to build on.

Where August II was planning to emulate Louis XIV was in the publication of a grand large-format festival book such as emanated from the Royal Press in Paris in the 1660s and 1670s. It would have 125 copper engravings by such artists as Carl Heinrich Jacob Fehling, Raymond Leplat, Alessandro Mauro, Pöppelmann, Zacharias Longuelune and Anna Maria Werner. But, though the Prints and Drawings collection contains many of the preparatory illustrations for this work, the book was never published, perhaps for lack of money. Like many of August II's projects, including the Zwinger, execution and idea did not quite match up.

We have seen how August took the traditions of his house in religion, in court culture, in the Ducal collections, in the development of alchemy and in court festivals and put his own distinctive mark on them. He made Dresden a European city, rather than just a German one, and left an artistic legacy which still makes it one of the artistic capitals of Europe.

Conclusion

This book begins with that moment in the middle of the sixteenth century when the Albertine branch of the House of Wettin wrested the Electorship of Saxony from the senior branch, the Ernestines. This was the moment when Dresden became a court city. It ends when the Electors of Saxony have become, if only for a few generations, Kings of Poland and Grand Dukes of Lithuania, dividing their time between their two capitals, Dresden and Warsaw.

One of the stories that this book seeks to tell is how a princely house uses art in its widest sense as part of its panoply of power, as a tool of government and as an expression of its political ambitions. But the understanding of power and of princely government, and indeed of art, is conditioned, not to say determined, by the ideas of the age. So at any one time there is a fruitful and dynamic interaction between the individual prince, the political situation and the intellectual and cultural world he inhabits. To take an example: of the eight Electors of Saxony this book discusses, seven were devout Lutherans. Crucial to their concept of government and of princely behaviour was Luther's vision of the role of the prince towards his subjects and of right Christian behaviour in general. In addition, the Electors of Saxony were regarded throughout Protestant Europe as guardians of the Reformation, initially because Luther's Wittenberg was on their territory and their ancestor Friedrich the Wise had been Luther's protector, but subsequently because they became the leaders of the *Corpus Evangelicorum*, the grouping of Protestant princes in the Holy Roman Empire. This widespread image of their role naturally influenced their own self-understanding and then crucially determined their patronage of church music and Lutheran biblical drama and their presentation of themselves throughout the sixteenth and seventeenth centuries as devout Lutherans in funerary monuments, paintings and *bas reliefs*.

Equally, once princes north of the Alps had become acquainted, particularly during the second half of the sixteenth century, with the extraordinary flowering of art, architecture, science and technology which had already taken place in Italy, Protestant princes for whom the Catholic south was by definition suspect became fascinated by all things Italian. That there was a tension between the constant importation of Italian artists, composers, musicians, architects and fortification engineers, the constant engagement with the official art of the Catholic Italian princes, and the pronouncedly German quality of official Lutheran culture, associated through Luther himself with the German language, only gave their fascination an added *frisson*.

The last of our Electors, Friedrich August I (August the Strong), visited Versailles at the age of seventeen, at a time when he was merely a younger son. He met Louis XIV, then a man of about fifty, and the French king made a lasting impression on the youth. Versailles became a cultural touchstone and Louis an ideal to be emulated for the rest of Friedrich August's life. Comparable is the year-long stay at a comparably young and impressionable age of another younger son, Johann Georg I, in Italy in 1601. When both of these men succeeded to the Electorship unexpectedly, their early cultural experiences expressed themselves in the art, architecture, music and theatre they commissioned in Dresden and, in the case of Friedrich August, in Warsaw.

The interest of the Electors of Saxony in some of the principal currents of thought of their age can be seen in the case of Elector August in the sixteenth century, whose personal interest in science and technology was so sustained and which manifested itself in the collections he founded and which bore such fruit in the economic expansion of his territory. The way this engagement with and understanding of science was developed further by Johann Georg I as one of the fruits of his stay in Italy is charted in chapter 2. The on-going interest of the Electors throughout at least two centuries in alchemy, that central branch of early modern science, manifested itself culturally in court festivals but also in what has become that cultural product known to most people throughout the world who have no other acquaintance with Dresden court culture, Meissen porcelain or, as it is often called, Dresden china.

The management of knowledge, as it is called in chapter 3, that is, the patronage of scientific enquiry, its organisation and its display were very much matters of princely concern in this period. The arrangement of the library, the organisation and re-organisation of the cabinet of curiosities down the centuries, the founding by Johann Georg I of a 'Chamber of Anatomy' – all of this activity has to do with the intellectual world the Electors inhabited but also with their understanding of their role as rulers.

The wider political scene was at times the determining factor for cultural production in Saxony. We might cite the decoration of the Riesensaal, the principal ceremonial space in the Palace in Dresden, discussed in chapter 5. At the height of the Thirty Years' War, Johann Georg I commissioned a whole new iconographic programme for this room. It was begun in 1628 and completed in 1638, though with a seven-year hiatus because of the war. This programme positioned Saxony within the Empire, the universe and indeed the cosmos, at a time when political certainties needed to be stoutly reaffirmed. Johann Georg II's installation as Garter Knight and his institution of a series of festivals on its anniversary enabled him to bolster his own personal position – he was, after all, called George himself – but also to demonstrate within the Empire, and particularly in competition with emerging Brandenburg, his political standing on the international stage. In similar vein, the great wedding festivals organised by August the Strong in 1719 for the marriage of his son and heir to the daughter of the Emperor celebrated the greatest diplomatic triumph of his reign, after his own election to the crown of Poland.

But at other times it was internal Albertine family politics that were the driving force. Both chapter 1 and chapter 5 chart the way in which Johann Georg II used drama and ballet to emphasise his pre-eminent position as heir and subsequently Elector in a life-long struggle with his three younger brothers.

The period charted in this book was not an age when decisions were taken by committee. It was the will of the individual prince that determined what got built or painted, what was bought in terms of art works, which musicians were employed, what plays were performed and in what space. Without the love of Christian I for horses, for instance, the great stable building in Dresden would not have been commissioned. Without the real taste and understanding of August the Strong for goldsmith work, indeed his passion for intricate beautifully crafted *objets de vertu*, the masterpieces produced by the Dinglinger brothers and which every visitor to Dresden today marvels over in the Green Vault would never have come into being.

This book has proceeded by taking soundings, by picking up particular cultural objects or manifestations at various times. It seeks to show the interaction between prince, politics and ideas over almost two centuries in the most important Protestant court in the Empire and the only such court with a continuous dynastic and cultural tradition. Electoral

Saxony's main borders, apart from those with Ernestine Saxony to the west, were with Bohemia to the east and Brandenburg to the north. Its political engagement with Poland reinforced its gaze eastwards rather than westwards. But its cultural engagement was with Italy and later with France, the influences from which it combined with its own strong local Lutheran German tradition. Court culture in Dresden exhibits a fruitful synthesis to be found nowhere else in the Empire, if not in Europe, in this form.

Notes

Chapter 1

1. See HStA OHMA C2 for accounts of these funerals, detailing the elaborate ceremonial that was employed.
2. Dirk Syndram (ed.) with Ulli Arnold and Jutta Kappel, *Das Grüne Gewölbe zu Dresden. Führer durch seine Geschichte und seine Sammlung*, second revised edition, Munich, Berlin, 1997, p. 11.
3. Wilhelm Ernst Tentzel, *Saxonia Numismatica, oder Medaillen-Cabinet. Dritter Theil der Albertinischen Linie/ Von Chur=Fürst Johann Georgen II. biß auff Den ietzigen Chur=Printzen*. Dresden/ gedruckt beym Kön. Hoffbuchdrucker/ Joh.Riedeln. 1705. BL 603.e.12,13. Tab. 68, no. I.
4. Ekkehard Henschke, *Landesherrschaft und Bergbauwirtschaft: zur Wirtschafts- und Verwaltungsgeschichte des Oberharzer Bergbaugebietes im 16. und 17. Jahrhundert*, Berlin, 1975. This monograph provides a detailed examination of early modern mining in general, its organisation and its legal, economic and administrative basis, with many comparisons with Saxony. See also Herbert Pforr, 'Der sächsische Silberbergbau in der Agricola-Zeit', in *Agricola-Ehrung 1994. Bergreviere im 16. Jahrhundert. Vorträge des historischen Kolloquiums*. Clausthal-Zellerfeld n.d., pp. 3–18.
5. Henschke, *Landesherrschaft*, p. 358.
6. *Bergbau und Kunst in Sachsen*, exh. cat., Staatliche Kunstsammlungen, Dresden 1989, p. 78.
7. See Helmut Bräuer, 'Zur wirtschaftlichen Entwicklung Sachsens nach dem Dreißigjährigen Krieg', *Dresdner Hefte* 33 (1993), 13–24.
8. See Hugh Torrens, 'Early collecting in the field of geology', in Oliver Impey and Arthur Macgregor, *The Origins of Museums. The Cabinet of Curiosities in Sixteenth- and Seventeenth-Century Europe*, Oxford, 1985, pp. 204–13, pp. 207–8.
9. See Klaus Thalheim, 'Die Suche nach "edlen Steinen" in Sachsen vom 16. bis zum 18. Jahrhundert', in Jutta Kappel, *Deutsche Steinschneidekunst aus dem Grünen Gewölbe zu Dresden*, exh. cat., Deutsches Steinschneidemuseum, Idar-Oberstein 1998, pp. 11–25.
10. See Karlheinz Blaschke, *Moritz von Sachsen, ein Reformationsfürst der zweiten Generaton*, Göttingen, 1983.
11. Heinrich Magirius, 'Das Moritzmonument im Freiberger Dom – ein Gemeinschaftswerk italienischer, niederländischer und deutscher Künstler zum Andenken an eine hervorragende Fürstenpersönlichkeit', in *Dresdner Hefte* 52 (1997), 87–92.
12. I am indebted to the study of the Freiberg Burial Chapel by Monika Meine-Schawe: *Die Grablege der Wettiner im Dom zu Freiberg. Die Umgestaltung des Domchores durch Giovanni Maria Nosseni 1585–1594*, Munich, 1992.
13. Meine-Schawe, *Die Grablege der Wettiner*, p. 106.

14 Wolfgang May, 'Die höfische Architektur in Dresden unter Christian I', in *Dresdner Hefte* 29 (1992), 63–71.
15 Meine-Schawe, *Die Grablege der Wettiner*, p. 32.
16 *Ein kurtzer Bericht/ Welcher gestallt von der Rhömischen Keyserlichen Mayestat/ Keyser Maximilian/ dis Namens dem Andern/ Der Churfürst Hertzog Augustus zů Sachssen/&c unser gnedigster Herr/ Seiner Churfürstlichen Gnaden Reichs Lehen unnd Regalien/ auff den jetzigen jhrer Key. May. Ersten Reichstag/ allhier zů Augspurg/ den vviij. des Monats Aprilis/ offentlich underm Himmel empfangen/ Und wie es allenthalben darmit zůgangen*. Getruckt zu Strasburg bey Peter Hug in S. Bartelgassen 1566.
17 See Jutta Bäumel, *Die Rüstkammer zu Dresden. Führer durch die Ausstellung im Semperbau*, Munich, Berlin, 1995, pp. 61–2.
18 See Béatrice Nicollier-De Weck, *Hubert Languet (1518–1581). Un Réseau politique international de Melanchthon à Guillaume d'Orange*, Geneva, 1995, p. 181f.
19 See Karlheinz Blaschke, 'Religion und Politik in Kursachsen 1586–1591', in Heinz Schilling (ed.), *Die reformierte Konfessionalisierung in Deutschland – Das Problem der 'Zweiten Reformation'*, Gütersloh, 1986, pp. 79–97.
20 See Blaschke, 'Religion und Politik', p. 86f.
21 See Ernst Koch, 'Der kursächsische Philippismus und seine Krise in den 1560er und 1570er Jahren', in Heinz Schilling (ed.), *Die reformierte Konfessionalisierung*, pp. 60–77. The contemporary suspicion is voiced among others by Iacobus Francus in his *Relatio Historica quinquennalis. Warhafftige Beschreibung/ aller fürnemmen unnd gedenckwürdigen Geschicht/ so sich jnnerhalb funff Jahren/ nemlich/ von anno 1590/ biß 1595. in hoch und nieder Teutchland ... zugetragen haben*, Frankfurt am Main: Brachfeldt, 1595, p. 92.
22 Meine-Schawe, *Die Grablege der Wettiner*, pp. 54–5.
23 See Axel Gotthard, '"Politice seint wir bäpstisch". Kursachsen und der deutsche Protestantismus im frühen 17. Jahrhundert', in *Zeitschrift für historische Forschung*, 20, 1993, 275–319.
24 See *Verborgene Schätze der Skulpturensammlung*, exh. cat. Staatliche Kunstsammlungen, Dresden 1992, p. 50, and Siegfried Asche, *Drei Bildhauerfamilien an der Elbe. Acht Meister des siebzehnten Jahrhunderts und ihre Werke in Sachsen, Böhmen und Brandenburg*, Vienna, Wiesbaden, 1961, p. 181f. In *Verborgene Schätze* it says that the relief was placed in the *Kunstkammer* on 30 September 1674. The date in fact is 30 November 1674.
25 Tentzel, *Saxonia Numismatica*, Tab. 58, no. 1, text pp. 572–4, and Julius und Albert Erbstein's *Verzeichniss der Hofrath Engelhardt'schen Sammlung sächsischer Münzen und Medaillen*, Dresden 1888 (part 1), 1890 (part 2), 1896 (part 3), 1903 (part 4), 1909 (part 5), No. 952 (part 3), p. 243.
26 HStA OHMA N I Nr.8: Ordnung Wie es an hohen Fest= und Sonntagen auch in der Wochen in der Residentz Dreßden, gehalten werden solte.
27 See Helen Watanabe-O'Kelly, *Triumphall Shews. Tournaments at German-speaking Courts in their European Context 1580–1730*, Berlin, 1992.
28 This is recorded in a magnificent manuscript tournament book in the SLUB (Mscr.Dresd.K 2) entitled: Contrafactur des Ringrennens. So Weilandt der Durchlauchtigste und Hochgeborne Furst und herr Augustus Hertzogk zu Sachssen, des Heiligen Römischen Reichs Ertzmarschalch und Churfürst Landgraue in Duringen, Margraue zu Meissen und Burggraue zu Magdeburgk,

Christseliger Gedechtnis den 23 February Anno 1574 im Fastnacht alhier zu Dreßden im Churfürstlichen Schlosse gehalten, auch mit wasserley Inuention einn Jede Parthei uf die Bahne kommen und daselbst gantz Ritterlich zierlich und herlich volbracht.

29 The sheet depicting David (fol. 23) has been missing from the manuscript since 1961.
30 See Jean-Louis Sponsel, *Der Zwinger, die Hoffeste und die Schloßbaupläne zu Dresden*, Dresden 1924, p. 14, and Irmgard Becker-Glauch, *Die Bedeutung der Musik für die Dresdener Hoffeste bis in die Zeit Augusts des Starken*, Kassel, Basel, 1951, p. 32 f.
31 A similar group of monks and nuns was presented at the running at the ring held in Cölln an der Spree by the Elector of Brandenburg in 1581 for the christening of his son Christian. Elector August of Saxony and his son Christian I, the Elector of Brandenburg's future son-in-law, were present. See the printed account by Philipp Agricola at SLUB Hist.Brand. 14, misc. 2, and at HStA OHMA B a, fol. 191f. and the manuscript tournament book by Friedrich Bercht [?] at SLUB Mscr.Dresd.J 17 (KA 500).
32 HStA OHMA B1 a and Ritterspiell 1581–1591 Nr 26a 10526. The manuscript tournament book by Daniel Bretschneider (SLUB Mscr.Dresd.K 1) is entitled: Contrafactur des Ringkrennens vndt anderer ritterspiell so vff Christiani Fürstlichen Beylager gehalten worden.
33 There is a volume of coloured engravings by Daniel Bretschneider with text at SLUB Hist.Sax.C.26 and just the engravings, again coloured, are included in SLUB Mscr.Dresd.K 1. This is discussed by Becker-Glauch, *Die Bedeutung der Musik*, p. 51.
34 This again is included in SLUB Mscr.Dresd.K 1.
35 SLUB Mscr.Dresd.J 9 and Sponsel, *Der Zwinger*, p. 20.
36 This is Abriß und Verzeichnus aller Inventionen und Aufzüge welche an Faßnachten Anno 1609 Als den Durchlauchtigsten Hochgeborenen Fürsten und Herrn, Herrn Christian den Anderen Herzogen und Churfürsten zu Sachsen die Durchlauchtige Hochgeborene Fürsten und Herrn, Herr Johann Casimir und Herr Johann Ernst Herzogen zu Sachsen sowol Herr Christian Marggraf zu Brandenburg freundlicherweise uff die im Churfl. Schloßhoff zu Dresden auffgerichtete Rennbahne gebracht worden. Verferttigt durch Daniel Bretschneider, Bürgern und Mahlern zu Dresden. SLUB Mscr.Dresd.J 18.
37 HStA OHMA A 3, Bildrolle Hierüber Nr.3 and Bildrolle Hierüber Nr. 13; Wolfgang Ferber, *Relation und umbständliche Beschreibung eines ansehnlichen und fürnehmen Stahlschiessens...*, Dresden: Gimel Bergen, 1615.
38 Georg Petzold, *Beschreibung Der Churfürstlichen Kindtauff/ und Frewdenfests zu Dreßden: den 18. Septemb. des verlauffenen 1614. Jahres/ wie auch der Ritterlichen Frewdenspiel/ folgende Tage uber/ Von Dem Durchlauchtigsten/ Hochgebornen Fürsten und Herrn/ Herrn Johann Georgen/ Hertzogen zu Sachssen... Gehalten... Auff gnedigstes begehren S. Durchlauchtigkeit/ aus dem Lateinischen vom Autore transferirt...*, Dresden 1615.
39 See Christoph Krummacher, *Musik als praxis pietatis. Zum Selbstverständnis evangelischer Kirchenmusik*, Göttingen, 1994.
40 See the exh. cat. *'Wunder Harfe'. 450 Jahre Sächsische Staatskapelle Dresden*, Staatliche Kunstsammlungen, Dresden, 1998, p. 13.

41 For church music in general at the Dresden court, see Eberhard Schmidt, *Der Gottesdienst am Kurfürstlichen Hofe zu Dresden. Ein Beitrag zur liturgischen Traditionsgeschichte von Johann Walter bis zu Heinrich Schütz*, Berlin, 1961.
42 See the many publications of Wolfram Steude, for instance, *Musikgeschichte Dresdens in Umrissen*, Dresden, 1978.
43 See the authoritative reworking by Greta Konradt of Walter Blankenburg's article 'Historia' in *Die Musik in Geschichte und Gegenwart*, second revised edition ed. by Ludwig Finscher, Kassel, Stuttgart 1994–, vol. 4, pp. 311–34.
44 They are entitled: *Historia des Leidens und Sterbens unsers Herrn und Heylandes Jesu Christi nach dem Evangelisten S. Matheum*; *Historia des Leidens und Sterbens ... Jesu Christi nach dem Evangelisten St. Lucam*; and *Historia des Leidens und Sterbens Jesu Christi nach dem Evangelisten St. Johannem* respectively.
45 See Konradt, 'Historia', p. 318.
46 On the printing industry in Zwickau see Kristina Leistner, '475 Jahre Buchdruck in Zwickau' in *500 Jahre Ratsschulbibliothek Zwickau*, exh. cat. Zwickau 1998, pp. 68–76, and on Meyerpeck and Biblical drama see Stephen L. Wailes, *The Rich Man and Lazarus on the Reformation Stage. A Contribution to the Social History of German Drama*, Susquehanna University Press, 1997, p. 169.
47 Registratur der bücher in des Churfürsten zu Saxen liberey zur Annaburg, SLUB Bibl.Arch.IB vol. 20.
48 The history of this library provided by a former librarian, Friedrich Adolf Ebert, *Geschichte und Beschreibung der königlichen öffentlichen Bibliothek zu Dresden*, Leipzig 1822, is still useful, but the best modern account, both of its development and its present-day holdings, is to be found in the article 'Dresden – Sächsische Landesbibliothek', in vol. 17, Sachsen A-K, pp. 95–155, ed. by Friedhilde Krause, of the *Handbuch der historischen Buchbestände in Deutschland* ed. by Bernhard Fabian, Hildesheim, Zurich, New York, 1997.
49 This work is still in the SLUB today at Theol. ev. mor.
50 The first edition is still in the SLUB at Lit.Lat.rec.A.1160.
51 This work is in the SLUB at 3 A 9739.
52 We know that the copy in the SLUB at Lit.germ.rec.2878.2 came from the Electoral Library.
53 SLUB Lit.Germ.rec.B 2878, 4.
54 The SLUB has 6 of his comedies at Lit. Rom. A.
55 SLUB Bibl.Arch.I 21 and Bibl. Arch. I 28, 29, 30. resp.
56 SLUB Lit.Germ.rec.B.1078.
57 The SLUB still holds this manuscript at Mscr.Dresd.M 227.
58 The text is preserved in the SLUB at Mscr.Dresd.M 224.
59 SLUB Mscr.Dresd.M261.
60 SLUB Mscr.Dresd.M 217.
61 Moritz Fürstenau, *Zur Geschichte der Musik und des Theaters am Hofe zu Dresden*, 2 vols., Dresden, 1861–1862; Robert Prölß, *Beiträge zur Geschichte des Hoftheaters zu Dresden in actenmässiger Darstellung*, Erfurt, 1880; Sponsel, *Der Zwinger*, Dresden, 1924.
62 *Englische Comedien und Tragedien/ Das ist: Sehr Schöne, herrliche und außerlesene, geist= und weltliche Comedi und Tragedi Spiel, Sampt dem Pickelhering, welche wegen ihrer artigen Inventionen, kurtzweiligen auch theils wahrhafftigen Geschicht halber, von den Engelländern in Deutschland an Königlichen, Chur= und Fürst= lichen Höfen, auch in vornehmen Reichs= See= und Händel=Städten seynd*

agiret und gehalten worden, und zuvor nie im Druck auß=gangen. An jetzo, Allen der Comedi und Tragedi lieb=habern, und Andern zu lieb und gefallen, der Gestalt in offen Druck gegeben daß sie gar leicht darauß/ Spielweiß widerumb angerichtet, und zur Ergetzligkeit und Erquickung des Gemüths gehalten wer=den können. Gedruckt im Jahr M.DC.XX. Leipzig: Gottfried Große 1620. This and collections of similar texts from 1630 and 1670 are reprinted in Manfred Brauneck (ed.), *Spieltexte der Wanderbühnen* (Ausgaben der deutschen Literatur des XV. bis XVIII. Jahrhunderts), Berlin/New York, 1970.

63 Wimmer, *Jesuitentheater*, and Jean Lebeau, *Salvator mundi. L'exemple de Joseph dans le théâtre allemand au XVIe siècle*, Nieuwkoop, 1977.

64 *Eine schöne Geistliche/Geistreiche Comoedi/von dem H. Joseph/...*, Dresden: Matthes Stöckel 1602. SLUB Lit.lat.rec.A.996. For the Goedelmann connection see Jörg Ulrich Fechner, 'Zur literaturgeschichtlichen Situation in Dresden 1627. Überlegungen im Hinblick auf die "Dafne"-Oper von Schütz und Opitz', in *Schütz-Jahrbuch* 1988, 5–29, p. 10.

65 HStA OHMA G 4, fol. 172b.

66 HStA OHMA A 11b, 489a–493a.

67 HStA OHMA NI Nr. 1.

68 HStA OHMA G 5a, fol. 460a–461b.

69 The archival documents are at HStA OHMA G 7. The printed account is: Gabriel Tzschimmer, *Die Durchlauchtigste Zusammenkunft/ Oder: Historische Erzehlung/ was der Durchlauchtigste Fürst und Herr/ Herr Johann George der Ander/...in...Dresden im Februario des MDCLXXVIII Jahren...auffühen und vorstellen lassen...*, Nürnberg, 1680. See Helen Watanabe-O'Kelly, 'Gabriel Tzschimmer's *Durchlauchtigste Zusammenkunft* (1680) and the German Festival Book Tradition', *Daphnis* 22 (1993), Heft 1, 61–72.

70 Tzschimmer, *Durchlauchtigste Zusammenkunft*, p. 132.

71 Tzschimmer, *Durchlauchtigste Zusammenkunft*, p. 138.

72 Tzschimmer, *Durchlauchtigste Zusammenkunft*, p. 151.

73 Tzschimmer, *Durchlauchtigste Zusammenkunft*, p. 160.

74 See Helen Watanabe-O'Kelly, 'Joseph und seine Brüder: Johann Georg II. und seine Feste zwischen 1660 und 1679', *Dresdner Hefte* 8 (1990), Heft 1, 29–38 and 'August von Sachsen-Weißenfels (1614–1680) und das Theater- und Festwesen am Dresdner Hof', in *Weltsicht und Selbstverständnis im Barock. Die Herzöge von Sachsen-Weißenfels – Hofhaltung und Residenzen. Protokoll des Wissenschaftlichen Kolloquiums am 24. und 25. April in Querfurt.* Halle 1999, 112–24.

75 Miscellanea Saxonica (Acta Streitigkeiten zwischen Chursachsen und Fürst August postuliertem Administrator des Stifts Magdeburg betreffend), SLUB Mscr.Dresd.J 180.

Chapter 2

1 See Stefan Delang, 'Das Renaissanceschloß', in *Das Dresdner Schloß. Monument sächsischer Geschichte und Kultur*, Dresden, 1992, pp. 68–73, and Ulrich Schütte, *Das Schloß als Wehranlage. Befestigte Schloßbauten der frühen Neuzeit*, Darmstadt, 1992, p. 48f.

2 Evelyn Korsch, 'Ein "heimlicher Vorschlag". Die politischen Beziehungen zwischen Dresden und Ferrara in der Mitte des 16. Jarhhunderts', in *Elbflorenz. Italienische Präsenz in Dresden 16–19. Jahrhundert*, ed. by Barbara Marx, Amsterdam and Dresden, 2000, pp. 37–64. My thanks are due to Professor Marx for allowing me to see this article and those by Dombrowski and Castor (see notes 6 and 12 below) from the same volume before publication.

3 In what follows I am indebted to the unpublished Master's dissertation by Sonja Karallus, 'Der "Riesensaal" im Dresdner Residenzschloß', Bonn, 1998.

4 Heinrich Magirius, 'Die bildkünstlerische Ausgestaltung der Fassaden des Schlosses', in *Das Dresdner Schloss*, pp. 74–7.

5 See the article on Scandello by Lothar Hoffmann-Erbrecht in *Grove Dictionary of Music and Musicians*, London, 1980, vol. XX, p. 547.

6 Damian Dombrowski shows how often Italian artists moved between Dresden and Prague in his article 'Dresden–Prag: Italienische Achsen in der zwischenhöfischen Kommunikation', in *Elbflorenz. Italienische Präsenz in Dresden 16–19. Jahrhundert*, ed. by Barbara Marx, Amsterdam and Dresden, 2000, pp. 65–99.

7 See Martin Ruhnke's article, 'Pinello di Gherardi', in *The New Grove Dictionary of Music and Musicians* ed. by Stanley Sadie, London, 1980, vol.14, pp. 754–5.

8 See the article by Hilda Lietzmann, 'Der kaiserliche Antiquar Jacopo Strada und Kurfürst August von Sachsen', in *Zeitschrift für Kunstgeschichte* 3 (1997), 377–99, where the relevant documents are reprinted.

9 See Werner Schade, *Dresdener Zeichnungen 1550–1650. Inventionen sächsischer Künstler in europäischen Sammlungen*, Dresden, 1969, p. 31.

10 See Dombrowski, 'Dresden–Prag', p. 71.

11 Barbara Marx, 'Künstlermigration und Kulturkonsum. Die Florentiner Kulturpolitik im 16. Jahrhundert und die Formierung Dresdens als Elbflorenz', in Bodo Guthmüller (ed.), *Deutschland und Italien in ihren wechselseitigen Beziehungen während der Renaissance*, Wiesbaden, 2000, pp. 211–97.

12 Markus Castor, 'Rocco di Linar und die *Mathematica Militaris* der Dresdner Fortifikation in italienischer Manier', in *Elbflorenz. Italienische Präsenz in Dresden 16–19. Jahrhundert*, ed. by Barbara Marx, Amsterdam and Dresden, 2000, pp. 101–34.

13 See Eva Papke, *Festung Dresden. Aus der Geschichte der Dresdner Stadtbefestigung*, Dresden, 1997, p. 66f.

14 See Monika Meine-Schawe, *Die Grablege der Wettiner im Dom zu Freiberg. Die Umgestaltung des Domchores durch Giovanni Maria Nosseni 1585–1594*, Munich, 1992, pp. 121–3, where both Sprintzenstein's letter of recommendation and Nosseni's letter of appointment are reprinted.

15 Wolfgang May, 'Die höfische Architektur in Dresden unter Christian I.', in *Dresdner Hefte* 29 (1992), 63–72.

16 Johann Sebastian Müller, *Des Chur= und Fürstlichen Hauses Sachsen/ Ernestin= und Albertinischer Linien/Annales von Anno 1400. bis 1700 . . .* , Weimar/ in Verlegung Johann Ludwig Gleditsch Buchhändlers in Leipzig/ Anno 1700, p. 192.

17 See the description by Laurentius Peccensteinius, *Theatrum Saxonicum, darinnen ordentliche warhaftige Beschreibung der . . . Könige, Chur- unnd Fürsten . . . Bisthumb . . . Schlösser . . . Ankunft, Auffnehmung . . . Thaten . . . in Obersachsen . . .*

ex archivis colligirt, In Verlegung Henning Grossen des Eltern/ Buchhendlern zu Leipzig Gedruckt zu Jehna durch Tobiam Steinman/ Anno MDCVIII.

18 See Wolfgang Götz, *Deutsche Marställe des Barock*, München, Berlin, 1964.
19 See the detailed discussion of the organisation of these storage arrangements in Claudia Schnitzer, *Höfische Maskaraden. Funktion und Ausstattung von Verkleidungsdivertissements an deutschen Höfen der Frühen Neuzeit*, Tübingen, 1999, p. 330f.
20 See Jutta Bäumel, *Die Rüstkammer zu Dresden. Führer durch die Ausstellung im Semperbau*, Munich, Berlin, 1995, pp. 6–9.
21 *Des Augsburger Patriciers Philipp Hainhofer Reisen nach Innsbruck und Dresden*, ed. by Oscar Doering, Vienna: Carl Graeser, 1901, p. 189.
22 Anton Weck, *Der Chur = Fürstlichen Sächsischen weitberuffenen Residentz= und Haupt=Vestung Dresden Beschreib: und Vorstellung/ Auf der Churfürstlichen Herrschafft gnädigstes Belieben in Vier Abtheilungen verfaßet/ mit Grund: und anderen Abrißen/ auch bewehrten Documenten erläutert durch Ihrer Churfürstlichen Durchl. zu Sachsen/ etc. Rath/ zu den Geheimen: und Reich=Sachen bestalten Secretarium und Archivarium Antonium Wecken*. Nürnberg/ In Verlegung Johann Hoffmanns/ Buch: und Kunsthändler/ Gedruckt daselbst bey Christian Sigismund Froberger. Anno MDCLXXX.
23 Quoted from Götz, *Deutsche Marställe des Barock*, p. 11.
24 Laurentius Peccensteinius, *Theatrum Saxonicum*, p. 12.
25 Jutta Bäumel, *Die Rüstkammer zu Dresden*, p. 67.
26 For an account of this festivity, see Iacobus Francus, *Relatio Historica quinquennalis. Warhafftige Beschreibung/ aller fürnemmen unnd gedenckwürdigen Geschicht/ so sich jnnerhalb funff Jahren/ nemlich/ von anno 1590/ biß 1595. in hoch und nieder Teutschland... zugetragen haben*, Frankfurt am Main: Brachfeldt, 1595, p. 286f.
27 See Marx, 'Künstlermigration und Kulturkonsum', pp. 289–90, where the relevant documents are transcribed.
28 See Marx, 'Künstlermigration und Kulturkonsum' p. 264.
29 Inv.No.U 267. See Bäumel, *Die Rüstkammer zu Dresden*, p. 58.
30 HStA Geheimes Archiv 8017/12, 16 June 1596, fol. 379b.
31 Naples 1550. See Helen Watanabe-O'Kelly, *Triumphall Shews. Tournaments at German-speaking Courts in Their European Context 1560–1730*, Berlin, 1992, in which Chapter III gives an overview of riding and horse-breeding in early modern Europe, as well as discussing the most important works of early modern hippological literature.
32 See Marx, 'Künstlermigration und Kulturkonsum', p. 263 and the relevant correspondence on pp. 281–2 of the same article.
33 See Julius Richter, *Das Erziehungswesen am Hofe der Wettiner Albertinischer (Haupt-) Linie*, Berlin, 1913, p. 134. He transcribes a letter from the Elector dated Cölln, 27 April 1598.
34 Federigo Grisone, *Künstlicher Bericht und allerzierlichte beschrybung der Edlen ... F. Grisonis. Wie die Streitbarn Pferdt... zum Ernst und ritterlicher Kurtzweil geschickt und volkommen zumachen. In sechs Bücher bester ordnung wolverstendlichem Teutsch und zierlichen Figuren... durch J. Fayser den Jüngern*, August 1573.
35 SLUB Bibl.Arch.I 21.
36 SLUB Bibl.Arch.I Ba 29, 'Bücher von Pferden und Roß Artzney' fol 146a f.
37 SLUB Bibl.Arch.I Ba 29, fol.155a f.

38 SLUB Bibl.Arch.I Ba 29 148b. Hörwart von Hohenburg, *Von der Hochberhümpten Adelichen und Ritterlichen* Kunst der Reyterey (Tegernsee, 1578).
39 Claudio Corte, *Il Cavallerizzo... nel qual si tratta della natura de' Caualli, delle Razze, del modo di gouernarli, domarli, & frenarli. Et di tutto quello, che a'Caualli, & a buon Cauallerizzo s'appartienne; Di nuouo dall'Auttore stesso corretto & emendato*, Venice 1562, and Lyons: Alessandro Marsilij, stampato per Pietro Roussin 1573. The Venetian edition is listed in the catalogue of the Frankfurt Book Fair for autumn 1573, so it was available in the Empire from at least this date.
40 The first edition appeared in Bologna in 1556. The SLUB inventory gives 1563 as the date and Venice as the place of publication.
41 Publius Vegetius Renatus, *I quattro libri della medicina de'cavalli et altri giumenti; overo dell'arte di Mariscalchi, tradotti della latina nella lingua volgare*, Venice, 1544.
42 This is to be found in SLUB Bibl Arch I 30, beginning at fol. 233a.
43 He also commissioned a manuscript tournament book from Heinrich Göding: Vorzeichnus vnd warhafftige eigentliche Contrafacturen aller Scharff rennen vnd Treffen, so der Durchlauchtigste hochgeborne Fürst vnd Herr Herr Augustus Hertzog zu Sachßen etc. vor vnnd inn S. Churf. G. Churfürstlichen Regierung mitt sonderlicher geschicklichkeit auch großer Lust vnnd verwunderung aller Zuseher gantz Ritterlich vnd rühmlich gethan vnd verbracht hat auch Zu wes Zeitt an welchem ortt vnnd mitt was Personen ein Jedes Rennen geschehen, Zu Ewigem löblichem gedechtnus S. Churf. G. geübtem mannlichen Ritterspielen deroselben Posteritet also fürgestellet. SLUB Mscr.Dresd.J 44. It suffered so badly in World War II that it can no longer be examined, though it is still in the possession of the SLUB in Dresden. Some pages from it are reproduced in Erich Haenel, *Der sächsischen Kurfürsten Turnierbücher*, Frankfurt a.M., 1910. See Helen Watanabe-O'Kelly, 'Chivalry and professionalism in Electoral Saxony in the mid-sixteenth century', in *The Chivalric Ethos and Military Professionalism*, ed. by David Trim, Leiden, in press.
44 For a more complete account of this development, see Helen Watanabe-O'Kelly, 'Tournaments and their Relevance for Warfare in the Early Modern Period', *European History Quarterly* 20 (1990), 451–63.
45 This is depicted in the illustrated manuscript account entitled Contrafactur des Ringrennens, So... Augustus Hertzogk zu Sachsen, des heiligen Römischen Reichs Ertzmarschalch vnd Churfürst..., den 23 February 1574 im Fastnacht alhier zu Dreßden im Churfürstlichem Schlosse gehalten, SLUB Mscr.Dresd.K 2. This magnificent manuscript is an oblong folio of 98 leaves, in pen, ink, wash, gouache and gilding on paper. It is probably by Daniel Bretschneider the Elder (1550–1623).
46 Antonio Bendinelli, *Il Nobilissimo et Richissimo Torneo Fatto nella Magnifica Città di Piacenza nella venuta del Serenissimo Don Giovanni D'Austria*, Piacenza, 1574.
47 See Jörg Jochen Berns, *Die Herkunft des Automobils aus Himmelstrionfo und Höllenmaschine*, Berlin, 1996.
48 See Schnitzer, *Höfische Maskeraden*, p. 310. It was already visible in the Ark of Venus, a float designed by Nosseni in 1581 for Christian I to take with him to the tournament for the christening of another Christian, the son of Johann Georg, Elector of Brandenburg, in Cölln (now Berlin).

49 HStA OHMA B1 a and b and Ritterspiell 1581–1591 Nr.26A. Daniel Bretschneider's manuscript depiction of these events entitled Contrafactur des Ringkrennens vndt anderer ritterspiell so vff Christiani Fürstlichen Beylager gehalten worden is at SLUB Msc.Dresd.K 1 and Hist.Sax.C.26 and Hist.Sax.C 25 = KA 827.
50 See HStA Ritterspiel 1581–1591 Nr 26a 10526.
51 See the depictions by Daniel Bretschneider the Elder in: Des Durchlauchtigsten Hochgebornen Fursten und Herrn Herrn Christiani Hertzogens vnd Churfursten zue Sachssen Ringk Rennen, welche S. Churf. G. an dero gelibten Jungen Tochter Freulein Dorotehenn/ Furstlichen Tauffe zue Dressden auffn Schloshoff den 26. 27. 28. vnd 29. January gehalten worden. Anno 1591. SLUB Mscr.Dresd.J 9. This is again an oblong folio of 87 leaves, in pen, wash, gouache and gilding on paper.
52 The archival documents are to be found at HStA OHMA G 1. See there too Bildrolle Nr. 6. See Daniel Bretschneider's 125-page tournament book in the SLUB, Mscr.Dresd.J 18. Its full title can be found in chapter 1, note 33.
53 See Helen Watanabe-O'Kelly, 'War and politics in early seventeenth-century Germany: The tournaments of the Protestant Union', in *Atti del Convegno del Centro di Studi Storici di Narni, La civiltà del torneo (sec. XII–XIII)*, Rome, 1990, pp. 231–45.
54 Schnitzer, *Höfische Maskeraden*, p. 315 and pp. 318–20.
55 HStA Geheimes Archiv 8017/2 Der Churfl. Jungen Herrschafften education belangende (Hoffmeister u. Praeceptorn Bestallung). Julius Richter discusses the entire education of these young princes, beginning before their father's death, in his detailed depiction of the princely education of the Albertines from the middle of the fifteenth century to the end of the eighteenth. See note 33 above. Far less detailed is Ernst Reimann, *Prinzenerziehung in Sachsen am Ausgange des 16. und im Anfange des 17. Jahrhunderts*, Dresden, 1904.
56 HStA Geheimes Archiv 8017/12, doc. 2.
57 HStA Geheimes Archiv 8017/12, doc.3.
58 HStA 8017/12 fol. 362a-401b. Richter prints a transcription of this in *Erziehungswesen*, pp. 456–76. Notker Hammerstein provides fascinating comparable information relating to the education of the Landgraves of Hesse-Darmstadt in his article, 'Prinzenerziehung im landgräflichen Hessen-Darmstadt', *Hessisches Jahrbuch für Landesgeschichte*, 33 (1983), 193–237.
59 HStA 8017/12, fol. 372a.
60 Vorzeichnus: Der Bücher/ welche in der Jungen Herrschafft Studirstüblein in dreÿ Tabulat sein gesetzet worden. SLUB Bibl.Arch.I Ba 27.
61 Vertzeichnuß der bucher welche die Jünge Herrschafft zum studiren gebraucht, unndt welche uff Ihrer F.G.Tischlein stehen. SLUB Bibl.Arch.I Ba 27 fol. 40af.
62 Richter, *Erziehungswesen*, p. 171f.
63 HStA Geheimes Archiv 8017/12, document 1.
64 HStA 8017/12, fol. 379b.
65 HStA 8017/12, fol. 378a.
66 The 1558 edition, in which *Galateo* appeared as part of *Rime e prose di Monsignor Giovanni Della Casa* published in Venice by Niccolò Bevilacqua, was only a partial one. The first full edition appeared a year later: *Trattato di Messer Giovanni Della casa [sic] nel quale sotto la persona d'un uecchio idiota*

ammaestrante un suo giovanetto, si ragiona de' modi, che si debbono ò tenere ò schifare nella comune conuersazione, cognominato Galatheo ovver de' costumi, Milan: Appresso à Giovanni Antonio de gli Antonij; imprimeuano i fratelli da Meda 1559.

67 *Io.Casææ V.Cl.Galateus. Seu de morum honestate & elegantia, liber ex Italico Latinus, Interprete Nathane Chytræo* . . . Rostochii Typis Iacobi Lucij Transyluani. Anno CIC.IC.LXXIIX. See Emilio Bonfatti, 'Johannes Caselius liest Giovanni della Casas *Galateo* (Bologna, 1565)', in *Respublica Guelpherbytana. Festschrift für Paul Raabe*, Chloe. Beihefte zum Daphnis, Amsterdam, 1987, pp. 357–81.

68 *Ioannis Casae Galateus seu de morum honestate, et elegantia, liber ex italico latinus, interprete Nathane Chytraeo, cum eiusdem notis, nuper additis*, Frankfurt 1597. HAB 5.4 Eth. (1).

69 *Io Casae Galateus. Das ist das Büchlein von erbarn/ höflichen und holdseligen Sitten. Inn welchem unter der Person eines alten wolerfahrnen Hofmannes/ ein Edler Jüngling unterweiset wird/ wie er sich in seinen Sitten/ Geberden/ Kleydung/ Reden/ Schweigen/ Thun/ Lassen/ und gantzem Leben also fürsichtiglich verhalten solle/ daß er bey jedermenniglich möge lieb und werth gehalten werden. Neuwlich auß Italianischer Sprach verteutscht von Nathane Chytraeo. Gedruckt zu Franckfurt/ Anno 1597*. This is available in a modern reprint: *G. della Casa, Galateus. Das Büchlein von erbarn/ höflichen und holdseligen Sitten, verdeutscht von Nathan Chytraeus 1507*, ed. by Klaus Ley, Tübingen 1984 (Deutsche Neudrucke, Reihe Barock, 34).

70 SLUB Mscr.Dresd.M 222.

71 See the impressive number of editions and translations listed in Antonio Santosuosso, *The Bibliography of G. Della Casa*, Florence, 1979, and the many additions to Santosuosso given by Emilio Bonfatti in the article cited in note 67.

72 See SLUB Bibl.Arch.I 30, fol. 231a–274b: Inuentarium Uber die Bücher, welche der Durchlauchtigste Hochgeborne Furst und Herr Herr Johans George hertzog zu Sachssen, Gulich, Cleue und Berge, des Heiligen Römischen Reichs in den Landen des Sächsischen Rechtens und an den Enden in solchen Vicariat gehörende dieser Zeit Vicarius, . . . Anno 1612. In die Churf. Bibliothec alhie zu Dresdden, einantwortenn und beysetzenn lassenn. 'Galatheus oder von Erbarkeit und Höffligkeit der Sitten . . .' is listed on fol 265a.

73 Weck, *Der . . . Residentz= und Haupt=Vestung Dresden Beschreib: und Vorstellung*, fol.142a ff. See chapter 5 for an assessment of this work as part of the propaganda effort of Johann Georg II. Barbara Marx discusses this journey in her article 'Die Italienreise Herzog Johann Georgs von Sachsen (1601-2) und der Besuch von Cosimo III de' Medici in Dresden (1668). Zur Kausalität von *Grand Tour* und Kulturtransfert' (in press). My thanks are due to her for sight of the manuscript pre-publication.

74 Weck, *Der . . . Residentz= und Haupt=Vestung Dresden Beschreib: und Vorstellung*, p. 142.

75 Details of this inventory are given in note 14 above.

76 In an appendix to the unpublished article by Barbara Marx cited in note 73 above.

77 See Hans Joachim Neidhardt, 'Italienbeziehungen in der Dresdner Malerei', in *Dresdner Hefte* 40 (1994/4), 15–31, p. 16.

78 See Michael Heinemann, 'Heinrich Schütz in Kassel und Venedig', in *Moritz der Gelehrte. Ein Renaissancefürst in Europa*, exh. cat. Eurasburg 1997, pp. 301–4.
79 Hainhofer, *Reisen*, p. 231f.
80 See Mathias Rank and Horst Seeger, '"Was Dafne gibt, das bleibt!". Der Kontinuitätsgedanke in der Dresdner Operngeschichte', in *Oper in Dresden. Festschrift zur Wiedereröffnung der Semperoper*, Berlin 1985, pp. 11–16.
81 The full title is *Glückwündschung des Apollinis und der neun Musen, Welche auff dem GeburtsTag Des Durchlauchtigsten/Hochgebornen Fürsten und Herrn/ Herrn Johan Georgen/ Hertzogen zu Sachsen... Von Ihrer Churf. Gn. Collegio Musico mit zwölff Cornetten und so viel lebendigen Stimmen/ benebens Trommeten und Heerpaucken zu unterthänigsten Ehren am 5. Martii repræsentiret worden/ In die Music ubersetzt Durch Henrich Schützen Capelmeistern/ Anno M.DC.XXI.* Gedruckt in der Churf. Sächs. BergkStadt Freybergk/ bey Georg Hoffman. SLUB Hist.Sax.C.863.
82 See Fürstenau, *Zur Geschichte der Musik*, vol. 1, p. 38.
83 Elisabeth Rothmund, '"Dafne" und kein Ende: Heinrich Schütz, Martin Opitz und die verfehlte erste deutsche Oper', *Schütz-Jahrbuch* 20 (1998), 123–47.
84 For an illuminating account of the circumstances under which this work came into being, see Jörg Ulrich Fechner, 'Zur literaturgeschichtlichen Situation in Dresden 1627. Überlegungen im Hinblick auf die "Dafne"-Oper von Schütz und Opitz', *Schütz-Jahrbuch* 1988, 5–29.
85 Weck, p. 39.
86 Quoted from *In Fair Verona. English Travellers in Italy and their Accounts of the City from the Middle Ages to Modern Times*, ed. by Nicholas Barker, Cambridge, 1972, p. 8.
87 Hainhofer, *Reisen*, pp. 185–6, note 1.
88 Paula Findlen, *Possessing Nature. Museums, Collecting, and Scientific Culture in Early Modern Italy*, Berkeley, Los Angeles, London, 1994.
89 Findlen, *Possessing Nature*, p. 9.
90 See Giuseppe Olmi, 'Science–Honour–Metaphor: Italian Cabinets of the Sixteenth and Seventeenth Centuries', in Oliver Impey and Arthur Macgregor, *The Origins of Museums. The Cabinet of Curiosities in Sixteenth- and Seventeenth-century Europe*, Oxford, 1985, pp. 5–16, p. 6.
91 The titles are respectively: Giovan Battista Olivi, *De reconditis et praecipuis collectaneis ab honestissimo, et solertissimo Francisco Calceolario Veronensi in Musaeo adservatis*, Venice 1584, and Benedetto Ceruti and Andrea Chiocco, *Musaeum Francesci Calceolari Iunioris Veronensis*, Verona, 1622.
92 See Walter May, 'Die höfische Architektur in Dresden unter Christian I.', in *Dresdner Hefte* 29 (1992), 63–71, p. 69.
93 See Dombrowski, 'Dresden-Prag', p. 52.
94 Manfred Zumpe, *Die Brühlsche Terrasse in Dresden*, Berlin, 1991, p. 45.
95 Hainhofer, *Reisen*.
96 See Jutta Kappel, 'Einige Nachrichten über Steinschneider in Dresden von der Mitte des 16. bis zum Ende des 18. Jahrhunderts', in *Deutsche Steinschneidekunst aus dem Grünen Gewölbe zu Dresden*, exh. cat. ed. by Jutta Kappel, Dresden, 1999, pp. 59–87, p. 64.
97 Zumpe, *Brühlsche Terrasse*, p. 44.
98 Zumpe, *Brühlsche Terrasse*, p. 216.

99 See Claudia Maué, '"Künstliche und artige Unordnung". Naturalien und Naturimitationen in künstlichen Grotten des 16. und 18. Jahrhunderts', *Anzeiger des Germanischen Nationalmuseums*, 1995, pp. 76–92.
100 Thomas Coryate, *Coryat's Crudities Hastily Gobled up in five Moneths travells in France, Savoy, Italy, Rhetia commonly called the Grisons country Helvetia alias Switzerland, some parts of high Germany and the Netherlands; Newly digested in the hungry aire of Odcombe in the County of Somerset, and now dispersed to the nourishment of the travelling Members of this Kingdome*. Glasgow 1905, 2 vols, vol. 2, p. 36. Coryate's account was first published in 1611.
101 Martin Opitz, *Die Schäfferey von der Nimfen Hercinie*, ed. by Karl F. Otto, Jr., Berne and Frankfurt, 1976.
102 See Leonard Forster, 'Martin Opitzens Schäffery von der Nimfen Hercinie: Eine nicht nur arkadische Pionierarbeit', in *Theatrum Europaeum. Festschrift für Elida Maria Szarota*, ed. by Richard Brinkmann and Karl-Heinz Habersetzer, Munich, 1982, pp. 241–51.
103 Opitz, *Schäfferey*, pp. 29–30.

Chapter 3

1 See Oliver Impey and Arthur MacGregor (eds), *The Origins of Museums. The Cabinet of Curiosities in Sixteenth- and Seventeenth-Century Europe*, Oxford, 1985.
2 On the collections in Kassel, see Birgit Kümmel, *Der Ikonoklast als Kunstliebhaber. Studien zu Landgraf Moritz von Hessen-Kassel (1592–1627)*, Marburg, 1996, p. 156.
3 Tobias Beutel, *Chur=Fürstlicher Sächsischer stets grünender hoher Cedern=Wald/ Auf dem grünen Rauten=Grunde Oder Kurtze Vorstellung/ Der Chur=Fürstl. Sächs. Hohen Regal=Wercke/ Nehmlich: Der Fürtrefflichen Kunst=Kammer/ und anderer/ Seiner Chur=Fürstl. Durchl. hochschätzbaren unvergleichlich wichtigen Dinge/ allhier bey der residentz Dreßden/ Aus schuldiger Danckbarkeit zu GOtt/ vor so grosse/ dem Durchleuchtigsten Chur=Hause Sachsen/ verliehene Wohlthaten und Schätze*..., Dresden: gedruckt bey den Bergischen Erben. Anno 1671.
4 *Law Sports at Gray's Inn (1594)*, edited by Basil Brown (pseud. Isabelle Kittson Brown), New York, 1921, pp. 46–7. The Prince of Purpoole was a fictitious title assigned to the master of the revels held in the Inns of Court at Christmas 1594.
5 Lorenz Seelig, 'The Munich *Kunstkammer*, 1565–1807', in Impey and MacGregor, *The Origins of Museums*, pp. 76–89, p. 10.
6 *Law Sports at Gray's Inn (1594)*, p. 46.
7 See Jutta Bäumel, *Die Rüstkammer zu Dresden*, Berlin, 1995, p. 5.
8 Inventarium uber des Churfürsten zu Sachsenn und Burggrauen zu Magdeburgk etc meines gnedigsten hern Kunst Cammernn in Ihrn Churf. Gnaden Schloß und Vehstunge zu Dreßden: Wie desselben Vornehme sachen, Kunststücke und Zugehoriger Vorradt iedes besondern Sortirt und Ordiniert wordenn und nachuolgendenn Orten Zubefinden. Inuentirtt vnd aufgericht Anno 1587. This is kept in the Grünes Gewölbe in Dresden.

9 See Joachim Menzhausen, 'Elector Augustus's *Kunstkammer*: An Analysis of the Inventory of 1587', in Impey and MacGregor, *The Origins of Museums*, pp. 69–75.
10 'Indianisch' in the inventory could indeed mean Indian. We know that the Medici had items from Gujarat datable to between 1540 and 1570. See Robert Skelton, 'Indian Art and Artefacts in Early European Collecting', in Impey and MacGregor, *The Origins of Museums*, pp. 274–80, p. 276.
11 No. 211 of the list of books on folio 188a of the inventory is entitled: 'Beschreibunge von den Effecten und wirckungen des Cristals, welches der Herzogk v. Saphoÿ dem Churfürsten Herzogen Augustus zu Sachßen seligen zugeschicket' (Description of the effects of the crystal which the Duke of Savoy sent to the late Elector Duke August of Saxony).
12 It can still be seen today, but now contains only four large and five small uncut emeralds, borne on a tray held by the wooden figure of a South American Indian, a work commissioned from Balthasar Permoser by Friedrich August II around 1724. See Syndram, *Das Grüne Gewölbe*, pp. 174–5.
13 Inventarium 1597, fol. 19b.
14 Inventarium 1587, fol. 40b.
15 Inventarium 1587, fol. 42a.
16 See Ludolf von Mackensen, 'Die Kasseler Wissenschaftskammer oder die Vermessung des Himmels, der Erde und der Zeit', in *Moritz der Gelehrte. Ein Renaissancefürst in Europa*. exh. cat. ed. by Heiner Borggrefe, Vera Lüpkes and Hans Ottomeyer, Lemgo, Kassel, 1998, pp. 385–412.
17 Jost Weyer, *Graf Wolfgang II. von Hohenlohe und die Alchemie. Alchemistische Studien in Schloß Weikersheim 1587–1610*, Sigmaringen, 1992.
18 Elisabeth Scheicher implies as much about Archduke Ferdinand of the Tyrol on p. 32 of her article 'The Collection of Archduke Ferdinand II at Schloss Ambras: its Purpose, Composition and Evolution', in Impey and MacGregor, pp. 29–38. In *Worldly Goods* (London, 1996) Lisa Jardine also shows that Cardinal Francesco Gonzaga did not necessarily understand either the objects or the books he collected (pp. 55–72 and p. 150).
19 See Fritz Bönisch, Hans Brichzin, Klaus Schillinger and Werner Stams, *Kursächsische Kartographie bis zum Dreißigjährigen Krieg*, Berlin 1990, pp. 228–9.
20 Klaus Maurice, *Der drechselnde Souverän. Materialien zu einer fürstlichen Maschinenkunst*, Zurich, 1985.
21 Menzhausen, in Impey and MacGregor, *The Origins of Museums*, p. 72.
22 See the excellent article on the Sächsische Landesbibliothek, Dresden, and its history in Bernhard Fabian (ed.), *Handbuch der Historischen Buchbestände in Deutschland*, vol. 17 Sachsen A-K, Friedhilde Krause (ed.), Hildesheim, Zurich, New York, 1997, p. 96. Still worth reading is Friedrich Adolf Ebert, *Geschichte und Beschreibung der königlichen öffentlichen Bibliothek zu Dresden*, Leipzig, 1822.
23 See Béatrice Nicollier-De Weck, *Hubert Languet (1518–1581). Un Réseau politique international de Melanchthon à Guillaume d'Orange*, Geneva, 1995, p. 181f
24 Nicollier-De Weck, *Hubert Languet*, p. 314, note 16.
25 SLUB Bibl.Arch.I B vol. 20.
26 See Bernhard Fabian (ed.), *Die Messkataloge Georg Willers. Herbstmesse 1564 bis Herbstmesse 1573*, Hildesheim, New York, 1972.

27 Georgius Draudius, *Bibliotheca classica, sive Catalogus officinalis. In Quo singuli singularum Facultatum ac professionum libri ordine alphabetica recensentur... Vsque ad annum M.DXXIV inclusive*. Frankfurt am Main, 1625.
28 Rudolf Zaunick, *Der sächsische Paracelsist Georg Forberger*, Wiesbaden, 1977.
29 I. Schunke, 'Die Pariser Büchersendung des Hubert Languet an Kurfürst August von Sachsen, 1566', in *Festschrift Martin Bollert zum 60. Geburtstag*, Dresden, 1936, pp. 49–66.
30 SLUB Bibl.Arch. I vol. 21.
31 SLUB Bibl.Arch. I Ba vol. 26.
32 SLUB Bibl.Arch. I B vols. 28, 29 and 30. Vols. 28 and 29 relate to 1595 and vol. 30 takes us up to 1629.
33 *Des Augsburger Patriciers Philipp Hainhofer Reisen nach Innsbruck und Dresden*, ed. by Oscar Doering, Vienna, 1901, p. 181.
34 Anton Weck, *Der Chur=Fürstlichen Sächsischen weitberuffenen Residentz= und Haupt=Vestung Dresden Beschreib: und Vorstellung/ Auf der Churfürstlichen Herrschafft gnädigstes Belieben in Vier Abtheilungen verfaßet/ mit Grund: und anderen Abrißen/ auch bewehrten Documenten/ erläutert durch Ihrer Churfürstlichen Durchl. zu Sachsen/ etc. Rath/zu den Geheimen: und Reichs=Sachen bestalten Secretarium auch Archivarium Antonium Wecken*. Nürnberg/ In Verlegung Johann Hoffmanns/ Buch: und Kunsthändler/ Gedruckt daselbst bey Christian Sigismund Froberger. Anno. MDCLXXX, p. 41.
35 See Barbara Gutfleisch and Joachim Menzhausen, '"How a Kunstkammer should be formed". Gabriel Kaltemarckt's advice to Christian I of Saxony on the formation of an art collection, 1587', *Journal of the History of Collections*, I (1989), 3–31. This contains a transcription and translation into English of Kaltemarckt's report.
36 Gutfleisch and Menzhausen, '"How a Kunstkammer should be formed"', pp. 73–4.
37 Inventarium über die kurfürstliche sächsische Kunstkammer in Schloß und Festung Dresden. Erneuert und aufgerichtet den letzten Decembris anno 1595. Kept in the Grünes Gewölbe in Dresden.
38 Inventarium 1595, fol. 394a.
39 Inventarium 1595, fol. 318a.
40 Inventarium über die kurfürstliche sächsische Kunstkammer in Schloß und Festung Dresden. Erneuert und aufgerichtet den 1. Augusti anno 1610. Kept in the Grünes Gewölbe in Dresden.
41 Inventarium über die kurfürstliche sächs. Kunstkammer in Schloß und Festung Dresden. Erneuert und aufgerichtet den 28. Junii anno 1619. Kept in the Grünes Gewölbe in Dresden.
42 See the illuminating article by Thomas Rahn, 'Geschichtsgedächtnis am Körper. Fürstliche Merk- und Meditationsbilder nach der Weltreiche-Prophetie des 2. Buches Daniel', in *Seelenmaschinen. Gattungstraditionen, Funktionen und Leistungsgrenzen der Mnemotechniken vom späten Mittelalter bis zum Beginn der Moderne*, ed. by Jörg Jochen Berns and Wolfgang Neuber, Vienna, Cologne, Weimar 2000, pp. 521–61.
43 Gutfleisch and Menzhausen, '"How a Kunstkammer should be formed"', p. 12.
44 See *Gemäldegalerie Dresden Alte Meister. Katalog der ausgestellten Werke*, Dresden, 1992, Nos. 1918 and 1919.

45 Inventarium über die kurfürstliche sächsische Kunstkammer in Schloß und Festung Dresden. Erneuert und aufgerichtet den 4. Augusti anno 1640. Kept in the Grünes Gewölbe in Dresden.
46 See Dirk Syndram, *Die Schatzkammer Augusts des Starken*, Leipzig, 1999, pp. 28–33.
47 See note 3 above for the full title.
48 Claudia Schnitzer, *Höfische Maskaraden. Funktion und Ausstattung von Verkleidungsdivertissements an deutschen Höfen der Frühen Neuzeit*, Tübingen, 1999, p. 341.
49 Hainhofer, *Reisen*, p. 194.
50 *Verzeichnis der Inventare der Staatlichen Kunstsammlungen Dresden 1568–1945* bearbeitet von Elfriede Lieber, Dresden, Staatliche Kunstsammlungen, 1979.
51 Dresden HStA Hausmarschallamt Lit.R. Kap XVI Nr. 254, 2. Inventarium über das Churfürstl. Sächß. Tapezereÿ=Gewölbe in Dresden, 1682.
52 Dresden HStA Hausmarschallamt Lit R. Kap. XVI 219: Inventarium über Ihrer Churfl. Durchl. Schlaff Cammer Gemach.
53 Dresden HStA Hausmarschallamt Lit R Kap. XVI, Nr. 193: Inventarium des HofBettmeisters Caspar Hanisch.

Chapter 4

1 See Lisa Jardine, *Ingenious Pursuits. Building the Scientific Revolution*, London, 1999, pp. 325–31.
2 R. J. W. Evans, *Rudolf II and his World. A Study in Intellectual History*, second edition, London, 1997.
3 Stanislas Klossowski de Rola, *Alchemy. The Secret Art*, London, 1973, p. 7.
4 See Gareth Roberts, *The Mirror of Alchemy. Alchemical Ideas and Images in Manuscripts and Books from Antiquity to the Seventeenth Century*, London, 1994, p. 45 f.
5 See Jost Weyer, *Graf Wolfgang II. von Hohenlohe und die Alchemie. Alchemistische Studien in Schloß Weikersheim 1587–1610*, Sigmaringen, 1992, p. 46 f.
6 Leonhard Thurneysser, *Quinta Essentia, Das ist/ Die höchste subtilitet/ krafft und wirckung/ beyder der fürtrefflichsten/ und menschlichem geschlecht am nützlichsten Künsten/ der Medicin und Alchemy/ Auch wie nahe diese beyde mit sipschafft gefreund und verwandt sind/ Und das eine ohn beystandt der andern nicht nütz sey/ oder in den menschlichen cörpern zu wircken kein krafft habe. ...Leipzig cum privilegio caesareo. Gedruckt zu Leipzig/Bey Hans Steinman/ Typis Voegelianis. M. D. Lxxiiij. SLUB Chemica 23.
7 See Harry J. Sheppard, 'European Alchemy in the Context of a Universal Definition', in Christoph Meinel (ed.), *Die Alchemie in der europäischen Kultur- und Wissenschaftsgeschichte*, Wolfenbütteler Forschungen Bd. 32, Wiesbaden, 1986.
8 Weyer, *Graf Wolfgang II.*, p. 272 f.
9 Weyer, *Graf Wolfgang II.*, p. 36.
10 See the discussion in Evans, *Rudolf II*, Chapter VI: 'Rudolf and the Occult Arts'; also György E. Szönyi, 'Scientific and Magical Humanism at the Court of Rudolf II', in *Rudolf II and Prague. The Imperial Court and Residential City as*

the *Cultural and Spiritual Heart of Central Europe*. Exh. cat. London, 1997, pp. 223–30.
11 See *Allgemeine Deutsche Biographie*, Berlin, 1967–71, vol. 38, pp. 226–9.
12 See Gerschom Scholem, *Alchemie und Kabbala*, Frankfurt am Main, 1984, p. 63, who bases his claim on the third document at Loc. 4418/5 in the HStA. This document details experiments carried out by August and Mardochaeus de Delle together and has many annotations in the margin signed 'August'. But the hand and the paper indicate that it is an eighteenth century copy, not one contemporaneous with August himself.
13 See Lothar Suhling, '"Philosophisches" in der Frühneuzeitlichen Berg- und Hüttenkunst: Metallogenese und Transmutation aus der Sicht montanistischen Erfahrungswissens', in Meinel (ed.), *Die Alchemie*.
14 Evans, *Rudolf II*, p. 212.
15 HStA Geheimes Archiv Loc. 4417/4.
16 HStA Geheimes Archiv Loc. 8310.
17 See Bruce T. Moran, *The Alchemical World of the German Court. Occult Philosophy and Chemical Medicine in the Circle of Moritz of Hessen (1572–1632)*, Stuttgart, 1991, and 'Moritz von Hessen und die Alchemie', in *Moritz der Gelehrte. Ein Renaissancefürst in Europa*. Exh. cat. ed. by Heiner Borggrefe, Vera Lüpke and Hans Ottomeyer, Eurasburg, 1992, pp. 357–60.
18 See Hartmut Broszinski, 'Die Katalogisierung der Kasseler alchemistischen Handschriften', in Meinel, *Die Alchemie*, pp. 19–31.
19 Heiner Borggrefe, 'Moritz der Gelehrte als Rosenkreuzer und die "Generalreformation der gantzen weiten Welt"', in *Moritz der Gelehrte*, pp. 339–44.
20 1595 Teil II – Bibl.Arch. I 29, fol. 120a.
21 Rudolf Zaunick, *Der sächsische Paracelsist Georg Forberger*, Wiesbaden, 1977.
22 Inventarium uber des Churfürsten zu Sachsenn und Burggrauen zu Magdeburgk etc meines gnedigsten hern Kunst Cammernn in Ihrn Churf. Gnaden Schloß und Vehstunge zu Dreßden: Wie desselben Vornehme sachen, Kunststücke und Zugehöriger Vorradt iedes besondern Sortirt und Ordiniert worden und nachuolgendenn Orten Zubefinden. Inuentirtt vnd aufgericht Anno 1587. Grünes Gewölbe, Dresden.
23 HStA Geheimes Archiv Loc. 4416/6-8, Loc. 4417/1-121, Loc. 4418/1-6, 4419/1-23. Some of this material is in very poor condition and at the time of writing could only be consulted by means of old, at times illegible, film from the GDR period. Some of it consulted by this author in 1998 could no longer be consulted at all.
24 The SLUB also possesses a large number of so-called 'Magische und alchymische Handschriften' (Magical and Alchemical Manuscripts – Section N in the printed manuscript catalogue), though many are later acquisitions.
25 See Scholem, *Alchemie und Kabbala*, who expresses intense scepticism about the connection between such alchemical works and the actual Jewish cabbala.
26 Claus Priesner has shown that Thölde is in all probability the author of those writings purporting to be by Basilius Valentinus, a Benedictine monk. See his article 'Johann Thoelde und die Schriften des Basilius Valentinus', in Meinel (ed.), *Die Alchemie*.
27 See Weyer, *Graf Wolfgang II.*, p. 273.
28 See *Allgemeine Deutsche Biographie*, Berlin 1967–1971, vol. 33, pp. 436–8.
29 Evans, *Rudolf II*, p. 216.

30 SLUB Mscr.Dresd.N 155: De Transmutatione Metallorum, et lapide phylosophorum. Von vorenderunge der Metallen vnd von dem Phylosophischen Stein. Wie vnd welcher gestallt... dis Gottlich Geheimnus... tzuerforschen vnd zuerlangen sey.dem Durchlauchttigen... Fursten... Iohanns Georgen Hertzogen zw Sachssen....
31 *Freudiger Glückwünschungs=Segen / Uber Das Hoch=Fürstliche Beylager Der zwoen Hoch=Fürstlichen Durchlauchtigkeiten/ Nemlich Des Durchlauchtigsten Fürsten und Herrn/ Herrn Christian Ernsten/ Marggrafen zu Brandenburgk... und Der Durchlauchtigsten Fürstin und Fräulein/ Fräul. Erdmuth Sophien/ Hertzogin zu Sachsen.... Wie unterthänigst=gehorsamst=wolmeynend also hertzlich gewünschet in Alt=Dreßden von Petro Colbovio, von Gadebusch aus Meckelnburg. Gedruckt durch Melchior Bergen/ Churfürstl. Sächs. Hoff-Buchdrucker.* SLUB Hist.Sax.C.158,57.
32 *Petri Colbovii, Gadeb. Megar. Wolmeynendliches Chymisch Carmen. Von unterschiedlichen noch unbekandten nothwendigen Königlichen Universal=Alkahest= Menstruis, zum unterschiedlichen Chaos der Philosophorum, und dem Lapide Philosophico selbsten; Mit sampt des Arteph. Und Pont secreten abbreviir. [sic] Feur: Medicis, Apotheckern/ Chymicis und Laboranten nützlich zu lesen. Dreßden/ Gedruckt durch Melchior Bergen/ Im Jahr/ 1667.* SLUB Chem.952. Colbovius is also the author of a pedagogical treatise which he addressed to Jan Amos Comenius, the great Bohemian educator. See Franz Hofmann (ed.), *Sendschreiben des Petrus Colbovius (1650) und Brief des J.A. Comenius an Colbovius (1650). Eine pädogische Korrespondenz aus dem 17. Jahrhundert*, Veröffentlichungen der Comeniusforschungsstelle Bochum, vol. 3, Düsseldorf, 1974.
33 See Jost Weyer, *Graf Wolfgang II*.
34 See the exhibition catalogue *Bergbau und Kunst in Sachsen*, Dresden 1989, p. 59.
35 HStA Loc. 10526, Bd. I, Bl.263b, quoted from *Bergbau und Kunst in Sachsen*, p. 59.
36 *Daniel Bretschneider, Bürger und Mahler zu Dressdenn, ein Buch von allerley Inuentionen, zu Schlittenfarthen, welche auff dergleichen arten, gar wol zugerichtet vnd leichtlich geführet werden können, für Fürstliche, Gräffliche, Herrn vnd Adelstands Personen, mehren theils von neuem visirt vnnd verferttigett.* SLUB Mscr.Dresd.B 104.
37 Anton Weck, *Der Chur = Fürstlichen Sächsischen weitberuffenen Residentz= und Haupt=Vestung Dresden Beschreib: und Vorstellung/ Auf der Churfürstlichen Herrschafft gnädigstes Belieben in Vier Abtheilungen verfaßet/ mit Grund: und anderen Abrißen/ auch bewehrten Documenten erläutert durch Ihrer Churfürstlichen Durchl. zu Sachsen/ etc. Rath/ zu den Geheimen: und Reich=Sachen bestalten Secretarium und Archivarium Antonium Wecken*. Nürnberg/ In Verlegung Johann Hoffmanns/ Buch: und Kunsthändler/ Gedruckt daselbst bey Christian Sigismund Froberger. Anno MDCLXXX, pp. 333–4, here p. 333.
38 See Weck, *Der Residentz Dresden Beschreib: und Vorstellung*, p. 360f.
39 See HStA OHMA B Nr. 13b, fol. 377b.
40 Now in the Rüstkammer in Dresden, Inv. No. H 100. The dimensions are 159 × 354 cm. The legend begins: Der durch Leuchtige Hochgeborne Fürst vnnd herr herr Johannes Georg Der Junger hertzog zu Sachsen Gülich Cleue

vnd Berg, zur Welt geboren vnd den 27 Juny hernach alhier zu Dresten Getaufft worden...

41 *Ballet Von Zusammenkunft und Wirckung derer VII. Planeten/ auf Ihr. Churfl. Durchl. Zu Sachsen großem Theatro gehalten Den 3. Februarii Anno 1678.* Dresden/ Gedruckt durch Melchior Bergens Churfl. Sächs. Hof=Buchdr. Seel. Nachgelassene Wittbe und Erben. SLUB Sign.B44a; HAB Textb.4 ° 28; UBL Hist.Sax.88.

42 See Marie-Claude Canova-Green, 'Le ballet de cour en France', in *Spectaculum Europaeum* ed. by Pierre Béhar and Helen Watanabe-O'Kelly, pp. 485–512, p. 488.

43 See Dirk Syndram with Ulli Arnold and Jutta Kappel, *Das Grüne Gewölbe zu Dresden. Führer durch seine Geschichte und seine Sammlungen*, 2nd revised edition, Munich, Berlin, 1997, p. 281 and pp. 321–3.

44 See Klaus Thalheim, 'Die Suche nach "edlen Steinen" in Sachsen vom 16. bis zum 18. Jahrhundert', in Jutta Kappel, *Deutsche Steinschneidekunst aus dem Grünen Gewölbe zu Dresden*, Dresden, 1999, pp. 11–25, p. 15, and Helmut Bräuer, 'Zur wirtschaftlichen Entwicklung Sachsens nach dem Dreißigjährigen Krieg', *Dresdner Hefte* 33 (1993), 13–24.

Chapter 5

1 HStA OHMA B Nr.10.

2 *Cartel des Feuer-Wercks Worinnen die Eroberung des Güldenen Fellis Durch den Jason außgebüldet wird/* ... Dresden: Christian & Melchior Bergen 1650. SLUB Hist.Sax.C.118, 24.

3 See *Inhalt Deß Von dem Durchlauchtigsten Chur=Printzen zu Sachsen/ etc. Hertzog Johann Georgen Dem Andern/ angestellten Feuer=Wercks/ von Eroberung des Güldenen Fellis/ An vor=hochgedachte Hoch=Fürstl. H.H. Gebrüdere Beylager.* This is reprinted in *David Schirmers Churfürstlichen Sächsischen Bibliothecarii Poetische Rauten=Gepüsche in Sieben Büchern.* Dresden/ In Verlegung Andreas Löflers Buchführers. Gedruckt bey Melchior Bergen/ Churf. Sächs. Hof=Buchdr. 1663, pp. 42–5.

4 François Dolivet, *Inhalt Des Balletts Welches dem Durchläuchtigsten Hoochgebohrnen Fürsten und Herrn/ Herrn Johann Georgen/ Hertzogen zu Sachsen/ Jülich/ Klev und Berg/ des Heyligen Römischen Reichs Ertzmarschallen und Kuhrfürsten ... Von Dero ältern Herrn Sohne Dem auch Durchläuchtigsten Hoochgebohrnen Fürsten und Herrn Herrn Johann Georgen/ Hertzogen zu Sachsen/ Jülich/ Klev und Berg Kuhrprintzen/&c. Zu Kindlichen gehorsamen Ehren gehalten und fürgestället worden In dem Kuhrfürstl. Schlosse zu Dreßden/ Auff dem Riesensaale den 3. Julii im Jahr 1653. Verfärtiget durch Ihrer Kuhrprintzl. Durchl. zu Sachsen Tantzmeistern François Dolivet.* Dresden: Bergen, Christian und Melchior, 1653. SLUB Hist.Sax.C.53.

5 Johann Georg I in fact functioned as Imperial Regent ('Reichsvicarius') in 1612 on the death of Rudolf II, in 1619 on the death of Matthias I and in 1637 on the death of Ferdinand II.

6 In what follows I am indebted to the unpublished Master's dissertation by Sonja Karallus, 'Der "Riesensaal" im Dresdner Residenzschloß', Bonn, 1998.

7 Norbert Oelsner, 'Der Riesensaal', in *Das Dresdner Schloß. Monument sächsischer Geschichte und Kultur*, Dresden, 1992, p. 86f.
8 Karallus, 'Der "Riesensaal"', p. 61.
9 At either side of this wall and below the balustrade are painted two baldachins with four bronze male statues on top of each of them. It is also possible to make out, below the baldachins, *grisaille* paintings of other male figures. Since our only evidence for the existence of these elements, in a room which has since been destroyed, is Johann Samuel Mock's gouache of 1693, it is impossible to say what they represented.
10 David Schirmer, *Drama. Liebes=Spiel der Nymphen/ und Satyren*, in: *Rauten-Gepüsche*, 241f. See also Ernst Geller, *Arkadischer Hürten-Aufzug Als Die Durchläuchtigsten Hoochgebohrnen Fürsten und Herren/ Herr Johann Georg/ Hertzog zu Sachsen...Kuhrfürst...Herr Johann Georg/ Hertzog zu Sachsen... Kuhrprintz...Herr Johann Georg/ Hertzog zu Sachsen...Dero allerseits Nahmenstag begiengen den 24. Julii/ im Jahr GOtt VVoLLe Lange ZeIt Der RaVten Krafft KVhrSaChsen ErhaLten/ aVCh Die ZVVeIg' an GlVkke VVaChsen. Verfärtiget von Ihrer Kuhrprintzlichen Durchlauchtigkeit zu Sachsen Kammerschreibern Ernst Gellern. Dresden: Christian und Melchior Bergen, 1653*. HAB Xb 4° 172.
11 For an exhaustive account of the Order see Diethard Schneider, *Der englische Hosenbandorden: Beiträge zur Entstehung und Entwicklunng des 'The most noble Order of the Garter' (1348–1702) mit einem Ausblick bis 1983*, 2 vols in 4 pts, Bonn, 1988.
12 Elias, Ashmole, *The history of the most noble Order of the Garter: and the several orders of knighthood extant in Europe. Containing I. The antiquity of the town, castle, chapel, and college of Windsor;...II. The habits, ensigns, and officers of the Order*, London: printed for A. Bell, E. Curll, J. Pemberton, and A. Collins, W. Taylor and J. Baker, 1715, p. 363.
13 Their letters of appointment and their credentials are to be found at Ashmolean MSS 1131 fol. 74a–76a (Bodleian Library, Oxford).
14 The orders to the Wardrobe and the Jewel House to have these and other necessities made for the investiture of Johann Georg II are to be found at Ashmolean MSS 1112, fol. 17261–173b (Bodleian Library, Oxford).
15 HStA OHMA N I, no. 1, fol. 1a–44b.
16 See HStA Hausmarschallamt Lit. R. Kap XV, Nr. 254: Inventarium über das Churfürstl. Sächs. Tapezereÿ Gewölbe in Dresden, 1683.
17 Benjamin Leuber, *Kurtzer Bericht von dem Königlichen Engelländischen hohen und vortrefflichsten Ritter=Orden/ S.Georgen/ Und des Garters, oder Hosen= Bands. In unterthänigster Schuldigkeit aufgesetzt Als den 26. Aprilis Alt. Cal. im 1671. Jahr der...Fürst und Herr/ Hr. Johann Georg der Andere/...zu Dreßden/ in Seiner Churfl. Residentz Des Glorwürdigsten Ordens=Fest gantz hochfeyerlichen hielte/ und herrlichen celebrirte* von D.B.L. Budißin/ In der churfl. Sächs. Haupt=Sechs=Stadt des Marggraffthums Ober=Lausitz/ druckts Christoph Baumann/ Im Jahr 1671. SLUB Hist.Sax.C 158 39,d.misc 1.
18 Wilhelm Ernst Tentzel, *Saxonia Numismatica, oder Medaillen-Cabinet. Dritter Theil der Albertinischen Linie/ Von Chur=Fürst Johann Georgen II. biß auff Den ietzigen Chur=Printzen.* Dresden/ gedruckt beym Kön. Hoffbuchdrucker/ Joh.Riedeln. 1705.BL 603.e.12,13. Tab 57, no. IV, text p. 571, though Tentzel

wrongly claims that William Swan came to Dresden in 1669, rather than in 1671.
19 See HStA OHMA NI, Nr.1., fol. 47a f.
20 'Sir William Swan's narration of his Journey to Dresden, Aprill & May 1671', Ashmole MSS 1112, fol. 150–155, Bodleian Library, Oxford.
21 *Hercules Britto-Saxonicus Welcher Bey des Chur-Fürsten zu Sachsen... Johann Georgen des Andern/ Begehenden Ritter-Fests St. Georgi in... Dreßden/ Bey deme auf dem hohen Walle angezündeten Feuer-Wercke Auf einer brennenden Ehren-Seule Sich zugleich mit vorstellte. Anno M.DC.LXXI.* Dresden: in der Churfl. Sächs. Hof-Druckerey, 1671. SLUB Hist.Sax.C.158, 39.d, misc.2.
22 OHMA N I No.1, fol. 72a says 'Jacob' for the second part of this play instead of Joseph, but it is clear what is meant from the context.
23 In the same volume of the Court Chamberlain's papers just mentioned, HStA OHMA N I No.1. This volume contains all the documentation on the so-called 'Georgs-Feste'.
24 See Schneider, *Der englische Hosenbandorden*, p. 829.
25 Joachim Menzhausen, 'Karl II. von England als Drachenkämpfer. Gottfried Leygebes angeblicher Eisenschnitt', in *Dresdner Kunstblätter* 7 (1963), pp. 27–31.
26 *Gloriam ordinis periscelidis in serenissimo ac potentissimo principe ac domino, domino Johanne Georgio Secundo, Duce Saxoniae, Juliaci, Cliviae ac Monatium, Sacri Romani Imperii Archimarschallo et Electore... annua memoria ac solemni oratione in academia panegyri Anno MDCLXXIII. Venerabatur,* Johann Henricus Sander, Wittenberg: Literis Michaelis Meyeri relictae Viduae.
27 The documentation on these two celebrations is to be found in a file entitled 'St.Georgen Fest' and laid loosely in at the back of the bound volume on the Garter Festivals already quoted, HStA OHMA N I no. 1.
28 Johann Caspar Horn, *Der Königliche Engelländische hochberühmte Ritter-Orden S. Georgen/ und des Garters/ Als... Hr. Johann Georg der Andere/ Hertzog zu Sachsen... und Chur-Fürst... Auch... Ritter und Gesellschaffter Des... Ritter-Ordens S. Georgens... das... Ritter-Ordens-Fest/ in Dero... Residentz... Dreßden/ am 23. April. 1678. mit herrlichen Solenniteten... begienge Aus D. Benjamin Leübers/ weyland Chur-Fürstl. S. Raths und Cammer-Procuratoris in der Ober-Lausitz/ und anderer berühmter Autorum, glaubwürdigen Schrifften... abgefasset Von Johann Caspar Horn/ D.* Dresden: Baumann, 1678. SLUB Hist.Sax.C.146, misc.1.
29 HStA OHMA N I No.2, fol. 58a-64a.
30 *Des Thessalier-Fürstens/ Iasons Helden-Thaten/ In Eroberung Des göldenen-Fließes Zu Colchos Durch ein Feuerwerck vorgestellet bey feyerlicher Begehung Des Ritter-Orden-Fests St. Georgens. Zu Dreßden/ Den 25. Aprilis 1678.* Dresden: Bergen 1678. SLUB Hist.Sax.C.146,misc.2.
31 Tentzel, *Saxonia numismatica*, vol. IV, Tab. 61, no. 1, text on p. 596.
32 See Julius und Albert Erbstein's *Verzeichniss der Hofrath Engelhardt'schen Sammlung sächsischer Münzen und Medaillen*, Dresden 1888 (part 1), 1890 (part 2), 1896 (part 3), 1903 (part 4), 1909 (part 5), part 3, No. 958, p. 247.
33 See Erbstein, *Verzeichniss der Hofrath Engelhardt'schen Sammlung*, part 3, No. 959, pp. 247–8.
34 The Court Chamberlain's records are to be found in HstA OHMA B Nr. 13 a and b.

35 See HStA OHMA G 5a.
36 See HStA OHMA G 7.
37 See HStA OHMA G 8.
38 This work first appeared in 1558: *De quatuor summis imperiis, Babylonico, Persico, Graeco & Romano*, Geneva: Barbier and Courteau 1558.
39 *Joh. Sleidani Vier monarchien/ Worinnen kurtz alles verfasset/ was nach Erschaffung der Welt denckwürdig befunden/ vermehret vor diesen durch Gabriel Tzschimmern/ Von neuen continuiret biß auffs Jahr 1676*. Durch Anton Christian Fabricium. Mit Churfl. Sächs. Privilegio. In Verlegung Andreae Löfflers Buchh. In Dreßden. Merseburg. Druckts Caspar Forberger/ Fürstl.Sächs. Hoff=Buchdrucker Im Jahr 1676, p. 3.
40 Tzschimmer, pp. 82–3.
41 See Thomas Rahn, 'Geschichtsgedächtnis am Körper. Fürstliche Merk- und Meditationsbilder nach der Weltreiche-Prophetie des 2. Buches Daniel', in *Seelenmaschinen. Gattungstraditionen, Funktionen und Leistungsgrenzen der Mnemotechniken vom späten Mittelalter bis zum Beginn der Moderne*, ed. by Jörg Jochen Berns and Wolfgang Neuber, Vienna, Cologne, Weimar 2000, pp. 521–61.
42 Now in the Rüstkammer in Dresden, Inv. No. H 100. The dimensions are 159 × 354 cm. The legend begins: Der durch Leuchtige Hochgeborne Fürst vnnd herr herr Johannes Georg Der Junger hertzog zu Sachsen Gülich Cleue vnd Berg, zur Welt geboren vnd den 27 Juny hernach alhier zu Dresten Getaufft worden...
43 See Tobias Beutel, *Chur-Fürstlicher Sächsischer stets grünender hoher CedernWald/ Auf dem grünen Rauten-Grunde Oder Kurtze Vorstellung/ Der Chur=Fürstl. Sächs. Hohen Regal=Werck*, Dresden 1671, fol. K3.
44 HStA OHMA 2 and Hierüber Nr.4 Bildrolle 2.
45 Helen Watanabe-O'Kelly, 'Gabriel Tzschimmer's *Durchlauchtigste Zusammenkunft* (1680) and the Festival Book Tradition', in *Daphnis*, 22 (1993), pp. 61–72.
46 See Helen Watanabe-O'Kelly, 'Festival Books in Europe from Renaissance to Rococo', in *The Seventeenth Century*, 3 (1988), No.2, pp. 181–201.
47 Wolfgang Ferber, *Relation und umbständliche Beschreibung ienes ansehnlichen und fürnehmen Stahlschiessens*... Dresden: Gimel Bergen 1615.
48 Georg Pezold, *Beschreibung der Churfürstlichen Kindtauff/ und Frewdenfests zu Dressden/ den 18. September. des verlauffenen 1614. Jahres/ wie auch der Ritterlichen Frewdenspiel/ folgende Tage über/*.... Dresden, 1615.
49 *Abdruck der Cartellen So bey denen/ auff dem Fürstl. Beylager Deß... Herren Friderichen/ Erben zu Norwegen/ Herzogen zu Schleßwig...Mit Frewlein Maria Elisabeth...Herzogin zu Sachsen...Gehaltenen ansehnlichen Auffzügen Ring-Rennen und FußThurnier zu Dreßden außgegeben worden Dabey auch die Beschreib- und Abbildung des Churfürstlichen Sächsischen gnädigst angeordneten FewerWercks so... am 5. Martii zu Ehren praesentirt und verbrand/ in Kupffer gestochen*. Dresden: Seyffert, 1630.
50 For instance, Giovanni Battista Maccioni, *Applausi Festivi Barriera Rappresentata in Monaco alla Venuta [di] Leopoldo Augusto Nell gran Teatro presso la Residenza dell' Ser. Ferdinando Maria Duca di Baviera*, Munich 1658 or Pietro Paolo Bissari, *Incoronata. Drama Regio Musicale. Attione Prima De gli Applausi fatti nell'Ellettorale Città di Monaco per la Nascita Dell'Altezza Ser.ma Di Massimiliano Emanuele*, Munich 1662; *Antiopa Giustificata. Drama Guerriero, Attione*

Seconda De gli Applausi fatti alla Nascità Dell' Altezza Ser:ma Di Massimiliano Emanuele, Munich 1662 and *Medea Vendicativa. Drama di Foco. Attione Terza De gli Applausi fatti per la nascità Dell' Altezza Ser.ma Di Massimiliano Emanuele*, Munich 1662.

51 The basis for this statement is the *c*. 3,000 works surveyed for *Festivals and Ceremonies. A Bibliography of Printed Works relating to Court, Civic and Religious Festivals in Europe 1500–1800*, ed. by Helen Watanabe-O'Kelly and Anne Simon (London, 2000).
52 Tzschimmer, Part II, p. 51.
53 Tzschimmer, Part II, p. 477.
54 Tzschimmer, Part II, pp. 3–4.
55 Ulrich Schütte, 'Das Fürstenschloß als "Pracht-Gebäude"', in *Die Künste und das Schloß in der frühen Neuzeit*, ed. by Lutz Unbehaun, Munich, Berlin 1998, pp. 15–29.

Chapter 6

1 This is reprinted as volume I of *Spieltexte der Wanderbühne*, ed. by Manfred Brauneck, Berlin, 1970.
2 See Jerzy Limon, *Gentlemen of a Company. English Players in Central and Eastern Europe, 1590–1660*, Cambridge, 1985, p. 3.
3 See Albert Cohn, *Shakespeare in Germany in the Sixteenth and the Seventeenth Centuries: an Account of English Actors in Germany and the Netherlands and of the Plays Performed by Them during the Same Period*, London and Berlin, 1865, p. xxv, where their contract of employment is reprinted.
4 See Moritz Fürstenau, *Zur Geschichte der Musik und des Theaters am Hofe zu Dresden*, 1861–1862, reprint Leipzig, 1971, p. 69.
5 Limon, *Gentlemen of a Company*, p. 71.
6 Cohn, *Shakespeare in Germany*, p. lxxxvii.
7 See Limon, *Gentlemen of a Company*, p. 113.
8 Limon, *Gentlemen of a Company*, p. 30.
9 Limon, *Gentlemen of a Company*, p. 138f.
10 Limon, *Gentlemen of a Company*, p. 54.
11 E. Herz, *Englische Schauspieler und englisches Schauspiel zur Zeit Schakespeares in Deutschland*, Hamburg and Leipzig, 1903, p. 56.
12 Limon, *Gentlemen of a Company*, p. 115.
13 W. Creizenach, in *Die Schauspiele der englischen Komödianten*, Deutsche National-Litteratur Bd.23, Berlin and Stuttgart 1889, has identified many of these titles.
14 Limon, *Gentlemen of a Company*, p. 57.
15 Fürstenau, *Zur Geschichte der Musik*, p. 96.
16 Fürstenau, *Zur Geschichte der Musik*, p. 102.
17 Cohn, *Shakespeare in Germany*, p. cxviii.
18 Creizenach, *Die Schauspiele der englischen Komödianten*, p. lxiv and Limon, *Gentlemen of a Company*, p. 58.
19 See Johannes Bolte, *Die Singspiele der englischen Komödianten und ihrer Nachfolger in Deutschland, Holland und Skandinavien*, Theatergeschichtliche Forschungen VII, Hamburg and Leipzig, 1893, p. 19f.

20 According to Cohn, *Shakespeare in Germany*, p. cxviii, though he also mentions an anonymous play called *Dioclesian* performed 1594 at the Rose Theatre in London.
21 Limon, *Gentlemen of a Company*, p. 115.
22 Creizenach, *Die Schauspiele der englischen Komödianten*, p.l.
23 The printed programmes with a detailed plot summary are preserved in HStA OHMA A Nr. 11/b, together with the programme of the 'Freuden=Spiel vom Jupitern und Amphyitryonen'.
24 Creizenach, *Die Schauspiele der englischen Komödianten*, p. xlviii.
25 See Henry W. Sullivan, *Calderón in the German Lands and the Low Countries: His Reception and Influence, 1654–1980*, Cambridge, 1983, p. 72f.
26 Sullivan, *Calderón in the German lands*, p. 73.
27 A quotation from the *Ballet de Flore* (1669), the last ballet danced by Louis XIV.
28 Marie Claude Canova-Green, 'Le ballet de cour en France', in *Spectaculum Europaeum. Theatre and Spectacle in Europe (1580–1750). Histoire du Spectacle en Europe (1580–1750)*, ed. by Pierre Béhar and Helen Watanabe-O'Kelly, Wiesbaden, 1999, pp. 485–512, p. 486.
29 Sara Smart, 'Ballet in the Empire', in *Spectaculum Europaeum*, pp. 547–70.
30 The subtitle gives a good idea of the plot: 'Wie dieselbigen nach manchem Scharmützel, und Schlachten, Entlichen den Frieden dahin beschlossen, das jeder Stadt drey Mahn erwehlen, und vor derselben Freyheitt kempfen lassen, undter welchen die Stadt Rohm, den endtlichen Sigk, mit glück erhalttenn' (How they [Rome and Alba] finally made peace after many skirmishes and battles, by each city choosing three men to do combat for the freedom of their city. Rome finally achieved victory by this means.)
31 Fürstenau, *Zur Geschichte der Musik*, p. 86; Robert Prölß, *Beiträge zur Geschichte des Hoftheaters zu Dresden in actenmässiger Darstellung*, Erfurt 1880.
32 See the article by Canova-Green mentioned above for definitions of the different types.
33 Werner Braun, 'Das Ballett zum großen Kopenhagener Beilager 1634', in *Heinrich Schütz und die Musik in Dänemark zur Zeit Christians IV. Bericht über die wissenschaftliche Konferenz in Kopenhagen 10–14. November 1985*, ed. by Anne Ørbaek Jensen and Ole Kongsted, Copenhagen, 1989, pp. 69–79, p. 78. The rhymed cartell – five fourteen-line poems in rhymed Alexandrines – which was distributed by Calliope, is reprinted in Weck, *Der Residentz=und Haupt=Vestung Dresden Beschreib: und Vorstellung*, pp. 366–7.
34 *Musicalische Darstellung/ So auf des... Herrn Johan Georgen/ Hertzogens zu Sachsen Höchsterfreulichen Geburths-Tag/ Als nehmlich Höchstgedachte Churfürstl. Durchl. mit Beywohnung Göttlicher Gnaden den 5. Martii Ihr Grosses Stuffen-Jahr zu rücke geleget/ und den 6. dieses... in das 64. Jahr des Alters eingetretten Bey einem von dero Fürstlichen Enckelein/ Fräulein Erdmuth Sophia/ Hertzogin zu Sachsen/ [et]c. zu gehorsambster Glückwünschung praesentirten Ballet/ Nachfolgender massen von denen Chur- und Fürstlichen sämbtlichen Musicis/ mit Beyfügung allerhand Instrumenten unterthänigst abgesungen worden/ auf dem Churfürstl. Schloß zu Dreßden / des 1648. Jahres*. Dresden: Bergen: Gimel II., Witwe, 1648. SLUB Hist.Sax.C.946, 101.
35 I am indebted to A. H. Harper (University of Strathclyde) for sight of the draft of the unpublished introduction to his edition of Schirmer's *Rosen-Gepüsche*.

36 *David Schirmers Singende Rosen oder Liebes- und Tugend=Lieder Jn die Music gesetzt Durch Philipp Stollen itzo Jhrer Hoch=Fürstl. Durchl. Des Herrn Administratoris des Ertz=Bischthumbs Magdeburg Cammer=Musicum.* Dreßden/ Jn Verlegung Wolffgang Seyfferts/ Jm Jahr 1654. *David Schirmers Churfürstlichen Sächsischen Bibliothecarii Poetische Rosen=Gepüsche. Von Ihm selbsten aufs fleißigste übersehen/ mit einem gantz neuen Buche vermehrt und in allem verbesserten heraus gegeben.* Dresden/ In Verlegung Andreas Löflers Buchführers. Gedruckt bey Melchior Bergen/ Churf. Sächs. Hof=Buchdr. 1657. *David Schirmers Poetischer Rosen=Gepüsche Neues oder Ander Buch/ Von Ihm selbsten herauß gegeben.* Dresden/ In Verlegung Andreas Löflers Buchführers. Gedruckt bey Melchior Bergen/ Churf. Sächs. Hof=Buchdr. 1657.
37 *David Schirmers Churfürstlichen Sächsischen Bibliothecarii Poetische Rauten= Gepüsche in Sieben Büchern.* Dresden/ In Verlegung Andreas Löflers Buchführers. Gedruckt bey Melchior Bergen/ Churf. Sächs. Hof=Buchdr. 1663.
38 Published separately as: *Dem Durchlauchtigsten/ Hochgebohrnen Fürsten und Herrn/ Herrn Johann Georgen/ hertzogen zu Sachsen ... und Churfürsten ... Als Ihre Churfürstliche Durchlauchtigkeit ... dem 5. Mertzens das Fünf und Sechzigste Jahr Ihres Alters hinterleget ... War in einer Singenden Darstellung durch die eingeführte Zeit/ Kindheit/ Jugend/ Mannheit/ Alter/ und Ewigkeit beygebracht/ was Ihrer Churfürstl. Durchl. ferner hertzlich gewünschet ... würd Von Dero unterthänigsten und gehorsamsten sämbtlichen Hoff-capell-Verwandten und dem Dichter David Schirmern.* Dresden: Bergen, Christian II und Melchior, 1650. SLUB Hist.Sax.C.39 *Rauten-Gepüsche*, pp. 25–36.
39 *Bey dem ersten Feuer-Wercke/ So an Derer Durchlauchtigsten/ Hochgebornen Fürsten und Herren/ H. Christiani u. H. Moritzen/ ... Beylagern/Auff dem Walle/ oder so genannten Müntzberge/ verbrennet wurde*, in *Rauten-Gepüsche*, pp. 37–40. Also separately printed, SLUB Hist.Sax.C.118,23.
40 *Rauten-Gepüsche*, pp. 41–5. See also *Cartel des Feuer-Wercks Worinnen die Eroberung des Güldenen Fellis Durch den Jason außgebüldet wird/ ...*, Dresden: Christian und Melchior Bergen. SLUB Hist.Sax.C.118, 24.
41 See Helen Watanabe-O'Kelly, 'Entries, fireworks and religious festivals in the Empire', in *Spectaculum Europaeum*, pp. 721–41, p. 732f.
42 *Eigentliche Abbild= und Beschreibung deß Churf. Sächs. Gnedigst angeordneten Fewerwercks, so uff den fürstlichen Beylager, des ... Herrn Friedrichen, Erben zu Norwegen, Herzogen zu Schleßwig ... mit ... Frewlein Maria Elisabeth ... Herzogin zu Sachsen ... am 5 Martii 1630 zu Ehren praesentieret.* SLUB Hist.Sax.C.958.d,misc.1.
43 HStA OHMA N I No. 7. The account is laid loosely in at the front of the volume. It is headed: Erstes Feuerwercklein So Ihr Fürstl. Durchlauchtigkeit Hertzogk Johanns Georg zu Sachssen ... An dero genedigen unnd Vielgeliebten Frau Müttern, der ... Churfürstin zu Sachssen ... Frawen Magdalenen Sybillen Nahmens tage, welches war den 22. July Anno. 1635. Alhier zue Dreßden uff dem Hohen Wahl verbrennet.
44 Weck, *Der Residentz= und Haupt=Vestung Dresden Beschreib: und Vorstellung*, p. 364.
45 *Rauten-Gepüsche*, pp. 46–7.
46 *Rauten-Gepüsche*, pp. 47–50.
47 *Rauten-Gepüsche*, pp. 50–104.

48 See, for instance, Judith P. Aikin, 'The musical-dramatic works of David Schirmer', in *Daphnis* 26 (1997), 401–35.
49 *Rauten-Gepüsche*, pp. 104.
50 See Mara Wade, *Triumphus Nuptialis Danicus. German Court Culture and Denmark. The Great Wedding of 1634*, Wiesbaden, 1996.
51 Ernst Geller, *Arkadischer Hürten-Aufzug Als Die Durchläuchtigsten Hoochgebohrnen Fürsten und Herren/ Herr Johann Georg/ Hertzog zu Sachsen... Kuhrfürst... Herr Johann Georg/ Hertzog zu Sachsen... Kuhrprintz... Herr Johann Georg/ Hertzog zu Sachsen... Dero allerseits Nahmenstag begiengen den 24. Julii/ im Jahr GOtt VVoLLe Lange ZeIt Der RaVten Krafft KVhrSachsen ErhaLten/ aVch Die ZVVelg' an GIVkke VVaChsen. Verfärtiget von Ihrer Kuhrprintzlichen Durchlauchtigkeit zu Sachsen Kammerschreibern Ernst Gellern*. Dresden: Christian und Melchior Bergen, 1653. HAB XB 4° 172.
52 *Entwurff... Etlicher Chur- und Hoch-Fürstlicher Ergötzlichkeiten Nach dem... Johann George I.... Mit dem... Herrn Georgen/ Land=Grafen zu Hessen Darmstadt/ etc. 1655 von Düben zu Dreßden einkommen war/ und allda Dero Chur= und Hoch-Fürstlich. Geburths=Tage begingen*. Dresden: Bergen, 1655. SLUB Hist. Sax. C.946, 105.
53 See Canova-Green, 'Le ballet de cour en France', pp. 498–9.
54 *Rauten-Gepüsche*, p. 282.
55 See Aikin, 'The musical-dramatic works of David Schirmer'.
56 Aikin dates the first of these to 1656 but I can see no evidence for this date. Schirmer himself dates it to 1659 in the *Rauten-Gepüsche*, p. 427.
57 Aikin,'The musical-dramatic works of David Schirmer', pp. 422–3.
58 François de La Marche, *Ballet der Glückseligkeit mit welchem Die... Frau Magdalena Sibylla/ Chur-Fürstin zu Sachsen... Die... Frau Anna Sophien/ gebohrne Königliche Erb-Princeßin zu Dännemarck... Nach dem Sie von Dero geliebten Herren Sohne... Herrn Johann Georgen dem Dritten/ Chur-Printzen zu Sachsen... heimgeführet... Dem 5. Martii 1667... empfangen wolte Inventiret von François de La Marche, Tantzmeister zu Straßburg*. SLUB Hist.Sax.C.178.
59 *Cartel zu dem Ballet des Atlas von den vier Theilen der Welt. Welches Die Durchleuchtigste Fürstin und Frau/ Frau Anna Sophia, gebohrne Erb=Printzeßin/ der Königreiche Dennemarck/ Norwegen etc. Vermählete Chur=Printzeßin ... Bey Dero Chur=Printzeßlichen Durchleuchtigkeit am 18. Octobr. 1668 neulichst gebohrnen und geliebten Jungen Printzens Herrn Johann Georgens des Vierdten/ dem 2. Hornungs=Tag in Dreßden angestelleter Hoch=Fürstlichen Einsegnung Denen Keyser=Königl. Chur= und Hoch=Fürstl. Durchleuchtigkeiten und hochansehnlichen Anwesenden Herren Abgesandten und Gästen zu annehmlicher Ergetzlichkeit den 21. Gedachten Hornungs 1669. Auf den Riesen=Saale/ in der Chur=Fürstl. Burg zu Dreßden vorstellig machen liesse. Gedruckt durch Melchior Bergens/ Churf. G.Hof=Buchdr. Sel. Witwe und Erben*. HStA OHMA A Nr.11 b, fol. 381f.
60 *Kurtzer Entwurff/ Was Bey Sr. Chur=Fürstl. Durchlaucht. Herrn Herrn Johann Georgens des Ander/... Zusammenkunfft Dero Herren Gebrüdere... Zu Ehren Deroselben angestellet worden/ Im Monat Februario M.DC.LXXII. Dresden/ gedruckt durch Melchior Bergens/ Churfl. S.Hof.Burchdr.* [sic] *nachgelassene Wittwe und Erben*. SLUB Hist.Sax.C.158 39f and HStA OHMA G Nr.5a fol. 458 f.

Notes 267

61 Cartel zum Ballete. Welches Der Durchlauchtigste Hochgebohrne Fürst und Herr Hr. Johann George der Dritte/ ... Benebenst Dessen Hertzvielgeliebtesten Gemahlin/ ... Fr. Annen Sophien Gebohrner Erb=Printzeßin der Königreiche Dennemarck/ und Norwegen etc. ... Denen Anwesenden ... Durchlauchtigkeiten zu Sachsen etc. Zu sonderbahren Ehren und angenehmer Ergetzung ... auff dem Riesen=Saale daselbst den 11. Februarii Anno 1672. Vorgestellet zu Dresden. Gedruckt durch Melchior Bergens/Churfl. Sächs. Hof=Buchdr.sel.nachgelassene Witwe und Erben. HStA OHMA G Nr.5a fol.462f.

62 Cartel zu dem Frauen-Zimmer und Mohren-Ballet, welches Die durchleuchtigste Chur-Fürstin zu Sachsen etc. Als der Durchleuchtigste Chur-Fürst zu Sachsen ... Dero Durchleuchtigsten Sämtlichen Herren Brüder Nebenst Dero Hoch-Fürstlichen Gemahlinnen/ und Herren Söhnen/ und Fräul. Töchtern Dem i. Febr. 1678. Durch einen Prächtigen Einzug/ in Dreßden glücklich eingeholet hatte/ Dem 3. Darauf höchst erfreulichst auf dem grossen Riesen-Saale/ Der anwesenden sämtlichen Herrschafft zu annehmlichen Gefallen/ vorstellig machen liesse/ von Francisco Maran, Hoch-Fürstl. Marggräfl. Bayreutischen Tantz-Meister. Dresden. HAB Textb. 4° 28. The libretto is reprinted in Tzschimmer's Durchlauchtigste Zusammenkunft, pp. 106–13.

63 Ballet Von Zusammenkunft und Wirckung derer VII. Planeten/ auf Ihr. Churfl. Durchl. Zu Sachsen großem Theatro gehalten Den 3. Februarii Anno 1678. SLUB Sign. B44a and HAB Textb. 4° 28. UBL Hist.Sax.88.

64 Tzschimmer, Durchlauchtigste Zusammenkunft, p. 67. The libretto he reproduces differs in various minor ways from the separately printed libretto.

65 SLUB Mus.2-F-31. Hans-Georg Hofmann (University of Berne) is of the opinion that the two Italian kapellmeisters in post at this date, Giovanni Battista Bontempi and Vincenzo Albrici, working in collaboration, are the most likely composers of the score. See his article 'Das Dresdner Planetenballet 1678/79: Aspekte einer Inszenierung', Basler Jahrbuch für historische Musikpraxis, vol. 23, forthcoming.

66 Cartel Zu dem Ballet der vortrefflichen Schäffer und Schäfferinnen/ Welches auff dem Churfl. Schlosse zu Dreßden gehalten wurde Den 27. Februar. 1679, n.p. 1679. SLUB Hist.Sax.C.158,41.s.

67 See August Adolph von Haugwitz, Prodromus Poeticus, Oder: Poetischer Vortrab 1684, ed. by Pierre Béhar, Tübingen, 1984.

68 This is a paraphrase of a line from the prologue sung by Ovidius at the beginning of Bontempi and Peranda's Dafne (1671/72), in which he sings: 'weiln die götter itzt sich bey den großen Sachsen finden ... ' (while the gods are to be found among the great Saxons). See p. xxiii of the modern reprint of the opera cited in note 66.

69 Werner Braun, 'Opera in the Empire', in Béhar and Watanabe-O'Kelly (eds.), Spectaculum Europaeum, pp. 437–64.

70 See her article 'Schütz' in The New Grove Dictionary of Opera, ed. by Stanley Sadie. Vol. IV, London, New York, 1992, p. 259.

71 Braun, 'Opera in the Empire', p. 438.

72 See Colin Timms, 'Giovanni Angelini Bontempi', in The New Grove Dictionary of Music and Musicians, ed. by Stanley Sadie, London, 1980, vol. 3, p. 37.

73 Drama. Oder. Musicalisches Schauspiel Von der Dafne. Mscr. Dresd. App. 17788, 1 (the libretto); SLUB Mus. 1750-F-1 contains the score. There is a modern reprint in: Giovanni Andrea Bontempi, Marco Gioseppe Peranda,

Drama oder Musicalisches Schauspiel von der Dafne. Hrsg. Von Susanne Wilsdorf, Leipzig, 1998. Denkmäler Mitteldeutscher Barockmusik, Serie II: Komponisten des 17. und 18. Jahrhunderts, Band 2, pp. vi–vii. The divergences between score and libretto are discussed here also.

74 See her introduction to the work cited in note 69 above, p. ix.
75 The libretto is preserved in manuscript in the SLUB as 'Opera von Jupiter und Io', Mscr.Dresd.Appp. 1788, 2.

Chapter 7

1 Wilhelm Ernst Tentzel, *Saxonia Numismatica, oder Medaillen-Cabinet. Dritter Theil der Albertinischen Linie/ Von Chur=Fürst Johann Georgen II. biß auff Den ietzigen Chur=Printzen*. Dresden/ gedruckt beym Kön. Hoffbuchdrucker/ Joh.Riedeln. 1705. BL 603.e.12,13. Tab. 73, No.I, text on p. 680.
2 See Jacek Staszewski, 'August der Starke, Kurfürst Friedrich August I. von Sachsen, König August II. von Polen', in *Unter einer Krone. Kunst und Kultur der sächsisch-polnischen Union*, exh. cat., Leipzig 1997, p. 45.
3 At this time, a different calendar was in operation in Saxony from that in use in Poland. The former still held to the Julian calendar, which was ten days behind the Gregorian calendar, introduced into Catholic territories by Pope Gregory XIII in 1582. The Gregorian calendar was not introduced in the Protestant German territories until 1 March 1700, these territories simply losing the days between 19 and 28 February in that year. Dates before the two calendars were unified are therefore given according to both calendars.
4 See Jacek Staszewski, *Unter* einer *Krone*, p. 71f.
5 See Jacek Staszewski, *Unter* einer *Krone*, p. 45.
6 Karlheinz Blaschke, *Der Fürstenzug zu Dresden*, Leipzig, 1991, p. 174.
7 For full details of the various manoeuvrings leading up to the election and coronation see Jutta Bäumel, *Auf dem Weg zum Thron. Die Krönungsreise Augusts des Starken*, Dresden, 1997.
8 *Die Weinende Mutter/ Der Christlichen Lutherischen Kirchen Uber den Verlust ihres Höchst-wehrten und allerliebsten Sohns/ welcher sich anjetzo in den Schoß einer andern Kirchen-Mutter gesetzet hat. Dabey auch höchst=sehnliche und grosse Klage über ihre annoch ungerahtene und böse Kinder ... Von einem Der die wahre Kirche und Gott liebet*. Gedruckt im Jahr 1697. BL 477.a.38.
9 Reprinted, for instance, in the *Theatrum Europaeum*, Frankfurt am Main: Johann Philipp Andreä 1707, vol. XV (1696–1700), 238b–240b, together with the various stipulations made by the Saxon Estates.
10 Richard Burridge, *The Apostate Prince: Or, A Satyr Against the King of Poland*, London 1700. BL 1346.m.42.
11 See the chronology of August's journeys in *Unter* einer *Krone*, pp. 49–53, from which the following information is taken.
12 See Charles W. Ingrao, *The Habsburg Monarchy 1618–1815*, Cambridge, 1994, pp. 142–4.
13 See Hans-Günther Hartmann, *Moritzburg. Schloß und Umgebung in Geschichte und Gegenwart*, Weimar 1988, p. 35f.
14 Hans-Joachim Kuke, *Die Frauenkirche in Dresden. 'Ein Sankt Peter der wahren evangelischen Religion'*, Worms, 1996.

15 See for instance the collection of engravings of both the Frauenkirche and the Catholic Hofkirche in 'Risse der Dresdner Frauen und Catholischen Kirchen', UBL Gr.Folio 426.
16 See Kuke, *Die Frauenkirche in Dresden*, p. 56.
17 See Kuke, *Die Frauenkirche in Dresden*, p. 32.
18 *Jöchers Gelehrten-Lexikon*, vol. D-L, Leipzig: Johann Friedrich Gleditschens Buchhandlung 1750, col. 1408.
19 *Gloriosa Electorum Ducum Saxoniae Busta, Oder Ehre Derer Durchlauchtigsten und Hochgebohrnen Chur=Fürsten und Hertzoge zu Sachsen Leichen=Grüffte, Bestehend in denen auf Ihr Absterben gehaltenen und verfertigten Leichen= Predigten, Lateinische und Teutschen Lob=Reden, Epitaphien, Epicedien, Begräbniß= Müntzen und Ihren aus guten Originalien in Kupffer gestochenen Bildnissen zu Erhaltung Ihres glorwürdigen Ehren=Gedächtnisse In diese Collection zusammengebracht, mit denen mangelnden Curriculis Vitae, Oder Lebens=Läufften aus bewährten Scribenten vermehret, und mit vollständigen Registern versehen von Christian August Hausen, Stadt=Predigern in Dreßden*. Dresden: Bey Joh. Christoph Zimmermann und Joh. Nic. Gerlachen. 1728.
20 See Julius Richter, *Das Erziehungswesen am Hofe der Wettiner Albertinischer (Haupt-)Linie*, Berlin, 1913, pp. 264–5.
21 Richter, *Erziehungswesen*, pp. 272 and 279 respectively.
22 Katrin Keller (ed.), *'Mein herr befindet sich gottlob gesund und wohl'. Sächsische Prinzen auf Reisen*, Leipzig 1994, reprints the travel diaries and associated correspondence of the Grand Tours of both Johann Georg IV and Friedrich August I.
23 Jutta Bäumel, 'Das "Rheingrafenkleid" Augusts des Starken', *Dresdner Kunstblätter* 1997, No. 3, 91–8.
24 Quoted from Bäumel, 'Das "Rheingrafenkleid"', p. 92.
25 Moritz Fürstenau, *Zur Geschichte der Musik und des Theaters am Hofe zu Dresden*, (1861–62), reprint Hildesheim, New York, 1971, vol. ii, p. 9.
26 *La Vie de Scaramouche. Par le Sieur Angelo Constantini, Comedien Ordinaire du Roy dans sa Troupe Italienne, sous le nom de Mezetin. A Paris, A l'Hôtel de Bourgogne. Et Chez Claude Barbin, aus Palais, sur le Perron de al Sainte Chapelle. Le prix est de trente-six sols.* 1695.BL 1094.cc.28. First edition, very rare. The later editions are not rare.
27 See Bäumel, *Auf dem Weg zum Thron*, p. 201.
28 See Bäumel, *Auf dem Weg zum Thron*, p. 201.
29 Fürstenau, *Zur Geschichte der Musik und des Theaters*, vol. ii, pp. 22–3.
30 *Le Theatre des plaisirs presenté a la Majesté de Frideric Auguste Second, Roy de Pologne et Electeur de Saxe. Par le Sr. Ange de Constantini... & Representé en Presence de Sa Majesté le Roy de Danemarck. a Dresden ce* (space left blank on title-page to insert actual day) 1709. SLUB Hist.Sax.C.1033.
31 *Les Quatre Saisons, Divertissement de Musique & de Dance pour célébrer le mariage de Son Altesse Royale de Pologne & Electorale de Saxe, 1719*. Dresden: Johann Conrad Stößel 1719. HAB Lo Sammelbd. 32 (7 and 19). The libretto is by 'Sieur Poisson, Comedien du Roy', the music by S. Schmidt, *kapellmeister*, and the choreography by Sieur de Bargues, the dancing master.
32 See *Vorstellung und Beschreibung Das von Sr. Königl. Majestät in Pohlen, Churfl. Durchl. Zu Sachsen, erbauten so genannten Zwinger Gartens Gebäuden, Oder Der Königl. Orangerie zu Dreßden, In Vier=und=Zwantzig Kupffer=Stichen*

Kunst= und Grund=Rissen abgezeichnet und herausgegeben von Matthäus Daniel Pöppelmann, Königl. Pohln. Und Churfl. Sächs. Ober=Land=Baumeister, Anno 1729. UBL Matthäus Daniel Pöppelmann, Gr.Folio 424. The title is given in French as: *L'Orangerie Royale de Dresden avec des Pavillons et embellissements Batue en 1711 Par Ordre de S.M.le Roy de Pol:Elect.de Saxe Vicaire du St Empire Sur les desseins et Sous la conduite du Sr.N.Pöppelmann premier Architecte de S.Maj.*

33 See Michael Kirsten, 'Der Dresdner Zwinger', in Harald Marx (ed.), *Matthäus Daniel Pöppelmann. Der Architekt des Dresdners Zwingers*, Leipzig, 1990, p. 148f.

34 Dirk Syndram, *Die Schatzkammer Augusts des Starken*, Leipzig, 1999. What follows is greatly indebted to this book.

35 Syndram, *Die Schatzkammer Augusts des Starken*, p. 37.

36 Jutta Bäumel, *Auf dem Weg zum Thron*, p. 67f., where the inventory of these pieces (HStA OHMA D Nr.7, fol. 248–56) is transcribed.

37 See Ulrich Müller and Margarete Springeth, 'Ein Indien-Reisebericht des Barock aus Gold, Edelsteinen und Perlen: Der *Hofstaat zu Delhi am Geburtstag des Gros-Moguls Aureng-Zeb* der Hofjuwelier-Werkstätte von Johann Melchior Dinglinger (Dresden 1701–1701)', in *Beschreibung der Welt. Zur Poetik der Reise- und Länderberichte*. Ed. by Xenja von Ertzdorff unter Mitarbeit von Rudolf Schulz, Chloe vol. 31, Amsterdam, 2000, pp. 345–66.

38 Syndram, *Die Schatzkammer Augusts des Starken*, p. 76.

39 Syndram, *Die Schatzkammer Augusts des Starken*, p. 86.

40 See Sonja Karallus, 'Der "Riesensaal" im Dresdner Residenzschloß', unpubl. MA thesis, University of Bonn, 1998, p. 85.

41 Gerhard Glaser, 'Das Grüne Gewölbe', in *Das Dresdner Schloß. Monument sächsischer Geschichte und Kultur*. Dresden, 1992, pp. 109–13, p. 109.

42 See Rudolph Zaunick, 'Einführung', in E.W. von Tschirnhaus, *Medicina mentis, sive Artis inveniendi praecepta generalia*, second edition, Leipzig, 1695. Erstmalig vollständig ins Deutsche übersetzt und kommentiert von Johannes Haussleiter, Leipzig 1963, pp. 5–28.

43 See Eduard Winter, *E. W. v. Tschirnhaus (1651–1708). Ein Leben im Dienste des Akademiegedankens*, Berlin, 1959.

44 See R. Forberger, 'Tschirnhaus und das sächsische Manufakturwesen', in *E.W. von Tschirnhaus und die Frühaufklärung in Mittel- und Osteuropa*, Berlin, 1960, pp. 214–22.

45 See HStA Loc.4417/14 where a manuscript account of this is to be found with a large quantity of alchemical and cabbalistic material.

46 See Forberger, 'Tschirnhaus', p. 220.

47 See *Porzellansammlung Dresden. Führer durch die ständige Ausstellung im Dresdner Zwinger*, Dresden, 1998, p. 103.

48 See E. Winter, 'Der Bahnbrecher der deutschen Frühaufklärung E. W. v.Tschirnhaus und die Frühaufklärung in Mittel- und Osteuropa', in *E. W. von Tschirnhaus und die Frühaufklärung*, p. 69.

49 *Porzellansammlung Dresden*, p. 104.

50 *Einleitung zum Saturnus-Feste*, Dresden: Johann Conrad Stössel, 1719. HAB Lo.Sammelbd. 32 (8). *Introduction a la Fete de Saturne*, Dresden: Johann Conrad Stössel, 1719. HAB Lo.Sammelbd. 32 (11 and 13). *Saturni Unterirrdischer Auffstand und Bericht zu einem Bergmännischen Festin*, Dresden: Johann Conrad Stössel, 1719. HAB Lo.Sammelbd. 32 (9). *Beschreibung des Gebäudes und*

der Illumination Zum Bergwercks=Festin [Dresden: Johann Conrad Stössel, 1719]. HAB Lo.Sammelbd. 32 (10). *Description De la maison & de l'Illumination pour La Fete des Mineurs.* Dresden: Johann Conrad Stössel, 1719. HAB Lo.Sammelbd. 32 (12). See the exhibition catalogue *Bergbau und Kunst in Sachsen*, Dresden: Staatliche Kunstsammlungen, 1989, pp. 58–62.
51 Kupferstichkabinett Dresden, Inv.No.C 201, 35. See Schnitzer, *Höfische Maskaraden*, p. 177f. and Fig. 187.
52 Kupferstichkabinett Dresden, pen and wash, Inv.Nr.C 773 (from Ca 201, 24). Six different machines are depicted here.
53 For an extensive account of tournaments in Dresden see chapter V of Helen Watanabe-O'Kelly, *Triumphall Shews. Tournaments at German-Speaking Courts in their European Context 1560–1730*, Berlin, 1992.
54 See *Specification Derer Festivitaeten So bey ietzigem Carnevall An dem Chur=Sächsischem Hofe sind gehalten worden*, Dresden 1695 and HStA OHMA G 12 and the gouache depictions in the Kupferstichkabinett in Dresden, Ca 189.
55 HStA OHMA B 18.
56 HStA OHMA G 9.
57 HStA OHMA G 8.
58 The gouache depictions are preserved in a tournament book in the Kupferstichkabinett in Dresden, Ca 188.
59 Martin Klötzel, *Heidnischer Götter und Göttinnen prächtiger Auffzug/ An.1695. gehalten in Dreßden.* There is also a manuscript tournament book of the same event in gouache by Klötzel (Kupferstichkabinett Dresden Ca 190).
60 Claudia Schnitzer has pointed out how Klötzel's engraved depictions differ from his gouaches of the same group in her book *Höfische Maskaraden*, p. 4.
61 See the tournament book at SLUB Mscr.Dresd.K 2.
62 See 'Tournaments in the Empire' by Helen Watanabe-O'Kelly in *Spectaculum Europaeum*, pp. 602–3, for further information about the ladies' running at the ring.
63 See Adam Olearius, *Auffzüge und Ritterspiele So bey Des Durchläuchtigen/ Hochgebornen Fürsten und Herrn/ Herrn Friedrich Wilhelms...Jungen printzen/ hertzog Christian, Fürstlichen Kindtauffs Feste/...gehalten worden...zu Altenburg im Monat Junio 1654*, Schleswig, 1658.
64 Schnitzer, *Höfische Maskaraden*, pp. 164–5.
65 Schnitzer, *Höfische Maskaraden*, p. 330f.
66 Elisabeth Mikosch, 'Court Dress and Ceremony in the Baroque Age. The Royal/Imperial Wedding of 1719 in Dresden: A Case Study', unpublished doctoral dissertation, New York University, 1998, p. 73.
67 The entry is described in *Accurate Beschreibung Des solennen Einzugs Ihrer Hoheit Des Königl. Pohln. Und Chur=Printzens von Sachßen, Mit Seiner aus Wien angekommenen Durchl. Gemahlin, Wie solcher in die Königl. Und Chur=Sächß. Residentz=Stadt Dreßden/ den 2. September. 1719. Nachmittags von 2 biß 5. Uhr gehalten worden*. Dresden: Johann Conrad Stößel 1719. HAB Lo Sammelbd. 32, (6).
68 *La Gara degli Dei, Festa Musicale rappresentata in uno de' Reali Giardini di Dresda per servire d'introduzione agli Spettacoli destinati da S. M. A. solennizare le Nozze De' Serenißimi Principi Federigo Augusto, Principe Reale di Pollonia, & Elettorale di Sassonia e Maria Gioseffa, Arciduchessa d'Austria.* Dresden: J. C. Stöessel, 1719. This prints *en face* a French prose translation

of the libretto entitled *L'Emulation parmy les divinitez*. HAB Lo Sammelbd. 32 (16 and 17).

69 Contrary to what the title might lead one to think, a German account of the above minus the libretto but with a lot of detail on the actual firework display is to be found in: *Ausführliche Beschreibung des unvergleichlichen Feuer=Wercks/ So Ihro Hoheit dem Königl. Und Chur=Printzen von Sachsen Und Dero aus Wien angekommenen Durchl. Gemahlin/ zu Ehren, In Gegenwart des gantzen Hofes und einer unzehligen Menge Zuschauer, Am 10. Septembr. Anno 1719 Zu Dreßden . . . angezündet worden*. HAB Lo Sammelbd. 32 (5).

70 Also published by Stössel in Dresden in 1719. HAB Lo Sammelbd. 32 (14, 15 and 19).

71 See Claudia Schnitzer, 'Zwischen Kampf und Spiel. Orientrezeption im höfischen Fest', in *Im Lichte des Halbmonds. Das Abendland und der türkische Orient*, exh. cat., Dresden, 1995, pp. 227–34.

72 Elisabeth Mikosch, 'Ein Serail für die Hochzeit des Prinzen. Turquerien bei den Hochzeitsfeierlichkeiten in Dresden im Jahre 1719', in *Im Lichte des Halbmonds*, pp. 235–43.

73 Thomas DaCosta Kaufmann, *Court, Cloister and City. The Art and Culture of Central Europe 1450–1800*, London, 1987, p. 325.

Bibliography

This bibliography does not aim to be exhaustive but to list those manuscripts, early printed books and scholarly works used in the writing of this study. 'Early printed books' have been defined as those works published up to 1730. Since such books can vary widely from copy to copy, library details and shelfmarks have been given for the copy the author consulted.

Sources

Manuscripts

Court festivals: HStA Oberhofmarschallamt OHMA A-G. and Ritterspiel 1581–1591 Nr 26a 10526.
Alchemy: HStA Geheimes Archiv Loc. 4416/6-8, Loc. 4417/1-21, Loc. 4418/1-17, Loc. 4419/1-23.
Inventories of various kinds relating to the Palace in Dresden (those of the various collections are listed separately below): HStA Hausmarschallamt Lit.R Kap. XVI.

Angelini Bontempi, Giovanni Andrea and Marco Gioseppe Peranda, Opera von Jupiter und Io, SLUB Mscr.Dresd.App. 1788, 2.
Ashmolean MSS 1131 and 1112, Bodleian Library, Oxford.
Bercht, Friedrich [?], Untitled. Tournaments for the christening of Christian, son of Johann Georg, Margrave of Brandenburg, in Cölln an der Spree, 1581. SLUB Mscr.Dresd.J 17 (KA 500).
Bretschneider, Daniel, the Elder, Contrafactur des Ringkrennens vndt anderer ritterspiell so vff Christiani Fürstlichen Beylager gehalten worden. SLUB Mscr.Dresd.K 1. and Hist. Sax. C 26 and Hist. Sax. C 25 = KA 827.
——, Des Durchlauchtigsten Hochgebornen Fursten und Herrn Herrn Christiani Hertzogens vnd Churfursten zue Sachssen Ringk Rennen, welche S. Churf. G. an dero gelibten Jungen Tochter Freulein Dorotehenn/ Furstlichen Tauffe zue Dressden auffn Schloshoff den 26. 27. 28. vnd 29. January gehalten worden. Anno 1591. SLUB Mscr.Dresd.J 9.
——, Bürger und Mahler zu Dressdenn, ein Buch von allerley Inuentionen, zu Schlittenfarthen, welche auff dergleichen arten, gar wol zugerichtet vnd leichtlich geführet werden können, für Fürstliche, Gräffliche, Herrn vnd Adelstands Personen, mehren theils von neuem visirt vnnd verferttigett. SLUB Mscr.Dresd.B 104.
——, Abriß und Verzeichnus aller Inventionen und Aufzüge welche an Faßnachten Anno 1609 Als den Durchlauchtigsten Hochgeborenen Fürsten und Herrn, Herrn Christian den Anderen Herzogen und Churfürsten zu Sachsen die Durchlauchtige Hochgeborene Fürsten und Herrn, Herr Johann Casimir und Herr Johann Ernst Herzogen zu Sachsen sowol Herr Christian Marggraf zu Brandenburg freundlicherweise uff die im Churfl. Schloßhoff zu

Dresden auffgerichtete Rennbahne gebracht worden. Verferttigt durch Daniel Bretschneider, Bürgern und Mahlern zu Dresden. SLUB Mscr.Dresd.J 18.

Cramer, Daniel, Areteugenia: Ein schön Lustig Spiel, darinnen fürnemblich von den Freyen Künstenn agirett vnnd gehandelt wirdt. Auss dem Lateinischen M. Danielis Crameri etc. ins Teutsche transferirtt vonn Burchard Grossman. SLUB Mscr.Dresd.226.

Contrafactur des Ringrennens. So Weilandt der Durchlauchtigste und Hochgeborne Furst und herr herr Augustus Hertzogk zu Sachssen, des Heiligen Römischen Reichs Ertzmarschalch und Churfürst Landgraue in Duringen, Margraue zu Meissen und Burggraue zu Magdeburgk, Christseliger Gedechtnis den 23 February Anno 1574 im Fastnacht alhier zu Dreßden im Churfürstlichen Schlosse gehalten, auch mit wasserley Inuention einn Jede Parthei uf die Bahne kommen und daselbst gantz Ritterlich zierlich und herlich volbracht. SLUB Mscr.Dresd.K 2.

De Transmutatione Metallorum, et lapide phylosophorum. Von vorenderunge der Metallen vnd von dem Phylosophischen Stein. Wie vnd welcher gestallt...dis Gottlich Geheimnus...tzuerforschen vnd zuerlangen sey. Dem Durchlauchttigen...Fursten..., Iohanns Georgen Hertzogen zw Sachssen.... SLUB Mscr.Dresd.N 155.

Der Churfl. Jungen Herrschafften education belangende (Hoffmeister u. Praeceptorn Bestallung). HStA, Geheimes Archiv 8017/2.

1.–3. Theil des Inventarii über die Churf. Sächss. Librarey zu Dresden, so auf Befehlich des...Herrn Friedrich Wilhelmen Hertzogen zu Sachssen, Vormundens und der Chur Sachssen, Administratorius etc.... Vonn Uns Graff Joachim Andreas Schlicken und Siegmundt Rölingen der Rechte Doctorn im 1595. Jahre angefangen und vollendett worden. SLUB Bibl.Arch.I B vols. 28–30.

Erstes Feuerwercklein So Ihr Fürstl. Durchlauchtigkeit Hertzogk Johanns Georg zu Sachssen...An dero genedigen vnnd Vielgeliebten Frau Müttern, der... Churfürstin zu Sachssen...Frawen Magdalenen Sÿbillen Nahmens tage, welches war den 22. Julÿ Anno. 1635. Alhier zue Dreßden uff dem Hohen Wahl verbrennet. HStA OHMA N I No 7.

Gelhorn, Friedrich von, Galatheus oder von Erbarkeit, vndt Höffligkeit der Sitten. Erstlichen in Welscher sprach geschrieben vndt itzundt erst, mit sonderem fleis aus dem Welschen in unsere hochdeutsche sprach vertiret vndt gebracht. SLUB Mscr.Dresd.M 222.

Göding, Heinrich, Vorzeichnus vnd warhafftige eigentliche Contrafacturen aller Scharff rennen vnd Treffen, so der Durchlauchtigste hochgeborne Fürst vnd Herr Herr Augustus Hertzog zu Sachßen etc. vor vnnd inn S. Churf. G. Churfürstlichen Regierung mitt sonderlicher geschicklichkeit auch großer Lust vnnd verwunderung aller Zuseher gantz Ritterlich vnd rühmlich gethan vnd verbracht hat auch Zu wes Zeitt an welchem ortt vnnd mitt was Personen ein Jedes Rennen geschehen, Zu Ewigem löblichem gedechtnus S. Churf. G. geübtem mannlichen Ritterspielen deroselben Posteritet also fürgestellet. SLUB Mscr.Dresd. J 44.

Hass, Martin, Philomena Tragoedia Germana. Eine schöne Historia, Tragoedien weise zugerichtet, Von sorglichem anfange, vndtt betrübtem aussgange der brinnenden Liebe in zwein personen, Gabriotten, eines jungen Ritters aus Franckreich, vnndtt Philomenen, eines Koniges aus Engeland Schwester. (1602). SLUB Mscr.Dresd.M 14.b.

Illustrissimi ac potentissimi principis ac domini Christiani Ducis Saxoniae etc. Illustris bibliotheca cum duobus indicibus in ordinem redacta. 1588. SLUB Bibl.Arch.I B vol. 24.

Inventarium über die kurfürstliche sächsische Kunstkammer in Schloß und Festung Dresden. Erneuert und aufgerichtet den letzten Decembris anno 1595. Grünes Gewölbe, Dresden.

Inuentarium Uber die Bücher, welche der Durchlauchtigste Hochgeborne Furst und Herr Herr Johans George hertzog zu Sachssen, Gulich, Cleue und Berge, des Heiligen Römischen Reichs in den Landen des Sächsischen Rechtens und an den Enden in solchen Vicariat gehörende dieser Zeit Vicarius, ... Anno 1612. In die Churf. Bibliothec alhie zu Dredden, einantwortenn und beysetzenn lassenn. SLUB Bibl.Arch.I 30, fol. 231a–274b.

Inventarium über die kurfürstliche sächsische Kunstkammer in Schloß und Festung Dresden. Erneuert und aufgerichtet den 1. Augusti anno 1610. Grünes Gewölbe, Dresden.

Inventarium über die kurfürstliche sächs. Kunstkammer in Schloß und Festung Dresden. Erneuert und aufgerichtet den 28. Junii anno 1619. Grünes Gewölbe, Dresden.

Inventarium über die kurfürstliche sächsische Kunstkammer in Schloß und Festung Dresden. Erneuert und aufgerichtet den 4. Augusti anno 1640. Grünes Gewölbe, Dresden.

Inventarium über das Churfürstl. Sächß. Tapezereÿ=Gewölbe in Dresden 1682. HStA Hausmarschallamt Lit.R. Kap XVI Nr. 254, 2.

Inventarium über das Churfürstl. Sächs. Tapezereÿ=Gewölbe in Dresden 1683. HStA Hausmarschallamt Lit. R. Kap XV, Nr. 254.

Inventarium über Ihrer Churfl. Durchl. Schlaff Cammer Gemach. HStA Hausmarschallamt Lit R. Kap. XVI 219.

Inventarium des HofBettmeisters Caspar Hanisch. HStA Hausmarschallamt Lit R Kap. XVI, Nr. 193.

Kunn, Heinrich, Eine Geistlige Gewissen ruerende Historische Comedia, von der Schweren Belagerung, vnd Wunderbar Erlösung zu Samaria, aus dem 2 Buch der Konigen am 6 vnd 7 Capittel genommen. Durch Heinrich Kunnen Anno 1588 beschrieben, vnd nicht am Tage gegeben worden. Nun aber abgeschrieben, durch Dauid Kirchium Pfarherrn zu Grossen Zieten im Teltow und ChurFurstlicher Brandenb./Sechsischer G. zum Newem Jar verehrt. Anno Christ 1604. Den 15 Sontag nach S. Trinitatis. SLUB Mscr. Dresd.M 224.

Nosseni, Ioh. Maria, Architect. Schlitten fahrt, Welche auff vorgegebnen beuehlich Christianj dis Namenns des andern, welcher ... nicht alleine solche verordenen lassen, sondernn auch derselben Figuren deutunge vnd schrifften in diesem angehenden Seculo des 1601. Ihares Iedermenniglich zum Beyspiegel vor Augenn gestellet sinndt worden, wie auch derselbenn erclerunng hernach zu befinndenn. 1601. SLUB Mscr.Dresd.K 371.

Realkatalog der Churf. Bibliothek. 1580. SLUB Bibl.Arch.I B vol. 21.

Registratur der bücher in des Churfürsten zu Saxen liberey zur Annaburg, SLUB Bibl.Arch.IB vol. 20.

Schonaeus, Cornelius, Triumphus Christi. Das ist Die historia von der Sieghafften Aufferstehung Jesu Christi von den todten Comoedien Weisse, Zuvorn in Lateinischer Sprache, vnnd stylo Terentiano geschrieben. Nunmehr beides der schull-Jugent, vnnd auch dem gemeine Manne fast nützlich, vnnd lustig zu lesen. SLUB Mscr.Dresd.M 261.

Sommer, Wolffgangus, Pfahrrer zu Alten Guttern, Comoedia, Dass ist, Einn fein Christliches Lustiges Spiel, vom Heiligenn Patriarchen Isaac... 1602. SLUB Mscr.Dresd.M 227.

Tragoedia der zweyer mächtiger Städt Rohm und Alba. Wie dieselbigen nach manchem Scharmützel, und Schlachten, Entlichen den Frieden dahin beschlossen, das jeder Stadt drey Mahn erwehlen, und vor derselben Freyheitt kempfen lassen, undter welchen die Stadt Rohm, den endtlichen Sigk, mit glück erhalttenn. SLUB Mscr.Dresd.M 225.

Ußlaub, David, Inventarium uber des Churfürsten zu Sachsenn und Burggrauen zu Magdeburgk etc meines gnedigsten hern Kunst Cammernn in Ihrn Churf. Gnaden Schloß und Vehstunge zu Dreßden: Wie desselben Vornehme sachen, Kunststücke und Zugehoriger Vorradt iedes besondern Sortirt und Ordiniert wordenn und nachuolgendenn Orten Zubefinden. Inuentirtt vnd aufgericht Anno 1587. Grünes Gewölbe, Dresden.

Vertzeichnuß der bucher welche die Jünge Herrschafft zum studiren gebraucht, unndt welche uff Ihrer F.G.Tischlein stehen. SLUB Bibl.Arch.I Ba 27 fol. 40a f.

Vorzeichnus ettlicher geschriebener Artzney Bücher im eim besondern Schranken in der Churfürstlichen Librarey stehenndt. Ca. 1590. SLUB Bibl.Arch.I B vol. 26.

Vorzeichnus: Der Bücher/ welche in der Jungen Herrschafft Studirstüblein in dreÿ Tabulat sein gesetzet worden. SLUB Bibl. Arch.I Ba 27.

Zihler, Hans, Schauspiele: Ruth; Ein Schöne Comöedij von der Vermählung vnd Heürathung Jsaacs; Tragedia die khindtheit Mose; Comöedia die Jael mit Sissera; Tragedia der Jephte mit seiner dochter. SLUB Mscr.Dresd.M 217.

Early printed books

Abdruck der Cartellen So bey denen/ auff dem Fürstl. Beylager Deß... Herren Friderichen/ Erben zu Norwegen/ Herzogen zu Schleßwig... Mit Frewlein Maria Elisabeth... Herzogin zu Sachsen... Gehaltenen ansehnlichen Auffzügen RingRennen und FußThurnier zu Dreßden außgegeben worden Dabey auch die Beschreibund Abbildung des Churfürstlichen Sächsischen gnädigst angeordneten FewerWercks so... am 5. Martii zu Ehren praesentirt und verbrand/ in Kupffer gestochen. Dresden: Seyffert, 1630. SLUB Hist.Sax.C.958.d,misc.1.

Accurate Beschreibung Des solennen Einzugs Ihrer Hoheit Des Königl. Pohln. Und Chur=Printzens von Sachßen, Mit Seiner aus Wien angekommenen Durchl. Gemahlin, Wie solcher in die Königl. Und Chur=Sächß. Residentz=Stadt Dreßden/ den 2. September. 1719. Nachmittags von 2 biß 5. Uhr gehalten worden. Dresden: Johann Conrad Stößel 1719. HAB Lo Sammelbd. 32, (6).

Agricola, Philipp, *Beschreibung des... Herren Johansen Georgens Marggraffens zu Brandenburgk/... gehaltenen Chur vnnd Fürstlichen celebration/ Uber seiner Churfürstlichen Gnaden... Sohns/... Herrn Christiani/... Tauffe... vnnd hierüber nachmals ein Herrlich schön Geprenge an lustigen Ringkrennen vnd Fußthurniren/ ... gehalten... worden.* 1581. SLUB Hist.Brand.14,misc.2.

Albinus, Petrus, *New Stammbuch und Beschreibung des Uhralten Königlichen/ Chur und Fürstlichen/ usw. Geschlechts und Hauses zu Sachsen/ Mit alten Bildnissen, ... Leipzig: Abraham Lamberg 1602.* HAB T 645.4° Helmst (1).

Angelini Bontempi, Giovanni Andrea, *Historien des Durchleuchtigsten Hauses Sachsen*, Dreßden/ Gedruckt bey Melchior Bergen 1666. UBL Hist.Sax.1431.

Angelini Bontempi, Giovanni Andrea and Marco Gioseppe Peranda, *Drama oder Musicalisches Schauspiel von der Dafne*. Hrsg. Von Susanne Wilsdorf, Leipzig 1998. Denkmäler Mitteldeutscher Barockmusik, Serie II: Komponisten des 17. und 18. Jahrhunderts, Band 2, pp.vi–vii.

Ashmole, Elias, *The history of the most noble Order of the Garter: and the several orders of knighthood extant in Europe. Containing I. The antiquity of the town, castle, chapel, and college of Windsor; . . . II. The habits, ensigns, and officers of the Order*, London: printed for A. Bell, E. Curll, J. Pemberton, and A. Collins, W. Taylor and J. Baker, 1715. Bodleian Gough Berks. 12.

Ausführliche Beschreibung des unvergleichlichen Feuer=Wercks/ So Ihro Hoheit dem Königl. Und Chur=Printzen von Sachsen Und Dero aus Wien angekommenen Durchl. Gemahlin/ zu Ehren, In Gegenwart des gantzen Hofes und einer unzehligen Menge Zuschauer, Am 10. Septembr. Anno 1719 Zu Dreßden . . . angezündet worden. HAB Lo Sammelbd. 32 (5).

Ballet Von Zusammenkunft und Wirckung derer VII. Planeten/ auf Ihr. Churfl. Durchl. Zu Sachsen großem Theatro gehalten Den 3. Februarii Anno 1678. Dresden/ Gedruckt durch Melchior Bergens/ Churfl. Sächs. Hof=Buchdr. Seel. Nachgelassene Wittbe und Erben. SLUB Sign.B44a; HAB Textb. 4° 28; UBL Hist. Sax.88.

Beschreibung des Gebäudes und der Illumination Zum Bergwercks=Festin [Dresden: Johann Conrad Stössel, 1719]. HAB Lo.Sammelbd. 32 (10).

Description De la maison & de l'Illumination pour La Fete des Mineurs. Dresden: Johann Conrad Stössel, 1719. HAB Lo.Sammelbd. 32 (12).

Beutel, Tobias, *Chur=Fürstlicher Sächsischer stets grünender hoher Cedern=Wald/ Auf dem grünen Rauten=Grunde Oder Kurtze Vorstellung/ Der Chur=Fürstl. Sächs. Hohen Regal=Wercke/ Nehmlich: Der Fürtrefflichen Kunst=Kammer/ und anderer/ Seiner Chur=Fürstl. Durchl. hochschätzbaren unvergleichlich wichtigen Dinge/ allhier beyder residentz Dreßden/ Aus schuldiger Danckbarkeit zu GOtt/ vor so grosse/ dem Durchleuchtigsten Chur=Hause Sachsen/ verliehene Wohlthaten und Schätze, . . .* Dresden: gedruckt bey den Bergischen Erben. Anno 1671. HAB Gm 1518 (1).

Birken, Sigmund von, *Chur- und Fürstlicher Sächsischer Heldensaal*. Nuremberg: Hofmann, Gerhard 1677. HAB Gm 3969.

Bissari, Pietro Paolo, *Fedra Incoronata. Drama Regio Musicale. Attione Prima De gli Applausi fatti nell'Ellettorale Città di Monaco per la Nascità Dell'Altezza Ser.ma Di Massimiliano Emanuele*, Munich 1662. BL 162.g.9.

——, *Antiopa Giustificata. Drama Guerriero, Attione Seconda De gli Applausi fatti alla Nascità Dell' Altezza Ser:ma Di Massimiliano Emanuele*, Munich 1662. BL 162 g.8.

——, *Medea Vendicativa. Drama di Foco. Attione Terza De gli Applausi fatti per la nascità Dell' Altezza Ser.ma Di Massimiliano Emanuele*, Munich 1662. BL 162.g.10.

Bontempi, *see under* Angelini Bontempi.

Burridge, Richard, *The Apostate Prince: Or, A Satyr Against the King of Poland*, London 1700. BL 1346.m.42.

Cartel zu dem Ballet des Atlas von den vier Theilen der Welt. Welches Die Durchleuchtigste Fürstin und Frau/ Frau Anna Sophia, gebohrne Erb=Printzeßin /

der Königreiche Dennemarck/ Norwegen etc. Vermählete Chur=Printzeßin ... Bey Dero Chur=Printzeßlichen Durchleuchtigkeit am 18. Octobr. 1668 neulichst gebohrnen und geliebten Jungen Printzens Herrn Johann Georgens des Vierdten/ dem 2. Hornungs=Tag in Dreßden angestelleter Hoch=Fürstlichen Einsegnung Denen Keyser=Königl. Chur= und Hoch=Fürstl. Durchleuchtigkeiten und hochansehnlichen Anwesenden Herren Abgesandten und Gästen zu annehmlicher Ergetzlichekti den 21. Gedachten Hornungs 1669. Auf den Riesen=Saale/ in der Chur=Fürstl. Burg zu Dreßden vorstellig machen liesse. Gedruckt durch Melchior Bergens/Churf. G.Hof=Buchdr. Sel. Witwe und Erben. HStA OHMA A Nr.11 b, fol. 381f.

Cartel Zu dem Ballet der vortrefflichen Schäffer und Schäfferinnen/ Welches auff dem Churfl. Schlosse zu Dreßden gehalten wurde Den 27. Februar. 1679, n.p. 1679. SLUB Hist.Sax.C.158,41.s.

Cartel zum Ballete. Welches Der Durchlauchtigste Hochgebohrne Fürst und Herr Hr. Johann George der Dritte/ ... Benebenst Dessen Hertzvielgeliebtesten Gemahlin/ ... Fr. Annen Sophien Gebohrner Erb=Printzeßin der Königreiche Dennemarck/ und Norwegen etc. ... Denen Anwesenden ... Durchlauchtigkeiten zu Sachsen etc. Zu sonderbahren Ehren und angenehmer Ergetzung ... auff dem Riesen=Saale daselbst den 11. Februarii Anno 1672. Vorgestellet zu Dresden. Gedruckt durch Melchior Bergens/Churfl. Sächs. Hof=Buchdr.sel. nachgelassene Witwe und Erben. HStA OHMA G Nr.5a fol.462 f.

Cartel zu dem Frauen-Zimmer und Mohren-Ballet, welches Die durchleuchtigste Chur-Fürstin zu Sachsen etc. Als der Durchleuchtigste Chur-Fürst zu Sachsen ... Dero Durchleuchtigsten Sämtlichen Herren Brüder Nebenst Dero Hoch-Fürstlichen Gemahlinnen/ und Herren Söhnen/ und Fräul. Töchtern Dem 1. Febr. 1678. Durch einen Prächtigen Einzug/ in Dresßden glücklich eingeholet hatte/ Dem 3. Darauf höchst erfreulichst auf dem grossen Riesen-Saale/ Der anwesenden sämtlichen Herrschafft zu annehmlichen Gefallen/ vorstellig machen liesse/ von Francisco Maran, Hoch-Fürstl. Marggräfl. Bayreutischen Tantz-Meister. Dresden. HAB Textb. 4° 28.

Ceruti, Benedetto and Andrea Chiocco, *Musaeum Francesci Calceolari Iunioris Veronensis*, Verona 1622. HAB 38 Phys.2° (1).

Chytraeus, Nathan, *Io.Casæ V.Cl.Galateus. Seu de morum honestate & elegantia, liber ex Italico Latinus, Interprete Nathane Chytræo ... Rostochii Typis Iacobi Lucij Transyluani.* Anno CIC.IC.LXXIIX. HAB O 240. 8° Helmst.(1).

——, *Ioannis Casae Galateus seu de morum honestate et elegantia, liber ex italico latinus, interprete Nathane Chytraeo, cum eiusdem notis, nuper additis*, Frankfurt 1597. HAB 5.4 Eth.(1).

——, *Io Casae Galateus. Das ist das Büchlein von erbarn/ höflichen und holdseligen Sitten. Inn welchem unter der Person eines alten wolerfahrnen Hofmannes/ ein Edler Jüngling unterweiset wird/ wie er sich in seinen Sitten/ Geberden/ Kleydung/ Reden/ Schweigen/ Thun/ Lassen/ und gantzem Leben also fürischtiglich verhalten solle/ daß er bey jedermenniglich möge lieb und werth gehalten werden. Neuwlich auß Italianischer Sprach verteutschet von Nathane Chytraeo. Gedruckt zu Franckfurt/* Anno 1597. This is available in a modern reprint: G. della Casa, *Galateus. Das Büchlein von erbarn/ höflichen und holdseligen Sitten, verdeutscht von Nathan Chytraeus 1507*, ed. by Klaus Ley, Deutsche Neudrucke, Reihe Barock, 34, Tübingen 1984.

Della Casa, Giovanni, *Trattato di Messer Giovanni Della casa [sic] nel quale sotto la persona d'un uecchio idiota ammaestrante un suo giovanetto, si ragiona de' modi, che si debbono ò tenere ò schifare nella comune conuersazione, cognominato Galatheo ovver de' costumi,* Milan: Appresso à Giovanni Antonio de gli Antonij; imprimeuano i fratelli da Meda 1559.

Colbovius, Petrus, *Freudiger Glückwünschungs=Segen/ Uber Das Hoch=Fürstliche Beylager Der zwoen Hoch=Fürstlichen Durchlauchtigkeiten/ Nemlich Des Durchlauchtigsten Fürsten und Herrn/ Herrn Christian Ernsten/ Marggrafen zu Brandenburgk ... und Der Durchlauchtigsten Fürstin und Fräulein/ Fräul. Erdmuth Sophien/ Hertzogin zu Sachsen.... Wie unterthänigst=gehorsamst=wolmeynend also hertzlich gewünschet in Alt=Dreßden von Petro Colbovio, von Gadebusch aus Mecklenburg.* Gedruckt durch Melchior Bergen/ Churfürstl. Sächs. Hoff-Buchdrucker. SLUB Hist.Sax.C.158,57.

Colbovius, Petrus, *Petri Colbovii, Gadeb. Megar. Wolmeynendliches Chymisch Carmen. Von unterschiedlichen noch unbekandten nothwendigen Königlichen Universal=Alkahest=Menstruis, zum unterschiedlichen Chaos der Philosophorum, und dem Lapide Philosophico selbsten; Mit sampt des Arteph. Und Pont secreten abbreviir.* [sic] *Feur: Medicis, Apotheckern/ Chymicis und Laboranten nützlich zu lesen.* Dreßden/ Gedruckt durch Melchior Bergen/ Im Jahr/ 1667. SLUB Chem.952.

Constantini, Angelo, *La Vie de Scaramouche.* Par le Sieur Angelo Constantini, Comedien Ordinaire du Roy dans sa Troupe Italienne, sous le nom de Mezetin. A Paris, A l'Hôtel de Bourgogne. Et Chez Claude Barbin, aus Palais, sur le Perron de al Sainte Chapelle. Le prix est de trente-six sols. 1695.BL 1094.cc.28.

——, *Le Theatre des plaisirs presenté a la Majesté de Frideric Auguste Second, Roy de Pologne et Electeur de Saxe. Par le Sr. Ange de Constantini ... & Representé en Presence de Sa Majesté le Roy de Danemarck. a Dresden ce* (space left blank on title page to insert actual day) 1709. SLUB Hist.Sax.C 1033.

Coryate, Thomas, *Coryat's Crudities Hastily Gobled up in five Monaths travells in France, Savoy, Italy, Rhetia commonly called the Grisons country Helvetsia alias Switzerland, some parts of high Germany and the Netherlands; Newly digested in the hungry aire of Odcombe in the County of Somerset, and now dispersed to the nourishment of the travelling Members of this Kingdome.* 2 vols, Glasgow 1905.

Curicke, Georg Reinhold, *Freuden=Bezeugungen Der Stadt Dantzig über die Höchst=erwünschte Königliche Wahl und darauf Glücklich=erfolgte Krönung Des Durchläuchtigsten/ Großmächtigsten Fürsten und Herrn/ Herrn Augusti des Andern/ Königes in Pohlen/... Wobey Höchst=gedachter Majestät Königlicher Einzug in besagte Stadt/ die daselbst aufgerichtete Ehren=Pforten/ Huldigungs=Actus, Gehaltenes Feuerwerck/ und sonsten denckwürdiges vorgefallen/ biß an Dero Königlichen Abzug/ wahrhafftig beschreiben/ und alles in schönen Kupfferen repraesentiret wird.* Verfasset und zum öffentlichen Druck befordert von G.R. Curicke. Dantzig/ Verlegt durch Gillis Jansson von Waesberge/ Buchhändl. Gedruckt bey Johann/Zacharias Stollen. Danzig 1698. BL 9930.h.25.

Dedekind, Constantin Christian, *Die Aelbianische Musen-Lust. Faksimiledruck der Ausgabe von 1657,* ed. by Gary C. Thomas, Bern, Berlin, Frankfurt am Main 1991.

——, *Neue geistliche Schau=Spiele, bekwehmet zur Music,* n.p. [Dresden] 1670. UBL 8-BST 166/2 and 8-BST 167/1.

——, *Heilige Arbeit über Freud und Leid der alten und neuen Zeit/ in Music-bekwehmen Schau=Spielen* ahngewendet, Durch Andräen Löfflers Verlag/gedruckt zu Dreßden 1676. UBL 8-BST 166/2 and 8-BST 167/2.

De La Marche, François, *Ballet der Glückseligkeit mit welchem Die ... Frau Magdalena Sibylla/ Chur-Fürstin zu Sachsen ... Die ... Frau Anna Sophien/ gebohrne Königliche*

Erb-Princeßin zu Dännemarck... Nach dem Sie von Dero geliebten Herren Sohne... Herrn Johann Georgen dem Dritten/ Chur-Printzen zu Sachsen... heimgeführet... Dem 5. Martii 1667... empfangen wolte Inventiret von François de La Marche, Tantzmeister zu Straßburg. SLUB Hist. Sax.C.178.

Dolivet, François, *Inhalt Des Balletts Welches dem Durchläuchtigsten Hoochgebohrnen Fürsten und Herrn/ Herrn Johann Georgen/ Hertzogen zu Sachsen/ Jülich/ Klev und Berg/ des Heyligen Römischen Reichs Ertzmarschallen und Kuhrfürsten... Von Dero ältern Herrn Sohne Dem auch Durchläuchtigsten Hoochgebohrnen Fürsten und Herrn Herrn Johann Georgen/ Hertzogen zu Sachsen/ Jülich/ Klev und Berg Kuhrprintzen/ &c. Zu Kindlichen gehorsamen Ehren gehalten und fürgestället worden In dem Kuhrfürstl. Schlosse zu Dreßden/ Auff dem Riesensaale den 3. Julii im Jahr 1653.* Verfärtiget durch Ihrer Kuhrprintzl. Durchl. zu Sachsen Tantzmeistern François Dolivet. Dresden: Bergen, Christian und Melchior, 1653. SLUB Hist.Sax.C.53.

Drandorff, August Adolf von, *Augenschein und Positur Derer Feuer-Wercks Stücken/ Welche Der... Churfürst zu Sachsen Hertzog Johann George der Andere in Gegenwart... Hertzogen Augusti zu Sachßen... Hertzogen Mauritii zu Sachßen ... Hertzogen Johann Adolphen/ zu Holstein... jenseits der Pleiße bey der Vestung Pleißenburgk den 8. Julii Anno 1667 gnädigst angeordnet An statt Einer Feuerwercks-Probe... abgeleget und gehorsamst verrichtet worden durch* Augustum Adolphum von Drandorff/ der Zeit bestalten Fendrich bey der Vestung Pleißenburgk vor Leipzigk. n.p. 1667. SLUB Hist.Sax.C.158,37,m.

Draudius, Georgius, *Bibliotheca classica, sive Catalogus officinalis. In Quo singuli singularum Facultatum ac professionum libri ordine alphabetica recensentur... Vsque ad annum M.DXXIV inclusive.* Frankfurt am Main, 1625. HAB 75 Quod. (1).

Dresser, Mathaeus, *Sächsisch Chronicon. Darinnen ordentlich begriffen die fürnembsten und denckwirdigsten Sachen, so von Anbeginn der Welt sich begeben, allermeist aber die in dem Römischen Reiche und Sachsen bis uff den Monat Majum 1596.* Wittenberg: bei M. Johan Krafft/ In Verlegung Johan Francken Buchführer zu Magdeburg 1596. HAB T 841. 2° Helmst.

Eigentliche Abbild= und Beschreibung deß Churf. Sächs. Gnedigst angeordneten Fewerwercks, so uff den fürstlichen Beylager, des... Herrn Friedrichen, Erben zu Norwegen, Herzogen zu Schleßwig... mit... Frewlein Maria Elisabeth... Herzogin zu Sachsen... am 5 Martii 1630 zu Ehren praesentieret. SLUB Hist.Sax.C.958.d,misc.1.

Engelische Comedien und Tragedien/ Das ist: Sehr Schöne, herrliche und außerlesene, geist= und weltliche Comedi und Tragedi Spiel, Sampt dem Pickelhering, welche wegen ihrer artigen Inventionen, kurtzweiligen auch theils wahrhafftigen Geschicht halber, von den Engelländern in Deutschland an Königlichen, Chur= und Fürst= lichen Höfen, auch in vornehmen Reichs= See= und Händel=Städten seynd agiret und gehalten worden, und zuvor nie im Druck auß=gangen. An jetzo, Allen der Comedi und Tragedi lieb=habenden, und Andern zu lieb und gefallen, der Gestalt in offen Druck gegeben daß sie gar leicht darauß/ Spielweiß widerumb angerichtet, und zur Ergetzligkeit und Erquickung des Gemüths gehalten wer=den können. Gedruckt im Jahr M.DC.XX. Leipzig: Gottfried Große 1620. Reprinted in Manfred Brauneck (ed.), *Spieltexte der Wanderbühnen* (Ausgaben der deutschen Literatur des XV. bis XVIII. Jahrhunderts), Berlin/New York 1970.

Ferber, Wolfgang, *Relation und umbständliche Beschreibung eines ansehnlichen und fürnehmen Stahlschiessens zum gantzen Stande..., welches... Johann-Georg, Hertzog zu Sachsen... 1614 in... Dreßden... gehalten hat,* Dresden: Gimel Bergen 1615. SLUB Hist.Sax.C.852 m.

Francus, Iacobus, *Relatio Historica quinquennalis. Warhafftige Beschreibung/ aller fürnemmen unnd gedenckwürdigen Geschicht/ so sich jnnerhalb funff Jahren/ nemlich/ von anno 1590/ biß 1595. in hoch und nieder Teutschland...zugetragen haben*, Frankfurt am Main: Brachfeldt, 1595.

Francolin, Hans, *Thurnier Buch Warhafftiger Ritterlicher Thaten, so in dem Monat Junij des vergangenen LX. Jars in und ausserhalb der Statt Wienn zu Roß und zu Fueß/ auff Wasser und Lannd gehalten worden/ mit schönen figuren contrafeet/ und dem Allerdurchleuchtigsten/ Großmechtigisten Fürsten und Herrn/ Herrn Ferdinando/ erweltem Römischen Kayser/ zu allen zeyten Mherer des Reichs etc. deren allergeliebsten Khindern/ dem gantzen Adel unnd hochberüembter Teutschen Nation/ durch Hannsen von Francolin Burgunder/ Hochstgedachter Rö: Kay: Mayt: Emholden ec. zu Ehren beschriben*. Gedruckt zu Wienn in Osterreich durch Raphael Hofhalter/ auff polnisch Skrzetusky genandt/ beym Gülden Wolff. Vienna, 1560. BL 608.k.15.

La Gara degli Dei, Festa Musicale rappresentata in uno de' Reali Giardini di Dresda per servire d'introduzione agli Spettacoli destinati da S.M.A. solennizare le Nozze De' Serenißimi Principi Federigo Augusto, Principe Reale di Pollonia, & Elettorale di Sassonia e Maria Gioseffa, Arciduchessa d'Austria. L'Emulation parmy les divinitez. Dresden: J.C. Stöessel 1719. HAB Lo Sammelbd. 32 (16 and 17).

Geller, Ernst, *Arkadischer Hürten-Aufzug Als Die Durchläuchtigsten Hoochgebohrnen Fürsten und Herren/ Herr Johann Georg/ Hertzog zu Sachsen...Kuhrfürst...Herr Johann Georg/ Hertzog zu Sachsen...Kuhrprintz...Herr Johann Georg/ Hertzog zu Sachsen...Dero allerseits Nahmenstag begiengen den 24. Julii/ im Jahr GOtt VVoLLe Zelt Der RaVten Krafft KVhrSaChsen ErhaLten/ aVCh Die ZVVelg' an GlVkke VVaChsen. Verfärtiget von Ihrer Kuhrprintzlichen Durchlauchtigkeit zu Sachsen Kammerschreibern Ernst Gellern.* Dresden: Christian und Melchior Bergen, 1653. HAB Xb 4° 172. *See also under* Schirmer, David.

Grisone, Federigo, *Künstlicher Bericht und allerzierlichte beschrybung der Edlen... F. Grisonis. Wie die Streitbarn Pferdt...zum Ernst und ritterlicher Kurtzweil geschickt und volkommen zumachen. In sechs Bücher bester ordnung wolverstendlichem Teutsch und zierlichen Figuren...durch J. Fayser den Jüngern*, August 1573. HAB O 107 Helmst. 2°.

Haugwitz, Adolph August von, *Prodromus Poeticus, Oder: Poetischer Vortrab 1684*, ed. by Pierre Béhar, Tübingen 1984.

Hausen, Christoph August, *Gloriosa Electorum Ducum Saxoniae Busta, Oder Ehre Derer Durchlauchtigsten und Hochgebohrnen Chur=Fürsten und Hertzoge zu Sachsen Leichen=Grüffte, Bestehend in denen auf Ihr Absterben gehaltenen und verfertigten Leichen=Predigten, Lateinischen und Teutschen Lob=Reden, Epitaphien, Epicedien, Begräbniß=Müntzen und Ihren aus guten Originalien in Kupffer gestochenen Bildnissen. zu Erhaltung Ihres glorwürdigen Ehren=Gedächtnisses In diese Collection zusammengebracht, mit denen mangelnden Curriculis Vitae, Oder Lebens=Läufften aus bewährten Scribenten vermehret, und mit vollständigen Registern versehen von Christian August Hausen, Stadt=Predigern in Dreßden.* Dresden: Bey Joh. Christoph Zimmermann und Joh. Nic. Gerlachen. 1728. BL 10703.ff.41.

Hercules Britto-Saxonicus Welcher Bey des Chur-Fürsten zu Sachsen .. Johann Georgen des Andern/ Begehenden Ritter-Fests St. Georgi in...Dreßden/ Bey deme auf dem hohen Walle angezündeten Feuer-Wercke Auf einer brennenden Ehren-Seule Sich zugleich mit vorstellte. Anno M.DC.LXXI. Dresden: in der Churfl. Sächs. Hof-Druckerey, 1671. SLUB Hist.Sax.C.158,39.d,misc.2.

Hoë von Hohenegg, Matthias (trans. from the original by Aegidius Hunnius), *Eine schöne Geistliche/Geistreiche Comoedi/von dem H. Joseph/...*, Dresden: Matthes Stöckel 1602. SLUB Lit.lat.rec.A 996.

Horn, Johann Caspar, *Der Königliche Engelländische hochberühmte Ritter-Orden S. Georgen/ und des Garters/ Als...Hr. Johann Georg der Andere/ Hertzog zu Sachsen...und Chur-Fürst...Auch...Ritter und Gesellschaffter Des...Ritter-Ordens S. Georgens...das...Ritter-Ordens-Fest/ in Dero...Residentz...Dreßden/ am 23. April. 1678. mit herrlichen Solenniteten...begienge Aus D. Benjamin Leübers/ weyland Chur-Fürstl. S. Raths und Cammer-Procuratoris in der Ober-Lausitz/ und anderer berühmter Autorum, glaubwürdigen Schrifften...abgefasset Von Johann Caspar Horn/ D.* Dresden: Baumann, 1678. SLUB Hist.Sax.C.146,misc.1.

Jöcher, Christian Gottlieb, *Allgemeines Gelehrten-Lexikon*, vol. D-L, Leipzig: Johann Friedrich Gleditschens Buchhandlung 1750. UBL AF 02071–2.

Klötzel, Martin, *Heidnischer Götter und Göttinnen prächtiger Auffzug/ An.1695. gehalten in Dreßden.* N.p., n.d. UBL Hist.Sax 97.

Ein kurtzer Bericht/ Welcher gestalt von der Rhömischen Keyserlichen Mayestat/ Keyser Maximilian/ dis Namens dem Andern/ Der Churfürst Hertzog Augustus zŭ Sachssen/ &c unser gnedigster Herr/ Seiner Churfürstlichen Gnaden Reichs Lehen unnd Regalien/ auff den jetzigen jhrer Key. May. Ersten Reichstag/ allhier zŭ Augspurg/ den vviij. des Monats Aprilis/ offentlich underm Himmel empfangen/ Und wie es allenthalben darmit zugangen. Getruckt zŭ Strasburg bey Peter Hug in S. Bartelgassen 1566. HAB 238 Quod. (1-21).

Kurtzer Entwurff/ Was Bey Sr. Chur=Fürstl. Durchlaucht. Herrn Herrn Johann Georgens des Ander/...Zusammenkunfft Dero Herren Gebrüdere...Zu Ehren Deroselben angestellet worden/ Im Monat Februario M.DC.LXXII. Dresden/ gedruckt durch Melchior Bergens/ Churfl. S.Hof.Burchdr. [sic] nachgelassene Wittwe und Erben. SLUB Hist.Sax.C.158 39f and HStA OHMA G Nr.5a fol. 458 f.

Leuber, Benjamin, *Kurtzer Bericht von dem Königlichen Engelländischen hohen und vortrefflichsten Ritter=Orden/ S.Georgen/ Und des Garters, oder Hosen=Bands. In unterthänigster Schuldigkeit aufgesetzt Als den 26. Aprilis Alt. Cal. im 1671. Jahr der...Fürst und Herr/ Hr. Johann Georg der Andere/...zu Dreßden/ in Seiner Churfl. Residentz Des Glorwürdigsten Ordens=Fest gantz hochfeyerlichen hielte/ und herrlichen celebrirte* von D.B.L. Budißin/ In der churfl. Sächs. Haupt= Sechs=Stadt des Marggraffthums Ober=Lausitz/ druckts Christoph Baumann/ Im Jahr 1671. SLUB Hist.Sax.C.158 39,d.misc 1.

Maccioni, Giovanni Battista, *Applausi Festivi Barriera Rappresentata in Monaco alla Venuta [di] Leopoldo Augusto Nell gran Teatro presso la Residenza dell' Ser. Ferdinando Maria Duca di Baviera.* Munich 1658. HAB Gm 3129.

Mentz, Balthasar, *Stambuch Dorinnen der Chur unnd Fürsten zu Sachsen Hochlöbliche/ Ritterliche Thaten/ Bildnüsse und Wapen/ von Fridrich dem ersten biß uff itzige Herrschafft. Sampt des Römischen Reichsgliedmassen/ Amptspersonen Circk/ Kreyssen/ Reichs unnd Freystadten. Und das der Keyser Thurnier und Cammergerichts zu Speyr/ neben der Churfürsten zu Sachsen Hoffgerichts zu Wittenberg/ wolbestalte ordnung/ kurtz zusamen/ unnd in druck gebracht/* Wittenberg: M. Georg Müller/ In vorlegung des Autoris, Anno 1598. HAB Gm 4097 (1).

——, *Kurtze Erzehlung Vom Ursprung und Hehrkommen der Chur unnd Fürstlichen Stämmen/ Sachsen/ Brandenburg/ Anhalt und Lauenburg sampt etlichen derselben Bildnussen/ wie sie im Schloß zu Wittenberg zu finden.* Wittenberg: bey M. Georg Müller 1697. HAB Gm 4097 (2).

Müller, Johann Sebastian. *Des Chur= und Fürstlichen Hauses Sachsen/ Ernestin= und Albertinischer Linien/ Annales von Anno 1400. bis 1700...*, Weimar/ in Verlegung Johann Ludwig Gleditsch Buchhändlers in Leipzig/ Anno 1700. HAB Gm 4° 928.

Münster, Sebastian, *Cosmographia, d.i. Beschreibung aller Lender durch Sebastianum Munsterum in welcher begriffen Aller Völcker Herrschafften/ Stetten/ und namhafftiger flecken/ herkommen.* Basel: Heinrichum Petri 1544. HAB T 10.2° Helmst (1).

Musicalische Darstellung/ So auf des... Herrn Johan Georgen/ Hertzogens zu Sachsen Höchsterfreulichen Geburths-Tag/ Als nehmlich Höchstgedachte Churfürstl. Durchl. mit Beywohnung Göttlicher Gnaden den 5. Martii Ihr Grosses Stuffen-Jahr zu rücke geleget/ und den 6. dieses... in das 64. Jahr des Alters eingetretten Bey einem von dero Fürstlichen Enckelein/ Fräulein Erdmuth Sophia/ Hertzogin zu Sachsen/ [et]c. zu gehorsambster Glückwünschung praesentirten Ballet/ Nachfolgender massen von denen Chur- und Fürstlichen sämbtlichen Musicis/ mit Beyfügung allerhand Instrumenten unterthänigst abgesungen worden/ auf dem Churfürstl. Schloß zu Dreßden / des 1648. Jahres. Dresden: Bergen: Gimel II., Witwe, 1648. SLUB Hist.Sax.C.946,101.

Olearius, Adam, *Auffzüge und Ritterspiele So bey Des Durchläuchtigen/ Hochgebornen Fürsten und Herrn/ Herrn Friedrich Wilhelms.. Jungen printzen/ hertzog Christian, Fürstlichen Kindtauffs Feste/... gehalten worden... zu Altenburg im Monat Junio 1654*, Schleswig 1658. HAB 36.13.2.Geom. 2°.

Olivi, Giovan Battista, *De reconditis et praecipuis collectaneis ab honestissimo, et solertissimo Francisco Calceolario Veronensi in Musaeo adservatis*, Venice 1584. BL 1044.c.1.(1.).

Opitz, Martin, *Die Schäfferey von der Nimfen Hercinie*, ed. by Karl F. Otto, Jr., Berne and Frankfurt 1976.

Peccensteinius, Laurentius, *Theatrum Saxonicum darinnen ordentliche warhaftige Beschreibung der... Könige, Chur- unnd Fürsten... Bisthumb... Schlösser... Ankunft, Auffnehmung... Thaten... in... Obersachsen ex archivis colligirt.* Leipzig: In Verlegung Henning Grossen des Eltern/ Buchhandlern zu Leipzig Gedruckt zu Jehna durch Tobiam Steinman/ Anno MDCVIII [1608]. HAB Gm 4° 397.

Petzold, Georg, *Beschreibung Der Churfürstlichen Kindtauff/ und Frewdenfests zu Dreßden: den 18. Septemb. des verlauffenen 1614. Jahres/ wie auch der Ritterlichen Frewdenspiel/ folgende Tage uber/ Von Dem Durchlauchtigsten/ Hochgebornen Fürsten und Herrn/ Herrn Johann Georgen/ Hertzogen zu Sachssen... Gehalten... Auff gnedigstes begehren S. Durchlauchtigkeit/ aus dem lateinischen vom Autore transferirt...*, Dresden 1615. Private collection.

Pöppelmann, Matthäus Daniel, *Vorstellung und Beschreibung Das von Sr. Königl. Majestät in Pohlen, Churfl. Durchl. Zu Sachsen, erbauten so genannten Zwinger Gartens Gebäuden, Oder Der Königl. Orangerie zu Dreßden, In Vier=und=Zwantzig Kupffer=Stichen Kunst= und Grund=Rissen abgezeichnet und herausgegeben von Matthäus Daniel Pöppelmann, Königl. Pohln. und Churfl. Sächs. Ober=Land=Baumeister, Anno 1729.* UBL Matthäus Daniel Pöppelmann, Gr. Folio 424.

Li quattro Elementi: Carrosello, Dresden: Johann Conrad Stößel 1719. HAB Lo Sammelbd. 32 (14, 15 and 19).

Les Quatre Saisons, Divertissement de Musique & de Dance pour célébrer le mariage de Son Altesse Royale de Pologne & Electorale de Saxe, 1719. Dresden: Johann Conrad Stößel 1719. HAB Lo Sammelbd. 32 (7 and 19).

Risse der Dresdner Frauen und Catholischen Kirchen, UBL Gr. Folio 426.

Sander, Johann Heinrich, *Gloriam ordinis periscelidis in serenissimo ac potentissimo principe ac domino, domino Johanne Georgio Secundo, Duce Saxoniae, Juliaci, Cliviae ac Monatium, Sacri Romani Imperii Archimarschallo et Electore... annua memoria ac solemni oratione in academia panegyri Anno MDCLXXIII*. Venerabatur, Johann Henricus Sander, Wittenberg: Literis Michaelis Meyeri relictae Viduae, 1673. SLUB Hist.Sax.C.138.

Saturni Unterirrdischer Auffstand und Bericht zu einem Bergmännischen Festin, Dresden: Johann Conrad Stössel, 1719. HAB Lo.Sammelbd. 32 (9).

Saturnusfest: *Einleitung zum Saturnus-Feste*, Dresden: Johann Conrad Stössel, 1719. HAB Lo.Sammelbd. 32 (8).

Introduction a la Fete de Saturne, Dresden: Johann Conrad Stössel, 1719. HAB Lo.Sammelbd. 32 (11 and 13).

Schirmer, David, *David Schirmers Erstes Rosen=Gepüsche*. Hall in Sachsen/ Gedruckt bey Melchior Oelschlegels S. Erben/ im Jahr 1650. BL 11521 de 2 (1).

——, *Dem Durchlauchtigsten/ Hochgebohrnen Fürsten und Herrn/ Herrn Johann Georgen/ hertzogen zu Sachsen... und Churfürsten... Als Ihre Churfürstliche Durchlauchtigkeit... dem 5. Mertzens das Fünf und Sechzigste Jahr Ihres Alters hinterleget... War in einer Singenden Darstellung durch die eingeführte Zeit/ Kindheit/ Jugend/ Mannheit/ Alter/ und Ewigkeit beygebracht/ was Ihrer Churfürstl. Durchl. ferner hertzlich gewünschet... würd Von Dero unterthänigsten und gehorsamsten sämbtlichen Hoff-capell-Verwandten und dem Dichter David Schirmern*. Dresden: Bergen, Christian II und Melchior, 1650. SLUB Hist.Sax.C.39.

——, *Inhalt und Erklärung Des Feuer-Wercks/ Welches auff dem Fürstlichen Beylager Der... Herrn Christian Und Hern Moritzen/ Gebrüdern/ Hertzogen zu Sachsen... Mit denen... Freulin Christiana/ Und Freulin Sophia Hedwig/ Geborhnen Hertzogin zu Schleßwig... Zu Dreßden Im Wintermonat des 1650sten Jahres gehalten und verbrennet worden ist*. SLUB Hist. Sax.C.118,23.

——, *Cartel des Feuer-Wercks Worinnen die Eroberung des Güldenen Fellis Durch den Jason außgebüldet wird/...*, Dresden: Christian und Melchior Bergen 1650. SLUB Hist.Sax.C.118,24.

——, *David Schirmers Singende Rosen oder Liebes- und Tugend=Lieder Jn die Music gesetzt Durch Philipp Stollen itzo Jhrer Hoch=Fürstl. Durchl. Des Herrn Administratoris des Ertz=Bischthumbs Magdeburg Cammer=Musicum*. Dreßden/ Jn Verlegung Wolffgang Seyfferts/ Jm Jahr 1654. SLUB Mus. 1741/K/1.

——, *Entwurff... Etlicher Chur- und Hoch-Fürstlicher Ergötzlichkeiten Nach dem... Johann George I.... Mit dem... Herrn Georgen/ Land=Grafen zu Hessen Darmstadt/ etc. 1655 von Düben zu Dreßden einkommen war/ und allda Dero Chur= und Hoch-Fürstlich. Geburths=Tage begingen*. Dresden: Bergen, 1656. SLUB Hist.Sax. C.946,105.

——and Ernst Geller, *Entwurf derer Chur- und Hoh-fürstlichen Ergetzlichkeiten, welche an denen... Zusammenkunften bey gleich mit eingefallenen... des... Fürstens... Johann Georgens, Hertzogens zu Sachsen... und auch des ... Fürstens... Georgens, Land Grafens zu Hessen... Geburts-Tagen... auf dem... Schlosse zu Dressden sind vorstellig gemachet, ietzung aber... zusammen getragen, und zum andern mal heraus gegeben worden*. Dresden: Christian und Melchior Bergen 1655. BL 11746.bbb.7.

——, *David Schirmers Churfürstlichen Sächsischen Bibliothecarii Poetische Rosen=Gepüsche. Von Ihm selbsten aufs fleißigste übersehen/ mit einem gantz neuen*

Buche vermehret und in allem verbesssert heraus gegeben. Dresden/ In Verlegung Andreas Löflers Buchführers. Gedruckt bey Melchior Bergen/ Churf. Sächs. Hof=Buchdr. 1657. UBL 8-BST 635.

——, *David Schirmers Poetischer Rosen-Gepüsche Neues oder Ander Buch/ Von Ihm selbsten herauß gegeben.* Dresden/ In Verlegung Andreas Löflers Buchführers. Gedruckt bey Melchior Bergen/ Churf. Sächs. Hof=Buchdr. 1657.

——, *David Schirmers Churfürstlichen Sächsischen Bibliothecarii Poetische Rauten= Gepüsche in Sieben Büchern.* Dresden/ In Verlegung Andreas Löflers Buchführers. Gedruckt bey Melchior Bergen/ Churf. Sächs. Hof=Buchdr. 1663. UBL 8-BST 631.

Schütz, Heinrich, *Glückwündschung des Apollinis und der neun Musen, Welche auff dem GeburtsTag Des Durchlauchtigsten/Hochgebornen Fürsten und Herrn/ Herrn Johan Georgen/ Hertzogen zu Sachsen... Von Ihrer Churf. Gn. Collegio Musico mit zwölff Cornetten und so viel lebendigen Stimmen/ benebens Trommeten und Heerpaucken zu unterthänigsten Ehren am 5. Martii repræsentiret worden/ In die Music ubersetzt Durch Henrich Schützen Capelmeistern/ Anno M.DC.XXI.* Gedruckt in der Churf. Sächs. BergkStadt Freybergk/ bey Georg Hoffman. SLUB Hist.Sax.C.863.

Sleidanus, Johannes, *De quatuor summis imperiis, Babylonico, Persico, Graeco & Romano,* Geneva: Barbier and Courteau 1558.

——, *Joh. Sleidani Vier monarchien/ Worinnen kurtz alles verfasset/ was nach Erschaffung der Welt denckwürdig befunden/ vermehret vor diesen durch Gabriel Tzschimmern/ Von neuen continuiret biß auffs Jahr 1676.* Durch Anton Christian Fabricium. Mit Churfl. Sächs. Privilegio. In Verlegung Andreae Löfflers Buchh. In Dreßden. Merseburg. Druckts Caspar Forberger/ Fürstl.Sächs. Hoff=Buchdrucker Im Jahr 1676. HAB T 177. 8° Helmst.

Specification Derer Festivitaeten So bey ietzigem Carnevall An dem Chur=Sächsischem Hofe sind gehalten worden, Dresden 1695. UBL Hist.Bor.47-z/30.

Tentzel, Wilhelm Ernst, *Saxonia Numismatica, oder Medaillen-Cabinet. Dritter Theil der Albertinischen Linie/ Von Chur=Fürst Johann Georgen II. biß auff Den ietzigen Chur=Printzen.* Dresden/ gedruckt beym Kön. Hoffbuchdrucker/Joh. Riedeln. 1705. BL 603.e.12,13.

Theatrum Europaeum, Frankfurt am Main: Johann Philipp Andreä 1707, vol. XV (1696–1700). Bodleian fol. DELTA 330–350.

Des Thessalier-Fürstens/ Iasons Helden-Thaten/ In Eroberung Des göldenen Fließes Zu Colchos Durch ein Feuerwerck vorgestellet bey feyerlicher Begehung Des Ritter-Orden-Fests St. Georgens. Zu Dreßden/ Den 25. Aprilis 1678. Dresden: Bergen 1678. SLUB Hist.Sax.C.146,misc.2.

Thurneysser, Leonhard, *Quinta Essentia, Das ist/ Die höchste subtilitet/ krafft und wirckung/ beyder der fürtrefflichsten/ und menschlichem geschlecht am nützlichsten Künsten/ der Medicin und Alchemy/ Auch wie nahe diese beyde mit sipschafft gefreund und verwandt sind/ Und das eine ohn beystandt der andern nicht nütz sey/ oder in den menschlichen cörpern zu wircken kein krafft habe. . . .* Leipzig cum privilegio caesareo. Gedruckt zu Leipzig/Bey Hans Steinman/ Typis Voegelianis. M.D.Lxxiiij. SLUB Chemica 23.

Tzschimmer, Gabriel, *Die Durchlauchtigste Zusammenkunft/ Oder: Historische Erzehlung/ was der Durchlauchtigste Fürst und Herr/ Herr Johann George der Ander/ ...Bey Anwesenheit Seiner...Herren Gebrüdere/ dero Gemahlinnen/ Prinzen/ und Princessinnen/ zu sonderbahren Ehren/ und Belustigung/ in Dero Residenz und Haubt=Vestung Dresden im Monat Februario, des M.DC.LXXVIIIsten Jahres An allerhand Aufzügen/ Ritterlichen Exercitien, Schau=Spielen/ Schiessen/ Jagten/ Operen, Comoedien, Balleten, Masqueraden, Königreiche/ Feuerwercke/ und andern/ Denkwürdiges aufführen und vorstellen lassen...*, Nürnberg/ In Verlegung Johann Hoffmanns/ Buch: und Kunsthändler/ Gedruckt daselbst bey Christian Sigismund Froberger. Anno MDCLXXX. BL 823.l.13.

Unckel, Johann Carl, *Pfaltz/ Sachsen/ Brandenburg. Historische Beschreybung/ dero dreyen Hochlöblichen/ Weltlichen Churfürstlichen/ Pfaltz/ Sachsen/ Brandenburg/ Ankunfft/ Geschlechten/ Succession, Gemahlin/ Kindern/ Geschichten/ Thaten/ Leben/ und endtlichen Absterben...* Frankfurt: Bey Johann Carl Unckeln/ Bürgern und Buchhändlern/ Im Jahr/ 1619. SLUB Hist.Rhen.Inf.130.

Weck, Anton, *Der Chur=Fürstlichen Sächsischen weitberuffenen Residentz= und Haupt=Vestung Dresden Beschreib: und Vorstellung/ Auf der Churfürstlichen Herrschafft gnädigstes Belieben in Vier Abtheilungen verfaßet/ mit Grund: und anderen Abrißen/ auch bewehrten Documenten erläutert durch Ihrer Churfürstlichen Durchl. zu Sachsen/ etc. Rath/ zu den Geheimen: und Reich=Sachen bestalten Secretarium und Archivarium Antonium Wecken.* Nürnberg/ In Verlegung Johann Hoffmanns/ Buch: und Kunsthändler/ Gedruckt daselbst bey Christian Sigismund Froberger. Anno MDCLXXX. BL 158.g.10.

Die Weinende Mutter/ Der Christlichen Lutherischen Kirchen Uber den Verlust ihres Höchst-wehrten und allerliebsten Sohns/ welcher sich anjetzo in den Schoß einer andern Kirchen-Mutter gesetzet hat. Dabey auch höchst=sehnliche und grosse Klage über ihre annoch ungerahtene und böse Kinder... Von einem Der die wahre Kirche und Gott liebet. Gedruckt im Jahr 1697. BL 477.a.38.

Wirre, Heinrich, *Ordenliche Beschreibung des Christlichen/ Hochlöblichen und Fürstlichen Beylags oder Hochzeit/ so da gehalten ist worden durch... Herrn Carolen, Ertzhertzog zu Oesterreich, Burgund, Steyr... etc. mit... Maria, geborne Hertzogin zu Bayrn, den XXVI. Augusti in der Kayserlichen Statt Wienn...*, Vienna, 1571. BL 9930.h.34; HAB 234.1 Hist. 2°.

Scholarly works

Aikin, Judith P., 'The musical-dramatic works of David Schirmer', in *Daphnis* 26 (1997), 401–435.

Das albertinische Herzogtum Sachsen-Weißenfels. Beiträge zur barocken Residenzkultur, Freyburg/Unstrut 1999.

Asche, Siegfried, *Drei Bildhauerfamilien an der Elbe. Acht Meister des siebzehnten Jahrhunderts und ihre Werke in Sachsen, Böhmen und Brandenburg*, Vienna, Wiesbaden 1961.

Barock in Dresden. Kunst und Kunstsammlungen unter der Regierung des Kurfürsten Friedrich August I. von Sachsen und Königs August II. von Polen genannt August der Starke 1694–1733 und des Kurfürsten Friedrich August II. von Sachsen und Königs August III. von Polen 1733–1763, exh. cat., Leipzig 1986.

Barker, Nicholas (ed.), *In Fair Verona. English Travellers in Italy and their Accounts of the City from the Middle Ages to Modern Times*, Cambridge 1972.

Bäumel, Jutta, 'Kleidung und Ausstattung zu den Hochzeiten des Herzogs Johann Georg (I.) von Sachsen 1604 in Dresden/ 1607 in Torgau', in *Jahrbuch der Staatlichen Kunstsammlungen Dresden* 1993, 25–32.

——, 'Der Kleider-Nachlaß des Kurfürsten Moritz von Sachsen' in *Waffen- und Kostümkunde* 1993, 65–106.

——, *Die Rüstkammer zu Dresden. Führer durch die Ausstellung im Semperbau*, Munich, Berlin 1995.

——,'Das "Rheingrafenkleid" Augusts des Starken', *Dresdener Kunstblätter* 41 (1997), 91–8.

——, *Auf dem Weg zum Thron. Die Krönungsreise Augusts des Starken*, Dresden 1997.

——, 'Das Prunkkleid des sächsischen Kurfürsten Johann Georg I. von dessen Bildnis in der Jagdchronik aus dem Jahre 1647', *Dresdener Kunstblätter* 43 (1999), 131–140.

—— and Claudia Schnitzer, 'Mit Kurhut und Krone. Zwei Heroldsstäbe zur Hochzeit des Kurprinzen 1719', *Dresdener Kunstblätter* 41 (1997), 114–121.

Becker-Glauch, Irmgard, *Die Bedeutung der Musik für die Dresdner Hoffeste bis in die Zeit Augusts des Starken*, Kassel, Basel 1951.

Béhar, Pierre, *Les langues occultes de la Renaissance. Essai sur la crise intellectuelle de l'Europe au XVIe*, Paris 1996.

—— and Helen Watanabe-O'Kelly (ed.), *Spectaculum Europaeum. Theatre and Spectacle in Europe (1580–1750). Histoire du Spectacle en Europe (1580–1750)*, Wiesbaden 1999.

Bergbau und Kunst in Sachsen. exh. cat. Staatliche Kunstsammlungen Dresden 1989.

Berns, Jörg Jochen, 'Orpheus oder Assaph? Bemerkungen zum biographischen Informationswert und zur ästhetischen Interpretationskraft der Epicedien auf Heinrich Schütz und dessen Familienmitglieder', *Schütz-Jahrbuch* 16 (1994), 49–66.

——, *Die Herkunft des Automobils aus Himmelstrionfo und Höllenmaschine*, Berlin 1996.

Blaschke, Karlheinz, *Der Fürstenzug zu Dresden. Denkmal und Geschichte des Hauses Wettin*, Leipzig, Jena, Berlin 1991.

——, *Moritz von Sachsen, ein Reformationsfürst der zweiten Generation*, Göttingen 1983.

——, 'Religion und Politik in Kursachsen 1586–1591' in *Die reformierte Konfessionalisierung in Deutschland – Das Problem der 'Zweiten Reformation'*, ed. by Heinz Schilling, Gütersloh 1986, pp. 79–97.

Bolte, Johannes, *Die Singspiele der englischen Komödianten und ihrer Nachfolger in Deutschland, Holland und Skandinavien*, Theatergeschichtliche Forschungen VII, Hamburg and Leipzig, 1893.

Bönisch, Fritz, Hans Brichzin, Klaus Schillinger and Werner Stams, *Kursächsische Kartographie bis zum Dreißigjährigen Krieg*, Berlin 1990.

Bonfatti, Emilio, 'Johannes Caselius liest Giovanni della Casas *Galateo* (Bologna, 1565)' in *Respublica Guelpherbytana. Festschrift für Paul Raabe*, Chloe. Beihefte zum Daphnis, Amsterdam: Rodopi 1987, pp. 357–81.

Borggrefe, Heiner, 'Moritz der Gelehrte als Rosenkreuzer und die "Generalreformation der gantzen weiten Welt"', in *Moritz der Gelehrte. Ein Renaissancefürst in Europa*. Exh. cat. ed. by Heiner Borggrefe, Vera Lüpke and Hans Ottomeyer, Eurasburg 1997, pp. 339–356.

Braun, Werner, 'Das Ballett zum großen Kopenhagener Beilager 1634', in *Heinrich Schütz und die Musik in Dänemark zur Zeit Christians IV. Bericht über die wissenschaftliche Konferenz in Kopenhagen 10.–14. November 1985*, ed. by Anne Ørbaek Jensen and Ole Kongsted, Copenhagen, 1989, pp. 69–79.

——, 'Opera in the Empire', in Béhar, Pierre, and Helen Watanabe-O'Kelly (eds.), *Spectaculum Europaeum*, pp. 437–464.

Brauneck, Manfred (ed.), *Spieltexte der Wanderbühnen* (Ausgaben der deutschen Literatur des XV. bis XVIII. Jahrhunderts), Berlin/New York 1970.

Bräuer, Helmut, 'Zur wirtschaftlichen Entwicklung Sachsens nach dem Dreißigjährigen Krieg', *Dresdner Hefte* 33 (1993), 13–24.

Broszinski, Hartmut, 'Die Katalogisierung der Kasseler alchemistischen Handschriften', in Meinel, *Die Alchemie*, pp. 19–31.

Canova-Green, Marie-Claude, 'Le ballet de cour en France', in *Spectaculum Europaeum* Béhar, Pierre, and Helen Watanabe-O'Kelly (eds), pp. 485–512.

Castor, Markus, 'Rocco di Linar und die *Mathematica Militaris* der Dresdner Fortifikation in italienischer Manier', in *Elbflorenz. Italienische Präsenz in Dresden 16.–19. Jahrhundert*, ed. by Barbara Marx, Dresden 2000, pp. 101–134.

Christensen, Carl C., *Princes and Propaganda: Electoral Saxon Art of the Reformation*, Sixteenth Century Essays & Studies XX, Kirksville, Missouri, 1992.

Cohn, Albert, *Shakespeare in Germany in the Sixteenth and the Seventeenth Centuries: an Account of English Actors in Germany and the Netherlands and of the Plays Performed by Them during the Same Period*, London and Berlin, 1865.

Conermann, Klaus 'Opitz auf der Dresdner Fürstenhochzeit von 1630: drei satirische Sonette des Boberschwans', *Daphnis* 27 (1998), 587–630.

Creizenach, Wilhelm, *Die Schauspiele der englischen Komödianten*, Deutsche National-Litteratur Bd.23, Berlin and Stuttgart 1889.

Czok, Karl, *August der Starke und Kursachsen*, Leipzig 1990.

DaCosta Kaufmann, Thomas, *Court, Cloister and City. The Art and Culture of Central Europe 1450–1800*, London 1987.

Delang, Stefan, 'Das Renaissanceschloß' in *Das Dresdner Schloß. Monument sächsischer Geschichte und Kultur*. Dresden 1992, pp. 68–73.

Doering, Oscar (ed.), *Des Augsburger Patriciers Philipp Hainhofer Reisen nach Innsbruck und Dresden*, Vienna 1901.

Dombrowski, Damian, 'Dresden–Prague: italienische Achsen in der zwischenhöfischen Kommunikation', in *Elbflorenz. Italienische Präsenz in Dresden 16.–19. Jahrhundert*, ed. by Barbara Marx, Dresden 2000, pp. 65–99.

'Dresden-Sächsische Landesbibliothek', in vol. 17, Sachsen A–K, 95–155, ed. by Friedhilde Krause, *Handbuch der historischen Buchbestände in Deutschland*, ed. by Bernhard Fabian, Hildesheim, Zurich, New York 1997.

Ebert, Friedrich Adolf, *Geschichte und Beschreibung der königlichen öffentlichen Bibliothek zu Dresden*, Leipzig 1822.

Erbstein, Julius and Albert, *Verzeichniss der Hofrath Engelhardt'schen Sammlung sächsischer Münzen und Medaillen*, Dresden 1888 (part 1), 1890 (part 2), 1896 (part 3), 1903 (part 4), 1909 (part 5), part 3.

Espagne, Michel and Matthias Middell (eds.), *Von der Elbe bis an die Seine. Kulturtransfer zwischen Sachsen und Frankreich im 18. und 19. Jahrhundert*, Leipzig 1993.

Evans, R. J. W., *Rudolf II and his World. A Study in Intellectual History*, second edition, London 1997.

Fabian, Bernhard (ed.), *Die Messkataloge Georg Willers. Herbstmesse 1564 bis Herbstmesse 1573*, Hildesheim, New York 1972.

Fechner, Jörg Ulrich, 'Zur literaturgeschichtlichen Situation in Dresden 1627. Überlegungen im Hinblick auf die "Dafne"-Oper von Schütz und Opitz', in *Schütz-Jahrbuch* 1988, 5–29.

Findlen, Paula, *Possessing Nature. Museums, Collecting, and Scientific Culture in Early Modern Italy*, Berkeley, Los Angeles, London 1994.
Forberger, Rudolf, 'Tschirnhaus und das sächsische Manufakturwesen', in *E. W. von Tschirnhaus und die Frühaufklärung in Mittel- und Osteuropa*, Berlin 1960.
Forster, Leonard, 'Martin Opitzens Schäffery von der Nimfen Hercinie: Eine nicht nur arkadische Pionierarbeit', in *Theatrum Europaeum. Festschrift für Elida Maria Szarota*, ed. by Richard Brinkmann and Karl-Heinz Habersetzer, Munich 1982, pp. 241–251.
Friedrich Christian, Elector of Saxony, *Das geheime politische Tagebuch des Kurprinzen Friedrich Christian 1751 bis 1757*, ed. by Horst Schlechte, Weimar 1992.
Fürstenau, Moritz, *Zur Geschichte der Musik und des Theaters am Hofe zu Dresden*, 2 vols., Dresden 1861–1862.
Gemäldegalerie Dresden Alte Meister. Katalog der ausgestellten Werke, Dresden 1992.
Glaser, Gerhard, 'Das Grüne Gewölbe', in *Das Dresdner Schloß. Monument sächsischer Geschichte und Kultur*, Dresden 1992, pp. 109–113.
Götz, Wolfgang, *Deutsche Marställe des Barock*, München, Berlin 1964.
Gotthard, Axel, '"Politice seint wir bäpstisch". Kursachsen und der deutsche Protestantismus im frühen 17. Jahrhundert', in *Zeitschrift für historische Forschung* 20 (1993), 275–319.
Gutfleisch, Barbara, and Joachim Menzhausen, "How a Kunstkammer should be formed". Gabriel Kaltemarckt's advice to Christian I of Saxony on the formation of an art collection, 1587', *Journal of the History of Collections* I (1989), 3–31.
Haenel, Erich, *Der sächsischen Kurfürsten Turnierbücher*, Frankfurt a.M. 1910. Hainhofer.
Hammerstein, Notker, 'Prinzenerziehung im landgräflichen Hessen-Darmstadt', *Hessisches Jahrbuch für Landesgeschichte*, 33 (1983), 193–237.
Harper, A. J., *David Schirmer – A Poet of the German Baroque. An examination of Schirmer's lyric poetry and its relationship to the literature of the time*, Stuttgart 1972.
Hartmann, Hans-Günther, *Moritzburg. Schloß und Umgebung in Geschichte und Gegenwart*, Weimar 1988.
Heinemann, Michael, 'Heinrich Schütz in Kassel und Venedig', in *Moritz der Gelehrte. Ein Renaissancefürst in Europa*, exh. cat. Eurasburg 1997, 301–304.
Held, Wieland, *Der Adel und August der Starke. Konflikt und Konfliktaustrag zwischen 1694 und 1707 in Kursachsen*, Cologne, Weimar, Vienna 1999.
Heldt, Kerstin, *Der vollkommene Regent. Studien zur panegyrischen Casuallyrik am Beispiel des Dresdner Hofes Augusts des Starken*, Tübingen 1997.
Henkel, Gabriele, 'Die Hoftagebücher Herzog Augusts von Sachsen-Weißenfels' in *Wolfenbütteler Barock-Nachrichten* 18 (1991), 75–114.
Henschke, Ekkehard, *Landesherrschaft und Bergbauwirtschaft: zur Wirtschafts- und Verwaltungsgeschichte des Oberharzer Bergbaugebietes im 16. und 17. Jahrhundert*, Berlin 1975.
Hertel, Christiane, 'Dis/Continuities in Dresden's Dances of Death', *The Art Bulletin* (82) 2000, 83–116.
Herz, Emil, *Englische Schauspieler und englisches Schauspiel zur Zeit Shakespeares in Deutschland*, Hamburg and Leipzig, 1903.
Hoffmann-Erbrecht, Lothar, 'Scandello', in *The New Grove Dictionary of Music and Musicians*, London 1980, vol. 16, pp. 547–548.

Hofmann, Franz (ed.), *Sendschreiben des Petrus Colbovius (1650) und Brief des J. A. Comenius an Colbovius (1650). Eine pädogische Korrespondenz aus dem 17. Jahrhundert*, Veröffentlichungen der Comeniusforschungsstelle Bochum, vol. 3, Düsseldorf 1974.

Hofmann, Hans-Georg, 'Das Dresdner Planetenballet 1678/79: Aspekte einer Inszenierung', *Basler Jahrbuch für historische Musikpraxis*, vol. 23. Forthcoming.

Impey, Oliver, and Arthur Macgregor (eds.), *The Origins of Museums. The Cabinet of Curiosities in Sixteenth- and Seventeenth-Century Europe*, Oxford 1985.

Ingrao, Charles W., *The Habsburg Monarchy 1618–1815*, Cambridge 1994.

Jardine, Lisa, *Worldly Goods*, London 1996.

——, *Ingenious Pursuits. Building the Scientific Revolution*, London 1999.

Kappel, Jutta, *Deutsche Steinschneidekunst aus dem Grünen Gewölbe zu Dresden*, exh. cat., Deutsches Steinschneidemuseum, Idar-Oberstein 1998.

Karallus, Sonja, 'Der "Riesensaal" im Dresdner Residenzschloß', unpubl. MA thesis, Bonn 1998.

Keller, Katrin, '"Dresden schien zu meiner Zeit ein rechtes bezaubertes Land . . .". Zur Festkultur am Hofe Augusts des Starken', in Espagne, Michel and Matthias Middell (eds.), *Von der Elbe bis an die Seine*, pp. 52–73.

—— (ed.), *'Mein herr befindet sich gottlob gesund und wohl'. Sächsische Prinzen auf Reisen*, Leipzig 1994.

——, 'La magnificence des deux Augustes. Zur Spezifik höfischer Kultur im Dresden des Augusteischen Zeitalters (1694–1763)', *Cahiers d'Études Germaniques. Transferts culturels et région. L'exemple de la Saxe* 28 (1995), 55–66.

——, 'Der sächsische Adel auf Reisen. Die Kavalierstour als Institution adliger Standesbildung im 17. und 18. Jahrhundert' in Katrin Keller and Josef Matzerath (eds.), *Geschichte des sächsischen Adels*, Cologne, Weimar, Vienna 1997, 257–74.

——, '". . . daß die auch bald reißen, und sich gleichfals geschickt und dero hohen gnade verdient machen möchten.' – Die Kavalierstour als adlige Bildungsreise', in Wolfgang Schmale and Reinhard Stauber (eds.), *Menschen und Grenzen in der Frühen Neuzeit*, Berlin 1998, pp. 259–282.

Klossowski de Rola, Stanislas, *Alchemy. The Secret Art*, London 1973.

Kobuch, Agatha, 'Neue Sagittariana im Staatsarchiv Dresden. Ermittlungen unbekannter Quellen über den kursächsischen Hofkapellmeister Heinrich Schütz', *Jahrbuch für Regionalgeschichte* 13 (1986), 79–124.

Koch, Ernst, 'Der kursächsische Philippismus und seine Krise in den 1560er und 1570er Jahren' in: *Die reformierte Konfessionalisierung in Deutschland – Das Problem der 'Zweiten Reformation'*, ed. by Heinz Schilling, Gütersloh 1986, pp. 60–77.

Köhler, Georg, 'Die Rituale der fürstlichen Potestas. Dresden und die deutsche Feuerwerkstradition', in Georg Köhler (ed.) with Alice Villon-Lechner, *Die schöne Kunst der Verschwendung. Fest und Feuerwerk in der europäischen Geschichte*, Zurich and Munich 1988, 101–134.

Königliches Dresden. Höfische Kunst im 18. Jahrhundert, exh. cat., Munich 1990.

Konradt, Greta (and Walter Blankenburg), 'Historia' in *Die Musik in Geschichte und Gegenwart*, second revised edition ed. by Ludwig Finscher, Kassel, Stuttgart 1994–, vol. 4, pp. 311–334.

Korsch, Evelyn, 'Ein "heimlicher Vorschlag". Die politischen Beziehungen zwischen Dresden und Ferrara in der Mitte des 16. Jarhhunderts', in *Elbflorenz. Italienische Präsenz in Dresden 16.–19. Jahrhundert*, ed. by Barbara Marx, Dresden 2000, pp. 37–64.

Kötzschke, Rudolf and Hellmut Kretzschmar, *Sächsische Geschichte. Werden und Wandlungen eines Deutschen Stammes und seiner Heimat im Rahmen der Deutschen Geschichte* (1935), repr. Frankfurt am Main 1977.

Krummacher, Christoph, *Musik als praxis pietatis. Zum Selbstverständnis evangelischer Kirchenmusik*, Göttingen 1994.

Kuke, Hans-Joachim, *Die Frauenkirche in Dresden. 'Ein Sankt Peter der wahren evangelischen Religion'*, Worms 1996.

Kümmel, Birgit, *Der Ikonoklast als Kunstliebhaber. Studien zu Landgraf Moritz von Hessen-Kassel (1592–1627)*, Marburg 1996.

Lebeau, Jean, *Salvator mundi. L'exemple de Joseph dans le théâtre allemand au XVIe siècle*, Nieuwkoop 1977.

Leistner, Kristina, '475 Jahre Buchdruck in Zwickau' in *500 Jahre Ratsschulbibliothek Zwickau*, exh. cat. Zwickau 1998. 68–76.

Lieber, Elfriede, *Verzeichnis der Inventare der Staatlichen Kunstsammlungen Dresden 1568–1945* bearbeitet von Elfriede Lieber, Dresden 1979.

Lietzmann, Hilda, 'Der kaiserliche Antiquar Jacopo Strada und Kurfürst August von Sachsen', in *Zeitschrift für Kunstgeschichte* 3 (1997), 377–399.

Limon, Jerzy, *Gentlemen of a Company. English Players in Central and Eastern Europe, 1590–1660*, Cambridge 1985.

Löffler, Fritz, *Das alte Dresden. Geschichte seiner Bauten*, Leipzig 1989.

Mackensen, Ludolf von, 'Die Kasseler Wissenschaftskammer oder die Vermessung des Himmels, der Erde und der Zeit', in *Moritz der Gelehrte*, pp. 385–390.

Magirius, Heinrich, 'Die bildkünstlerische Ausgestaltung der Fassaden des Schlosses', in *Das Dresdner Schloss. Monument sächsischer Geschichte und Kultur*. Dresden 1992, pp. 74–77.

——, 'Das Moritzmonument im Freiberger Dom – ein Gemeinschaftswerk italienischer, niederländischer und deutscher Künstler zum Andenken an eine hervorragende Fürstenpersönlichkeit', in *Dresdner Hefte* 52 (1997), 87–92.

Marx, Barbara (ed.), *Elbflorenz. Italienische Präsenz in Dresden 16.–19. Jahrhundert*, Dresden 2000.

——, 'Künstlermigration und Kulturkonsum. Die Florentiner Kulturpolitik im 16. Jahrhundert und die Formierung Dresdens als Elbflorenz', in Bodo Guthmüller (ed.), *Deutschland und Italien in ihren wechselseitigen Beziehungen während der Renaissance*, Wiesbaden 2000, pp. 211–297.

——, 'Die Italienreise Herzog Johann Georg von Sachsen (1601-2) und der Besuch von Cosimo III de' Medici in Dresden (1668). Zur Kausalität von *Grand Tour* und Kulturtransfert mit einer Dokumentation von Kristina Popova, Barbara Marx und Juliane Schmidt'. In the press.

Marx, Harald (ed.), *Matthäus Daniel Pöppelmann. Der Architekt des Dresdner Zwingers*, Leipzig 1990.

Maué, Claudia, '"Künstliche und artige Unordnung". Naturalien und Naturimitationen in künstlichen Grotten des 16. und 18. Jahrhunderts', *Anzeiger des Germanischen Nationalmuseums*, 1995, 76–92.

Maurice, Klaus, *Der drechselnde Souverän. Materialien zu einer fürstlichen Maschinenkunst*, Zurich 1985.

May, Wolfgang, 'Die höfische Architektur in Dresden unter Christian I', in *Dresdner Hefte* 29 (1992), 63–71.

Meine-Schawe, Monika, *Die Grablege der Wettiner im Dom zu Freiberg. Die Umgestaltung des Domchores durch Giovanni Maria Nosseni 1585–1594*, Munich 1992.

Meinel, Christoph (ed.), *Die Alchemie in der europäischen Kultur- und Wissenschaftsgeschichte*, Wolfenbütteler Forschungen Bd. 32, Wiesbaden 1986.
Menzhausen, Joachim, 'Elector Augustus's *Kunstkammer*: An Analysis of the Inventory of 1587', in Impey and MacGregor, *The Origins of Museums*, 69–75.
——, 'Karl II. von England als Drachenkämpfer. Gottfried Leygebes angeblicher Eisenschnitt', in *Dresdener Kunstblätter* 7 (1963), 27–31.
Michael, Wolfgang F., *Das deutsche Drama der Reformationszeit*, Bern, Frankfurt am Main, Nancy 1984.
——, *Ein Forschungsbericht. Das deutsche Drama der Reformationszeit*, Bern, Frankfurt am Main, New York, Paris 1989.
Mikosch, Elisabeth, 'Court Dress and Ceremony in the Baroque Age. The Royal/Imperial Wedding of 1719 in Dresden: A Case Study', unpubl. Doctoral dissertation, New York University, 1998.
Moran, Bruce T., *The Alchemical World of the German Court. Occult Philosophy and Chemical Medicine in the Circle of Moritz of Hessen (1572–1632)*, Stuttgart 1991.
—— (ed.), *Patronage and Institutions. Science, Technology, and Medicine at the European Court 1500–1700*, Rochester NY, 1991.
——, 'Moritz von Hessen und die Alchemie', in *Moritz der Gelehrte*, pp. 357–360.
Müller, Ulrich, and Margarete Springeth, 'Ein Indien-Reisebericht des Barock aus Gold, Edelsteinen und Perlen: Der *Hofstaat zu Delhi am Geburtstag des Gros-Moguls Aureng-Zeb* der Hofjuwelier-Werkstätte von Johann Melchior Dinglinger (Dresden 1701–1707)', in *Beschreibung der Welt. Zur Poetik der Reise- und Länderberichte*. Ed. by Xenja von Ertzdorff unter Mitarbeit von Rudolf Schulz, Chloe vol. 31, Amsterdam 2000, pp. 345–366.
Neidhardt, Hans Joachim, 'Italienbeziehungen in der Dresdner Malerei', in *Dresdner Hefte* 40 (1994), 15–31.
Nicollier-De Weck, Béatrice, *Hubert Languet (1518–1581). Un Réseau politique international de Melanchthon à Guillaume d'Orange*, Geneva 1995.
O'Byrn, Freiherr, *Die Hofsilberkammer und die Hofkellerei zu Dresden*, Dresden 1880.
Oelsner, Norbert, 'Der Riesensaal', in *Das Dresdner Schloß. Monument sächsischer Geschichte und Kultur*, Dresden 1992, pp. 86–91.
Olmi, Giuseppe, 'Science-Honour-Metaphor: Italian Cabinets of the Sixteenth and Seventeenth Centuries', in Impey and Macgregor, *The Origins of Museums*, 5–16.
Porzellansammlung Dresden. Führer durch die ständige Ausstellung im Dresdner Zwinger, Dresden 1998.
Pforr, Herbert, 'Der sächsische Silberbergbau in der Agricola-Zeit', in *Agricola-Ehrung 1994. Bergreviere im 16. Jahrhundert. Vorträge des historischen Kolloquiums*. Clausthal-Zellerfeld n.d., pp. 3–18.
Priesner, Claus, 'Johann Thoelde und die Schriften des Basilius Valentinus', in Meinel (ed.), *Die Alchemie in der europäischen Kultur- und Wissenschaftsgeschichte*.
Prölß, Robert, *Beiträge zur Geschichte des Hoftheaters zu Dresden in actenmässiger Darstellung*, Erfurt 1880.
Rahn, Thomas, 'Geschichtsgedächtnis am Körper. Fürstliche Merk- und Meditationsbilder nach der Weltreiche-Prophetie des 2. Buches Daniel', in *Seelenmaschinen. Gattungstraditionen, Funktionen und Leistungsgrenzen der Mnemotechniken vom späten Mittelalter bis zum Beginn der Moderne*, ed. by Jörg Jochen Berns and Wolfgang Neuber, Vienna, Cologne, Weimar 2000, pp. 521–561.

Rank, Mathias and Horst Seeger, '"Was Dafne gibt, das bleibt!". Der Kontinuitätsgedanke in der Dresdner Operngeschichte', in *Oper in Dresden. Festschrift zur Wiedereröffnung der Semperoper*, Berlin 1985, pp. 11–16.
Retemeyer, Kerstin, *Vom Turnier zur Parodie. Spätmittelalterliche Ritterspiele in Sachsen als theatrale Ereignisse*, Berlin 1993.
Richards, Sarah '"A true Siberia": Art in Service to Commerce in the Dresden Academy and the Meissen Drawing School, 1764–1838', *Journal of Design History* 11 (1998), 109–126.
Richter, Julius, *Das Erziehungswesen am Hofe der Wettiner Albertinischer (Haupt-) Linie*, Berlin 1913.
Rifkin, Joshua et al., 'Schütz', in *The New Grove Dictionary of Music and Musicians*, ed. by Stanley Sadie, London 1980, vol. 17, 1–37.
Roberts, Gareth, *The Mirror of Alchemy. Alchemical Ideas and Images in Manuscripts and Books from Antiquity to the Seventeenth Century*, London 1994.
Rothmund, Elisabeth, '"Dafne" und kein Ende: Heinrich Schütz, Martin Opitz und die verfehlte erste deutsche Oper', *Schütz-Jahrbuch* 20 (1998), 123–147.
Ruhnke, Martin, 'Pinello di Gherardi', in *The New Grove Dictionary of Music and Musicians* ed. by Stanley Sadie, London 1980, vol.14, 754–755.
Sachsen und Polen zwischen 1697 und 1765. Beiträge der wissenschaftlichen Konferenz vom 26. bis 28 Juni 1997 in Dresden, Dresden 1998.
Santosuosso, Antonio, *The Bibliography of G. Della Casa*, Florence 1979.
Schade, Werner, *Dresdener Zeichnungen 1550–1650. Inventionen sächsischer Künstler in europäischen Sammlungen*, Dresden 1969.
Scheicher, Elisabeth, 'The Collection of Archduke Ferdinand II at Schloss Ambras: its Purpose, Composition and Evolution', in Impey and MacGregor, *The Origins of Museums*, pp. 29–38.
Schlechte, Monika, 'Der barocke Tiergarten Moritzburg – Planung der Gesamtanlage', *Jahrbuch der Staatlichen Kunstsammlungen Dresden* 1984, 23–42.
——, 'Barocke Festkultur – Zeremoniell – Repräsentation. Ein Ausgangspunkt kunstwissenschaftlicher Untersuchungen', *Wissenschaftliche Zeitschrift der Technischen Universität Dresden* 35 (1986), 29–32.
——, 'Die Festkultur am Hofe Augusts des Starken in ihrem Verhältnis zur Kunst', *Kunst der Bachzeit. Wissenschaftliche Konferenz der Zentralen Kommission Bildende Kunst des Präsidialrates des KB-DDR, Dresden, am 25. und 26. Oktober 1985*, Berlin 1986, 26–33.
Schlenker, Gerline, Artur Schellbach and Wolfram Junghans, *Auf den Spuren der Wettiner in Sachsen-Anhalt*, Halle 1998.
Schmidt, Eberhard, *Der Gottesdienst am Kurfürstlichen Hofe zu Dresden. Ein Beitrag zur liturgischen Traditionsgeschichte von Johann Walter bis zu Heinrich Schütz*, Berlin 1961.
Schneider, Diethard, *Der englische Hosenbandorden: Beiträge zur Entstehung und Entwicklung des 'The most noble Order of the Garter' (1348–1702) mit einem Ausblick bis 1983*, 2 vols in 4 pts, Bonn 1988.
Schnitzer, Claudia, 'Zwischen Kampf und Spiel. Orientrezeption im höfischen Fest', in *Im Lichte des Halbmonds. Das Abendland und der türkische Orient*, exh. cat., Dresden 1995, 227–234.
——, 'Ein "Spionagebericht in Bildern" aus Istanbul. Das Ungnadsche Türkenbuch und seine Kopie von Zacharias Wehme', *Dresdener Kunstblätter* 39 (1995), 98–105.

——, *Höfische Maskaraden. Funktion und Ausstattung von Verkleidungsdivertissements an deutschen Höfen der Frühen Neuzeit*, Tübingen 1999.
—— and Petra Hölscher, *Eine gute Figur machen. Kostüm und Fest am Dresdner Hof*. Exh. cat. Dresden 2000.
Scholem, Gerschom, *Alchemie und Kabbala*, Frankfurt am Main 1984.
Schütte, Ulrich, *Das Schloß als Wehranlage. Befestigte Schloßbauten der frühen Neuzeit*, Darmstadt 1992.
——, 'Das Fürstenschloß als "Pracht-Gebäude"', in: *Die Künste und das Schloß in der frühen Neuzeit*, ed. by Lutz Unbehaun, Munich, Berlin 1998, pp. 15–29.
Schunke, I., 'Die Pariser Büchersendung des Hubert Languet an Kurfürst August von Sachsen, 1566' in *Festschrift Martin Bollert zum 60. Geburtstag*, Dresden 1936.
Seelig, Lorenz, 'The Munich *Kunstkammer*, 1565–1807, in Impey and MacGregor, *The Origins of Museums*, pp. 76–89.
Sheppard, Harry J.,'European Alchemy in the Context of a Universal Definition', in Meinel, *Die Alchemie*.
Skelton, Robert, 'Indian Art and Artefacts in Early European Collecting', in Impey and MacGregor, *The Origins of Museums*, pp. 274–80.
Smart, Sara, 'Ballet in the Empire', in *Spectaculum Europaeum*, Béhar, Pierre, and Helen Watanabe-O'Kelly (eds), pp. 547–70.
Smith, Pamela H, *The Business of Alchemy: Science and Culture in the Holy Roman Empire*, Princeton 1994.
Spagnoli, Gina, '"Nunc dimittis": The Royal Court Musicians in Dresden and the Funeral of Johann Georg I', *Schütz-Jahrbuch* 10 (1988), 30–40.
Sponsel, Jean-Louis, *Der Zwinger, die Hoffeste und die Schloßbaupläne zu Dresden*, Dresden 1924.
Steude, Wolfram, *Musikgeschichte Dresdens in Umrissen*, Dresden 1978.
Suhling, Lothar, 'Philosophisches in der Frühneuzeitlichen Berg- und Hüttenkunst: Metallogenese und Transmutation aus der Sicht montanistischen Erfahrungswissens', in Meinel, *Die Alchemie*.
Sullivan, Henry W. Sullivan, *Calderón in the German Lands and the Low Countries: His Reception and Influence, 1654–1980*, Cambridge 1983.
Syndram, Dirk, *Der Thron des Großmoguls. Johann Melchior Dinglingers goldener Trauma vom Fernen Osten*, Leipzig 1996.
——, *Der 'Apis-Altar' Johann Melchior Dinglingers. Die Ägyptenrezeption unter Auguwst dem Starken*, Mainz 1999.
——, *Die Schatzkammer Augusts des Starken*, Dresden 1999.
—— (ed.) with Ulli Arnold and Jutta Kappel, *Das Grüne Gewölbe zu Dresden. Führer durch seine Geschichte und seine Sammlungen*. 2nd revised edition, Munich, Berlin 1997.
—— with Ulrike Weinhold, ' . . . *und ein Leib von Perl'. Die Sammlung der barocken Perlfiguren im Grünen Gewölbe*, Dresden 2000.
Szönyi, György E., 'Scientific and Magical Humanism at the Court of Rudolf II', in *Rudolf II and Prague. The Imperial Court and Residential City as the Cultural and Spiritual Heart of Central Europe*. Exh. cat. London 1997, pp. 223–230.
Thalheim, Klaus, 'Die Suche nach "edlen Steinen" in Sachsen vom 16. bis zum 18. Jahrhundert', in Jutta Kappel, *Deutsche Steinschneidekunst aus dem Grünen Gewölbe zu Dresden*, exh. cat., Deutsches Steinschneidemuseum, Idar-Oberstein 1998, pp. 11–25.

Timms, Colin, 'Giovanni Angelini Bontempi' in *The New Grove Dictionary of Music and Musicians*, ed. by Stanley Sadie, London 1980, vol. 3, p. 37.
Torrens, Hugh, 'Early collecting in the field of geology', in Impey and Macgregor, *The Origins of Museums*, Oxford 1985, pp. 204–213.
Unter einer Krone. Kunst und Kultur der sächsisch-polnischen Union, exh. cat., Leipzig 1997.
Verborgene Schätze der Skulpturensammlung, exh. cat. Staatliche Kunstsammlungen Dresden 1992.
Vermißte Kunstwerke des Historischen Museums Dresden, exh. cat. Staatliche Kunstsammlungen Dresden 1990.
Vocelka, Karl, *Habsburgische Hochzeiten 1500–1600. Kulturgeschichtliche Studien zum manieristischen Repräsentationsfest*, Vienna, Cologne, Graz 1976.
Wade, Mara, 'Schütz', in *The New Grove Dictionary of Opera*, ed. by Stanley Sadie, vol. IV, London New York 1992, p. 259.
——, *Triumphus Nuptialis Danicus. German Court Culture and Denmark. The Great Wedding of 1634*, Wiesbaden 1996.
——, 'Invisible Bibliographies: Three Seventeenth-Century German Women Writers', *Women in German Yearbook* 14 (1998), 41–69.
Wailes, Stephen L., *The Rich Man and Lazarus on the Reformation Stage. A Contribution to the Social History of German Drama*, Susquehanna University Press 1997.
Watanabe-O'Kelly, Helen, 'Festival Books in Europe from Renaissance to Rococo', in *The Seventeenth Century*, 3 (1988), No. 2, 181–201.
——, 'Joseph und seine Brüder: Johann Georg II. und seine Feste zwischen 1660 und 1679', *Dresdner Hefte* 8 (1990), 29–38.
——, 'Tournaments and their Relevance for Warfare in the Early Modern Period', *European History Quarterly* 20 (1990), 451–463.
——, 'War and Politics in Early Seventeenth Century Germany: The Tournaments of the Protestant Union', in *Atti del Convegno del Centro di Studi Storici di narni, La civiltà del torneo (sec.XII-XIII)*, Rome 1990, pp. 231–245.
——, *Triumphall Shews. Tournaments at German-speaking Courts in their European Context 1580–1730*, Berlin 1992.
——, 'Gabriel Tzschimmer's *Durchlauchtigste Zusammenkunft* (1680) and the German Festival Book Tradition', *Daphnis* 22 (1993), Heft 1, 61–72.
——, 'Fireworks and Illuminations – Precursors of Cinema?', in *German Life and Letters* 48 (1995), 338–353.
——, 'Entries, fireworks and religious festivals in the Empire', in Pierre Béhar and Helen Watanabe-O'Kelly (eds.), *Spectaculum Europaeum*, pp. 721–41.
——, 'August von Sachsen-Weißenfels (1614–1680) und das Theater- und Festwesen am Dresdner Hof', in *Weltsicht und Selbstverständnis im Barock. Die Herzöge von Sachsen-Weißenfels – Hofhaltung und Residenzen*. Protokoll des Wissenschaftlichen Kolloquiums am 24. und 25. April in Querfurt. Halle 1999, 112–124.
——, 'Chivalry and professionalism in Electoral Saxony in the mid-sixteenth century', in *The Chivalric Ethos and Military Professionalism*, ed. by David Trim, Leiden. In the press.
—— and Anne Simon, *Festivals and Ceremonies. A Bibliography of Printed Works relating to Court, Civic and Religious Festivals in Europe 1500–1800*, London 2000.
Weyer, Jost, *Graf Wolfgang II. von Hohenlohe und die Alchemie. Alchemistische Studien in Schloß Weikersheim 1587–1610*, Sigmaringen 1992.

Wimmer, Rudolf, *Jesuitentheater. Didaktik und Fest. Das Exemplum des ägyptischen Joseph auf den deutschen Bühnen der Gesellschaft Jesu*, Frankfurt am Main 1982.
Winter, Eduard, *E. W. v.Tschirnhaus (1651–1708). Ein Leben im Dienste des Akademiegedankens*, Berlin 1959.
——, 'Der Bahnbrecher der deutschen Frühaufklärung E. W. v.Tschirnhaus und die Frühaufklärung in Mittel- und Osteuropa', in *E. W. von Tschirnhaus und die Frühaufklärung*, Berlin 1960.
'Wunder Harfe'. 450 Jahre Sächsische Staatskapelle Dresden, exh. cat. Staatliche Kunstsammlungen Dresden 1998.
Wunderlich, Herbert, *Kursächsische Feldmeßkunst, artilleristische Richtverfahren und Ballistik im 16. Und 17. Jahrhundert*, Berlin 1977.
Zaunick, Rudolf (ed.), E. W. von Tschirnhaus, *Medicina mentis, sive Artis inveniendi praecepta generalia*, second edition, Leipzig 1695. Erstmalig vollständig ins Deutsche übersetzt und kommentiert von Johannes Haussleiter, Leipzig 1963.
——, *Der sächsische Paracelsist Georg Forberger*, Wiesbaden 1977.
Zumpe, Manfred, *Die Brühlsche Terrasse in Dresden*, Berlin 1991.
Zurück in Dresden. Ehemals vermisste Kunstwerke aus Dresdener Museen. Exh. cat., Dresden 1998.

Index

Aesop, 55
Agricola, Georg, 107
Agricola, Philipp, 28
Albert, Duke of Teschen, 200
Albertus Magnus, 102
Albrecht, Duke of Bavaria, 41, 71, 72
Albrecht, Duke of Saxony, 8, 157, 204
Albrecht-Alcibiades, Margrave of Brandenburg-Kulmbach, 9
Albrici, Vincenzo, 191
Alchemy, 100–29, 123, 239, *Figures 22–4*
　books on, 83, 108
　manuscripts in Dresden, 109–15
　philosopher's stone, 102, 109, 115
　porcelain and, 223–5
　see also 'Goldhaus' *under* Dresden
Alciati, Andrea, 56
Aldovrandi, Ulisse, 64
Alfonso II d'Este, Duke of Ferrara, 42
Altenburg, 26, 179
Altranstädt, Peace of, 198
Ammirato, Scipione, 61
Amsterdam, 222
Androuet du Cerceau, Jacques d', 88
Angelini Bontempi, Giovanni, 191–2
Anna, Princess of Denmark, Electress of Saxony, 11, 12, 85, 88, 115, 167
Anna, Holy Roman Empress, 62
Anna, Duchess of Saxony, 121
Anna Sophia, Princess of Denmark, 182, 183, 184, 193, 196
Annaburg, 27, 85, 115
Anton Egon, Prince of Fürstenberg, 223
Antonio of Navarre, 93–4
Antwerp, 9, 54, 60, 85
Appollonius, 56
Archer, William, 168
Aristophanes, 56
Aristotle, 56, 101, 102, 104
Armour, 73
Arnald of Villanova, 102

Arnold, Johann, 141
Assaying, *see* Minting
Astrology, 83, 104, 108, 120–9
Astronomy, 78, 82, 123
Aue, near Schneeberg, 224
Augsburg, 46, 59, 78, 91
Augsburg, Peace of, 9
August II, King of Poland (August the Strong), *see* Friedrich August I, Elector of Saxony
August III, King of Poland, *see* Friedrich August II, Elector of Saxony
August, Duke of Saxony, (son of Christian I), 29, 46, 57
August, Elector of Saxony, 1, 3, 8, 9, 10, 14, 15, 20, 40, 42, 106, 167, 204
　alchemy and, 105, 113, 115–16, 119, 120
　ivory-turning, 80, 84, 95
　Kunstkammer, 73, 74–84, 92, 94, 95, 96
　library, 84–8
　tournaments 49–50, 121
August, Duke of Saxony-Weissenfels, 21, 33, 34, 35, 124, 139, 158, 181, 184
Augustusburg, Palace of, 42
Auracher, Georg, 109
Austria, 199
Avicenna (Abu Ali ibn Sina), 102
Ayrer, Jakob, 171
Azelt, Johann, *Figures 12 and 38*

Bachmann, Daniel, 115
Bacon, Francis, 72, 101, 102
Baden, near Vienna, 195
Bähr, George, 201–3, *Figure 43*
Baia, 59
Baif, Antoine de, 174
Ballet, 30, 132–40, 146, 154, 161, 162, 166, 174–89, 208, 209
Banzland, Dr, 114

Barbara Sophia, Margravine of Brandenburg, Duchess of Württemberg, 53
Barnaud, Nicolas, 105
Beaujoyeulx, Balthasar de, 174
Beaumont, Francis, 171, 173
Benteley, George, 183
Bergen, Melchior, 116–17, 163, 176
Berlin, 225
Bernhard, Christoph, 25, 177, 191, 192
Bernstein, Hans von, 109
Besozzi, Cerbonio and Mattia, 40
Beutel, Tobias, 63, 71, 89, 95, 97, 98
Beuther, David, 112, 113, 115
Biblical drama, 24, 30–4, 166
Binche, 54
Biringoccio, Vanuccio, 110
Bischoff, Johann, 28
Boccaccio, 56
Boener, J.A., 160
Böhme, Johann Heinrich, the Elder, *Figure 8*
Bohemia, Kingdom of, 241
Bologna, 59, 199
Bologna, Giovanni di, 12
Bolzano, 59
Book fairs, 85
Borelli, Giovanni Alfonso, 222
Börner, Bartholomäus, 65
Boschi, J., 235
Boselli, Pietro, 12
Böttger, Johann Friedrich, 221, 223–5
Böttger stoneware, 223, *Figure 49*
Bottschild, Samuel, 160
Boyle, Robert, 101, 222
Brahe, Tycho, 89
Brandenburg, 17, 198, 199, 241
Brandenburg-Bayreuth, 17
Braunschweig, 25
Brehme, Christian, 98
Brescia, 39, 41, 59
Breslau, 26
Bretschneider, Daniel, the Elder, 21, 123, 125, 153, *Figures 10, 16, 25 and 26*
Browne, Robert, 168
Brunn, Lucas, 98
Brussels, 54

Bryan, George, 167
Buchner, August, 157, 178, 190
Buchner, Paul, 43
Bugenhagen, Johannes, 24
Bünau, Rudolf von, 21
Buonomia, Giovan Battista, 41
Buontalenti, Bernardo, 52
Burridge, Richard, 196–7
Buzoli, 59

Cabala, 113
Cabinet of Curiosities, *see* Kunstkammer
Calceolari, Francesco, 64
Calderón de la Barca, Pedro, 173
Calmbach, Georg, 26
Calvinism, 15–17, 36, 55
 books on, 89
Campana, Cesare, 61
Capua, 59
Caracciolo, Pasquale, 48
Carissimi, Giacomo, 191
Carlo Emanuele I, Duke of Savoy, 46
Carlos III, King of Spain, 200
Carpzov, Samuel Benedict, 148
Cartari, Vincenzo, 54
Cartography, 78, 79–80, 84
 books on, 82
Catholicism, 5, 8
Catullus, 56
Cavalieri, Emilio de', 63
Cavalli, Francesco, 190, 191
Celle, 207
Ceruti, Benedetto, 64
Cesare, Carlo di, 12, 42, 52, 67, *Figures 5 and 6*
Charles I, King of England, 142
Charles II, King of England, 141, 142, 143, 144, 145, *Figure 32*
Charles V, Holy Roman Emperor, 9, 54, 79, 86
Chemistry, 102, 106, 113
Chemnitz, 8, 137
Chettle, Henry, 170
Chiaveri, Gaetano, 201
Chiocco, Andrea, 64
Christian, Duke of Anhalt, 52, 122
Christian, Margrave of Brandenburg, 52
Christian III, King of Denmark, 79
Christian V, King of Denmark, 141

Christian I, Elector of Saxony, 1, 12, 54, 98, 167, 204, *Figures 5 and 7*
  alchemy under, 105, 106, 113, 116
  architecture under, 42, 43, 44, 65, 73, 156
  Calvinism and, 15, 17, 36
  horsemanship and, 45, 46, 47, 88, 240
  Kunstkammer of, 79, 83, 90–1, 94
  tournaments and, 21, 49–52, 122
Christian II, Elector of Saxony, 1, 17, 29, 42, 46, 52, 167, 189, 204
  alchemy and, 113
  education of, 54–9
  Kunstkammer of, 90–1
Christian, Duke of Saxony-Merseburg, 33, 95, 124, 130, 148, 158, 177, 184
Christian Albrecht, Duke of Saxony, 29
Christian August, Duke of Saxony-Zeitz, Bishop of Raab (Györ), 195
Christian Ernst, Margrave of Brandenburg-Bayreuth, 31, 117, 124, 151, 158, 182, 191
Christian Wilhelm, Margrave of Brandenburg, 52
Christiane, Duchess of Schleswig-Holstein, Duchess of Saxony-Merseburg, 130, 131, 139
Christina, Queen of Sweden, 169, 196
Christine, Archduchess of Austria, 200
Christine Eberhardine, Margravine of Brandenburg-Bayreuth, Electress of Saxony, 196
Christine, Princess of Lorraine, 52
Chryseus, Johann, 27, 28
Chytraeus, Nathan, 57, 58
Cicero, 55, 56, 61
Cicognini, Giacinto Andrea, 173–4
'Civil conversazione', 54–9
Clocks, 78
Coburg, 8
Colbert, Jean-Baptiste, 222
Colbovius, Petrus, 116, 117
Cölln an der Spree, 46
Colombre, Agostino, 48
Comines, Philippe de, 56
Comte de Granville, 141
Constantini, Angelo, 207, 208
Conti, Natale, 86
Copenhagen, 24, 167, 189

Corneille, Pierre, 173, 207
Corpus Evangelicorum, 196, 238
Corsi, Jacopo, 63, 189
Corte, Cesare, 48
Coryate, Thomas, 68
Cosimo I de' Medici, Duke of Florence, 41, 42
Craco, Dr Georg, 15
Cracow, 54
Cranach, Lucas the Elder, 3, 93
Cranach, Lucas the Younger, 3, 93
Cuma, 59

Dancing, 57, 174, *see also* Ballet
Danzig (Gdańsk), 169, 198, *Figure 42*
Darmstadt, 174
Dedekind, Constantin Christian, 34–6, 144
Dee, John, 106
Dekker, Thomas, 169
Delft, 223
Della Casa, Giovanni, 57–9
Delle, Mardochaeus de, 105
Demosthenes, 56
Denmark, 17, 167
  King of, 80
Descartes, René, 221
Dilich, Wilhelm, 54, 145
Dinglinger, Johann Melchior, Georg Friedrich and Georg Christoph, 216–19, 234, 240, *Figures 20 and 48*
Dolivet, François, 132, 180, 181
Doncourt, Dieudonné, 204
Döring, Gottfried, 216
Dorothea, Duchess of Saxony, 21, 42, 122
Draudius, Georg, 85
Dresden
  alchemical laboratories ('Goldhaus'), 109, 112, 118–20
  Armoury ('Rüstkammer'), 45, 50, 73, 74, 156, 205, 232
  Chamber of Anatomy, 63–5, 89, 93, 156, 240
  Coin Collection ('Münzkabinett'), 73, 96, 156
  Collection of Silver and Plate ('Silberkammer'), 73

Dresden – *continued*
  collections, 2, 90; storage of, 96
  Corner Saloon ('Eckgemach'),
    170, 173
  Council Chamber ('Ratsstube'),
    96, 156
  Electoral Palace ('das Schloß'), 37,
    39, 96, 99, *Figure 12*
  Frauenkirche, 201–3, 204
  Georgenbau, 216
  Green Vault ('Grünes Gewölbe'),
    96, 99, 113, 215–19, 220
  Hofkirche, 201
  Holländisches Palais, 219, 235
  Japanisch-Ost-Indisches Palais,
    219, 235
  Langer Gang, 43, *Figures 44 and 49*
  Lion House, 89
  Lusthaus, 64–70, 90, *Figures 17 and 18*
  Mathematisch-Physikalischer Salon,
    99, 220
  Picture Gallery ('Gemäldegalerie
    Alte Meister'), 3, 99, 220
  Playhouse, 89, 156, 182, 186, 186,
    191, *Figure 40*
  Porcelain Collection, 99, 220
  Portrait Gallery, 43–5, 156
  Powder Tower, 156
  Printroom ('Kupferstichkabinett'),
    99, 220
  Redoutensaal, 219
  Riding School, 125, 156
  Riesensaal, 38, 69, 132–40, 141,
    147, 156, 178, 182, 184,
    185, 240, *Figures 13, 29,
    30 and 38*
  room near the church ('Kirchsaale'),
    170, 176
  Sophienkirche, 203
  Stables ('Stallhof'), 43–5, 50, 153,
    240, *Figure 14*
  Stone Saloon ('Steinern Saal'), 137,
    181, 182
  Treasury ('Schatzkammer'), 73
  Weapons Store ('Zeughaus'), 97,
    125, 156
  Zwinger, 209–12, *Figures 44–7*
  See also Kunstkammer; Library
Druida, Michael, 29

Du Mesniel, Charles, 183, 184
Dürer, Albrecht, 54, 87
Dürr, Ernst Caspar, 19

Education, princely, 54–9
Edward III, King of England, 145
Elbe, River, 9, 201, 235
Eleonore, Duchess of Saxony-Eisenach,
  Electress of Saxony, 193
Elisabeth, Duchess of Saxony, 52
Emanuele Filiberto, Duke of Savoy, 76
Erasmus, 56
Ercker, Lazarus, 105
Ercole d'Este II, Duke of Ferara, 37
Erdmuthe Sophie, Duchess of
  Saxony, Margravine of
  Brandenburg-Bayreuth, 31, 117,
  124, 151, 158, 176, 182, 191
Erfurter Springer, 171
Erich, Duke of Braunschweig and
  Lüneburg, 94
Ernst, Elector of Saxony, 8
Erzgebirge, 5, 128, 224, *Figure 2*
Euripides, 56

Fabricius, Georg, 88
Fabritius, Kilian, 61, 68, 69, 135
Faust, Johann, 111–12
Fayser von Arnstein, Johann, 47
Ferbecq, Guillaume, 217
Fehling, Carl Heinrich Jacob, 226, 237,
  Figures 44 and 50–4
Ferdinand III, Holy Roman Emperor,
  94, 116, 139
Ferdinand IV, Holy Roman Emperor, 139
Ferdinand of Tyrol, Archduke, 71, 73
Ferdinand Albrecht, Duke of
  Braunschweig-Lüneburg, 79
Ferdinando I de' Medici, Grand Duke
  of Florence, 52
Ferrara, 37, 40, 42, 47, 59, 205, 215
Ferraro, Giovanni Battista, 48
Fetzer, Matthaeus, 60
Fiaschi, Cesare, 48
Figulus, Benedikt, 105, 109
Fink, Johann, 151
Fiorilli, Tiberio, 207, 208
Firearms, 80
  books on, 82

Fireworks, 131, 143, 146, 148, 152, 155, 177, 235, 236
Fischer von Erlach, Johann Bernhard, 209
Flacius Illyricus, 15
Fletcher, John, 170, 171, 173
Florence, 3, 12, 41, 42, 47, 60, 205
  Belvedere, 65, 68
  Boboli Gardens, 68
  Duke of, 60, 76, 79, 90
  Kunstkammer, 128, 212
  Palazzo Vecchio, 12
  San Lorenzo, 12
  Tribuna, 68
  Villa Medici, 68
Fondi, 59
Forberger, Georg, 86
Förster, Caspar, 189
France, 193, 194
  cultural impact of, 204–12, 241
Francesco I de' Medici, Duke of Florence, 12, 46
Francke, August Hermann, 222
François, Prince of Lorraine, Holy Roman Emperor, 200
François Louis de Bourbon, prince de Conti, 195, 197
Frankenhausen, 109
Frankfurt am Main, 217
Franz, Duke of Pomerania, 30
Franz Karl, Duke of Lauenburg, 117
Fraustadt, Battle of, 198
Fredrik, King of Denmark, 79, 208, 233
Freiberg, 5–8, 12, 18, 26, 137, 223
  Cathedral ('Dom St. Marien'), 5, 9
  Electoral Burial Chapel 5–15, 17, 37, *Figures 3–6*
  Palace, 42
  St. Anna mine, 6, *Figure 2*
Frey, Jacob, 28
Freybergische Springer, 171
Friedrich, Duke of Holstein-Gottorp, 162
Friedrich, Elector Palatine, 15, 42, 141
Friedrich the Wise, Elector of Saxony, 203, 238
Friedrich III, Duke of Schleswig-Holstein, 30, 124, 168, 177

Friedrich, Count of Hohenlohe, 76, 78
Friedrich, Duke of Saxony-Altenburg, 179, 234
Friedrich I, Duke of Württemberg, 105
Friedrich August I, Elector of Saxony (August II, King of Poland), 1, 5, 8, 17, 73, 89, 99, 189, 192, 193–237, 239
  alchemy under, 220–5
  architecture under, 210–12
  art collections under, 212–20, 240
  conversion to Catholicism of, 195–7, 199–201
  festivals under, 121, 129; on accession, 232–3; Saturnsfest, 225–9, *Figures 50–4*; Imperial wedding, 232, 234–7; Procession of Gods and Goddesses, 232, 234, *Figure 55*; visit of Danish King, 232–4; visit of Prussian King and Crown Prince, 232; reign in Poland, 197, *Figure 42*
Friedrich August II, Elector of Saxony (August III, King of Poland), 3,
  art collections under, 220
  conversion to Catholicism of, 199
  as King of Poland, 200
  marriage of, 200, 205
Friedrich Ludwig, Duke of Württemberg, 235
Friedrich Wilhelm, Elector of Brandenburg, 141
Friedrich Wilhelm, Duke of Saxony-Weimar, 12, 17, 42, 52, 54, 55, 56, 60, 90, 109
Friedrich, Amadeus, 117
Friedrichsthal, 223
Froberger, Sigismund, 155
Fromm, Andreas, 26
Fugger family, 41
Fugger, Marx, 48
Furchheim, Johann Wilhelm, 25

Gabrieli, Giovanni, 62
Gardening, *see* Horticulture
Garter, Order of, 140–51, 154, 217, 240, *Figures 29, 30*
Gdańsk, *see* Danzig

Geber (Jabir ibn Hayyan), 201
Gelhorn, Friedrich von, 57
Geller, Ernst, 180
Genoa, 215
Geological museum, 8
Geology, 84
Georg II, Landgrave of
  Hesse-Darmstadt, 30, 63,
  168, 175, 180
Georg, Duke of Saxony, 204
Georg Friedrich, Margrave of
  Brandenburg-Ansbach, 105
Georg Wilhelm, Duke of
  Braunschweig and Lüneburg, 207
Georg, Jonas, 110
Gerlach, Elias, 29
Geyer, 8
Giambologna, 46, 79
Giovio, Paolo, 56, 86
Giusti, Agostino, Count, 68
Giusti Gardens, *see* Verona
Glass-making, 6
Glücksburg, 223
Göding, Heinrich, 44, 49
Goedelmann, Johann Georg, 31
Goethe, Johann Wolfgang von, 111
Goetze, Master of Horse, 126, 141
Goldsmith work, 99
Gotha, 8, 26
Graef, Hendrik de, 173
Green, John, 168
Greene, Robert, 170
Grisone, Federigo, 47, 48
Gryphius, Andreas, 174
Guarini, Gian Battista, 180
Guerini, Rocco, Conte di Linar, 41–2
Guglielmo Gonzaga, Duke of Mantua, 46
Guicciardini, Francesco, 56, 86
Gustavus Adolphus, King of
  Sweden, 196

Habsburg, House of, 17, 200, 215, 235
Häsel, Theodosius, 91, 93, 98
Hagedorn, Friedrich, *Figure 18*
Hagen, Heinrich von, 47
Hainhofer, Philipp, 44, 62, 64, 89,
  91–2, 95, 97, 98
Halle, 139, 181, 222
  Franckesche Anstalt, 222

Hamburg, 9
Hamburg Players, 173
Hanover, 25, 222
  Elector of, 206
Harms, Johann Oswald, 161, 184,
  Figures 27, 39 and 40
Harnisch, O.S., 25
Hartmann, Andreas, 29
Harz mountains, 6
Hass, Martin, 189
Haugwitz, August Adolph von, 174,
  187, 189
Haugwitz, Friedrich August von, 187
Haupt, Jacob, 23
Hausen, Christian August, 203
Hedwig, Princess of Denmark, 29, 52,
  167, 189
Heermann, Paul, 217
Heideler, David, 115, 118
Heinichen, Johann David, 235
Heinrich, Duke of Saxony, son of
  Duke Albrecht, 8, 12, 17, 204
Heinrich, Duke of Saxony, son of
  Johann Georg I, 124
Helmstedt, 57
Henri II, King of France, 50, 54
Henri IV, King of France, 79
Henri Charles de la Trémoille, Prince
  de Tarente, 141
Herman, David, 117
Hermersberg, 105
Herodotus, 86
Heros, Johannes, 28
Hessus, Eobanus, 56
Higgins, Sir Thomas, 140
Hildebrand, Lucas von, 209
Hildesheim, 25
Historia (musical genre), 22–6
Hoby, Thomas, 64
Hoë von Hohenegg, Matthias, 31
Hörsellen, Eusebius, 119
Hoffmann, Johann, 155
Homer, 56
Horace, 56, 191
Horn, Johann Caspar, 147
Hornkens, Henricus, 61
Horticulture, 84, 88
Huber, Wenceslaus, 29
Huguenots, 15, 42, 85, 217

Hungary, 109, 194
Hunnius, Aegidius, 31
Hutter, Elias, 112
Huygens, Christiaan, 222

Innsbruck, 59, 91
Inventories, 98–9
Irmisch, Hans, 43
Italy, 24, 90, 204, 241
Ivory-turning, 80, 84, 98, *Figure 21*

Jakub Ludvik Sobieski, 195
Jamnitzer, Wenzel, 87
Jan III Sobieski, King of Poland, 195
Jena, 8
Jeniss, Hans, 41
Joachim II, Elector of Brandenburg, 105
Joachim Friedrich, Elector of Brandenburg, 47
Joachimsthal (Jáchymov), 116
Johann the Constant, Elector of Saxony, 203
Johann Adolf, Duke of Saxony-Weissenfels, 33, 235
Johann Casimir, Count Palatine, 15
Johann Casimir, Duke of Saxony-Coburg, 52
Johann Ernst, Duke of Saxony-Eisenach, 52
Johann Friedrich the Magnanimous, Elector of Saxony, 1, 3, 9, 14, 203
Johann Friedrich II, Duke of Saxony, 14
Johann Friedrich, Duke of Württemberg, 53
Johann Georg, Duke of Anhalt, 52
Johann Georg, Elector of Brandenburg, 17, 42, 46, 54, 105, 116
Johann Georg I, Elector of Saxony, 1, 17, 29, 30, 33, 42, 44, 46, 48, 89, 146, 167, 176, 181, 204
  alchemy under, 116
  Chamber of Anatomy of, 63–5
  education of, 54–9
  festivals and, 123
  as Imperial Regent, 133, 139
  Italian journey of, 59–70, 190, 239

Kunstkammer of, 91–6
  library of, 88–9, 98
  'Lusthaus' and, 65–70
Johann Georg II, Elector of Saxony, 1, 3, 17, 18, 19–20, 25, 27, 30–6, 44, 99, 204
  alchemy and, 109, 113, 116, 117–18, 120
  'Bergsmannsgarnitur' of, 126, 226, *Figure 28*
  biblical plays and, 30–4
  christening of, 153–4, 158
  drama under, 172
  festivals under, 232; 'Durchlauchtigste Zusammenkunft', 124–9, 152, 153, 154, 158, 184–7, 235, *Figure 35*; 'Georgsfest', 142, 146, 147; 'Johannestag', 140; 'Vertrauliche und Fröliche Zusammenkunfft', 152, 184, 191
  'Hausmannsturm' erected by, 156
  as Jason, 130–2, 148
  as Mars, 134
  as Nimrod, 151–4
  self-fashioning of, 130–65
  as St George, 140–51
Johann Georg III, Elector of Saxony, 1, 17, 148, 151, 176, 193, 195, 204
  alchemy and, 118
  ballet and, 184
  as Cupid, 134, 179
Johann Georg IV, Elector of Saxony, 1, 30, 31, 118, 158, 172, 183, 187, 193, 204, 223
Johann Sigismund, Elector of Brandenburg, 167
Johanna of Austria, 12
Johanneum, 43
Johanngeorgenstadt, 5, 228
Jolly, George, 168
Jones, Richard, 168
Joseph I, Holy Roman Emperor, 199, 200, 205
Josepha, Duchess of Saxony, Dauphine, 200
Jüdiger, Simon Joachim, 118
Julius, Duke of Braunschweig-Lüneburg, 105

Julius Heinrich, Duke of Lauenburg, 117
Justinian, 86

Kaltemarckt, Gabriel, 90, 93
Kannen, Marshall, 141
Karl, Archduke of Austria, 80
Karl VI, Holy Roman Emperor, 199, 200
Karl XI, King of Sweden, 117
Karl XII, King of Sweden, 198
Kassel, 3, 54, 79, 106, 168
Katharina, Duchess of Mecklenburg, Duchess of Saxony, 12
Kentmann, Johann, 8
Kepler, Johannes, 89
Khunrath, Heinrich, 105
Kieslingswalde, 221, 222
Kilian, Philipp, 150, 161
King, Thomas, 167
Kircher, Athanasius, 222
Klemm, Samuel, 126, *Figure 28*
Klengel, Wolf Caspar von, 8, 19, 128, 148, 200, 223
Klisów, Battle of, 198
Klötzel, Martin, *Figure 55*
Knoch, Hans Ernst von, 204, 206
Knöffel, Johann Christoph, 201
Kobenhaupt, Hans, 65
Köhler, Christoph, 117
Kölbel, Jacob, 87
Königsberg, 167, 169
Königsmark, Aurora von, *Figure 55*
Königstein, Fortress of, 17, 208
Kötschenbroda, Peace of, 169
Krause, Jakob, 88
Krell, Nicolaus, 15, 17
Krieger, Adam, 177
Krüginger, Johann, 28
Krumlov, 105
Kunckel, Johann, 117
Kunn, Heinrich, 29
Kunstkammer, 71–3
  Bevern, 79
  Dresden, 71, 73–88, 90–6, 97, 156, 215, 220, 239; books in, 78, 81–3, 87; geology in, 92; tools in, 83
  Florence, 128

Munich, 71
Schloss Ambras, Innsbruck, 71, 74, 79
Kyd, Thomas, 170, 171

La Marche, François de, 182, 183
La Marche, Louis, 183
Landtag, Saxon, 135, 137, 157
Langensalza, 137
Languet, Hubert, 15, 85, 87
Lauremberg, Johann von, 189
Lausitz, 26, 34, 133, 221, *Figure 11*
Leibniz, Wilhelm Gottfried, 222
Leiden, 221
Leipzig, 85, 105, 132, 207
Leipzig Partition, 8, 73
Le Maistre, Matthaeus, 40
Lentulo, Scipione, 61
Leonhart, Sebastian, 55, 98
Leopold I, Holy Roman Emperor, 199
Lepanto, Battle of, 50
Leplat, Baron Raymond, 219, 237
Leszczyński, Stanislas I, King of Poland, 198, 200
Leuber, Benjamin, 142
Leygebe, Gottfried, 144, *Figure 42*
Leyser, Polycarp, 24
Library, Electoral, 74, 81, 83, 88–9, 96, 98, 156, 220, 239
  books on architecture, 82, 87
Lille, 208
Linar, Rocco di, *see* Guerini, Rocco
Lindemann, Christian Philipp, 202
Lisbon, 209
Livonia, 198
Löbenigk, Egidius, 75, 80
Lochar, 42
London, 168, 221
Longuelune, Zacharias, 201, 237, *Figure 56*
Lonicerus, Adam, 113
Lotichius Secundus, Petrus, 56
Lotti, Antonio, 235
Louis XIV, King of France, 180, 181, 195, 205–6, 208, 212, 215, 221, 222, 237, 239
Louis, Dauphin, 200
Louis, Grand Dauphin, 212
Louis Henri, prince de Condé, 221
Löwendal, Woldemar, Freiherr von, 226

Lubomirski, Prince, 209
Lucretius, 56
Ludwig Wilhelm, Margrave of Baden, 195
Lugano, 8, 42
Lull, Ramon, 102
Lully, Jean-Baptiste, 189, 207
Lusatia, *see* Lausitz
Luther, Martin, 8, 22, 23, 26, 40, 56, 86, 196, 238, 239
Lutheran sacred music, 22–6
Lutheranism 5–36, 37, 196, 201–4, 241
Lyons, 54, 222

Macedonia, Patriarch of, 83
Madruzzi, Cardinal Christoph, Archbishop of Trent, 39
Magdalena Sibylle, Margravine of Brandenburg, Electress of Saxony, 123, 137, 175, 177, 181
Magdalena Sibylle, Duchess of Saxony, Princess of Denmark, Duchess of Saxony-Altenburg, 179, 234
Magdeburg, 26, 109, 139
Maier, Michael, 104, 106
Mandeville, John de, 54
Manni, Agostino, 63
Mantua, 37, 42, 47, 60
  Duke of, 79, 83
  Palazzo del Tè (Sala dei Giganti), 38
Manutius, Aldus, 61
Maran, François, 183, 187
Maria Amalia, Duchess of Saxony, Queen of Spain, 200
Maria Anna, Princess of Bavaria, Electress of Saxony, 200
Maria Anna, Duchess of Saxony, Electress of Bavaria, 200
Maria Elisabeth, Duchess of Saxony, Duchess of Holstein-Gottorp, 30, 162, 168, 177
Maria Josepha, Princess of Austria, Electress of Saxony, Queen of Poland, 201, 234–5
Maria Theresa, Holy Roman Empress, 200
Marie Casimire Louise de la Grange, Queen of Poland, 195
Marino, Hypolido de, 47

Marlowe, Christopher, 111, 169
Marston, John, 170
Martial, 56
Massinger, Philip, 169, 172
Mathematics, 78, 109
  books on, 82, 87, 89
Matthias, Holy Roman Emperor, 62, 168
Mauro, Alessandro, 237
Maximilian I, Holy Roman Emperor, 54, 86, 128
Maximilian II, Holy Roman Emperor, 15, 40, 75, 76, 79, 94
Maximilian III Joseph, Elector of Bavaria, 200
Mazarin, Cardinal Jules, 180, 207
Medicine, 88, 102, 109
  books on, 86, 113, 114
  surgery, 84
Medici court, 12
Meissen, 8, 135, 157
  Albrechtsburg, 223, 225
  see also Porcelain manufacture
Melanchton, Philipp, 15, 203
Mercator (Gerhard Kremer), 89
Merian, Matthaeus, the Younger, 65, *Figure 17*
Merseburg, 139
Mestre, 59, 60
Metal industries, 6, 225–9
Metallurgy, 102, 106, 113, 221
Merseburg, 33
Meyerpeck, Wolfgang, 26
Mézétin, *see* Constantini
Michael, Rogier, 24, 62
Michelangelo, 12, 79
Michelspacher, Steffen, 112
Milan, 37, 60, 205, 215, *Figure 7*
Miltitz, Nicol von, 52, 121
Mining, 5–8, 87, 105, 107, 109, 221, *Figure 2*
  books on, 107
  festivals and, 120–9, 225–9, *Figures 27, 28 and 51–3*
Minting, 113, 114
  assaying, 107, 109, 114, 119
Mock, Johann, *Figures 29 and 30*
Möhlich, Gabriel, 175
Molière (Jean-Baptiste Poquelin), 172–3, 189, 207

Möller, Johann, 25
Montargon, Gentleman of the Chamber to Friedrich August I, 205
Monteverdi, Claudio, 191
Moritz, Landgrave of Hesse-Kassel, 62, 105, 106, 135
Moritz, Elector of Saxony, 1, 9, 12, 17, 23, 37–9, 40, 42, 59, 69, 135, 156, 204
  monument to, 10–11, *Figures 3–4*
Moritz, Duke of Saxony-Zeitz, 33, 34, 124, 130, 139, 148, 151, 158, 184
Moritzburg, 19, 30, 36, 200, *Figure 9*
Morrison, Fynes, 168
Mühlberg, Battle of, 1, 9, 15, 204
Müller, Marcus, 110, 113, 115
Munich, 3, 54, 91, 130, 163
Münster, Sebastian, 56
Music
  books on, 89
  'Churfürstliche Cantorey', 23
  'Historia', the, 22–6
  secular court, 23, 62
  Venetian church, 62

Naogeorg, Thomas (*pseud.* of Thomas Kirchmayer), 27, 28
Naples, 59
Naumann, Johann Christoph, 200
Naumburg, Treaty of, 9, 139
Nebuchadnezar, effigy of, 92
Nehmitz, Michael von, 223
Neitschütz, Magdalena Sibylla von, 193
Neri, Antonio, 117
Netherlands, 90, 193, 207, 221
Newton, Isaac, 101
Nienburg, Johann, 98
Nijmegen, Peace of, 152
Nissmitz, Johann von (*pseud.* of Johann Georg I), 59
Nissmitz, Georg von, 59
Nola, 59
Northern War, 198–9, 209, 219, 229
Nosseni, Giovanni Maria, 8, 11, 12, 41, 42, 43, 44, 50, 52, 54, 65, 79, 83, 92, 128, 174, 223
Novara, 61
Novels, early German, 86

Nuremberg, 40, 59, 60, 116, 155, 172, 193
Nystad, Peace of, 198

Oberschlema, 6
Occult arts, 100
Öder, Matthias, 80
Odescalchi, Livio, 195
Oginski, Count, 209
Ohain, Gottfried Papst von, 223
Opera, 30, 63, 146, 154, 161, 166, 175–6, 180, 181
  La Gara degli Dei, 235
  Il Paride, 189
  Teofane, 235
Opitz, Martin, 63, 69–70, 175, 191
Oppel, Johann David von, 156
Orthelius, Andreas, 113, 116
Ottoman Empire, 38
Ovid, 56, 63, 191

Pachmann, Daniel, *see* Bachmann, Daniel
Pacta Conventa, 195
Padua, 59, 192
Pallavicino, Carlo, 192
Papin, Denis, 221
Paracelsus (Theophrastus Bombast von Hohenheim), 86, 87, 102, 103, 107, 128
Paris, 3, 54, 172, 180, 204, 205, 206, 207, 209
  Académie royale des Sciences, 222
  Chantilly, 209
  Comédie Française, 206
  Comédie Italienne, 206, 207
  Hôtel de Bourgogne, 207
  Petit Bourgon, 207
  St Cloud, 206, 209, 223
Parma, 60
Parmigianino, 93
Paruta, Paolo, 61
Passau, Treaty of, 9
Paulsen, Carl Andreas, 172
Pavia, 60, 205
Peccensteinius, Laurentius, 45
Peele, George, 170
Peffenhauser, Anton, 45, 46

Peranda, Marco Giuseppe, 25, 191, 192
Peri, Jacopo, 63, 189
Permoser, Balthasar, *Figure 77*
'Persten', Rupert, 167
Pescetti, Orlando, 60
Petrarch, 70
Petrus Appianus, 78
Petzold, Georg, 22
Pezold, Georg, 162
Peucer, Caspar, 15
Pfeifer, D., 109
Pfund, Georg, 29
Pharmacology, 88, 102
Philipp II, Duke of Orléans, 221
Philipp II, King of Spain, 54
Philippi, Christian, 98
Piacenza, 50
Pickelhering, 168
Pillnitz, Schloß, 119
Pinello di Gerardi, Giovanni Battista, 40
Protestant Union, 17
Pirna, 144
Pistoris, Hartman, 109
Plautus, 56, 169
Plays, 146, 175
   biblical, 24, 30–4, 166
   strolling players, of, 166–74
Plutarch, 56, 86
Polybius, 86
Pope, Thomas, 167
Pöppelmann, Matthäus Daniel, 209–12, 220, 237, *Figures 45–7*
Porcacchi, Tommaso, 61
Porcelain manufacture, 221–5, 239
Poitiers, Louis de, 207, 208
Portugal, 205, 209, 215
Poussin, Nicolas, 219
Praetorius, Christian, 118
Prague, 65, 105, 106, 110, 116, 128, 169, 171, 209, 215
   Belvedere, 65
Preusen, Christian, 119
'Pritschmeister' accounts, 162
Propertius, 56
Protestant Union, 53
Ptolemy, 78
Pultusk, Battle of, 198
Puritans, 168

Quiccheberg, Samuel, 72

Racine, Jean, 207
Raetel, Heinrich, 28
Rasis (Abu Bakr Muhammad ibn Zakariyya A-Razi), 102
Rasser, Johann, 28
Rechenberg, Georg, Freiherr von, 217
Reformation, 8, 17, 199, 203, 204, 238
Reichenbach, 228
Reichenstein, 105
Reinhart, Elias, 55, 56
Reinhold, Johannes, 78
Reisiger, Hans, 94
Religious feast-days, 20
Reyna, Francisco de la, 48
Reynolds, Robert, 168
Rhine, 193, 194
Ricchino, Francesco, 39
Ricci, Cardinal, 222
Richelieu, Cardinal Armand Jean du Plessis, duc de, 181
Riding, 46–8, 57, 86, 88
Riese, Adam, 109
Riesengebirge, 69
Riga, 198
Rinuccini, Ottavio, 63, 70, 189
Ripa, Cesare, 54
Rodewisch, 6
Roe, William, 168, 169, 171
Röhling, Sigmund, 55
Roll, Georg, 78
Romano, Giulio, 38
Rome, 54, 59, 60, 61, 63
Rosicrucianism, 106
Rostock, 57
Rousseau, Jean, 204
Rožmberk, Vilém (Wilhelm von Rosenberg), 105, 112
Rückert, Thomas, 78
Rudolf II, Holy Roman Emperor, 76, 79, 101, 105, 109, 112, 116, 215
Ruexner, Georg, 54, 164
Ruffo, Giordano, 48
Rusius, Laurentius, 48
Russia, 195, 198

Sachs, Hans, 171
Salt extraction, 109

Sander, Johann Heinrich, 145
Sannazaro, Jacopo, 69, 70
Sarachi workshop, *Figure 19*
Sarmoneta, 59
Savoy, Duke of, 60, 76
Scaliger, 56, 70
Scandello, Antonio, 24, 25, 40
Scarron, Paul, 173
Schaffgotsch, Hans Ulrich, Freiherr von, 69, 70
Schiebling, Christian, 135
Schiessler, Christoph, 87
Schirmer, David, 131, 176–87
Schirmer, Melchior, 115
Schleswig-Holstein, 131
Schmalkaldic League, 9, 204
Schmidt, Johann Christian, 208
Schmidt, Johann Georg, 202, 212, *Figures 46–7*
Schneeberg, 6, 128
Schober, H.W., 148, 150, 161, *Figures 33–4*
Schonaeus, Cornelius, 29
Schönberg, Christoph von, 119, 122
Schönberg, Heinrich von, 122
Schönberg, Wolf von, 121
Schütz, Christian, 15
Schütz, Heinrich, 24–5, 62–3, 175, 176, 177, 178, 190
Schuward, Johann, 27
Schwabe, Nicol, 93
Schwenckfeldt, Caspar, 69
Schwertzer, Sebald, 105, 112, 116
Sebottendorf, Hans von, 109
Seneca, 56
Serabaglio, Giovanni Battista, 46
Servi, Constantino de', 42
Settala, Manfredo di, 222
Settizonio, Lauro, 61
Shakespeare, 169, 170, 172, 173
Sharpe, Lewis, 172
Shooting contests, 146, 152
Sibylle Elisabeth, Duchess of Württemberg, 123, 137, 175
Sicily, Kingdom of, 59
Sievershausen, Battle of, 1, 9, 40
Sigismund, King of Poland, 93
Silvestre, Louis de, 219
Sitzenroda, 42

Sleidanus, Johannes, 86, 152
Solis, Vergil, 87
Sommer, Wolfgang, 29
Sophie, Duchess of Saxony (daughter of Christian I), 21, 30, 51
Sophie, Margravine of Brandenburg, Electress of Saxony, 16, 21, 51, 55, 116, 167
Sophie Charlotte, Queen of Prussia, 221
Sophie Eleonore, Duchess of Saxony, Landgravine of Hesse-Darmstadt, 30, 63, 168, 175, 181
Sophie Hedwig, Duchess of Schleswig-Holstein, Duchess of Saxony-Zeitz, 130
Spain, 205, 209, 215
Spencer, John, 167, 168
Spener, Philipp Jakob, 196, 222
Speyer, Peter von, 46
Spranger, Bartholomäus, 90
Sprintzenstein, Count Hans Albrecht von, 42
St. George, Thomas, 140
Stephens, Thomas, 167
Stockholm, 169
Stolle, Philipp, 177, 181
Stolpen, 144
Strada, Jacopo, 41
Strasburg, 109
Strolling players, theatre of, 166–74
Strungk, Nicolaus Adam, 25
Stumpfeldt, Elias, 115
Sturm, Johann, 56
Stuttgart, 53, 54, 65, 91, 175, 236
Suetonius, 56
Swan, Sir William, 143, 144, 147
Sweden, 195, 198, 199

Tacitus, 61, 86
Tapestries, 98
Taubescher Garten, 173
Terence, 56
Terracina, 59
Thaw, Valentin, 83, 87
Theti, Carlo, 42, 47
Thirty Years' War, 7, 130, 135, 146, 168, 240
Thucydides, 86
Thuringia, 8

Thurneisser, Leonhard, 87, 102, 105, 116, 128
Tintoretto (Jacopo di Robusti), 93
Titian (Tiziano Vecellio), 41, 93
Tola, Benedetto, Gabriele and Guerino, 9, 38–9, 135, *Figure 13*
Torgau, 8, 9, 23, 29, 63, 85, 137, 173, 174, 189
Tournaments, 20–2, 49–54, 86, 97, 121–3, 164
 foot tournament, 147
 giuoco de' caroselli, 236
 joust, 20, 49
 ladies' running at the ring, 234, 235
 running at the head, 49, 235
 running at the ring, 20, 49, 123, 124, 125, 131, 147, 151, 153, 161, 186
 running at the quintain, 20, 146, 147, 155, 186, 232
 tilt, 20
Trent, 59, 60
Treviso, 60
Trieste, 59
Tschirnhaus, Ehrenfried Walther von, 8, 221–5
Turin, 205, 215
Turks, 194
Tzschimmer, Gabriel, 32–3, 128–9, 150, 152, 155, 158–65, 185, *Figures 12, 14, 34, 35, 37 and 38*

Ulm, 60
Ußlaub, David, 74, 98, 113, 119
Utrecht, 169

Valla, Lorenzo, 56
Valturio, Roberto, 56
Vegetius, Renatus, 48
Velten, Johannes, 172–4
Venice, 37, 59, 60, 61, 62, 192, 205, 215
Ventura, Comin, 61
Venuti, Filippo, 61
Vercelli, 60
Verona, 60, 61, 63, 64, 207
 Giusti Gardens, 68
Versailles, 206, 209, 212, 219, 239
Vienna, 41, 54, 85, 86, 130, 168, 193, 209, 212, 235

Villette, F., 222
Virgil, 56, 86
Vitruvius, 56, 88
Vladyslav IV, King of Poland, 168
Vogtland, the, 8
Vondel, Jost van den, 35

Wackerbarth, Count Anton Christoph von, 201
Wagner, Hans, 54
Wagner, Valentin, *Figure 13*
Walther, Johann, the Elder, 23, 40
Warsaw, 168, 198, 207, 217, 238, 239
Watzdorf, Margarethe von, Abbess of Weissenfels, 113
Wayde, John, 168, 171
Wechinger, Johann, 92
Weck, Anton, 43, 59, 60, 61, 63, 94, 95, 155–8, 165, 161, 177, *Figures 15 and 36*
Weckhardt (Wecker), Georg, 80, *Figure 21*
Wehme, Zacharias, 15, *Figure 7*
Weikersheim, 105, 119
Weimar, 3, 8, 60
Weise, Christian, 222
Weissenfels, 25, 26, 33
Werner, Anna Maria, 237
Werner, Johann Christoph, 93
Werthern, Dietrich von, 88
Wessel, Hans, 9
Wettin, House of, 1, 8, 137, 178, 200, 223, 235, 238
Wild, Sebastian, 27
Wilhelm V, Duke of Bavaria, 105
Wilhelm, Landgrave of Hesse-Kassel, 76, 78, 105
William, Prince of Orange, 121, 141
Windsor, 142
Wittenberg, 3, 8, 9, 26, 85, 111, 132, 137, 145, 172, 176, 223, 238
Wolffius, Johannes, 113
Wolfframsdorff, Hermann von, 141
Wolfgang II, Count of Hohenlohe, 78, 104, 105, 119
Wortmann, Christian Albrecht, 211, *Figure 45*
Württemberg, 17, 175
 Dukes of, 162

Xenophon, 48, 56, 86

Zacaire, Denys, 86
Zeitz, 26, 33, 139
Zellische Comoedianten, 207
Zerroen, Antonius van, 9
Zihler, Hans, 29

Zimmermann, Balthasar, 80
Zittau, 222
Zöblitz, 65, 128
Zorn, Friedrich, 225
Zucchi, Bartholomeo, 61
Zuzschky, Georg, 117
Zwickau, 26, 137